A Century of
Carnival Glass

Glen and Stephen Thistlewood

Schiffer Publishing Ltd

4880 Lower Valley Road, Atglen, PA 19310 USA

Dedication

For Angie and Andrew

With particular thanks to the skilled and devoted glass craftsmen from both the past and the present for giving so much beauty to the world

The sun is still in the sky and shining above you
Let me hear you sing once more like you did before
Sing a new song . . .
Try once more like you did before
Sing a new song.

—Extract from lyrics of "Chiquitita" 1979 (Andersson/Ulvaeus), sung by Abba.

Cover: Almost a century of Carnival Glass from all corners of the world is represented here. Top left, from the USA, echoes of the Rococo style in this splendid, smoke *ACANTHUS* plate made by the Imperial Glass Company. Top right, three superb *ROSE GARDEN* vases from the European manufacturers Brockwitz and Eda Glasbruk. From both Europe and the USA, the *TORNADO* vases (center left) are a combination of the European originals and the splendid Northwood vase they inspired. Center right, *DIANA THE HUNTRESS*, the magnificent Roman goddess, is portrayed on a bowl from Europe, while bottom left, Adam and Eve feature on this superb *GARDEN OF EDEN* plate made by the Fenton Art Glass Company in the 1980s. Mystical and full of symbolism, the vases and tumblers made in India (bottom right) bring a touch of the exotic to the magic of Carnival Glass.

Title Page: Three Classic Carnival Glass manufacturers who have carried on the legacy that their forefathers began. Left: the Northwood Art Glass Company's superb blue *DOLPHIN* card receiver was made in 1999. Center: Imperial produced this *STORYBOOK MUG* in the early 1970s; the color of this example is the rich cobalt blue that Imperial called "Aurora Jewels." Right: the amazing *JEFFERSON COMPOTE* from Fenton, made in Independence Blue for the Bicentennial in 1976.

Library of Congress Cataloging-in-Publication Data

Thistlewood, Glen.
A century of carnival glass / Glen and Stephen Thistlewood.
p. cm.
ISBN 0-7643-1209-X (hardcover)
1. Carnival glass—Catalogs. 2. Carnival glass—Collectors and collecting—United States—Catalogs.
I. Thistlewood, Stephen. II. Title
NK5439.C35 T556 2001
748.2913-dc21
00-010149

Designed by Bonnie M. Hensley
Type set in Shelley Allegro BT/Korinna BT

ISBN: 0-7643-1209-X
Printed in China
1 2 3 4

Published by Schiffer Publishing Ltd.
4880 Lower Valley Road
Atglen, PA 19310
Phone: (610) 593-1777; Fax: (610) 593-2002
E-mail: Schifferbk@aol.com
Please visit our web site catalog at **www.schifferbooks.com**

In Europe, Schiffer books are distributed by Bushwood Books
6 Marksbury Avenue Kew Gardens
Surrey TW9 4JF England
Phone: 44 (0) 20-8392-8585; Fax: 44 (0) 20-8392-9876
E-mail: Bushwd@aol.com
Free postage in the UK. Europe: air mail at cost.

This book may be purchased from the publisher.
Include $3.95 for shipping. Please try your bookstore first. We are always looking for people to write books on new and related subjects. If you have an idea for a book please contact us at the above address.
You may write for a free catalog.

Contents

Acknowledgments

In the course of researching and writing this book, we have been helped by many individuals and organizations from all over the world. Researchers and scholars, libraries and museums, manufacturers and glass collectors—the response and support has been tremendous. Many people share with us the desire to not only faithfully record, but also to "showcase" the true beauty of the glass that is Classic Carnival's Legacy. We hope that we have done that in the pages of this book. Now we wish to pay a tribute to all those who have helped us so much. This book would not have been written without them.

Joan Doty has always "been there" to help, support, and proofread the trickiest bits! **Janet and Alan Mollison** have helped to edit and support throughout. **Bob Smith** has helped to search out archives and catalogs from all over the world, we owe him many thanks. Our family and our close circle of friends have helped more than they will ever know—thanks also to Dave Doty and Tom and Sharon Mordini for their support.

We also wish to thank:

Siegmar Gieselberger for his outstanding research and provision of crucial archive information.

For allowing us access to photograph their wonderful glass collections, we wish to give particular thanks to the following: **Ann and David Brown, Carol and Derek Sumpter, Rita and Les Glennon, Gerd and Lars Erik Olsson, Anne Marie and Lennart Skoglands.**

Michael Whitten for his photography of the tumblers in Bob Smith's collection.

Thanks also to Rick McDaniel and Susan Brewer.

We have also had much information and tremendous support from libraries, museums and glass manufacturers. Our grateful thanks to:

Frank. M. Fenton
David and Mary McKinley, Northwood Art Glass Co.
Susan Haddad, Director of Northwood Art Glass Co.
John Boyd and Sue Boyd, Boyd's Crystal Art Glass
Terry and Donna Crider, Crider Art Glass
Russel and JoAnn Vogelsong of Summit Art Glass
Gary and Dodie Levi
Mosser Glass Inc.
Mahavir Jain, Director Jain Glass Works
Ray and Judy Steele (for the archives of the late Bob Gallo)
John and Pat Resnik (for the archives of the late Don Moore)
Howard Seufer
Nick Dolan, Shipley Art Gallery, Gateshead
Kaisa Koivisto, Curator, and Aija Avnery, Finnish Glass Museum, Riihimaki
Gunnel Holmer, Smalands Museum, Vaxjo, Sweden
Annet van der Kley-Blekxtoon, Curator, Stichting National Glasmuseum, Leerdam, Holland

Tiina Aaltonen, Iittala Glasmuseum
Milan Hlaves, Museum of Decorative Arts, Prague, Czechoslovakia
Manchester Central Library
Dr. Bernard Mossner, Director of Public Relations and Culture, Stadt Coswig
Gail Bardhan and Kelly Bliss, Corning Museum of Glass
Dr. Sylva Petrova, Curator, Museum of Decorative Arts, Prague, Czechoslovakia
Gerard Roots, Curator, Church Farmhouse Museum, Barnet, London
Diane Foulds, author and Czech glass researcher
Bob Murray, Johnson Matthey Ltd.
Ivo Haanstra
Jon Saffell
J. M. Smith, International Bottle Company
Anthony Pike, Divisional Director *Tableware International* (formerly *Pottery Gazette and Glass Trade Review*)

There are many others who have also allowed their glass to be photographed. We are deeply grateful to all. Sincere thanks to:

Frank and Shirley
Elaine and Fred Blair
John and Frances Hodgson
Sue and Ray McLaren
Jim Nicholls
Gale Eichorst
Sue Foster
Brian and Doreen Lapthorne
Phyllis and Don Atkinson
Fiona Melville
Nigel Gamble
Maureen Davies
Pat and Alex Chalmers
Jeri Sue Lucas
Pat Thornton
Steve and Trudy Auty
John Kerr and Rob Innes
Alan Henderson
Charles and Jeanette Echols
Carolyn and Paul Walkden
Janet and Peter Rivers
Mrs. Harry Habberley
Kay Hoffman and Howard Shosted

Finally, even more help in many ways from the following:

Fred Stone
Brian Pitman
Diane Rosington
Pam and Mike Mills
Harry and Jean Barrett
Hank Powers

Karen McIntyre
Gwilym Elis Jones
Janet Dickson
Treva Mauch
Clinton Arsenault
Bob and Imogene Grissom
Lennart Anderson
Dixie Nichols
David Cotton
Ray and Jean Rogers
Annie Rooks
Lois Langdon
Ron and April Duncan
John and Margaret McGrath
Lance and Pat Hilkene
Wayne Delahoy
Mary Hare
Darrell and Kelly Markley
Robert Truitt
Alan Fullrich

Last, but by no means least, we wish to thank our publisher, Peter Schiffer and our editor, Donna Baker. Their friendship and support has been outstanding.

Photography for the book (with the exception of those noted in the captions) is by Stephen Thistlewood. Equipment used was a Canon EOS 500N camera and Sigma Macro lens, using twin 500 watts tungsten floodlights and an 80B filter. Film used was Fujichrome Sensia II ISO 200. Drawings and sketches (unless stated otherwise) are by Glen Thistlewood.

Further Resources

As the Internet becomes more accessible for all, we would like to mention two websites that are of great help to the Carnival Glass collector.

The Woodsland Carnival Glass Website—http://www.woodsland.com/carnivalglass—is run by Fred Stone and Brian Pitman and is a free resource. A daily mailing list on Carnival Glass and a further Educational site is available by annual subscription to the collector's club, Woodsland World Wide Carnival Glass Association (www.cga).

John Valentine's Contemporary Carnival Glass website—http://www.carnivalglass.net/—provides (for an annual subscription) an excellent resource on Modern Carnival Glass and is recommended.

We would urge all collectors to join local or international Carnival Clubs. The knowledge and friendship gained will be worth it. Educational resources such as *NetworK* (the quarterly journal published by the authors) are also of great value to keep abreast of current information and research. Information and contact addresses for clubs can be found in various resources, e.g. the Woodsland website mentioned above, Mordini's *Auction Reports,* and Doty's *Field Guide to Carnival Glass.*

Part One

Reprise

"The history book on the shelf is always repeating itself."
—Extract from lyrics of "Waterloo" 1974 (Anderson, Andersson and Ulvaeus), sung by Abba.

Carnival Glass had its origins and inspirations in the iridized art glass produced first in Europe, then in the USA. Stimulated by its beauty and appeal, the Classic Carnival manufacturers went on to create a product that took the world by storm and reached out to millions. The stroke of genius was that it was not only affordable, but also astonishingly ornamental, gracing many a humble home. The production of Classic Carnival in the USA itself became the inspiration for the subsequent rebirth of iridized glass in Europe (other countries such as Argentina and Australia also followed). It is fascinating to note the European origin of the product and then to observe the way in which it was produced again in Bohemia, Germany, England, and Scandinavia with such dazzling success in the 1920s. The full story of how this came about, and the incredible amount of wonderful Carnival Glass that was produced, is told in full, for the first time, in this book. Years of research, and the international co-operation of collectors and scholars alike, have resulted in the creation of this tribute to the skillful artistry and dedication of craftsmen from a past era—this is *A Century of Carnival Glass*.

Chapter One
Inspirations

"Popular music is popular because a lot of people like it."
—Irving Berlin (1888-1989) American composer.

In 1907, a young Russian immigrant working as a singing waiter in New York's Chinatown had a small success with his first song. Four years later, having changed his name from Israel Baline to Irving Berlin, the one time waiter wrote "Alexander's Ragtime Band." Tin Pan Alley had a hit! At the same time, the glassware that was quietly introduced in 1907 as "Golden Sunset Iridescent" quickly gained favor. By 1911 the wholesale catalogs were full of ads for iridized glass, proclaiming it to be gorgeous "Wonder Glassware," "Monarch Glassware," and a "remarkable seller." Carnival Glass was a hit!

Classic Carnival Glass is press moulded, iridized glass that was produced in the United States of America from about 1907 to around 1925. The main manufacturers in the USA were Fenton, Northwood, Imperial, Dugan/Diamond, and Millersburg, with smaller amounts being produced by various other companies such as Westmoreland. The new iridized glassware was sold by major wholesalers and distributors such as Butler Brothers, and Premium Houses like Lee Manufacturing Co. based in Chicago. Water sets, table sets, punch sets, plates, vases, compotes, bowls, and more bowls were arrayed on the pages to tempt the buyers. Carnival Glass was a resounding success, though at the time it didn't bear that name—it was given its nickname in later years as it became a popular collectible. The full story of Classic Carnival is explained in great detail in *Carnival Glass: The Magic and the Mystery*.[1]

Classic Carnival Glass was transported by rail and by boat. Indeed, that Herculean feat, the construction of the Panama Canal, chopped 9,000 miles off the sea journey from New York to San Francisco, thus facilitating trade with the Pacific coast of North America and beyond. The export trade with Europe, and the United Kingdom in particular, also flourished. In 1911, the first ads for Imperial's *RIPPLE* vase and various *IMPERIAL GRAPE* items were placed by the agent Markt & Co. of London, in the British *Pottery Gazette*—the new glass met with instant success. Though the dark years of World War One intervened, Classic Carnival was back in the UK with a flourish in the early 1920s in the form of a splendid full color ad in the *Pottery*

Gazette for Imperial's *HEAVY GRAPE*. Fenton's Carnival lines were also heavily promoted by Charles Pratt, who represented the National Glass Company. Carnival from Dugan/Diamond and Northwood was also very popular (both companies had commercial and personal ties with England and naturally utilized them).

In Part Two, entitled *The First Movement*, you will read the story of European Carnival Glass—the legacy handed down by the producers of Classic Carnival, which was grasped with eager hands by those "waiting in the wings." The background to the production of Carnival Glass in Europe is one that mirrors many cataclysmic events. The relative stability of the early 1920s was followed by the doom of the Wall Street crash in 1929 and the shock waves that reverberated around the world. The subsequent Depression was followed within years by the first stirrings of another war looming on the horizon. Although Fenton and Imperial were still actively producing Classic Carnival through the 1920s, and exporting to Europe (which continued until around 1929), it was during this period that several European glass manufacturers began to produce Carnival Glass themselves. Other countries also carried on the Classic Carnival legacy, including Australia, Argentina, Mexico, and India. With the exception of Australia[2] the Carnival output of all these countries will be examined in detail in this book.

In Part Three, entitled *The Second Movement*, the course of iridized glass (Late Carnival Glass) in the USA during the Depression Years is carefully traced.

The legacy left by the producers of Classic Carnival Glass is still burning strongly, indeed, it has come full circle again. Part Four, entitled *The Encore*, assesses how Carnival Glass production returned to the USA in the 1960s, and provides an invaluable, detailed examination of production (including reproduction) in recent years.

[1] Glen and Stephen Thistlewood, *Carnival Glass: The Magic and the Mystery* (Atglen, Pennsylvania: Schiffer Publishing Ltd., 1999).
[2] The reader is referred to *Carnival Glass: The Magic and the Mystery* by the authors, for a thorough overview of Australian Carnival. Also see *Carnival Glass of Australia* by the Australian Carnival Enthusiasts Association Inc., 1988.

Flanked by illustrations for "Accordion Pleated Sateen Petticoats" and "Soft, Fluffy, Warm Blankets" is a Northwood *CHERRIES AND LITTLE FLOWERS* enameled water set in rich cobalt blue Carnival Glass. This gorgeous set was described in the ad as reflecting "all the Lovely Colors of the Rainbow. . . Made of strong royal blue glass in iridescent finish; richly hand painted." This Lee Manufacturing Company ad from one of their 1916 catalogs is unusual in that it is in full color. It was offered free as a special extra premium with an order of $10.00 or over to Lee's lady agents.

Fenton Art Glass was the first manufacturer to market Carnival Glass in around 1907. This beautiful amethyst *AUTUMN ACORNS* plate was found in the UK. SP $2500-3500.

Another rare plate from Fenton is the spatula footed *DRAGON AND LOTUS* in amethyst—this one was discovered in Oregon. SP $4500-5500.

More Carnival in color from Lee Manufacturing in 1916—a complete Imperial *LUSTRE ROSE* water set and table set in marigold. The ad stated that "we have endeavoured to show you the wonderful colors in this picture but the set itself is far more gorgeous than we can illustrate or describe." $1.50 would have secured either a full water set or table set. Note that the table set was described as a "Tea Set."

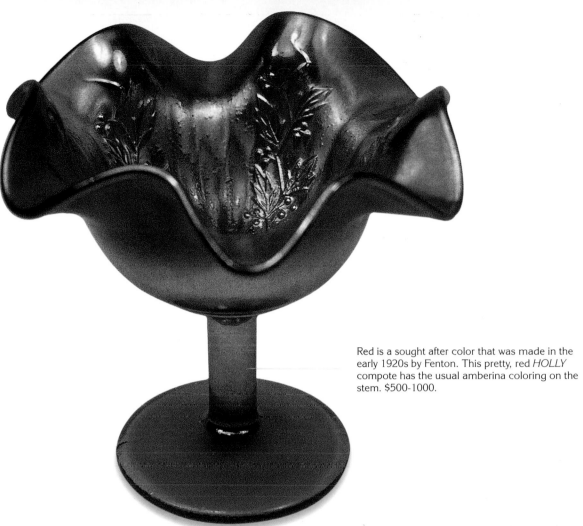

Red is a sought after color that was made in the early 1920s by Fenton. This pretty, red *HOLLY* compote has the usual amberina coloring on the stem. $500-1000.

Flowers, fruits, and birds were favorite motifs on Carnival. Animals were used too, as on this wonderful *PANTHER* centrepiece bowl in blue by Fenton. SP $800-1600.

Water sets were popular shapes in Classic Carnival—this is an unusual enameled set from Fenton. The pattern is *ENAMELED WINDFLOWER* (the pitcher has also been called *ENAMELED CLOVERS*). $550-750 for a full set.

Punch sets were popular (and useful) shapes too. Shown here is Northwood's *PEACOCK AT THE FOUNTAIN* set in rich marigold. $600-900.

A pair of Northwood *THIN RIB* vases in sapphire blue. These were discovered on a street market in Provence, France. SP $300-500 each.

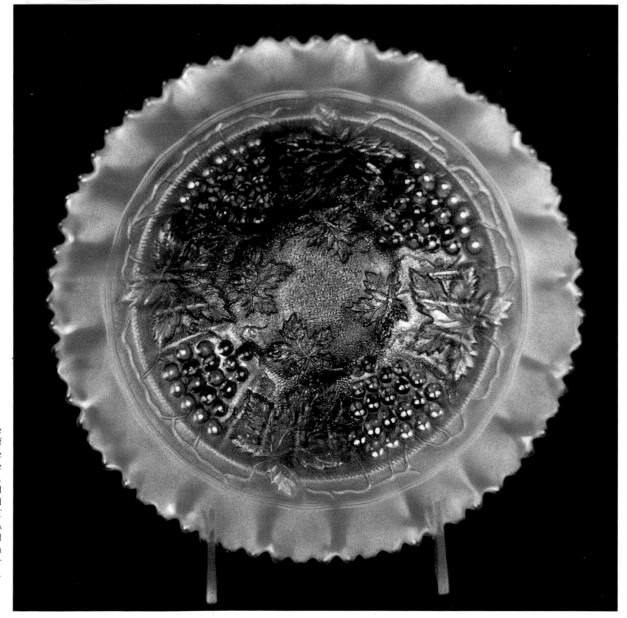

Two of the signature characteristics of Northwood are the pie crust edge and the delicious aqua opal color. Here they are combined on this fabulous stippled *GRAPE AND CABLE* bowl, found in the UK. A similar example was sold at auction in the USA in February 2000 for $3450.

The ever popular *PEACOCKS* from Northwood, seen here on a stippled blue plate. $900-1500.

The discovery by Karen MacIntyre in early 2000 of a Baltimore Bargain House catalog finally proved that Northwood was indisputably the maker of the *POPPY SHOW* and *ROSE SHOW* items. Until then, though Northwood was the prime candidate, no proof of attribution had been found. Shown here is a purple *POPPY SHOW* bowl. $750-1200.

Imperial marketed their Carnival Glass in the UK with a strong advertising campaign in the British *Pottery Gazette*. Several of these gorgeous purple *LOGANBERRY* vases have been found in the UK. $2000-3000.

The *IMPERIAL FLUTE* pattern, though plain, showcases the iridescence magnificently on this purple tumbler. The punch cup also has the *FLUTE* pattern on the exterior, but is known as *HEAVY GRAPE* for its splendid interior design. A purple tumbler sold at auction in the USA for $500 in 1999. The punch cup is seldom offered for sale: SP $150-250.

Both Imperial and Northwood made a pattern that featured the *STAR OF DAVID*. This is Imperial's, seen here in green—an unusual color for this pattern. $100-175.

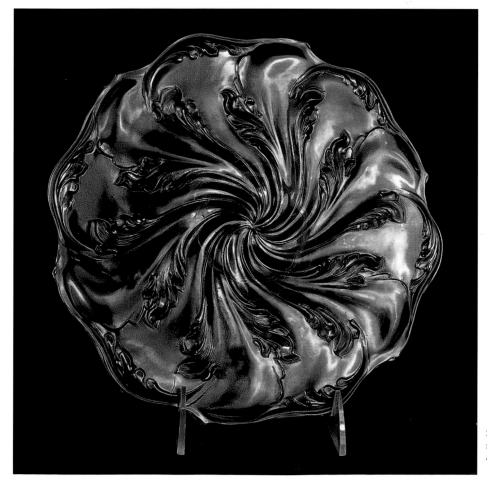

Smoke was used by Imperial with great success, seen here on a lovely *ACANTHUS* plate. One sold at auction in 1999 for $725.

If only it didn't have a chip! Imperial's fabulous *OPEN ROSE* plate in purple sells for around $2000 or more, when perfect. This slightly flawed beauty was found on a flea-market stall in the north of England, so the price was right.

Individual tumblers by Millersburg are popular with collectors. From left: green *DIAMONDS* ($80-120), marigold *FEATHER AND HEART* ($60-90), and a green *HANGING CHERRIES* ($100-200).

SEAWEED is the pattern name of this Millersburg bowl with its wonderful Rococo swirls. In marigold and with the crimped 3 in 1 edge, $200-350.

Millersburg's SWIRLED HOBNAIL was used on cuspidors, rose bowls, and vases. This marigold vase, $150-250.

Millersburg made several peacock patterns; this one is the PEACOCK AND URN design, shown here in a green ice cream shaped bowl. $750-1200.

An unusual color for Dugan/Diamond was this deliciously frosty celeste blue. Made in the early 1920s, celeste items were exported to the UK and Australia, judging by the high proportion of examples found there. This *VINTAGE* bowl with a domed foot was found in the north of England. $800-900.

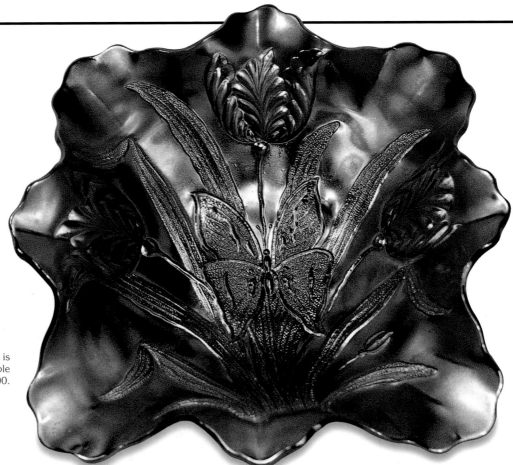

The massive *BUTTERFLY AND TULIP* bowl is a collectors' favorite. This square, purple example from Dugan/Diamond, $1000-2000.

A gorgeous lavender effect is seen on this *FANCIFUL* plate by Dugan/Diamond. SP $500-1000.

An uncommon pattern is Dugan/Diamond's *FLOWERS AND SPADES*. A peach opal example like this, $400-500.

Links and Connections

During the century before World War One, over 50 million people emigrated from Europe to North America: this constituted the greatest migration of human beings the world has ever seen. The inscription at the foot of the Statue of Liberty, seen by many immigrants as they sailed to Ellis Island, reads "Give me your tired, your poor, your huddled masses yearning to breathe free"—and "breathe free" they did. They came from all over Europe: from the United Kingdom, Germany, Austria, France, Italy, and Scandinavia. In many instances they left behind hunger, repression, and overcrowding, though some were simply seeking fresh opportunities and pastures new. They brought with them their culture and their history, their skill and their imagination. This European heritage found a natural foothold in the thriving focus of the American glass industry—the Ohio Valley. Harry Northwood and his young cousin, Thomas Dugan, were among the many talented craftsmen who brought their skills from Stourbridge (one of England's main centers of glassmaking) to Pennsylvania, West Virginia, and Ohio.

When Classic Carnival Glass was first made in the USA around 1907, it was imitating the iridized art glass that had been made previously by Loetz in Bohemia, Tiffany in the USA, and Thomas Webb and Sons in England, to name just a few. Early ads for the glass we now call Carnival described the new iridized ware as "Bohemian Iridescent," "Pompeiian," "Venetian Art" and "Parisian," indicative of a recognized link with the sources of inspiration. The similarities didn't stop there, for a large number of the patterns and shapes that were produced in Classic Carnival Glass also had links with patterns and shapes made previously in Europe. Harry Northwood in particular derived many ideas and inspirations from his formative years in Stourbridge. Northwood's GRAPE AND CABLE candle lamp, the TORNADO vase, the splendid WIDE PANEL EPERGNE, and the LEAF AND BEADS rose bowl were almost certainly inspired by similar items made in the Stourbridge area of England. The NAUTILUS (aka ARGONAUT SHELL) pattern was another English inspiration for Northwood that is fully documented.[1] The NAUTILUS was first made by Northwood in ivory glass, imitative of china, in 1900. (It was later made in Carnival Glass by Dugan, who took over the moulds.) The NAUTILUS was modelled on a Royal Worcester china vase, made in 1888, that looks almost identical to Northwood's version—the features of the large shell, the tiny shells adorning the base—all the details are there. Miss Elizabeth Robb, Harry Northwood's granddaughter, remembers[1] her grandmother "relating that Harry Northwood returned from England with the Worcester vase, vowing that he would recreate it in glass." The Royal Worcester china vase still remains with the Northwood family. Also see Part Two, Chapter Two for further details on Stourbridge Carnival Glass.

Two examples of Classic Carnival that had their inspirations in items originally made in England. On the left, a purple NAUTILUS, $150-250 (note: the NAUTILUS was first made in glass by Northwood, the Carnival examples were made later by Dugan/Diamond); and right, a purple TORNADO by Northwood, $600-1000.

It should come as no surprise to realize that following the subsequent mass production of iridized ware in the USA, events would go full circle and return to Europe. The American Carnival Glass manufacturers had exported great quantities of their products to Europe; the United Kingdom in particular had received huge amounts. During the 1920s however, England, Sweden, Finland, Germany, and Czechoslovakia all followed the American lead and began to produce their own Carnival Glass. Australia too had been importing large amounts of Carnival from the USA and in common with Europe, began to produce a splendid, iridized home product. Argentina and Mexico followed suit, not only importing as well as imitating the USA Classic Carnival, but also importing and imitating the European produced Carnival. Indeed, Argentina had quite complex trade relationships with many European countries as well as the United States.

It is most interesting to study the names given in the various European Carnival Glass manufacturers' catalogs to some of their lines. The names chosen obviously reflected the trade links they had and quite possibly some of their export destinations. There was Balmoral, Lincoln, Melbourne, Pall Mall, Lille, Lyon, Rio, Florida, Espagne, Bodega, Colon, Argentina, Hudson, Hungaria, Rumania, Essex, and Cambridge—all names used for glassware produced in Europe. A study of the actual pattern designs used by both the original Classic Carnival manufacturers and the European manufacturers also reveals many links, as plagiarism and possibly even mould movements took place. Some United States Glass Co., Cambridge Glass, and Dugan/Diamond patterns have European counterparts. Several Imperial patterns too, for example, *SCROLL EMBOSSED* (used by Sowerby) and *TIGER LILY* (used by Riihimaki, see Part Two, Chapter Seven for details) were made in European Carnival Glass.

Imperial did it first! On the left is the Imperial version of the *TIGER LILY* water pitcher in teal ($200-400), while on the right is Riihimaki's version in blue ($450-600).

Just as USA Classic Carnival Glass is found in many countries around the world, so European and other "foreign" made glass turns up just about anywhere! Indeed, a great deal of European, South American, and Indian Carnival has been found in the USA. Much of it was exported at the time of manufacture, though since the 1960s, a substantial amount of Carnival Glass has also been traded around the world as a collectible. With international business on the Internet at auction websites like *eBay*, this trend will undoubtedly continue. German Carnival is found in Scandinavia and the United Kingdom as well as mainland Europe and North and South America. Scandinavian Carnival is found in North and South America as well as the United Kingdom and Australia. Czechoslovakian Carnival has been found in the USA, United Kingdom, mainland Europe, Scandinavia, and South America and Australia. Carnival produced in England has been found just about everywhere. It will be noted in the text describing the Carnival Glass patterns below where (when known) such items have been found. Part of the "magic and the mystery" of Carnival is that it can turn up anywhere, anytime!

[1] William Heacock, James Measell, and Berry Wiggins, *Harry Northwood. The Early Years* (Marietta, Ohio: Antique Publications, 1990).

Imperial did it first again! The *SCROLL EMBOSSED* pattern on the interior of a stunning purple compote. $100-200.

This time it was Sowerby who did the copying—here's *SCROLL EMBOSSED* on the interior of a small Sowerby bonbon dish. $30-50.

Part Two

The First Movement

"There goes that song again"
—Cahn and Styne, 1944.

Chapter One

The Production of Iridized Glass in Europe

Europe's position at the center of the world economy was deeply damaged by World War One. In the years of instability that ensued, mainland Europe (and Czechoslovakia in particular) struggled. In the glass trade, many were soon out of work. Other parts of Europe, especially Sweden, that had remained largely untouched by the war were able to increase the number of their glassworks and a struggle set in for control of foreign markets. Czechoslovakia was "overrun with foreign agents who were not on the look out for merchandise, but for qualified workers who, in the depressed conditions then prevailing, they easily won over, so that Bohemia was exporting skilled craftsmen instead of goods."[1] Such mixing of skills across Europe no doubt laid the ground for the many connections that are continually being uncovered within the industry.

In *Collectible Bohemian Glass 1880-1940*, Robert and Deborah Truitt note[2] that "the process of iridizing the finish (on glass) was first developed in 1856 at Zlatno. It was first exhibited in Vienna in 1873. By 1900, there was hardly a single manufacturer that did not, or at least could not, produce iridized glass." Ludwig Lobmeyer is often thought to have been the first to exhibit commercially produced iridescent glass. Thomas Webb of Stourbridge, England soon followed suit. At the Paris Exhibition of 1878, Webb's "Bronze" glass was shown—a deep green, based glass, iridized in shades of purple. Later, Webb produced their "Iris" range that was close in appearance to marigold Carnival. The Austrian glassmaker, Loetz, has a name that is synonymous with iridescent art glass, in fact, Loetz ware resembles in many ways the finest of Tiffany's output. Indeed, the European glass manufacturers had a fine legacy of producing iridized glass, however, it been aimed at a totally different market than that which American Carnival Glass had satisfied. During the 1920s everything changed. The production of mass produced Carnival Glass began in Europe. It came from England, Sweden, Finland, Germany, and Czechoslovakia. Europe was about to witness a flowering of some of the most beautiful Carnival Glass ever made.

The quantity of Carnival Glass produced by the European manufacturers is astonishing: almost three hundred European patterns are detailed within this book. There are probably more. The quality of much European Carnival is superb; the major producers were important glasshouses with fine reputations to uphold. Eda Glasbruk in Sweden produced Carnival of breathtaking beauty—sadly, its output continued for only a short period of time. Brockwitz A.G. was a major factory in Germany that produced truly superb Carnival reflecting its fine reputation. Josef Inwald A.G. in Czechoslovakia produced Carnival with an iridescence that upheld Bohemia's reputation for excellence in glass, while Sowerby in England made some stunning pieces reminiscent of the company's past glories. These are just a few of the factories in Europe that made Carnival, the very best examples of which were probably produced in the years 1925 to circa 1929. As with Classic American Carnival Glass, however, there are also some inferior items; lower end glass with poor iridescence, perhaps manufactured towards the end of the "flowering" of European Carnival.

Opposite page:
The superb *ROSE GARDEN* pattern was made by both Brockwitz in Germany and Eda Glasbruk in Sweden. But which shapes were made by Brockwitz and which by Eda? (see Chapter Three, Germany and Chapter Six, Sweden for more information). Back, from left: marigold pitcher, SP $500-900; 12" high, marigold cylinder vase, SP $700-900; 9" high, large, blue oval vase (one sold at auction in 1999 for $6000); marigold chop plate, NP (only marigold example reported); and blue pitcher, SP $800-1000. Foreground, from left: large blue rose bowl, SP $300-900; mid-size blue rose bowl, SP $300-900; 5" high, blue oval vase (one sold at auction in 1999 for $2000); and large marigold rose bowl (one sold at auction in 1995 for $1950). Please note that there have been very few auction and private sales for these items so values are extremely hard to judge.

There was also much plagiarism between the European manufacturers. Just as the Europeans had copied some of the Classic American patterns, they also copied each other. To further complicate the situation, moulds were also sold, glass was exported, and patterns were registered in one country and made in another. All in all, much cross fertilization of ideas took place. Patterns that are believed to have been made by more than one manufacturer include *ROSE GARDEN, CURVED STAR, ELEKTRA, PINWHEEL*, and *SUNFLOWER & DIAMOND*—there are probably more besides.

Two very different *CURVED STAR* vases from different makers. On the left is the blue Brockwitz version (SP $650-1000), while on the right is the Eda Glasbruk version known as *LASSE*. The vase had its own name within the pattern range—*DAGNY* (SP $800-1100). *Courtesy of Ann and David Brown.* For more detail, see Chapter Three on Germany and Chapter Six on Sweden.

Four vases with very similar patterns that could easily be confused, yet the manufacturers are very different. From left, Sowerby's *DERBY* aka *PINWHEEL* in marigold, SP $250-400; Riihimaki's *TENNESSEE STAR* in amber, SP $400-650; Brockwitz *CURVED STAR* in marigold, SP $400-900; and Inwald's tiny (just under 5" high) *PINWHEEL* in marigold, SP $400-600.

Signature Characteristics of European Carnival

Much European Carnival Glass is simply stunning. From intricate geometrics to classic Art Deco, and with iridescence and color of the highest quality, European Carnival has a true magic of its own combining beauty with practicality.

• Most items only have one patterned surface—usually the exterior. On plates and bowls, the inside is often plain, possibly to facilitate use. Most patterns described in the following chapters are exterior only and this will not be noted further as it is the norm. Where a pattern is interior or where there are two patterned surfaces, this **will** be noted in the text.

• As the pattern is usually exterior, shapes are designed in order to show it to maximum effect.

• The designs are frequently intaglio and geometric in style.

• Where flowers feature in the design, they are stylized and are usually (not always) executed in a "Near Cut" manner.

• Carnival colors are limited. Marigold was the most common color, with blue also being used in Scandinavia and Germany. However, there are variations and exceptions (the complete details for each factory are given in the relevant chapters). In Sweden, for example, an iridized, opaque white milk glass called pearl (*parlemorlystrad*) was used on some scarce examples of Eda Glasbruk's Carnival. Rare examples of purple and lilac Carnival were also used from time to time in Scandinavia, though amethyst was regularly used by Sowerby in England. Teal, aqua, smoke, pink, black, vaseline, and amber are all Carnival colors that are known to have been made in Europe.

• The base of the items are often ground and typically exhibit tiny chips due to this method of manufacture. This is a feature of the glass.

• Iridescence is often of very high quality (there are exceptions).

• Little hand finishing (there are some exceptions).

• Vases may be blown or pressed into moulds, but not swung, and only very occasionally have hand finishing or ruffling to the mouths.

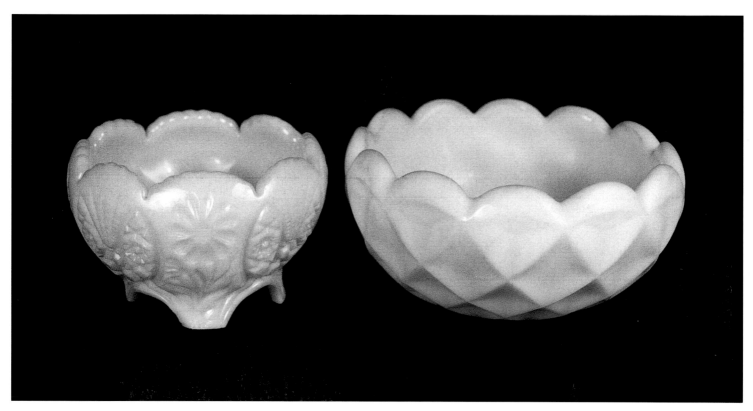

Marigold and blue are the most frequently seen colors from the European manufacturers, but other colors were used too—lilac, black, aqua, and smoke are some of the more unusual shades. Pearl, known in Sweden as *parlemorlystrad*, was used on occasion by Eda Glasbruk. The iridescence is soft and shimmers with delicate pinks and greens; the base color is opaque white. On the left is a small *SUNK DAISY* rose bowl, on the right is a small *SVEA* rose bowl. *Courtesy of Ann and David Brown.* NP.

Shapes were often designed for practical use and to show the exterior pattern to best effect. In the Brockwitz catalog dated 1931, all illustrated shapes were given their contemporary names in both English and German. These shapes were common to most European manufacturers and are listed below. For information, the German names are also noted in parenthesis.

• **Table sets** consisted of three items: covered butter (sometimes the pattern is inside the lid), sugar bowl (may or may not be stemmed), and cream jug. The creamer may sometimes seem to be disproportionately small compared to the large sugar bowl.
• **Celery vases** (*traubenspuler*)—tall, cylindrical containers, often on a pedestal foot. These items were also used for washing fruit, especially grapes, at the table.
• **Flower-bowl** (*blumenbowl*)—shaped rather like a squat, wide vase and came complete with a metal grille or a glass frog, to hold the blooms in place.
• **Footed cake stands** (*tortenplatten*)—also known as salvers, displayed gateaux (cakes) well.

• **Cheese stand** (*kaseglocken*)—may be mistaken for the butter dish, which is quite a bit smaller. The cheese stand is a substantial, large covered item. The pattern is usually exterior on the lid on these showy items.
• **Two piece fruit dish** (*fruchtshale*)—an imposing shape rather like a punch bowl, comprising an upturned stemmed sugar (compote) or an upturned stemmed celery vase, with a large bowl on top. The base of the bowl had a custom shaped, circular groove into which the pedestal foot of the upturned sugar or celery snugly fitted. These, of course, were multi-purpose, as the items that made up the fruit dish were also used separately in their own right.
• **Jardinières**—large oval flower bowls. These were popular shapes and were often placed on window ledges filled with small potted plants.
• **Table centers** (*tafelaufsatze*)—were the splendid epergnes that decorated the center of the dining table.
• **Wine, cordial or liqueur sets** (*likorsatze*)—these were made up of a decanter or carafe, stemmed wine glasses and sometimes, a matching undertray.

A table set In Europe Is made up of a covered butter dish (which sometimes has the pattern on the inside of the lid, as here), creamer and sugar (stemmed or flat based). This marigold set is in the *CURVED STAR* pattern and was made by Brockwitz. Butter dish SP $75-125; creamer $50-75; stemmed sugar $50-75.

A two piece fruit dish, or *fruchtshale*, was an imposing centrepiece for the table. The height of the *fruchtshale* could be varied by using either a large upturned celery (as here) or a smaller stemmed sugar, combined with a large, flat bottomed bowl on top. These *CURVED STAR* items are from Brockwitz. Marigold celery $50-75; large bowl $50-75.

The Going Down of the Sun

In the aftermath of World War Two, mainland Europe witnessed unprecedented, forced mass movements of populations, including many deportations and mass expulsions. Many boundaries were totally re-written. European society has always been in flux, fragmented, and diverse and during the twentieth century it became more fragmented and diverse than ever. Factories were destroyed, many records and archives were lost forever. Further, as Czechoslovakian glass researcher Diane Foulds aptly put it, in correspondence with the authors, "European glass is ultimately a study in cross-fertilization." Factories copied each others' patterns, bought each others' moulds and even took each others' workers. The lack of complete catalog records does not help to unravel the remaining mysteries and consequently, many puzzles still exist and will continue to do so.

How To Use This Book / Sources of Information

Part Two of this book is arranged by country—within each country the manufacturer(s) are considered and all known patterns that can be attributed to that manufacturer based on catalog evidence are detailed alphabetically. For each pattern, shapes and colors that are known have been listed. Where the authors have not actually seen the item, shape, or color themselves, the term "reported" is used. We have listed known colors for each pattern in general and not for each individual shape—this information represents the best of current knowledge, consequently, the reader should be aware that not *all* shapes mentioned are necessarily known in *all* the stated colors for that particular pattern. Please note that where measurements are given they are approximate. The attributed pattern listing is followed by a listing of patterns that are thought to be by that manufacturer based on circumstantial (rather than catalog) evidence and "house style." All countries in Europe are first considered, following which the Carnival output of Argentina, Mexico, Peru, India, and China is also itemized.

Collections containing European Carnival Glass that are located within the USA, the UK, and Scandinavia have been photographed for the purposes of this book. The surviving catalogs of most European and Argentinean Carnival Glass manufacturers have been studied: illustrations from them and full details are included within the text. It should be stressed that the catalogs available are only a very small proportion of what must have been issued at the time. We do not have a full complement of catalog information for any manufacturer. Sourcing them has been a long and difficult task and a great deal of credit must go to Robert Smith of Boston. German glass researcher Siegmar Gieselberger has also been instrumental in providing important Brockwitz archives. The discovery of some of these catalogs has resulted in much re-writing and constant re-thinking. Information and catalogs have also been acquired through museums in England, Scandinavia, and mainland Europe as well as the Boston City Library. Also listed within the text for each pattern are the countries where examples of the Carnival Glass items have been found.

Throughout the book, value ranges are given for all photographed items where possible. Value is assessed for items with excellent iridescence and no damage, and in the color and shape photographed only. Values are based on known auction prices and private sales. Lower values would naturally be attributed to items with damage and poor color or iridescence. Condition, color, iridescence, availability, and indeed subjective judgment all play a major part in determining value. The reader is referred to David Doty's *A Field Guide to Carnival Glass*[3], Tom and Sharon Mordini's *Carnival Glass Auction Prices*[4] and similar guides to gain further pricing information. Please note that many of the items shown in this book have never or only rarely appeared at public auction, therefore price assessment is not easy. Furthermore, many patterns are being named and attributed for the very first time in this book; therefore, although they may have been sold at auction in the past, they have been sold unidentified. For some exceptionally rare and unusual items, no price (NP) is shown. This is because the item concerned has not, to our knowledge, changed hands either at auction or in a private sale, for many years—indeed it may never have changed hands. A speculative price category (SP) has been used purely as a guide, where the value has been assessed based on similar, though not necessarily identical, items. Neither the authors nor the publishers can be liable for any losses incurred when using the values attributed within this book, as the basis for any transaction.

[1] Dr. Jindrich Cadik, *Modern Glassmaking in Czechoslovakia* (Prague, 1931).

[2] Robert and Deborah Truitt, *Collectible Bohemian Glass. 1880-1940* (Kensington, Maryland: B & D Glass, 1995).

[3] David Doty, *A Field Guide to Carnival Glass* (Marietta, Ohio: The Glass Press Inc., 1998).

[4] Tom and Sharon Mordini, *Carnival Glass Auction Price Reports* (Freeport, Illinois: by authors, 1984-1999).

England

"This royal throne of kings, this sceptred isle"
—William Shakespeare

Glassmaking was established in England as long ago as the twelfth century. Originally the focus of the industry was in the south of the country, but with the discovery of plentiful supplies of coal for fuel, the glass industry, along with many other "heavy" industries, was drawn north. It developed and grew in two main areas: one was in the Midlands around the area known as Stourbridge, the other was in the northeast around the Tyne Valley. As time went on, the developing canal and navigable river networks in both areas served the industry well for the transport of both raw materials and finished goods. Pressed glass dominated the Tyne glassworks while the Stourbridge area became better known for its blown "art glass" product.

Sowerby's Ellison Glass Works Ltd., Gateshead-on-Tyne

"The land of far horizons"
—G. M. Trevelyan.

The ancient kingdom of Northumbria was home to Sowerby's Ellison Glassworks. Situated in the northeast of England, the region encompasses Durham, Northumberland, and the river basins of the Tees, Tyne, and Wear. To the east lies the North Sea: at times wild and inhospitable, witness to many tragedies and shipwrecks, yet also a provider of jobs, livelihoods and indisputable beauty—"the glories of surf and foam" (Lord Byron). Rich in history, the area played host to the Roman occupation—the Emperor Hadrian ordered the build-

ing of a great wall to run from the banks of the Tyne in the east of England right across to the Solway Firth in the west. Its purpose was to keep out the Scots, for the border land was traditionally one of great unrest. Indeed right up to the end of the sixteenth century the area was part of the "Border Reivers"—an area of fortified towns and farms that was constant witness to the clash of steel and the thunder of hooves and where cattle rustling was rife.

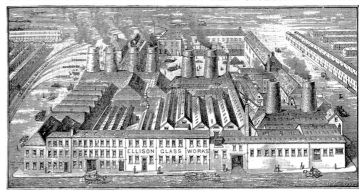

Familiar visual symbols of Tyneside are the bridges that span the River Tyne, joining Newcastle to Gateshead.

Sowerby's Ellison Glass Works in Gateshead-on-Tyne was opened in 1852. This ad is from the British *Pottery Gazette* of 1887 and clearly shows the rail and road links that Sowerby's utilized. The river Tyne, just a few hundred yards away, provided further transport facilities. Note the six huge chimneys in the middle of the factory; these were the six ten-pot furnaces, all under one roof.

Glassmaking was one of the area's many industries. Cheap local coal supplies as well as the navigable waterway of the Tyne were major inducements for its location. In the midst of a rapid industrial boom, Sowerby's Ellison Glassworks opened in 1852 at East Street, Gateshead, on the south bank of the river Tyne: within fifteen years it had become the largest pressed glass manufacturer in Europe, with offices and showrooms in London, in Germany (Hamburg), and France (Paris). Indeed, a contemporary account noted that it was "the largest pressed glass manufacturer in the world." Towards the end of the 1800s and in the early years of the twentieth century the situation was not so good for the company. Sowerby lost their lead. Foreign competition was fierce and as the cataclysmic years of World War One loomed, many of the work force left their jobs to enlist.

A fresh start was needed in the post war gloom. In the early 1920s, Sowerby brought in an innovative chemist, Percival Marson, who had experimented with iridescence on glass in the Stourbridge glassmaking region several years earlier.[1] The United Kingdom was no stranger to Carnival Glass, having had huge quantities shipped into the country from the USA via agents such as Charles Pratt, from around 1910. Supplies had dried up during the war years, but in the early 1920s had resumed again with vigor. The National Glass Co. Ltd., were pushing Fenton's "Iridescent Art Ware" through ads in the *Pottery Gazette*, stating in 1923 that the product was "the original iridescent glassware which still holds first place for beautiful colour effects—golden, green, violet and royal blue—high grade quality—at moderate prices." In April 1925, an article by the National Glass Co. in the *Pottery Gazette* noted that "In the old iridescent ware, which was at one time chiefly supplied in a golden orange tint, a new celeste blue, having a kind of satin sheen finish, is being offered." Carnival Glass was undoubtedly popular in Britain and it sold well. Sowerby needed a boost for their sales—the way forward was obvious. Sowerby launched iridescent glass in the early 1920s and it was a success, for Marson's lustre effects were of high quality. They took a full page ad in the *Pottery Gazette* in October 1926 that proclaimed in large type: "Sowerby's Ellison Glassworks beg to announce the Opening on October 1st, of their New London Showroom". . . and on offer was "Iridescent" Glass.

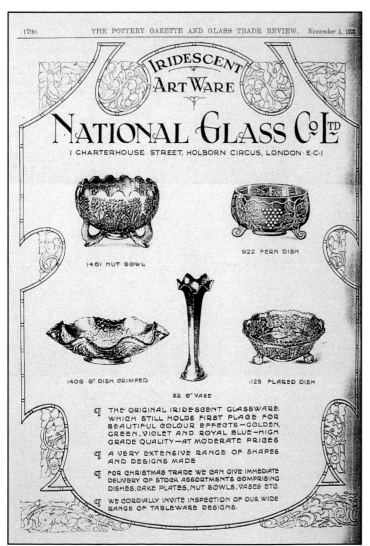

A 1923 British *Pottery Gazette* ad for the National Glass Co. Ltd., in London, featuring Fenton's Classic Carnival. These lines were still very popular in the UK and helped to create the demand for similar items from Sowerby.

Sowerby's announced their new London showroom in the British *Pottery Gazette* in 1926. Iridescent Glass— Sowerby's Carnival— was on offer.

Carnival was a success and Sowerby's business looked up. In 1929, they listed offices in Australia (Sydney), New Zealand (Auckland), South Africa (Johannesburg), South America (Buenos Aires), and India (Bombay). The greatest part of the company's general output went to the former British Colonies, with orders constantly coming from the War Office, the Admiralty, and the RAF lists as well. In the British *Pottery Gazette* of April 1931 it was reported that Sowerby had a big selection of glass on show: "There was also a full range of pieces in orange flame iridescent ware, suitable for the needs of special markets." Britain's Queen Mary undoubtedly liked Sowerby's glass. We can't be certain that she purchased their Carnival Glass, but we can be sure that when she visited Sowerby's stands at the British Industries Fairs in the early 1930s she ordered several of Sowerby's lines: rose bowls, vases, and trinket sets. Indeed, her namesake, the *R.M.S. Queen Mary* (now at Long Beach, California), was fitted out in 1936 with glass lighting and passenger tableware made by Sowerby.

The *R.M.S. Queen Mary* was fitted out with glass lighting and tableware made by Sowerby.

A contemporary writer in the 1930s[2] described the factory processes in this way: "From out of the furnace, clumps of glass are extracted by long steel rods. These are clamped into a press. Within a few moments out comes a butter dish or jug as the case may be. These articles are then attached to another rod and poked into the glory hole where they are re-heated. Another skilled worker then gives the correct shaping touch and they are passed into the cooler where they lie for about eight hours—then are examined for faults, finally cleaned and polished. Altogether, from furnace to packing room, the products pass through about sixteen or seventeen different hands."

The good times were not to last. The press moulded glass tableware market was being filled by cut-price imports from countries such as Czechoslovakia. World War Two brought problems to the northeast and Sowerby's output, in common with other glass manufacturers, was severely curtailed. When peace returned, high taxes were imposed by many of Sowerby's previous overseas markets so as to protect their own trade. Sowerby lost more business. Further, they were slow to change either their production methods (they had been using manual techniques to manufacture press moulded glass since the nineteenth century) or their product styles. Difficulties began: Sowerby's mould shop closed in 1952; in 1956 the Official Receiver was called in; and in 1957, Sowerby was taken over by Suntex Safety Glass Industries. The company entered a period of slow decline: signal lamps and safety glass were produced in Gateshead, while the manufacture of fancy glass ceased in 1972. The Nazeing Glassworks in Essex purchased almost four hundred of Sowerby's moulds. Most of them were in such poor condition that they were left to rot and disintegrate. Nazeing report that they were only interested in the signal moulds and saved some twenty or thirty moulds in total

from eventual destruction. In 1982, the original Ellison works was demolished. The one surviving connection is an industrial glass plant in Gateshead called Tynesyde Safety Glass. It represents all that is left of the original links with Suntex and Sowerby. Sadly, that company report that all their archives were destroyed in 1998. All that remains of Sowerby's Carnival Glass legacy are the beautiful items that they made: the *DIVING DOLPHINS*, the *COVERED SWANS*, and more—preserved by collectors in homes and museums around the world.

Signature Characteristics of Sowerby's Carnival Glass

• Generally high quality glassware, though as the factory clung on into the 1950s and early 1960s, some later examples of the common items such as *CHUNKY* are not up to the standard of Sowerby's earlier output.

• Some of Sowerby's glass has a ground base, some doesn't; also Sowerby sometimes used one-piece moulds—see below for more explanatory detail on these characteristics.

• Marigold and amethyst were the main colors used for Carnival, however, blue, green (as well as intermediate shades of aqua), vaseline, black amethyst, and amber were also used —see below for more explanatory detail on color.

• Use of old moulds, some dating back to the 1880s, as well as moulds gradually introduced through 1927. Patterns are not exclusively exterior—Sowerby frequently used interior patterns as well.

• Most of Sowerby's Carnival was "as moulded"—however there was hand finishing, in the form of ruffling, on a few items such as the *DIVING DOLPHINS* bowls and some *PINEAPPLE* items. This is somewhat uncommon in European Carnival.

• Unlike most other European factories, Sowerby used both cameo and intaglio designs (most European factories used mainly intaglio, "near-cut" patterns).

Sowerby's peacock head trademark, moulded in the glass, is familiar to most collectors. Not seen so often, however, is the paper label marked BRITISH MADE. Other labels are known marked TYNESYDE GLASSWARE.

When Sowerby began to manufacture Carnival Glass in the mid 1920s they utilized many of their existing moulds. Some of them dated back to the 1880s, though a few had only been in production for ten or twenty years. Some re-vamping took place, as a plagiarized version of Imperial's *SCROLL EMBOSSED* was made as an interior for various items, notably the *DIVING DOLPHINS* bowls. One of Sowerby's patents, dating from June 1885, serves to identify some of the company's items. It was a characteristic mould design, whereby the handles of the item (a small sweetmeat or bonbon dish) are moulded all in one-piece across the top section.[1] The little *SCROLL EMBOSSED* bonbons that are sometimes called ashtrays exhibit this unusual feature. Sowerby's delightful peacock head trademark can very occasionally be found on their Carnival lines.

Though Sowerby are credited with introducing iridized glass to England in the mid 1920s, Simon Cottle reports[1] that the 1912 trade catalog, which had many new lines, showed "photo-set illustrations of many unusual 'cut' designs, some of which appear to have an iridescence." *PINEAPPLE, DIAMOND PEAKS, SOWERBY WIDE PANEL* and *SEA THISTLE* were all new lines in 1912 and indeed, there are examples of *PINEAPPLE* with weak marigold iridescence that may well date from this early era of production. Further, Cottle notes that iridized glass was actually developed at Sowerby in 1905, but didn't go into full commercial production for another twenty years (see entry on *TINY DAISY* below).

The real glories of Sowerby's Carnival stem from the 1920s, and full credit must be given to Percival Marson, the original Stourbridge developer of iridized glass. The iridescent effects that they used were known as "Sunglow" (a golden iridescence like marigold found on clear base glass) and "Rainbo" (a deeper, darker effect usually found on amethyst, blue, blue/green, and black base glass). Sowerby's blue base glass varies tremendously from a consistent cobalt coloring seen on the *FLORA* bowls, to a wide variety of blue/greens.

Typical shapes for Sowerby were tableware and novelty items, sometimes called "fancy goods." Vases (often the same pattern in several sizes) were also produced by the company. The base on some items is ground, though on others there is a collar base. One-piece moulds were also used by the company from time to time. This type of mould has no joints and therefore cannot be opened to remove the hot glass. Therefore, once the plunger (which shapes the inside of the item) has been withdrawn, the mould is turned upside down and the hot glass is simply dropped out. It would have been caught by a glassworker, using wooden paddles and would then have been attached ("stuck-up"—see Appendix One) to a hot metal punty rod for finishing, iridising etc. Such items often have tiny chips on the base due to the grinding—in our opinion such minor chips are not "damage" but are simply characteristics of the method in which the glass was made.

Carnival lines were shown in the 1927 Sowerby catalog. It is interesting to note that prices for many of the popular items were quoted at that time. A comparison between them indicates which items were costlier to produce than others. Prices were, of course, quoted in pounds sterling and were pre-decimalization. Thus amounts are shown in shillings (there were twenty shillings to the pound and twelve pence to the shilling). A contemporary US dollar estimate is given after each price.

Note: amounts quoted are for wholesale quantities and are per dozen.

The *PINEAPPLE* rose bowl cost six shillings per dozen: six pence each. 6d. (4 cents).

The *WICKERWORK* plate and stand cost twelve shillings per dozen for the plate and eight shillings per dozen for the stand. A single plate and stand would have cost a shilling for each plate and eight pence for each stand. The pair would have been one shilling and sixpence. 1/6d. (12 cents).

The *DIVING DOLPHINS* bowls cost eighteen shillings per dozen: one shilling and sixpence each. 1/6d. (12 cents).

The smallest of the *HOBSTAR AND CUT TRIANGLES* bowls cost eight shillings and sixpence per dozen: eight pence half-penny each. 8½d. each. (6 cents).

The *DAISY BLOCK ROWBOAT* cost ten shillings per dozen: ten pence each. 10d. (7 cents).

Sowerby Catalogs

Those patterns that have been attributed to Sowerby have been identified from the following editions of Sowerby catalogs (by year of issue): 1882 (Book 9), 1895, 1900 (Book 17), 1907, 1912 (Book 20), 1927, 1933 (Book 30), plus Books 35 through 41, which cover the 1940s through the early 1960s. All are stored at the Shipley Art Gallery, Gateshead on Tyne. Sincere thanks to the past curator, Nick Dolan, for his outstanding help.

Sowerby Patterns Known in Carnival Glass

AFRICAN SHIELD

Just one shape was made in this pattern (Sowerby's #2639), a tiny, eight sided, violet vase complete with a wire mesh grille across the top to hold the flowers in place. Sometimes it may be found with a chrome lid, complete with small hole to fit a spoon (to be used as a mustard pot or similar). The pattern is reminiscent of the late 1920s or early 1930s style, featuring bold, simple lines and elongated ovals. It's not an easily found item, though as you would expect, it turns up more in England than elsewhere. Examples have also been reported in the USA and Australia.

Shape: vase
Color: marigold

This dainty little posy or violet vase is Sowerby's *AFRICAN SHIELD* and comes complete with a wire mesh grille to hold the blooms in place. Fully complete with the metal grille, these marigold vases range from $100-150.

CANE AND SCROLL see *SEA THISTLE*

CHUNKY aka *ENGLISH HOB AND BUTTON*

Sowerby's pattern #2266 is a simple, geometric exterior pattern that was well established in the factory's line when Carnival Glass came on the scene in the 1920s. A wide range of tableware items was illustrated in the company's catalogs in 1907 and 1912. *CHUNKY* was produced in marigold during the mid 1920s and then again in the 1950s when it was made in a range of bowls and plates that are sometimes fitted with a variety of unusual metal stands. Two and three tiers are known with the stands frequently formed as female figures. Sowerby's catalog Number 37 (dating from 1954) states that the bowls were available in "Sunglow Iridescent shade . . . with or without chromium fittings." Interestingly, the Indiana Glass Company, Dunkirk, Indiana, reproduced this pattern in the 1970s in blue and amber Carnival bowls and plates (see Part Four).

Shapes: bowls, plate, epergne with various metal fitments
Colors: marigold and amethyst

Sowerby's *CHUNKY* was their pattern number 2266 and made its first appearance in the 1907 catalog illustration shown.

Known to collectors as *CHUNKY* or *ENGLISH HOB AND BUTTON*, some of the shapes were amazingly exotic. Here is a two-part marigold epergne, the upper level supported by a chrome figure in the Art Deco style. One with a metal lily on the top sold at auction in the USA in 1995 for $450. Simple marigold bowls will sell for much less.

COVERED HEN

A fascinating item, the lid to this butter dish is formed as a hen surrounded by her family of chicks. First seen in the Sowerby catalogs in 1928 with the catalog #2551, this novelty butter dish was called the "Chic butter." No examples are known to us bearing the Sowerby peacock head trademark, however, some examples have been seen bearing a paper label marked Sowerby. There are variations with regard to the little chicks and the rocks that surround the seated hen. This item was also made again in Sunglow (marigold) by Sowerby in the 1950s and possibly later. Examples have been found in the USA, UK and Australia. (An interesting, controversial account of the *COVERED HEN* butter dish can be found in O. J. Olson's "News and Views" Volume 20, #5, July 10, 1982 and also the Carnival Glass Society (UK) Ltd., Journal #4 1984.)

Shape: hen novelty covered butter dish
Colors: marigold and blue

Sowerby's *COVERED SWAN* and *COVERED HEN*, both in blue. Compare this *SWAN* to the ones in the following illustration—they are different. The blue one in this picture is thought to be a newer re-cut version of the old 1880s original mould. The delicate neck (surely the cause of much breakage in manufacture) is filled in with glass. There are also minor differences in the body and the edge shape of the base. All are hard to find. Blue *COVERED SWAN* $100-300: blue *COVERED HEN* $80-150.

COVERED SWAN

Almost a twin to the *COVERED HEN*, this was made in the 1920s, using an early 1880s mould (Sowerby pattern #2031.) It is a masterpiece, a breathtakingly beautiful item that makes one marvel at the skills of the mouldmakers and glassmakers. The neck of the swan gracefully curves right back until it almost touches the swan's body. The whole shape of the piece is elegant and satisfying. The item was designed to be a butter dish, the swan being the lid that nestled into a scalloped base. On the inside of some of the lids, faint registration details (the letters RD and barely discernible numbers) as well as a peacock head trademark, can sometimes be very faintly seen. Sowerby's catalog from 1927 lists the *SWAN* butter as being made in Sunglow (marigold) and Rainbo lustre (amethyst).

There is also another *COVERED SWAN* from Sowerby that is similar in overall concept to the one detailed above, though the actual execution of the design has many differences. It is a newer version, though it is not possible to be certain when it was made. The color is blue, the space between neck and body is filled in with glass. The edge to the base is smooth, not scalloped and the lid fits on the outside of the base, not the inside as in the older version. Overall, it sits a little taller than the older *COVERED SWAN* and its base is identical to that on the *COVERED HEN*. All versions have been found in the USA, the UK, and Australia.

Shape: swan novelty covered butter dish
Colors: marigold and rare amethyst for the older version, blue only for the newer version with the filled in neck

The first version of Sowerby's *COVERED SWAN* that utilized the 1880s mould has a scalloped edge to the base. Compare this with the smooth edge of the re-cut version as shown in the previous photograph of the blue *COVERED SWAN* and *COVERED HEN*. None of the *COVERED SWANS* are easy to find. In marigold $100-300; in amethyst SP $200-400.

CROSSHATCH

This is a typical hobnail type of pattern and was given the Sowerby pattern #2377. *CROSSHATCH* probably dates from the early 1920s and is only known in Carnival in a small creamer and stemmed sugar that were part of a wide range of tableware items. The butter dish was probably also made in Carnival but has not yet been reported. Examples are usually marked with the peacock head trademark and are not too easy to find.

Shapes: creamer and stemmed sugar (compote)
Color: marigold

CROSSHATCH is known in only a few shapes, such as the sugar and creamer illustrated in this 1920s Sowerby ad. Other shapes may well be found one day.

SERVICE No. 2377

2377 Cream.   2377½ Cream.   2377 Sugar.

CYNTHIA (LADY CYNTHIA) see *SOWERBY DRAPE*

DAISY BLOCK ROWBOAT

The name for this item comes from the stylized daisy design that adorns its exterior. The interior of these boats usually has a ribbed design though rare examples are reported with a plain interior and the peacock head trademark plus a moulded Registered Design (RD) #42947. The mould for this item was originally made in 1886; its Sowerby pattern was #1874. Three sizes of these boats were made at that time in crystal glass. A single stand was also designed to fit all of them. When the mould was revived in the 1920s, however, only the mid size boat was made in Carnival. No Carnival stand has yet been found, though it is a possibility, of course. The *DAISY BLOCK ROWBOAT* was probably intended as a table decoration, to be used for flowers or candies. It has been reported in the USA, UK, and Australia, though it is not an easy pattern to find.

Shape: boat novelty
Colors: marigold, amethyst, and rare aqua shades

The *DAISY BLOCK ROWBOAT* (pattern #1874) was first shown in Sowerby's catalogs in 1886. Though three sizes were originally made in crystal, only the 12" boat is known in Carnival Glass

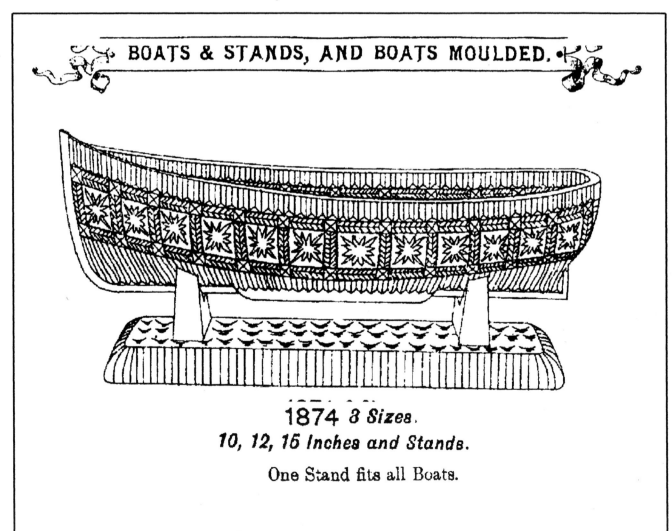

BOATS & STANDS, AND BOATS MOULDED.

1874 3 Sizes.
10, 12, 15 Inches and Stands.
One Stand fits all Boats.

DERBY aka PINWHEEL

A broad, intaglio geometric pattern, its dominant feature being an 8-pointed star, DERBY (Sowerby's #2414) has been found in a variety of shapes. Of particular interest is the fact that an almost identical pattern was produced by Josef Inwald of Czechoslovakia, though the range of shapes is not exactly the same. The item found most often (though it should be stressed that this is actually rather a scarce item) is the vase, which Sowerby produced in three heights: 6.5", 8", and 10.5". The Inwald vases, though similar in appearance, are in fact at different heights to the Sowerby ones—indeed, the smallest Inwald PINWHEEL stands only a fraction over 4" high. The bases are also different. The Sowerby vases have a domed base whilst the Inwald version has a flat base, features a star pattern, and is ground to a polished mirror shiny finish.

The DERBY rose bowl has been seen in the rare color of black amethyst. An unusual shape, this Sowerby rose bowl is not the typical shape collectors generally expect, as can be seen in the photograph. Examples of DERBY have been found in the USA and Australia, though the widest range of shapes and colors has been found (not surprisingly) in the UK. Note that the name DERBY was given to this range by Sowerby during the early 1930s; prior to that it had simply been known by its pattern number.

Shapes: vase (three sizes), cookie jar (biscuit barrel), bowls in various sizes and rare rose bowl. It is possible that table set items exist in this pattern, too.

Colors: marigold, amethyst, rare black amethyst, and two examples (to date) of the blue 8" vase

A most unusual shape and color, this is Sowerby's DERBY rose bowl in black amethyst. *Courtesy of Frank and Shirley.* NP.

DERBY aka PINWHEEL vases came in three sizes: 6.5", 8" and 10.5". The three examples shown are all amethyst. $300-500 (for the 6" vase)—similar prices are likely for the other sizes, though this is speculative as few have sold at public auction.

Another seldom seen shape in Sowerby's DERBY pattern is this covered cookie jar in marigold. *Courtesy of Don and Phyllis Atkinson.* SP $100-200.

DIAMOND PEAKS

Extensively featured in Sowerby's 1912 catalog in a range of fifteen different tableware shapes, this geometric pattern (#2334) was made in Carnival a few years later, during the 1920s. In common with many other European shapes, the bowl in this pattern fits neatly onto the upturned, stemmed sugar, creating an attractive table center. Not an easy pattern to find, most examples are from the UK and only a few shapes in the range are currently known in Carnival.

Shapes: stemmed sugar (compote), butter dish, and large bowl. A creamer is likely.

Color: marigold

The typically European match of an upturned stemmed sugar (compote) underneath a large fruit bowl makes up the intentional shape of the two piece fruit dish—an attractive table centrepiece. The pattern here is Sowerby's *DIAMOND PEAKS* in marigold. *Courtesy of Carol and Derek Sumpter.* SP $100-150.

Sowerby's 1912 catalog had a wide range of shapes in the newly introduced #2334 pattern. Known today as *DIAMOND PEAKS*, this was made in Carnival during the 1920s. A stemmed sugar (compote) like that shown in the illustration, is reported bearing a paper label that says TYNESYDE GLASSWARE.

DIAMOND PINWHEEL

The maker of this pattern had long been a mystery until Janet and Alan Mollison found a *DIAMOND PINWHEEL* butter dish complete with a cream colored paper label, edged with gold, at an antique fair in the United Kingdom in 1991. The wording on the label read "British Made" and above it was the Sowerby peacock head logo. Our recent research has discovered this pattern (#2295) illustrated in Sowerby's catalog in 1907 in sixteen different tableware shapes (not made in Carnival at that time). The butter dish is listed in the 1927 catalog as being made in both marigold and amethyst (Sunglow and Rainbo) though currently, no amethyst examples are known.

The pattern is a simple geometric and the shape is fundamentally practical. The exterior of the bottom section carries a pinwheel pattern, flaring out to form the scalloped edge of the butter dish with its diamond design. The same diamond pattern is found on the **inside** of the lid. The significance of the mix of interior and exterior patterns only becomes apparent when the top and bottom sections are fitted together. The diamond pattern on the bottom, when viewed from above, is then seen through the glass, because of the way the pattern fans out to form the edge of the butter dish. In a similar fashion, the interior pattern of the top half is seen through the glass. It is a clever use of design, coupled with excellent color and iridescence throughout. On the ground base of the dish is a slightly indented, 20-rayed intaglio star.

Shapes: butter dish and cake stand
Color: marigold

The swirling pattern of Sowerby's *DIAMOND PINWHEEL* is easy to see on the base of this cake stand (salver). *Courtesy of Carol and Derek Sumpter.* SP $75-125.

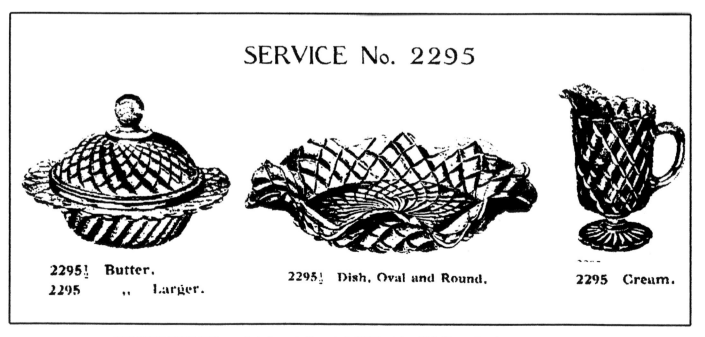

DIAMOND PINWHEEL was first shown in Sowerby's 1907 catalog. This illustration, however, comes from one of their 1920s catalogs, where the item was listed as being made in *Sunglow* (marigold Carnival). Two sizes of butter dish were made, but only the smaller size (#2295½) was listed in *Sunglow*.

DIVING DOLPHINS

DIVING DOLPHINS was made from one of Sowerby's old moulds dating back to 1882. In 1846, in the days of the young Queen Victoria, the British held a fabulous festival at the fashionable south coast resort of Brighton. A splendid fountain was built in Victoria's honor—the Victoria Fountain—that is an astonishing life sized twin to the DIVING DOLPHINS bowl. The dolphin is an ancient symbol of the sea and has long been associated with maritime power, so it was a natural choice for use in Brighton. The style of the fountain was typical of its time—the era of the Rococo Revival. Other craftsmen at the time were also using similar motifs. Glass and ceramic manufacturers on both sides of the Atlantic began to use dolphin and shell motifs. It's quite likely that when Sowerby originally made the DIVING DOLPHINS mould in 1882, they were reflecting the fashion of the era—the designer may even have styled it after the Victoria Fountain.[3]

The DIVING DOLPHINS bowl stands on three feet, each styled to form the shape of a dolphin's head. Their bodies curve up and round, onto the main part of the bowl. Around the sides of the bowl are stylized flowers and leaves, the combination of elements forming a most attractive, overall design. Note that this pattern is cameo (raised up off the surface of the glass). In the 1920s, when Sowerby began to make iridized glass, DIVING DOLPHINS (Sowerby #1544) was one of the moulds that they revived, but one change was made. The interior of the original bowls had no pattern, but Sowerby decided to update the old mould by adding their version of Imperial's SCROLL EMBOSSED pattern. This is an undoubted copy that Sowerby subsequently also utilized on several other small Carnival items.

This pattern has been found in the USA, the UK, and Australia. A splendid amber bowl was the second piece of Carnival Glass that the authors owned! Found at a small, local antique fair back in the early 1980s, it cost £5 (about $8)—quite a bargain.

Shapes: ruffled or smoothly flared bowl, as well as rare square and tri-corn bowl and rose bowl, all shaped from the same mould

Colors: marigold, amethyst, rare aqua/teal blue shades, and amber.

ENGLISH HOB AND BUTTON see CHUNKY

ENGLISH HOBSTAR

The maker of the boat shaped ENGLISH HOBSTAR has been a mystery for many years, but our discovery of the Sowerby catalog from 1933 finally came up with the answer in late 1999. It is Sowerby's pattern #2480 and was made in two boat shapes: sides incurved or straight up. Carnival examples are sometimes found in chrome handled, basket fittings, decorated with leaves. An attractive and useful item, it was probably made from the late 1920s through the mid 1930s. Examples have been found in the UK and Australia.

Shape: boat
Color: marigold

The iridescence on this Sowerby ENGLISH HOBSTAR marigold jardinière (oval bowl) is truly astonishing. Pinks, limes, and purples flash hotly as the glass catches the light, proving that Sowerby could produce an iridescence to rival anyone's! SP $50-100 for an example with this kind of superb iridescence; much less, however, for a pale example, perhaps $20-50.

Here's a most unusual color for Sowerby's DIVING DOLPHINS—blue! The regular, ruffled marigold bowl in this pattern would be $125-225; for this teal blue color, however, no prices at auction are recorded but they would almost certainly be considerably higher than the marigold examples. *Courtesy of Don and Phyllis Atkinson.*

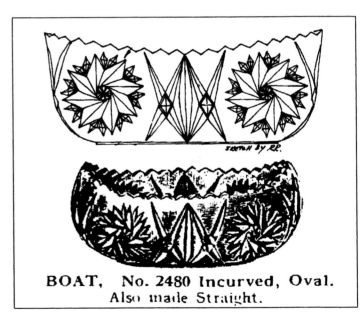

BOAT, No. 2480 Incurved, Oval. Also made Straight.

ENGLISH HOBSTAR is shown here in a drawing (top, courtesy Ray Rogers of Australia) and from the Sowerby 1933 catalog (below).

FLORA

A beautiful, intaglio exterior pattern of roses and leaves distinguishes this unusual bowl (Sowerby #2565). It was manufactured in England, probably in the 1920s and 1930s, yet the Carnival examples are very hard to find in that country, indeed, most have been found in the United States. In Carnival, it is only known in a rich cobalt blue, though the mould was used for later production in various non-iridized colors that often have a matt finish (sand blasted). In fact, the pattern was available as a fruit set with six matching small bowls, though none of these have yet been reported in Carnival.

A *FLORA* bowl (not iridized) can be seen in Sowerby's Pattern Book as late as 1956, with a central glass female figurine and a separate plinth. The figurine has holes around the bottom for fixing flower stems into. The whole set was described as "floating bowl with figurine and plinth. Bowl and figure supplied with or without sandblast decoration." The plinth, or base stand, was separate and was made of black glass. It appears that these bowls (though probably not the iridized ones) were actually bought in large quantity by a major British chocolate manufacturer who then sold them with confectionery inside, topped off with a pretty ribbon.[1]

    Shape: bowl
    Color: blue

GATESHEAD

A rare item indeed, this was reported in the CGS (UK) Pattern sheets in October 1984. The notes that accompany the illustration of this item indicate that it was made in the mid 1920s. It is a classical and elegant, tall candlestick with a plain panelled design. The Sowerby pattern number was #2445. Found in the UK.

    Shape: candlestick
    Color: black amethyst

Should you first see an example of Sowerby's *FLORA* with its base down, you would be unimpressed, as the bowl is quite plain. What a surprise when you turn it over to reveal the magnificent, intaglio, floral pattern that lies underneath! Only known in blue, $75-150.

The *GATESHEAD* candlestick is a most imposing item in rich, black amethyst. *Courtesy of Frank and Shirley.* NP.

GOODNIGHT

Another rare candlestick, this is a small, handled, plain panelled item that was in production during the late 1920s and early 1930s. The original Sowerby name for the item was the *GOODNIGHT* candlestick and it had the pattern #2434. The correct name for this shape is actually a "chamber stick," as it was used to light one's way to the "bed chamber."

Shape: candlestick
Color: black

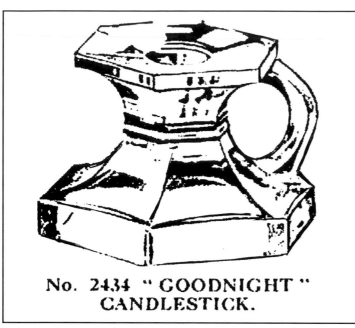

Sowerby's #2434 was their *GOODNIGHT* candlestick (or chamber stick)— a seldom seen item.

HANS aka *DIAMOND SHIELD*

This pattern has been incorrectly attributed[4] to Leerdam, and given the Dutch sounding name *HANS* (then re-named elsewhere as *DIAMOND SHIELD* and further incorrectly attributed to Brockwitz or Inwald)—so, as it has already been named, we will stay with the pattern name even though it would be more fitting to call it "Henry"— for this is an English made item from Sowerby. Illustrated in Sowerby's catalog number 38 dating from the 1950s, *HANS* was shown in the shape of a preserve set (catalog #2681), complete with chrome metal handle and preserve spoon. The stemmed sugar bowl or compote is also known on a chrome base. The pattern features file panels separated by notched ribs—the only examples we have studied had a pale iridescence. Known with a metal base. Found in the UK.

Shapes: stemmed compote (both with and without chrome base), bowl, and creamer

Color: marigold

A seldom seen pattern, *HANS* is shown here in the form of a small, marigold bowl. *Courtesy of Carol and Derek Sumpter.* SP $30-50.

HOBSTAR AND CUT TRIANGLES

An elegant contrast of diamond file-filled peaks, and smooth, rounded cup shapes is repeated six times around the *HOBSTAR AND CUT TRIANGLES* items. On the base is a large, intricate hobstar, angled off on six edges. The interior is ribbed with a bulls-eye effect of concentric rings in the very center. The ruffling on some bowls follows the pattern and is cupped outward in six equal scallops. *HOBSTAR AND CUT TRIANGLES* is not too hard to find in the regular bowl shape, but the cupped in rose bowls are quite scarce. Two further pattern variations were made: one has a complex hobstar in place of the plain panels around the sides (see *STELLAR* below); the other has a fan shape in the same location and is not yet reported in Carnival.

HOBSTAR AND CUT TRIANGLES had the Sowerby pattern #2411. In the Sowerby catalog of 1927 no less than twenty different shapes of bowl were offered in Carnival Glass in this pattern, each with slight variations to the basic shape, size, and ruffling. The pattern has been found in the USA, the UK, and Australia.

Shapes: bowls, plates, and rose bowls in various shapes and sizes from 5" to 8-9" diameter

Colors: marigold, amethyst, and rare aqua/teal. Black amethyst is also reported.

Aqua is a rare color for Sowerby and this is the only example currently reported in the *HOBSTAR AND CUT TRIANGLES* pattern. Marigold bowls do not usually sell for more than $50 or so, however, an aqua example like this would no doubt sell for quite a lot more. *Courtesy of Carol and Derek Sumpter.*

HONEYPOT

The base to this covered pot is some-times found and thought to be a Sowerby tumbler. In fact, it has a lid, too—the item is a lidded pot, though there is no hole for a spoon. A honeypot, perhaps? The lower half of the pot has a ribbed pattern; on the base is a 20-rayed intaglio star with (usually) a Sowerby peacock trademark moulded into the center. The lid has a matching ribbed pattern on the inside—the outside is smooth. Found in the UK.

Shape: lidded honeypot
Color: marigold

JAGGED EDGE

Sowerby's #2643 is an easily recog-nized pattern, distinguished by the vertical prism bands that form the shape of the piece as well as the pattern. In Carnival, the only shape reported to us is the boat—some-times found in a metal holder. Found in the UK and Australia.

Shape: boat
Color: marigold

JEWELLED PEACOCK

An intricate geometric design found on the exterior of the *SCROLL EMBOSSED* sweet dish or bonbon (sometimes errone-ously termed an ashtray). The name refers to the Sowerby peacock head trademark found in the center of this pattern. Introduced in the late 1800s, the pattern had the Sowerby pattern #8005. The *SCROLL EMBOSSED* interior was added in the 1920s when the Carnival ver-sions were made. Four distinctive, open-work handles are an inter-esting feature on this item. Found mainly in the UK, but also in the USA and Australia.

Shape: sweet dish
Color: marigold

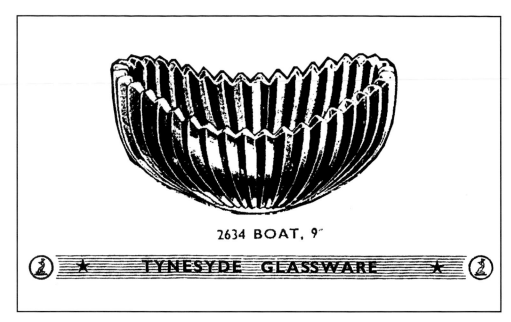

2634 BOAT, 9″

TYNESYDE GLASSWARE

JAGGED EDGE was illustrated in Sowerby's catalog #39 (dating from the 1950s) and was probably made in Carnival around that time. The *Sunglow* (Carnival) *COVERED HEN* was also illustrated in that catalog.

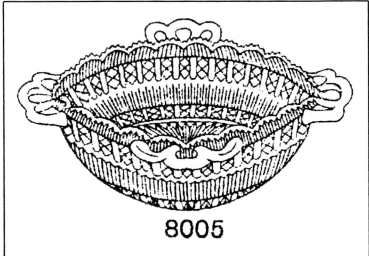

8005

Taken from a Sowerby catalog dated 1895, this illustration shows the *JEWELLED PEACOCK* exterior clearly on this pretty little bonbon (sweet) dish, pattern #8005. The *SCROLL EMBOSSED* interior was added some thirty years later when it was made in Carnival.

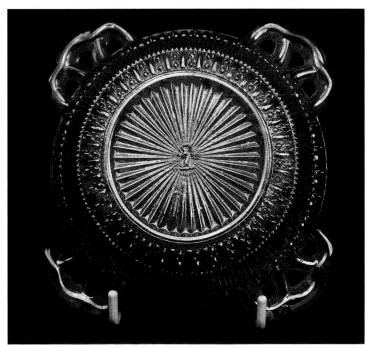

JEWELLED PEACOCK is an intricate Sowerby pattern that dates from the late 1800s. Seen here on a marigold bonbon (sweet) dish that is sometimes referred to as an ashtray. Note the Sowerby peacock head trademark in the center. $30-50.

LEA and variants

A simple combination of wide stippled band and a bordering notched band, this pattern has quite a history. Though the Carnival examples date from the 1920s, this pattern first appeared in the shape of a handled boat (now called a pickle dish) in Sowerby's catalogs in the late 1800s with the pattern #1322. The sugar and creamer shapes had the Sowerby pattern #1493. They are known in various, unusual non-iridized colors. The creamer and sugar often have a distinctive, stylized flower design inside that is also on the interior of the *RIBBONS AND LEAVES* sugar bowl. Note that there are knob feet on the sugar and creamer, but not on the pickle dish. There is a variation to the basic pattern where the stippled band is plain and punctuated with bold, upward pointing chevrons. This variation is only reported on the sugar and creamer shapes. Found in the UK, Australia, and USA.

Shapes: creamer, sugar dish, handled boat (pickle dish)

Color: marigold (amethyst is reported but we cannot confirm)

LINDISFARNE

An intricate and complex star design on the wide base is the main feature of this unusual bowl, dating from the very start of the 1900s. The sides of the bowl are upright and feature panels, topped off with a scalloped edge. Its first appearance (to our knowledge) was in Sowerby's 1907 catalog, where it was given the pattern #2240. Its production in Carnival was probably during the 1920s and was no doubt very limited, as only one example (found in the northeast of England) is currently known to us.

Shape: large bowl
Color: marigold

This illustration is taken from Sowerby's catalog #11, dated 1885, and shows the *LEA* sugar and creamer. The diamond mark shown in the illustration is the British Design Registry mark. The Carnival versions were probably made in the 1920s.

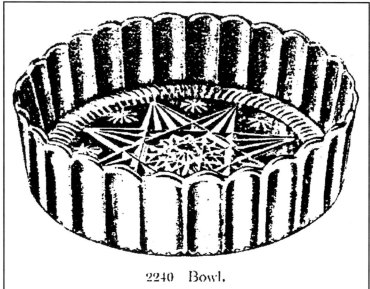

2240 Bowl.

Sowerby's 1907 catalog carried this illustration of their *LINDISFARNE* bowl (named by the authors). Though the intricate star pattern appears to be on the interior, in fact it is underneath the bowl. The inside is smooth and plain, making the bowl very practical for everyday use.

A stunning, intricate geometric design covers the base of Sowerby's *LINDISFARNE* bowl. NP.

PINEAPPLE

Sowerby's pattern #2349, *PINEAPPLE* was illustrated in the company's 1912 catalog. The pattern takes its name from the main motif in the design, which appears to be an upside-down pineapple! Some pieces are trademarked with the Sowerby peacock head. It is known in several unusual colors including blue and vaseline Carnival. A popular and attractive pattern that is found in the USA, UK, and Australia.

Shapes: creamer, sugar bowl, stemmed sugar, butter dish, rose bowl, plate, and stemmed cake plate

Colors: marigold, amethyst, aqua (rare), blue (rare), and vaseline (rare)

An amethyst, stemmed, ruffled sugar (or compote) alongside a creamer, in Sowerby's popular *PINEAPPLE* pattern. The smooth portions of the pattern contrast delightfully with the intricate file sections and allow the iridescence to produce different effects. A butter dish would make up the typical three-part table set, but they are exceptionally hard to find in this pattern. Indeed, an amethyst butter dish has not yet been reported. Stemmed sugar/compote $40-75; creamer $40-75.

PINWHEEL vases, see *DERBY*

PINWHEEL

This pattern, known in small bowls only, has no connection with the Sowerby pattern *DERBY* (pattern #2414) despite the fact that the name *PINWHEEL* has also been given to the *DERBY* vases. *PINWHEEL* is named after the whirling star on the base and is a twin to *PINEAPPLE*—the difference being that the pineapple motif is missing (a kind of "absentee pineapple"!) Mainly found in the UK.

Shape: bowls

Color: marigold (and possibly amethyst)

PORTCULLIS

Sowerby's pattern #2381, known to collectors as *PORTCULLIS*, is not a particularly interesting pattern. Its main design motif is a repeated block pattern. In Carnival, it is seldom seen and seldom recognized, though a wide range of tableware items in clear glass was illustrated in the company's 1927 catalog. Mainly found in the UK.

Shapes: various tableware items are known

Color: marigold

SERVICE
No. 2381

2381 Cream.   2381¾ Sugar.   2381½ Cream.

PORTCULLIS items, as depicted in Sowerby's 1927 catalog: shown are two shapes of creamer and a stemmed sugar (compote).

PORTSMOUTH

A geometric pattern known in the form of a handled bonbon. It is Sowerby's #2320 and was shown in their catalog dated 1907. Little is known about the availability of this item as only one example has been reported so far—there must be more but possibly they are currently going unidentified. For more information see the illustration at the end of this chapter.

Shape: handled bonbon
Color: amethyst

PRISM AND CANE

This design was first seen in Sowerby's catalogs in 1907 (pattern #2269) and is a variation on Sowerby's *CHUNKY* (aka *ENGLISH HOB AND BUTTON*). It features a similar prismatic, all-over design, though with elongated panels in the central section. Small bowls are found with Sowerby's *SCROLL EMBOSSED* on the interior. Mainly found in the UK.

Shape: bowl
Color: marigold

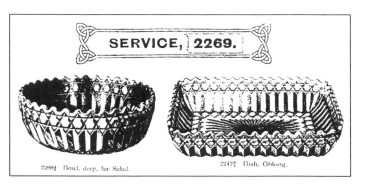

A seldom seen Sowerby pattern, *PRISM AND CANE* made its debut in Sowerby's 1907 catalog. The Carnival versions were made nearly twenty years later.

RIBBONS AND LEAVES

Raymond Notley reported (HOACGA 1984) that this item was "borrowed" from the firm of Davidson (also of Tyneside). It seems that Davidson had issued a covered butter in this pattern; Sowerby, however, only used the handled base and, unlike Davidson, Sowerby produced the pattern in Carnival. A distinctive, cameo, stylized lazy leaf pattern was added to the interior—it can also be seen on the interior of the *LEA* sugar and creamer.

Shape: handled sugar bowl
Color: marigold

ROYAL SWANS

ROYAL SWANS is a particularly lovely item. The centre section is an oval, boat shaped container, either side of which is a swan with outstretched wings. A waterlily and cattail type of pattern covers the side of the boat shape. This rare item had the Sowerby pattern #1328 and was first shown in the Sowerby 1882 catalog. Westmoreland's "Swan" sugar and creamer set are very possibly modelled on this Sowerby original. *ROYAL SWANS* is a novelty item, to be used as a posy vase or spill holder. It stands 5" long and is 3" high. Known in various Sowerby non-iridized colors from the 1880s, it was re-used in the 1920s for Carnival production. Found in the UK and Australia.

Shape: swan vase
Colors: marigold and amethyst

A number of Sowerby items (not all known in Carnival) featured swans, the inspiration for their designs being the art of Walter Crane. *ROYAL SWANS* was first made in the late 1880s; the very few Carnival examples known date from the 1920s.

SEA THISTLE aka CANE AND SCROLL

SEA THISTLE is a stylized, abstract pattern that also bears many similarities to Sowerby's *PINEAPPLE* design. It has the Sowerby pattern #2371. An astonishingly wide range of items in the pattern was illustrated in Sowerby's 1912 catalog, though Carnival examples are actually quite hard to find. *SEA THISTLE* items have been reported from the UK, Australia, and the USA.

Shapes: creamer, sugar, and rose bowl (cupped in)
Color: marigold

SEA THISTLE is not a pattern that is easily found; it is seen here in the form of a marigold, cupped in rose bowl. SP $100-175.

SERVICE 2371.

2371½ Cream.   2371½ Sugar.   2371 Cream.

SEA THISTLE was first illustrated in Sowerby's 1912 catalog.

SCROLL EMBOSSED

Known as the interior of the *DIVING DOLPHINS* bowls and also on several small sweet or bonbon dishes (sometimes called ashtrays), where *SCROLL EMBOSSED* is seen in conjunction with *JEWELLED PEACOCK* (an intricate geometric design that features the Sowerby peacock head trademark in the centre of the base). The sweet dish was also used with two other exterior patterns: *PRISM AND CANE* and *PINEAPPLE*.

Shapes: bowl and small sweet dish (bonbon)
Colors: for *DIVING DOLPHINS* colors see relevant entry. For *JEWELLED PEACOCK* and other exteriors, marigold and amethyst.

SOWERBY DRAPE aka (LADY) CYNTHIA

In 1929 the British *Pottery Gazette* ran an ad for Sowerby stating that they would be showing their glassware at "The Industries Fair" in London. In the center of the ad was the splendid *SOWERBY DRAPE* vase—a new design for Sowerby, not a revival of one of their old Victorian moulds. This magnificent item stands almost 10" high and in Carnival, it is found only in a dense black amethyst. So dark is the color that it is exceptionally difficult to see any purple coloration at all, even when held to a very intense light source. The panelled pattern itself is essentially very simple, the vase stands on a pedestal and the top may be either cupped in or flared out. But what distinguishes this vase is its astounding, electric iridescence. The few scarce examples that we have seen have all had this incredible effect. The

combination of dense, black amethyst base glass and electric iridescence makes this one of Sowerby's most impressive pieces of Carnival Glass. It had the Sowerby pattern #2437. In William Heacock's *The Glass Collector* #5 1983, an example of this vase was shown that had been found by Cynthia Nagy in the USA. Other examples have been reported from the UK and Australia.

Shape: vase
Color: black amethyst

SOWERBY'S RIB

A classically simple ribbed pattern that was illustrated in crystal glass in Sowerby's 1865 catalog (pattern #2153). Few examples are currently known and all studied have a rich, marigold iridescence. Quite possibly there are many more examples of this pattern.

Shape: creamer and handled bonbon
Color: marigold

SOWERBY'S RIB is the pattern on this little creamer. SP $30-50.

Black amethyst was a signature color of Sowerby's, though it was used only occasionally. Seen here at its best in the form of two splendid *SOWERBY DRAPE* vases: one cupped in and one slightly flared. $500-900 each.

43

SOWERBY WIDE PANEL aka ESSEX

A simple design, the exterior of items having plain wide panels, each topped off with a scalloped edge. Bowls in this pattern may have a ground base—indeed a medium sized bowl, which the authors have personally examined, has a 30-rayed star with a Sowerby peacock moulded right in the center. The bowl has no mould seams and has been made from a "stuck-up" one-piece mould (see Appendix One for definition). This is an unusual feature, as most Carnival Glass bowls and plates are made from three or four piece moulds. Other similar Carnival bowls are the Australian *KING-FISHER* master and berry bowl and the mysterious *FOUR FLOWERS VARIANT* items. Carol and Derek Sumpter from England own an interesting dark example, almost black—a dense purple-blue shows through only when held to a very bright light. Only the interior of the bowl is iridized, showing gold with pink and green highlights. The exterior looks very elegant, with a matte black effect and gilding along the top edge.

Sowerby initially only used pattern numbers to denote their glassware, but during the early 1930s they assigned actual pattern names to some of their best selling lines. Their #2370 became the "*ESSEX*" pattern. Examples have so far only been reported in the UK.

Shapes: bowls in varying sizes are known. It is very likely that a wider range of tableware shapes was made in Carnival.

Colors: marigold and black amethyst (may be gilded on the edge)

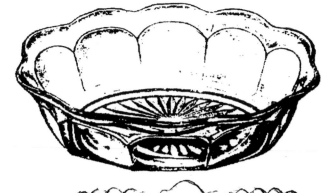

"ESSEX" DISH.
Oval. 6 Sizes.
Round. 7 Sizes.

"DERBY" DISI
Oval. 5 Sizes.
Round. 4 Size

"SURREY" BUTTER.

"ESSEX" BUTTER.

SOWERBY WIDE PANEL (later known as *ESSEX*, as noted in this Sowerby catalog illustration) was simply introduced as pattern #2370 in the 1920s. A few years later, however, Sowerby introduced a range of geographical names to their glass: "Norwich" and "Durham," for example, were assigned to ranges that were not made in Carnival. However *DERBY* (aka *PINWHEEL*), *SURREY*, and *ESSEX* were names given to patterns known in Carnival.

2348 Dish, oval and round.

SPOOL

Similar to *SOWERBY WIDE PANEL*, *SPOOL* is another plain bowl that has a notched band around the outer edge but, in this case, no wide panels. It was illustrated in Sowerby's 1912 catalog (pattern #2348). Also from a one-piece mould, it is known in black amethyst glass with a ground, star base and Sowerby peacock trademark. So far it has only been reported in the UK.

Shape: bowl
Colors: black amethyst and possibly marigold

A plain pattern, *SPOOL* (Sowerby's #2348) was illustrated in their 1912 catalog.

STAR

First illustrated in Sowerby's 1927 catalog (pattern #2409), *STAR* is a plain exterior design with two encircling rows of notches and a large, distinctive cut star (hence the name) on the base. Examples are known in marigold where the base is clear, thus making the central star motif into a prominent feature.

    Shape: bowl
    Color: marigold

STELLAR

A seldom seen pattern, *STELLAR* (named by the authors) was illustrated in Sowerby's 1927 catalog (pattern #2413). The pattern is all exterior and features alternating large, complex hobstars with triangular file filled motifs. The concept is very similar to *HOBSTAR AND CUT TRIANGLES*—on *STELLAR*, the smooth intervening spaces between the cut triangles (as found on *HOBSTAR AND CUT TRIANGLES*) are instead filled with the massive hobstars.

    Shape: bowl
    Color: marigold

STELLAR was named by the authors whilst researching for this book. This marigold bowl is the only example (there must be more) that we have seen. *Courtesy of Carol and Derek Sumpter.* SP $60-100.

SURREY

The *SURREY* butter dish was first shown in a 1927 Sowerby catalog ad, where it was simply given the pattern #2402. A fairly plain design, it is however occasionally found in Carnival Glass. ("Surrey" is the name of an English county—the actual name was assigned to pattern #2402 in the early 1930s.) So far, *SURREY* has only been reported in the UK.

    Shape: butter dish
    Color: marigold

TINY DAISY

The first example of this pattern (named by the authors) in Carnival Glass was found in the form of an exquisite little creamer in November 1999 in Somerset, England. The creamer stands just 2.5" high and features a pattern comprising tiny stylized daisy motifs and vertical ribs. The color is a vivid vaseline with a marigold iridescence that allows the green of the glass to show strongly though. Simon Cottle notes[1] that Sowerby did, in fact, produce iridescent glass at around the same time it was first introduced in the USA. He states that "although the development in 1905 of iridescent glass—otherwise known as Carnival Glass—was considered a failure, it was successfully achieved before the project was curtailed." Cottle goes on to observe that it was only when Percival Marson "its (i.e. iridized glass) original Stourbridge developer became a chemist at Sowerby's in the early 1920s" that Carnival lines became a viable proposition for the company.

It is very likely, given the somewhat inconsistent iridescence on the *TINY DAISY* and the shape in which it is found, that this was indeed an early, circa 1905, example of Sowerby's Carnival. Diminutive little creamers were popular in the late 1800s through the early 1900s in England, and Sowerby produced a wide range of them. By the 1920s, however, the trend was away from the tiny individual cream jugs and all Sowerby creamers from the 1920s onward are much larger in size. A faint Sowerby's peacock head trademark can just be made out on the inside of the creamer at the bottom.

    Shape: creamer
    Color: vaseline

TINY DAISY (named by the authors) is an exquisite, diminutive creamer that has a marigold iridescence on a very vivid, vaseline base glass. NP.

TYNESIDE STAR

Illustrated in a Sowerby catalog dated 1933, this pattern (#2455) is all exterior and features a curving starred base, topped off with a wide ribbed band. The pattern was used extensively through the 1950s. Only reported in the UK.

Shapes: bowls, cake stand, and footed bowl (comport) with metal fitting

Color: marigold

A two-part plate and stand make up the scarce item known as Sowerby's *WICKERWORK*. $300-500 for the complete item in marigold.

TYNESIDE STAR boasts a magnificent starburst design covering the whole of its base. The inside of the bowl, however, is plain and was obviously intended for practical use as a serving dish. SP $30-50.

WICKERWORK

WICKERWORK is an intricately moulded item; an open lattice like plate and matching, three-footed stand, it had the Sowerby pattern #1102. The pattern was first used by Sowerby in the 1880s. Interestingly, it is often possible to find the Sowerby peacock's head trademark on the three-legged base. Oddly, the stand usually has two peacocks' heads on it while the plate top usually has none. Early non-Carnival versions of the plate and stand were often stuck together; the iridized versions, however, were separate. The 1927 Sowerby catalog shows "1102 Plate and Stand (Loose)"—to ensure that wholesalers who were familiar with previous examples of the item, understood clearly that the *WICKERWORK* plate and stand were no longer available glued together. The catalog indicates that the top half was available as either a cupped up bowl shape (seldom found) or a flat plate. The three-legged base was available as a matching stand and was actually sold separately as well, as a pin tray. In fact, the stand fits several other Sowerby items, including some *PINE-APPLE* bowls, and was a useful multi-purpose item. *WICKERWORK* is found in the USA, Australia, and UK.

A similar item (not iridized) was also made by Eda Glasbruk in Sweden circa 1890. The most likely explanation is that they simply copied the design—Sowerby and Eda had fairly close ties.

Shapes: flat plate, rare bowl, and three-footed stand

Colors: plate, bowl, and stand are known in marigold, however, the plate only is also known in amethyst

Possible Sowerby Patterns in Carnival Glass

FOUR FLOWERS VARIANT and the *MYSTERY GRAPE*

Because these two patterns are inextricably linked (in particular with regard to unraveling the mysteries surrounding them both) they have been grouped together.

• *FOUR FLOWERS VARIANT*

The *FOUR FLOWERS* pattern was originally made by Dugan/Diamond in the United States; a similar pattern was certainly produced in iridized form in Scandinavia. However, the *FOUR FLOWERS VARIANT* is different from both of these. It is distinctive in that it has four extra stems between the interlocking pincers. It also has a ground base—as it was made by the "stuck-up" method (see Appendix One for definition)—with a star marie and (usually) a *THUMBPRINT* pattern on the exterior. It has no mould seams as it is made from a one-piece mould. It is found in a very wide range of Carnival colors yet is only known in three sizes of bowls and two sizes of plate. These are: 9" bowl and plate (most easily found size), the scarce 11" bowl and plate, plus the rare 7" bowl.

The *FOUR FLOWERS VARIANT* items have, on occasion, been found on metal stands. A silver plated cupid base is known as the stand for an emerald green *FOUR FLOWERS VARIANT* bowl. Other bowls and plates in the pattern have been found with holes drilled through the center as if to accommodate a metal stand. Examples have been found in the USA, UK, Ireland, and Australia, with by far the greatest majority being found in England. An amethyst example was found in a most unusual location by an Australian collector—on the Pakistani border!

Dugan/Diamond's Classic version of *FOUR FLOWERS*, seen here on a rare ice cream shaped bowl in deep purple. NP.

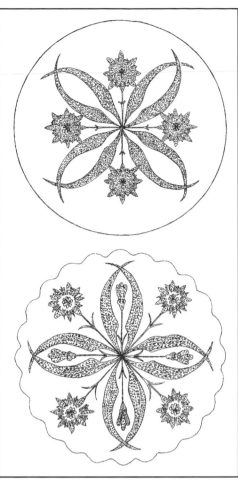

The *FOUR FLOWERS VARIANT* design (bottom) is identical to its inspiration, Dugan Diamond's *FOUR FLOWERS* (top), except for one thing—the addition of the intervening stems and flower buds between the "pincers."

A beautiful *FOUR FLOWERS VARIANT* bowl in a most unusual color—a pale, almost frosty yellow with a hint of amber. SP $100-250.

• *FOUR FLOWERS HYBRID*

The *FOUR FLOWERS HYBRID* is an oddity. The few scarce examples of the bowl have a 7.5" diameter and are teal green, sometimes with an uneven iridescence. The pattern fills the face of the bowl right up to the outside edge, however the most striking difference is that there are no extra stems between the interlocking pincers. As these extra stems are the distinguishing feature of the *VARIANT*, their absence makes this pattern much more like the original *FOUR FLOWERS* pattern. However, the *HYBRID* has the *THUMBPRINT* exterior, a ground base, and is made from a one-piece mould. Quite a paradox. On the examples we have studied, the glass is full of streaks and bubbles and the mould work is sometimes shallow and poor.

So why do we consider that the *FOUR FLOWERS VARIANT* and the *HYBRID* could be Sowerby products? Neither the *VARIANT* nor the *HYBRID* appears in any of that company's catalogs (though to be fair, there are few Sowerby catalogs known and many years are not covered). Let's examine the evidence:

• The items are made from a one-piece mould—most other examples of Carnival made in this way are from Sowerby and one or two pieces from Crown Crystal (Australia).
• The base of the items is ground, indicating that the "stuck-up" method was used (see Appendix One for definition). This is found on quite a number of Sowerby items.
• The colors used for the *FOUR FLOWERS VARIANT* and the *HYBRID* were those used by Sowerby—indeed they used purple and amethyst quite often. Various shades of green, aqua, and teal as well as amber were also used by Sowerby for their Carnival—albeit somewhat infrequently. Further, green and amber/yellow were greatly used by Sowerby on their non-iridized glass output.
• In an international survey carried out via the Internet Carnival Club, Woodsland World Wide, in November 1999, it was found that the majority of examples were sourced in the UK.
• The pattern is a plagiarized design—Dugan/Diamond used it in Classic Carnival. Eda in Sweden made an almost identical copy of the *FOUR FLOWERS* pattern—this is interesting as Sowerby are thought to have had links with Eda. Sowerby copied Imperial's *SCROLL EMBOSSED*, so the principle of plagiarism was a well established one.
• The trademark on the "sister" pattern to the *FOUR FLOWERS VARIANT*, the *MYSTERY GRAPE* (see below) that appears to be the remnants of a Sowerby peacock head.
• Similarities to other items felt to be Sowerby (*LEAFY TRIANGLE* and *OXFORD CROSS*, see below).
• Sowerby often used metal stands and fittings.

So when was *FOUR FLOWERS VARIANT* manufactured? Quite possibly it was a slightly later product of the factory, maybe the 1930s—the quality of *FOUR FLOWER VARIANT* and *HYBRID* items is very inconsistent and sometimes very poor indeed. The glass often exhibits streaks, bubbles, and "dirt," yet some examples are stunning, breathtaking, and have incredibly good iridescence—characteristics of a factory encountering troubled times—yet a factory that was once great and knew how to make wonderful glass.

Shapes: bowls in three sizes and plates in two sizes; scarce examples on metal mounts are known

Colors: many shades of purple from pale lilac to a deep purple and black amethyst. Shades of green including an ice-like green, apple green, vivid teal green, emerald green, olive green, and dark green slag. Also yellow and amber.

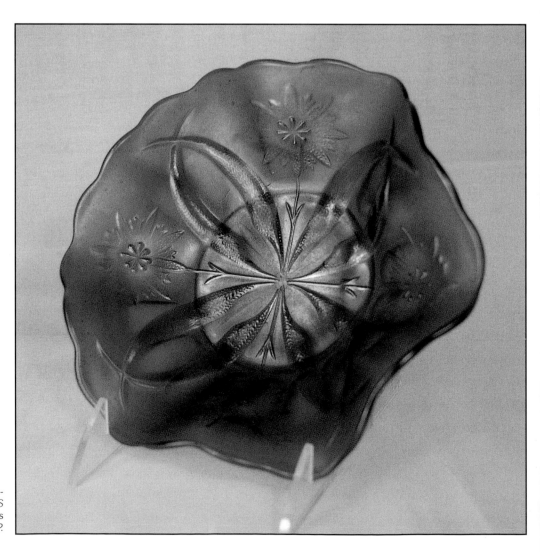

The *FOUR FLOWERS HYBRID* is a cross-over between the Classic *FOUR FLOWERS* and the *FOUR FLOWERS VARIANT*. This example is green. NP.

• *MYSTERY GRAPE*

Yet another intriguing pattern from what appears to be the same manufacturer as the *FOUR FLOWERS VARIANT*. Like the *FOUR FLOWERS VARIANT*, the *MYSTERY GRAPE* is cameo and is from a one-piece mould. Both patterns share a ground base and the exterior *THUMBPRINT* pattern, though the *MYSTERY GRAPE* bowl, measuring 6" in diameter, is a little smaller in size. The main design, however, is a grape and leaf pattern very similar to Fenton's *VINTAGE*. This item has also been found mounted on metal stands. The pattern is very hard to find with no more than around six examples known to us in both the USA and UK.

Possibly the most intriguing and significant detail about the *MYSTERY GRAPE* is that on the two examples that we have studied there is the remnant of what appears to be a trademark in the center of the interior of the bowl. The mark shows as proud (cameo) and the features that are discernible correspond exactly to the shape of the Sowerby peacock's head trademark. The dimensions and proportions are all correct. When this fact is added to the circumstantial evidence regarding both the *FOUR FLOWERS VARIANT* and the *MYSTERY GRAPE*, it makes a powerful case for asserting that the manufacturer of both was, indeed, Sowerby.

Shape: bowl
Color: emerald green with a somewhat "frosty" appearance

KOKOMO

The pattern on this familiar chunky rose bowl is a simple geometric. The unusual squared off feet are very similar to items seen in Sowerby's 1950s catalogs (see also *OVAL STAR AND FAN* and *SPEARS AND CHEVRONS*). Found in the USA and UK.

Shape: footed rose bowl
Color: marigold

LEAFY TRIANGLE

An unremarkable pattern that has a Sowerby "feel" to it, though it is hard to be certain: *LEAFY TRIANGLE* has an interior design that features a group of leaves arranged in a triangle shape. It does possess an interesting feature in that it was made from a one-piece mould in much the same manner as the *FOUR FLOWERS VARIANT* and the *MYSTERY GRAPE*. It also has a "sister" pattern that we have christened *OXFORD CROSS*. Fairly easy to find in the UK.

Shape: bowl
Color: marigold

MITRED DIAMONDS AND PLEATS

This pattern has long been a mystery as to the manufacturer, but we are cautiously attributing it to Sowerby by virtue of its shape and pattern.

Shape: handled sweet dish (bonbon)
Color: marigold

OVAL STAR AND FAN

This design is found on a rose bowl that is very similar to *KOKOMO* and *SPEARS AND CHEVRONS*. It stands on three squared off feet and has a geometric pattern of elongated ovals, filled with a star design and separated by swag motifs. The whole item, stylistically and in weight and appearance is very suggestive of Sowerby's 1950s output. Found in the USA and UK.

Shape: rose bowl
Color: marigold

The scarce and enigmatic *MYSTERY GRAPE* bowl has only been found in this gorgeous, rich blue-green color. SP $150-250.

OXFORD CROSS

The strange design on the interior of this scarce bowl has captivated the thoughts of all who have seen it. It has been variously suggested that this distinctive cross motif is an auspicious symbol, bringing good luck and good health. Similar patterns have been noted in northern India, Afghanistan, and Persia. The bowl is also intriguing in that it bears many similarities to the *LEAFY TRIANGLE* bowl; further, the item was made from a one-piece mould and has no mould seams (akin to the mode of manufacture of the *FOUR FLOWERS VARIANT*). It is impossible to draw firm conclusions at this juncture; research into the likely manufacturer continues, though Sowerby remains a distinct possibility. Examples have been found in the UK and Australia.

　Shape: bowl
　Color: marigold

Whilst browsing through a small antique shop in the old University town of Oxford, the authors came across this unusual marigold bowl—and named it *OXFORD CROSS* for obvious reasons. SP $40-60.

SPEARS AND CHEVRONS

Bearing a simple intaglio design on heavy glass, the most distinctive feature of this rose bowl is its three, squared off feet. The heaviness of the glass, the unusual style of the feet and the overall concept of the pattern are very characteristic of the 1950s Sowerby output. Several similar rose bowls (shown in Sowerby's 1950s catalogs) all share the same distinctive squared off feet. Found in the UK.

　Shape: footed bowl
　Color: marigold

Lesser Known English Carnival Producers

BAGLEY AND CO.—THE CRYSTAL GLASS COMPANY, Knottingley

Bagley began their operations in a small way in 1871 at Knottingley, West Yorkshire. Some forty years later, in 1913, they launched the Crystal Glass Company for the production of containers for preserves and confectionery. In the early 1930s, the company made a range of glass called "Crystaltynt." The colors quoted included "Sunglow," which was quite possibly an iridized marigold (note that Sowerby called their marigold "Sunglow"). It is possible that some of the un-attributed Carnival items found in the United Kingdom came from factories such as this, but this is currently un-confirmed.

CANNING TOWN GLASS WORKS, London

Small amounts of Carnival Glass were made by other manufacturers in England. One of them, Canning Town Glass Works Limited, was located on the Isle of Sheppey near London, though its head office was in the city itself. Most examples of Carnival made by Canning Town Glass Company are marigold, but a handful of very rare items are also known in a beautiful smoky grey-blue base glass with light blue/purple iridescence.

Canning Town Patterns Known in Carnival Glass

THISTLE VASE

The mould of the *THISTLE VASE* was found at the Canning Town Glass Works, London, in the 1970s. (Another set of moulds for a dressing table set was also discovered at the same time.) The *THISTLE VASE* is a chunky, blow moulded vase in the shape of a thistle flower, and stands about 6" high. It's fairly easily found in the United Kingdom in marigold, though two rare examples are also known in smoky grey-blue. Canning Town Glass Company was incorporated into the Bells Whisky Group, making bottles and subsequently becoming part of United Glass.

　Shape: vase
　Colors: marigold and a rare smoky grey-blue

Fairly easy to find in marigold (and often with a very light, silvery iridescence) the *THISTLE* vase is exceptionally rare in the smoky grey-blue color shown. Indeed, only two examples in this color have been reported. Marigold vase $30-50. NP for the smoky grey-blue vase.

Possible Canning Town Patterns in Carnival Glass

ROYAL PINEAPPLE

Though we are listing this vase under Canning Town Glass Company, we have no absolute proof that it was made there—however, there is sufficient similarity between the items to be fairly sure of the attribution. *ROYAL PINEAPPLE* is a chunky, blow moulded vase that stands about 8" high: its top section has a plain panelled design whilst the bottom, bulbous section features a looped design—the whole giving the appearance of a pineapple. Around the top is a notched pattern that has been interpreted as a crown (hence the name). A single smoky grey-blue example is known, which adds to the evidence it was made by Canning Town Glass Works. This rare item was found by Pat Thornton in the UK.

    Shape: vase
    Colors: marigold and a rare smoky grey-blue

JACKSON BROTHERS LTD., Knottingley

Jackson Brothers trademarked their post war glass production with a distinctive, entwined, moulded JBK—bottles and jars were their main lines. Lightly iridized jars or vases in plain shapes are known with this trademark. Pale smoke, lilac, and marigold have all been seen.

JOHN WALSH WALSH, Birmingham

John Walsh Walsh of the Soho and Vesta Glassworks, Birmingham, England, was established in the early 1800s. Their first experiments with iridescence were in 1907 when they selected a number of their free-blown lines for iridescence. They registered an iridized line called "Vesta-Venetian" that ranged in color from yellow to blue. Then, during the late 1920s and early 1930s, they issued another line in iridized glass that was described glowingly in their ads: "for just as a Persian carpet changes color in different lights, so does the Iridescent glass vary in shade and lustre." The colors they made were "Amber iridescent," "Blue iridescent," and "Blue Pompeian." The shapes, however were simple, classic, and functional, with little moulded relief. Simple panelled designs in bowls and vases, these do turn up from time to time, sometimes with an EPNS (electro plated nickel silver) base attached. These metal bases were also made in the Birmingham area, possibly by Elkingtons, who were renowned for that type of manufacture.

MOLINEUX, WEBB AND CO. LTD., Manchester

The Manchester firm of Molineux Webb was a distinguished glass manufacturer, dating back to 1827, though their designs were not registered until 1846. Situated in the northwest of England, they also made small amounts of Carnival in the mid 1920s. They finally ceased trading in 1927.

Molineaux Webb Patterns Known in Carnival Glass

LANCASTRIAN

The first bowl in this pattern (to be identified) was found in early 2000 by Ray and Jean Rogers in Australia. The item was illustrated in a 1925 British *Pottery Gazette* ad for *Lancastrian Crystal Best Quality Pressed Glass*. In appearance it is very similar to the Crown Crystal (Australia) *HEAVY BANDED DIAMOND* pattern. However, the Rogers report that all the diamonds and ribs on the English piece are concave (go in) and there is an additional row of ribs not seen on the Crown Crystal item. On the Australian piece, the diamonds and ribs are all convex (stand out). Further, the Rogers explained that "there are 15 flats (or patterns) around the periphery and the bowl measures approx. 8.5 across the top and is almost 4" high. There is a 30-point star in the base. The base diameter is a shade over 4.5". There are 3 grooves below the diamond pattern similar to those above the diamonds. When I compare the *AUSTRALIAN HEAVY BANDED DIAMOND* tumbler to the bowl, the tumbler pattern design is identical. Makes you wonder if there was close co-operation between the companies, copycats or if a mould designer migrated to Australia?"

    Shape: bowl
    Color: marigold

The *ROYAL PINEAPPLE* vase (seen here) has stylistic similarities with the *THISTLE* vases (previous photo). $30-50 for a marigold example such as this.

MANCHESTER

The British *Pottery Gazette* ad from 1925 mentioned above also showed this item—an unusual vase with a scalloped base and a horizontal ribbed design. This distinctive item is known, though is rather scarce, in Carnival.

Shape: footed vase
Color: amber

This amber posy vase (subsequently named *MANCHESTER* after the location of the firm) was illustrated in the ads of Molineux, Webb and Company Limited of Manchester. *Courtesy of Carol and Derek Sumpter.* $30-50.

STEVENS AND WILLIAMS

Stevens and Williams had the distinction of having Harry Northwood's father, the great glass artist John Northwood I, as their Art Director. One of the company's specialties was "Matso-No-Ke" Japanese style decoration[5]—applied flowers and leaves. Several of their exquisite rose bowls dating from the late 1800s have three curved feet that form a twig and leaf pattern on the side of the bowl—almost exactly like the feet on Harry Northwood's Classic Carnival *LEAF AND BEADS* rose bowls! After John's death in 1903, his eldest son John II (Harry's brother) followed his father as Art Director. Stevens and Williams are known to have produced free-blown lilies and trumpets for epergnes as well as a variety of salt cellars that are typically iridized (in marigold) only at the top. They are often found on a variety of metal mountings that are sometimes marked EPNS for electro plated nickel silver.

Stevens and Williams Patterns in Carnival Glass

FOUNTAIN EPERGNE and similar examples

The *FOUNTAIN EPERGNE* and other, similar items were made by Stevens and Williams around 1910 or 1911. Often these were mounted on fancy metal stands made by local Birmingham or Stourbridge firms such as Elkingtons or the Britannic Manufacturing Company. The *FOUNTAIN EPERGNE* is found on a marked silver plated frame and has an elegant, large, central lily surrounded by four smaller lilies. The glass is rich marigold around the upper edge,

but clear further down—very typical of these blown items from Stevens and Williams. Harry Northwood's *WIDE PANEL EPERGNE* was almost certainly modelled on similar items made in Stourbridge. Concurrence as to Northwood's inspiration can be read in *Harry Northwood The Wheeling Years.*[6]

Shape: epergne
Color: marigold

Three epergne lilies from Stevens and Williams; note that the marigold iridescence was only applied around the top of the lily. *Courtesy of Rita and Les Glennon.* SP from around $30-50 for individual lilies.

THOMAS WEBB AND SONS

The British Midlands is famous for its glass legacy. It was also the birthplace of Harry Northwood and was the source of his early experiences in glass making and its associated craftsmanship. In fact, several of Harry Northwood's Classic Carnival patterns were inspired and influenced by the glass that was made by both Webb, Stevens & Williams, and others (see above). Thomas Webb and Sons of Stourbridge is fully credited with using surface iridescence. The company produced free-blown, iridized lustre ware in the late 1800s, making a deep green glass, iridized in shades of purple that they called "Bronze" glass, and later an iridized golden effect called "Iris." Queen Victoria herself bought some of Webb's iridized "Bronze" glass. Other iridized items were almost certainly produced by Webb.

Possible Webb Patterns in Carnival Glass

PEACOCK FEATHER

A superbly decorative item, this rare, pedestal footed vase (one example only—belonging to Nigel Gamble—is known to us) features elegant, peacock feather motifs as its moulded design. The rich marigold iridescence is applied only around the upper section of the vase. It has the characteristics of Stourbridge manufacture and is almost certainly a Webb product.

Shape: pedestal footed vase
Color: marigold

This rare and magnificent vase is known as *PEACOCK FEATHER* and is almost certainly a product of one of the Stourbridge manufacturers—possibly Thomas Webb and Sons. *Photo courtesy of Nigel Gamble.*

TORNADO VARIANT

Undoubtedly the model for Northwood's *TORNADO* vase, this exquisite item is exceptionally hard to find. These blown vases are around 6" to 7" high and there is always a pontil mark on the base. The slight variation in size is typical of the method of manufacture. The glass is of exceptionally high quality and the marigold iridescence is Tiffany-like and quite superb. As with Northwood's *TORNADO* vase, there are three "tornado" motifs around the vase and the top is pulled into three ruffles.

The manufacturer is not absolutely certain, but study of a Harrods catalog from 1909 (reprinted in *The Journal of the Glass Association: Volume 5, 1997*) showing glass made in Stourbridge indicates that this vase was very possibly a Stourbridge product. Illustrated in the catalog extract were vases that were identical in shape to the *TORNADO VARIANT*. The pedestal foot, the shapely curved sides and the distinctive mouth—the vases illustrated and described as "Hand Made English Glass" were almost certainly Webb's production. Further, some of the vases had what was termed "peacock decoration"—bold, feather like swirls that look exactly like the motifs (the "tornadoes") on the Classic Northwood *TORNADO* vases. Harry Northwood's home town was, of course, Stourbridge, where the Webb factory was located. Almost certainly he modelled the Northwood *TORNADO* vase on this design made in England just a year or two before he would have produced his own version. These were superior vases being sold through a high quality store (Harrods) that commanded high prices: the price of a large 12" high vase would have easily purchased the entire week's groceries for an average family.

The "missing link" that adds further weight is the rare press moulded *TORNADO VARIANT* (see photo on next page) that is thought to be a Northwood product. This item has a pedestal base, and is almost identical to the blown *VARIANT* in shape. The likely chain of events is that Harry Northwood saw the Webb vases and attempted to make his own press moulded version. His first attempt had a pedestal base and was very possibly somewhat hard to produce and remove from the mould. His subsequent attempt had a modified foot—the Classic Carnival Northwood *TORNADO* vase.

Shape: pedestal footed vase

Colors: marigold and marigold with both green and vaseline applied "peacock" feather decoration (the "tornadoes"). These green "tornadoes" were in fact called "Emeraldene Decoration" in the Harrods ad.

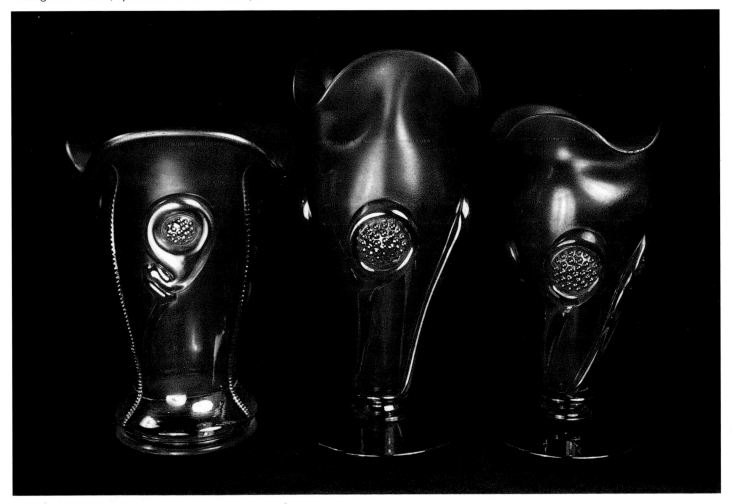

Did Harry Northwood model his famed *TORNADO* vase on similar blown vases produced in Stourbridge? The similarity is undeniable. Northwood marigold *TORNADO* vase (left) $650-900. *TORNADO VARIANT* (center and right) SP $900-2000.

The "missing link"—the *TORNADO VARIANT* seen here is yet another variation on the Classic Carnival version by Northwood. The interesting thing is that this vase is press moulded, unlike the *VARIANTS* in the previous illustration. The general consensus of opinion is that Northwood made this vase. The likely sequence of events is that this was Northwood's first attempt to copy the blown Stourbridge vases (shown in the preceding photo). Maybe the pedestal foot proved too difficult to remove from the mould and so the familiar version with the wide base evolved. SP $1000-2000.

Possible English Carnival Glass Patterns

In the past, much Carnival produced outside the USA used to be vaguely termed "English" when the researcher or writer had little or no idea of the origin of the item. Within the pages of this book we present years of research that enables the sources of many past mysteries to be known and shared. However, puzzles remain and there are still a number of patterns that we cannot, with certainty, trace to a manufacturer. Below is a list of those that we believe are probably English by virtue of their signature characteristics.

HOBSTAR REVERSED

A plain pattern that features a repeated hobstar enclosed within an oval shape. The rose bowl complete with its glass flower holder or frog is fairly easy to find in the UK, though all other shapes are scarce. Davidsons of Tyneside, England, have been suggested as the maker, but there is no evidence to support this, and the company is not recorded as having produced Carnival Glass. The maker is currently unknown, though we strongly suspect an English source.

Shapes: footed flower or rose-bowl with glass frog, celery vase, and small pitcher
Color: marigold

INTAGLIO MUMS

A scarce and rather attractive design, *INTAGLIO MUMS* features four large stylized chrysanthemum heads linked by deeply serrated chrysanthemum leaves. Only the cake plate is known in this pattern, a hole having been drilled through the center and the ruffled glass plate then mounted onto a metal stand—a typical Sowerby device. Scarce examples have been found in the UK—the manufacturer was quite possibly Sowerby.

Shape: metal footed cake stand
Color: marigold

MAY BASKET aka *MAPLE LEAF, DUCHESSE,* and other baskets

Several handled baskets are known; the patterns include the *MAY BASKET* aka *MAPLE LEAF* (featuring a large maple leaf on the upper surface, with "lacy" style beading underneath) and *DUCHESSE* (featuring an elegant stylized plume motif). Yet another basket is known that has British Coronation Commemorative lettering. It is impossible to be totally certain, but the overall style, coupled with the characteristic marie pattern on the *MAY BASKET* that was used in some of Sowerby's patterns, reinforce the fact that these items are very possibly English.

Shape: handled basket
Color: marigold

REISLING

A familiar Carnival motif—the grape vine—yet unusual for European manufacture, even more so because the pattern is all cameo on this scarce item. The grape motif is repeated on the base. It has a "sister" pattern called *SERPENTINE ROSE*. The two shapes in which it is known are curiously at odds with one another—the creamer being very tiny while the sugar is very large. Found in the UK, the manufacturer is currently unknown, though an English source is very possible.

Shapes: creamer and sugar
Color: marigold

Three individual size creamers whose maker remains uncertain. Top: *SPLIT DIAMOND;* bottom, left to right: *REISLING* and *SERPENTINE ROSE*. $20-50 each.

Little creamers are very collectible, so before we leave this section on England, here are some more Sowerby items, courtesy of Rita and Les Glennon. Top row, left to right: *PINEAPPLE* and *CROSS HATCH;* bottom row, left to right: *SEA THISTLE* and *LEA VARIANT*. In marigold, $25-55 each.

SERPENTINE ROSE

This is a "sister" pattern to *REISLING*, known in only a tiny creamer and a larger footed sugar bowl. The pattern is cameo and features a pretty trailing rose and leaves against a stippled background. The rose motif is repeated on the base. The design on the sugar bowl is clumsily interpreted and is not as well executed as that on the exquisite little creamer. Found in the UK, the manufacturer is currently unknown, though we suspect that it is English.

    Shapes: creamer and sugar
    Color: marigold

SPLIT DIAMOND

Possibly one of the most frequently found patterns in the UK, *SPLIT DIAMOND* has not yet been traced to a manufacturer, though some suggest Sowerby. A simple intaglio design featuring alternating fan and diamond motifs.

    Shapes: creamer, stemmed sugar, butter dish, and bowls in various sizes
    Color: marigold

THISTLE AND THORN

Found in the USA and Australia as well as all over the UK, *THISTLE AND THORN* is a familiar pattern to most British collectors, yet surprisingly has not yet been attributed with certainty to a manufacturer. Similar, older examples of glass were made by Greener in the UK, but no proof exists to suggest that the Carnival examples were made by them. The pattern is cameo, featuring thistles and deeply serrated leaves; the handles and feet are in a bark effect.

    Shapes: footed creamer, footed dish/plate, and footed bowl
    Colors: marigold and rare examples of an odd milky green

Nichols Buttons

Though existing somewhat later than the other glass companies listed above, the one man production company run by Lionel Nichols is interesting for its contribution to one aspect of Carnival Glass that is frequently overlooked: the production of pressed, iridized buttons. The buttons produced in the 1950s by Lionel Nichols are somewhat on the fringe of Carnival production. Nichols started making his glass buttons after World War Two; before that he had been a button salesman. His whole approach was experimental; he had no industrial experience, but his unique and attractive products soon began to be highly sought after by the London fashion houses of the post war era. As his daughter, Dixie, explains "the twin establishment pillars of Norman Hartnel and Hardy Amies" were his customers. She says fondly, "like all craftsmen he had no regard for his own time. When at work he was as happily absorbed as a child."

Nichols produced his buttons with a huge variety of unusual and unique designs—many were decorated and often custom iridized. He used iridescent coatings in the form of liquid lustres which could be either painted or sprayed on before gentle re-heating. The finished iridescent buttons from Nichols are distinctive—heavy with a stuck on metal shank, the iridescence is either a deep bronze sheen or a lighter, mother-of-pearl lustre.

[1] Simon Cottle, *Sowerby Gateshead Glass* (Gatshead, England: Tyne and Wear Museums Service, 1986).

[2] *Gateshead Weekly Pictorial Post*, April, 1939.

[3] Angela, Glen and Stephen Thistlewood, "The Diving Dolphins of Brighton, England." *The Carnival Pump* (Official publication of the International Carnival Glass Association Inc., June 1993).

[4] Marion Quintin-Baxendale, *Collecting Carnival Glass* (London, England: Francis Joseph, 1998).

[5] Cyril C Manley, *Decorative Victorian Glass* (England: Ward Lock, 1981).

[6] William Heacock, James Measell, and Berry Wiggins, *Harry Northwood. The Wheeling Years* (Marietta, Ohio: Antique Publications, 1991).

A *THISTLE AND THORN* footed sugar bowl in a most unusual color—a pale, milky-green. Only a few examples in this color are known, yet marigold examples of the pattern in several shapes are quite common in the UK. NP for this rare color. Marigold items in *THISTLE AND THORN*, however, would be $20-50 (similar prices for all three known shapes). *Courtesy of Janet and Alan Mollison.*

Mysteries keep on cropping up. This handled bonbon proved enigmatic; we even considered that it might be from Argentina until a 1907 Sowerby catalog gave us the answer. This is a Sowerby pattern (#2320) that was first listed in that year though the date of its actual production in Carnival Glass is uncertain. No pattern name was given, so we will take the liberty of calling it *PORTSMOUTH*, after the place in which it was found. There must be more examples in existence to help document this unusual English item. *Courtesy of Carol and Derek Sumpter.* NP.

Chapter Three

Germany

"We must always change, renew, rejuvenate ourselves."
—Johann Wolfgang von Goethe.

Today's Germany has evolved through many political and economic upheavals. Crucial parts of the country's rich glass history are buried beneath many layers of the past and may never be unearthed. Fortunately for us, documentation exists for the Brockwitz factory, which was situated in the region known as Saxony. Until only recently, just one catalog, the Brockwitz *Musterbuch* (Book of Patterns) from 1931, has been the main source of information. However, in 1999, German glass researcher, Siegmar Gieselberger, sourced catalogs dating from 1921, 1928, and 1929. He kindly shared them with the authors in early 2000. Further interesting information that has helped to provide background detail to the Brockwitz factory is the visit, in 1928, by a group of British glass-workers to the *Aktien-Gesellschaft Brockwitz*, which was documented in great detail in the British *Pottery Gazette* of that year.

Brockwitz A.G., Coswig

"A scientific planning seems to lie at the very foundation of the factory's success."
—Editorial article on Brockwitz in the British *Pottery Gazette*, 1928.

Today, the town of Brockwitz does not exist. To discover the area where the great Brockwitz glass factory once stood, you would need to locate the present town of Coswig. The area has a significant industrial past, situated near the navigable river Elbe and close by a rich source of fuel: machinery of various types, leather goods and glass manufacture were its main industries. Production at the Glasfabrik, Aktiengesellschaft, Brockwitz began on the first day in January 1904. Employment grew from just 300 at its inception to over 1,200 in 1927, when Carnival Glass was being produced. Efficiency and high quality were important standards. Brockwitz were proud that they made all their own moulds and indeed, "had a huge engineering shop, employing an army of engineers and mechanics" (British *Pottery Gazette* July 1928). Some of their moulds were used by other factories. Eda Glasbruk in Sweden certainly also used Brockwitz moulds (*ROSE GARDEN* in particular, was of German origin). Brockwitz was a major factory, producing a significant amount of consistently high quality and very beautiful glass.

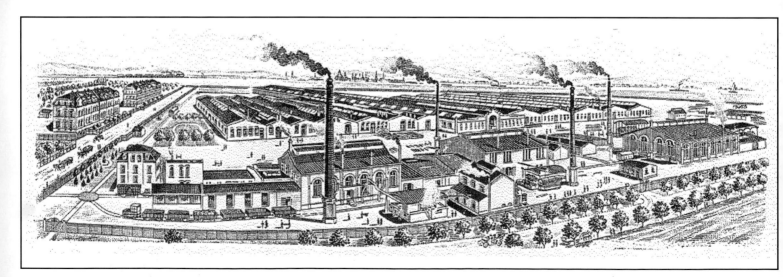

The Brockwitz factory in 1921, as illustrated on the front of their catalog.

Carnival Glass "fashioned in the American style"[1] was produced at Brockwitz mainly during the mid to late 1920s and possibly into the very early 1930s. In a price list dated 1926, iridized glass was mentioned. At that time, the factory was in its heyday, with eight furnaces in operation, each containing about fourteen pots. The good times were not to last; the lean years of the Depression began to be felt and in 1932 Brockwitz was forced to cut production. Then, only a few years later, the harsh reality of World War Two meant that the factory was given over to the production of glass weaponry. Sadly, following the War, much machinery was dismantled and taken away; the few valiant efforts at revival were in vain—the days of glory for Brockwitz were over.

A wide range of shapes in strong, well designed patterns feature in Brockwitz catalogs through the 1920s. A feature of the factory is that they adapted several of their most popular patterns (*CURVED STAR, TARTAN, ASTERS* and *NORTHERN LIGHTS*) to suit different shapes. So, the pattern may look a little different on certain shapes, yet it is still part of the same range—just interpreted in a slightly altered way. For example, *NORTHERN LIGHTS, STAR AND HOBS,* and the *TEXAS TUMBLER* are all the same pattern range (Brockwitz actually called the range *IMPERAT*)—just altered to fit the form of different items.

Signature Characteristics of Brockwitz Carnival Glass

• High quality glassware. Brockwitz cut their own moulds using an electrolytic process and coated them with a layer of aluminum to guard against a too rapid wearing of the sharp edges. This also ensured a finished article of better quality.
• Ground base, smoothly polished (typically may have small chips caused by the grinding).
• Carnival colors are blue and marigold only.
• Intaglio, "near-cut" geometric designs or stylized florals—usually exterior. These are sometimes very intricate and detailed.
• Whole suites of glassware in single patterns, though the pattern may have a slightly different interpretation to fit individual shapes.
• High quality iridescent finish.
• Some items may occasionally be hand finished (mainly bowls and compotes) with ruffling. Vases are always "as moulded" with no extra shaping.

Many Brockwitz items exhibit intricate mould work—as shown in the detail on this *SUPERSTAR* jardinière.

Brockwitz Catalogs

Brockwitz catalogs from 1921, 1928, and a further supplement from 1929 have all been sourced by Siegmar Gieselberger. They have enabled the authors to obtain a clear picture of the output of the factory and to sort out many previous mysteries. In the Brockwitz *Musterbuch* (Book of Patterns) issued in 1931, all items are noted in four languages—German, English, French and Spanish—which indicates the areas that Brockwitz exported to. Note that the Spanish was probably for their South American customers rather than those in Spain itself. Thanks to Bob Smith for sourcing the 1931 catalog, parts of the 1926 catalog, and further information direct from the town of Coswig itself. Thanks also, to Michael Whitten for his German translation of various significant documents.

This catalog illustration from the Brockwitz 1928 catalog may help to identify the *ANTIGONE* pattern—a complex geometric comprised of whirling stars and fans. The vases and tray illustrated are not yet known in Carnival (so far as we are aware).

Brockwitz Patterns Known in Carnival Glass

ANTIGONE aka WARDANCE aka SHOOTING STAR

A full range of goods was made in *ANTIGONE* (the Brockwitz factory name) though it is currently only reported in just a few Carnival shapes. A typical intaglio, geometric pattern comprising whirling buzz stars and fans, *ANTIGONE* has been found in both the USA and the UK.

Shapes: creamer, stemmed sugar (compote), and butter dish
Color: marigold

The pattern is on the inside of this marigold butter dish lid in the Brockwitz pattern *ANTIGONE*. $75-125.

ASTERS aka MARGUERITE (Germany) aka BLOMSTOR (Sweden)

The appearance of a butter dish in this pattern in an Oskar Hallberg (Orebro, Sweden) catalog dated 1914 led the authors to suspect that it might be a Swedish product, possibly from Eda. Indeed, the pattern is known by Eda collectors as *BLOMSTOR*. However, Siegmar Gieselberger's discovery of Brockwitz catalogs from the 1920s helps to put the pattern firmly at the door of Brockwitz— for in those catalogs was a very wide range of goods in all the known shapes of *ASTERS*.

ASTERS is an intaglio, stylized floral pattern. Note that the bowls and plates feature a distinct scallop and flute edge. The pattern is all exterior and the marie has a distinctive star that is also found on pieces that are variously called *NORTHERN LIGHTS, TEXAS TUMBLER*, and *STAR AND HOBS*. A scarce pattern, it has been found in the UK, mainland Europe, the USA and Sweden. Interestingly, the *SUNFLOWER AND DIAMOND* vase (see illustration at right) was actually part of Brockwitz' *ASTERS* pattern range. The interpretation of the stylized floral pattern was similar rather than exactly identical.

Shapes: bowls, rose bowls and plates in various sizes from a diminutive 3.5" diameter bowl to a full sized chop plate. Salvers (footed cake stands) in various sizes and a rare, small size, oval vase are also known.

Colors: marigold and blue (vase and salver only known in marigold so far)

In Brockwitz' 1928 catalog, the pattern known to collectors as *ASTERS* was illustrated and called *MARGUERITE*. Note that the *SUNFLOWER AND DIAMOND* vase (bottom left) was illustrated as part of this pattern range.

ASTERS is seen here in a large, blue bowl (turned upside down) and a small marigold cake stand or salver. Blue bowl $200-400. Marigold cake stand $80-100.

A rare treat—a pair of small, marigold *ASTERS* vases in the delightful oval (or fan) shape. *Courtesy of Don and Phyllis Atkinson.* SP $800-1100.

ARIADNE see ROSE BAND

BERTHA

This pattern features oval, shield-like shapes, alternately filled with stylized floral motifs. A range of shapes in the pattern was shown in the 1928 Brockwitz catalog, though only the bowl is currently known in Carnival. Hard to find, it has been reported in the USA and UK.

Shape: bowl
Color: marigold

BERTHA was the Brockwitz name for this unusual pattern. *Courtesy of Carol and Derek Sumpter.* SP $80-150.

BOND aka BOSTON (Germany)

This pattern, featuring interlocking, elongated chevrons, was made by Brockwitz in a range of shapes, however only the vase is currently known in Carnival. The design was actually called *BOSTON* by Brockwitz—an interesting choice of name. Four sizes of the vase were noted in Brockwitz catalogs: 6", 7.5", 8.5", and 10"—only the 6" vase is currently known in Carnival. This is a very scarce item, so far found only in the UK.

Shape: vase
Color: blue

Interlocking chevrons make a satisfying pattern on this Brockwitz blue *BOND* vase. SP $150-300.

BREMEN

What a surprise when a wine glass in this pattern was shown to us in Las Vegas, Nevada in 1999 by Kay Hoffman and Howard Shosted. The pattern was unlisted in Carnival at the time and our research subsequently discovered the item to be part of an extensive suite of table items in the *BREMEN* pattern. Kay had found the wine (one of a pair) back in the early 1990s in Salt Lake City, Utah. She had been antiquing with her mother and they passed Squire's Antique Store, a shop that deals mainly in imported furniture from Europe. The Hoffmans went in on a whim and came out with two wines, priced at $15 each. Quite a deal!

A full range of other shapes, not yet listed in Carnival, but shown in the Brockwitz catalog supplement in 1929 include: decanter, vases of various sizes, celery, stemmed sugar, jardinière, handled bonbon, bowls, oval platter, and a covered punch bowl and ladle with custard cups. Two fruit set "marriages" are also shown; one comprises a large fruit bowl with an upturned celery beneath it, the other comprises a fruit bowl with an upturned sugar bowl beneath it. It is very likely that any of these items may exist in Carnival.

Shape: wine glass
Color: marigold

A full page of items in the Brockwitz pattern *BREMEN* from their 1929 catalog supplement. Only the wine glass has been reported so far, but there are sure to be other shapes in existence.

CATHEDRAL ARCHES

A splendid geometric design, so typical of Brockwitz, with its elaborate near-cut file and star motifs. This pattern was illustrated in the Brockwitz catalogs during the 1920s and is occasionally found in Carnival Glass. The two shapes in which this pattern is known are both very imposing: one is a massive fruit dish, reminiscent of a punch set, comprising a large bowl on a stand. The other is a one piece compote with a long, slender stem.

    Shapes: compote and fruit dish
    Color: marigold

CHICAGO

We were most surprised when Don Atkinson, a fellow British collector, showed us a superb marigold creamer in this classical pattern. It was identical to the "Chippendale" pattern that was originally made in crystal in the early 1900s by the Jefferson Glass Company of West Virginia, then in later years by Davidsons in the UK. *CHICAGO* is a classic, simple design characterized by plain panels and with a very distinctive shape to the handled items. It is also very similar to the *COLONIAL* style of pattern and Imperial's *FLUTE* and *CHESTERFIELD*. However, Brockwitz also produced an exceptionally wide range of shapes in this pattern, though only the creamer is so far known in Carnival. The pattern range was extended by the addition of a variety of frosted floral and fruit motifs on the base of some items (mainly bowls) in the range, though these have not yet been reported in Carnival. Only reported in the UK.

    Shape: creamer
    Color: marigold

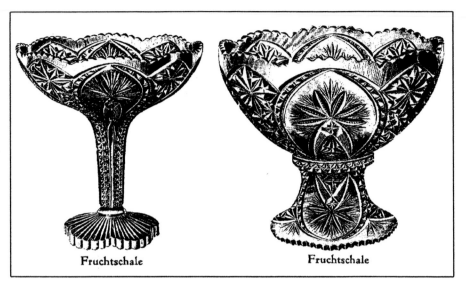

Fruchtschale   Fruchtschale

CATHEDRAL ARCHES, in the two impressive shapes that it is known, were illustrated in Brockwitz catalogs through the 1920s.

CHARLOTTE

Named after the Danish lady who discovered a compote in this pattern in Scandinavia. The pattern features four massive hobstars, dazzling in their intricacy—dividing the stars are four elegant fan shapes. A truly magnificent item with a wonderful iridescence, there is only one known example of the compote at present, though marigold bowls are also known.

    Shape: compote and bowl
    Color: marigold and blue

Nr.	11112	11114
cm	12	14
M	190.—	240.—

A classic shape in a classic pattern—this is Brockwitz *CHICAGO* pattern in a marigold creamer. *Courtesy of Don and Phyllis Atkinson.* NP.

CHARLOTTE features massive and very intricate hobstars—this illustration is from the Brockwitz 1928 catalog.

CHRIST and MARY aka SAINT CANDLESTICKS

Back in 1972, Sherman Hand in his "Colors in Carnival Glass" series, first illustrated one example of this curious and rare item. Another example of these unusual items was reported in 1999. England was the source and the lucky collector who found it, Jim Nicholls, was eager to learn more. The candlesticks are clearly shown in the Brockwitz catalogs. Made in two different sizes (approximately 10" and 12") and each featuring different figures, they were given the following names and catalog numbers: *MARIA* #8193 (10") and #8195 (12"); *CHRISTUS* #8194 (10") and #8196 (12"). Currently, only the smaller 10" versions have been reported to us in Carnival. Both *CHRIST* and *MARY* are known in this size.

Shape: candlestick
Color: marigold

Maria	Nr. 8195	Maria	Nr. 8193
Christus	Nr. 8196	Christus	Nr. 8194
cm	30	cm	25

The *CHRIST* and *MARY* candlesticks were featured in Brockwitz catalogs through the 1920s, yet they are exceptionally rare "finds" in Carnival.

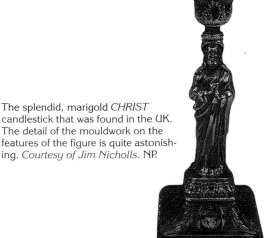

The splendid, marigold *CHRIST* candlestick that was found in the UK. The detail of the mouldwork on the features of the figure is quite astonishing. *Courtesy of Jim Nicholls.* NP.

COSMOS AND HOBSTAR

An intriguing item, *COSMOS AND HOBSTAR* has only been found in the form of a marigold bowl mounted on a metal stand. Examples found in the USA and UK have both been teamed up in this manner. The pattern is a beautiful intaglio geometric that features a blend of stylized flowers and geometric motifs interpreted in much the same manner as on the Brockwitz pattern, *ROSE GARDEN*. *COSMOS AND HOBSTAR* is illustrated in the Brockwitz 1928 catalog.

Shape: mounted bowl
Color: marigold

The scarce examples of marigold *COSMOS AND HOBSTAR* have only been reported on metal mounts. *Courtesy of Sue Foster.* NP.

Detail of the *COSMOS AND HOBSTAR* pattern.

CURVED STAR aka *ZURICH* (Germany)

A complex, intaglio geometric design that has been attributed to a variety of manufacturers over the years and indeed has been confused with other patterns. In fact it is clearly illustrated in the 1921, 1928, and 1931 Brockwitz catalogs where it had the pattern name *ZURICH*. The interpretation of the pattern by Brockwitz is distinctive in that the claw shapes are filled with a file pattern. A very wide range of shapes was illustrated, including various "associated" designs (see *SUPERSTAR* jardinière below). Undoubtedly, *CURVED STAR* was one of Brockwitz' main sellers and must have been very popular at the time.

Other shapes in the *CURVED STAR* pattern were also illustrated in the Swedish Eda catalog in 1929 and in the 1934 and 1938 Finnish Karhula catalogs. See Chapter Six on Sweden for detailed consideration of this pattern and its manufacturers. Found in the USA, UK, Scandinavia, mainland Europe, South America, and Australia.

Shapes: bowls in a very wide range of sizes and shapes (including square bowl), plates in various sizes, epergne, creamer, cylinder vase (three sizes; approx. 7", 9" and 11" high), stemmed celery, stemmed sugar (compote) in two different shapes, covered stemmed sugar, fruit stand, pitcher, small salt, butter dish (two versions—pattern inside the lid and outside the lid), cheese dish

Colors: marigold and blue

A selection of blue *CURVED STAR* items from Brockwitz, From left: celery vase ($80-150), bowl (cupped in, $80-150), and two different styles of the stemmed sugar ($70-120 for the larger one, $150-250 for the small, delicate example, which is a hard-to-find shape). Note the celery vase has been termed *CATHEDRAL CHALICE* in the past—however, this item was a simple domestic object and not meant for religious use.

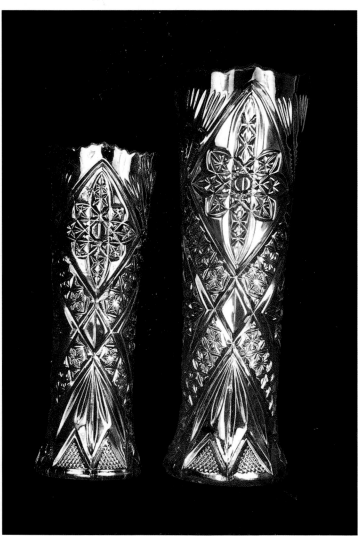

A *CURVED STAR* marigold bowl from Brockwitz in a most unusual shape—square. *Courtesy of Carol and Derek Sumpter.* SP $90-200.

Service „Zürich"

Kompottschale, rund   Kompottschale, eingezogen

CURVED STAR is a geometric design of great complexity that is shown to great advantage in these marigold cylinder vases by Brockwitz. The smaller one stands a little over 7" high, the larger one is around 9". SP $400-900 for either.

CURVED STAR was actually named *ZURICH* by Brockwitz. The file filled claws are a characteristic of the Brockwitz version of this pattern.

CURVED STAR FLOWER BOWL

This item has been given a separate pattern identification as it is a slightly different design to *CURVED STAR*, however it was illustrated in the Brockwitz 1928 catalog as part of the *CURVED STAR (ZURICH)* range. The curved star motif is still present, however there are no fan motifs and no claw shapes. Instead there is a continuous, zig-zag file band and a starburst motif. Known in the flower bowl (sometimes called a flower block) shape in various sizes (four sizes were noted in the Brockwitz 1928 catalog) with Carnival Glass flower "frogs" or metal grilles, as well as with a handled metal basket cover. Found in the USA and UK.

Shapes: flower bowls with assorted metal ware tops and glass "frogs"
Color: marigold

The *CURVED STAR FLOWER BOWL* sometimes has a glass frog for holding blooms in place; this marigold example, however, has a metal grille to support them. SP $100-150.

DAISY AND CANE see *TARTAN*

DIAMOND CUT SHIELDS

A rare pattern, *DIAMOND CUT SHIELDS* is a bold geometric; its main motif, the shield, is almost reminiscent of Zulu art. Isolated, individual examples (usually with stunning iridescence) have been found in the USA, Australia, and Argentina; however the first known, complete water set was discovered in the USA by Darrell and Kelly Markley in 1999. The pitcher is a stately, heavy item that features a distinctive notched handle. The pattern was a mystery for several years until Bob Smith identified it in the Brockwitz catalog (#6450 pitcher and #6451 tumbler).

Shapes: pitcher and tumbler
Color: marigold

The iridescence on this *DIAMOND CUT SHIELDS* pitcher and tumbler is of the highest quality and very typical of the superb output from this German factory. SP Pitcher $350-500; tumbler $150-200.

The addition of a metal handle and cover gave the *CURVED STAR FLOWER BOWL* shape a different use. First example known shown here courtesy of Doreen and Brian Lapthorne. SP. $100-150.

DRAPED ARCS

Just one example of this beautiful and elegant pattern is currently reported. There must surely be other examples in existence. The single example known is a bowl, found by Carol and Derek Sumpter; it was found by them in the UK in 1997. In the Brockwitz catalogs, the bowl is shown married up with an upturned, stemmed sugar in the same draped pattern. The combination produces what the catalog terms a "Fruchtschale" or fruit-dish. Another shape in the same pattern was also illustrated: an oval jardinière 8" long (not currently known in Carnival).

Shape: bowl
Color: blue

This is currently the only example known of the Brockwitz *DRAPED ARCS* pattern: the blue bowl shown here is courtesy of Carol and Derek Sumpter. NP.

ELEKTRA aka SHOOTING STAR aka HOBSTAR WHIRL aka WHIRLI-GIG

The puzzle here (aside from all the names!) is who made this pattern. It features in both the Brockwitz and Riihimaki (Finland) catalogs. The answer could well be that both manufacturers produced their own version. Examples have been found in the USA, UK, and Scandinavia. A full range of shapes was depicted in the Brockwitz catalogs, including oval jardinières and vases. A splendid oval bonbonniere, reminiscent of a Faberge egg, is illustrated—to find that item in Carnival would be remarkable. Only a few shapes, however, are currently known in Carnival—there may well be more.

Shapes: creamer and stemmed sugar (compote)
Color: marigold

Service „Elektra"

Butterdose mit Überfalldeckel   Kompottschale, eingezogen

EUROSTAR

Named by Sue Foster, this pattern is currently known in the shape of a splendid epergne—the only complete example so far reported. Its shape is impressive—a splendid three-part epergne featuring an all-over, interlocking star pattern. The connections between the separate parts are made by threaded glass screws that are part of the actual fittings—an amazing example of glass craftsmanship. Illustrated in the Brockwitz 1928 catalog (pattern #53900), it was made in the epergne, a scroll footed bowl, and a scroll footed, handled bonbon. A rare pattern, so far only found in the UK.

Shape: epergne
Color: marigold

Tafelaufsatz

The magnificent *EUROSTAR* epergne as illustrated in the Brockwitz catalog (1928).

Carnival examples of *ELEKTRA* are known in the stemmed sugar and creamer shape. The butter dish and bowl here, as illustrated in the Brockwitz 1928 catalog, have not yet been reported in Carnival, but they show the pattern well and—who knows—there may be examples in existence.

This is the only complete example of the *EUROSTAR* epergne known so far. *Courtesy of Sue Foster.* NP.

FOOTED PRISMS aka *FOOTED PRISM PANELS*

An attractive combination of teardrop like panels and geometric stars comprises this simple pattern. The pedestal vase in the smaller 9" size is found fairly often in the UK—less often in the USA. The taller vase is a rare find indeed. *FOOTED PRISMS* has the Brockwitz pattern #9233. Found in the USA, UK, and Australia mainly in marigold.

Shape: vase in two sizes: 9" and 13"
Colors: marigold and blue

Brockwitz *FOOTED PRISMS* pedestal footed vase is hard to find in this gorgeous shade of cobalt blue. A blue example like this one sold at the 1998 HOACGA auction for $400.

FILIGRAN

An open edge pattern, not unlike Northwood's *WILD ROSE*, this is only known to us in the large bowl shape, although stemmed items were also depicted in the Brockwitz 1931 catalog. The single documented example was found in the UK.

Shape: bowl
Color: marigold

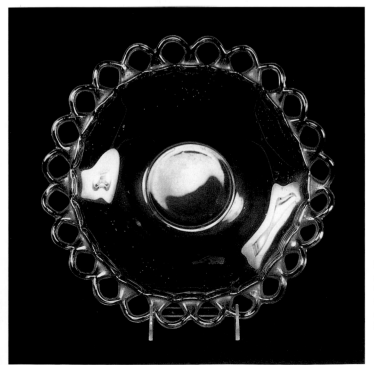

Clearly illustrated in the Brockwitz 1931 catalog—where it was named *FILIGRAN*—was this massive, low, light marigold bowl (measuring about 14" across) with a most distinctive "lacy" open edge. *Courtesy of Frank and Shirley.* NP.

FOOTED PRISM PANELS see FOOTED PRISMS

GALACTIC BEAUTY

Found and named by British collector, Jim Nicholls, this is the first reported, handled basket confirmed as a Brockwitz product. Illustrated in that company's 1928 catalog, this magnificent item features a complex, interlocking pattern of stars, fans, and file panels. A stately item, made taller by the elegant, applied handle, this basket was discovered in Scandinavia. Currently this is the only known example.

Shape: handled basket
Color: marigold

Blumenkorb

This pretty item was described in the Brockwitz catalog as a *Blumenkorb*, which literally means flower basket.

GLOBUS see MOONPRINT

HEN

Brockwitz made a covered hen that was very similar in concept to the Sowerby example. Illustrated in their catalogs through the 1920s, there appear to have been several sizes made. Other covered dishes included a covered rabbit and a covered duck—all were covered sugars. It is not possible to say whether all or any, were made in Carnival.

HOBSTAR PANELS aka GENUA (Germany)

Illustrated in the Brockwitz 1928 catalog, HOBSTAR PANELS is a geometric that has many similarities with the Imperial patterns,

DIAMOND LACE and CHATELAINE. Bowls, plates, and table set items were all illustrated—though only the creamer and handled sugar are currently reported, we feel sure that more shapes will be found. Certainly the possibility of a covered butter is most likely, to make up the complete three part table set.

Shape: creamer and sugar
Color: marigold

Genua

The HOBSTAR PANELS pattern, as seen in the Brockwitz 1928 catalog, is shown here in the form of a creamer, handled sugar, and covered butter. Only the creamer and sugar are currently reported in Carnival.

LATTICE AND LEAVES

A 9" high, pedestal footed vase, very similar in shape to FOOTED PRISMS. The pattern, however, is simpler and is only around the top. It's a seldom seen piece, rarely found in either color, though scarce examples have been reported in the USA, UK, and Australia. LATTICE AND LEAVES has the Brockwitz pattern #1063.

Shape: vase
Colors: marigold and blue

LATTICE AND LEAVES is hard to find in any color! The marigold examples have sold at auction for $100-200: a blue example like this has not yet sold at auction in the USA but would undoubtedly reach a much higher figure. *Courtesy of Carol and Derek Sumpter.* NP.

LUISE

Named *LUISE* in the Brockwitz 1928 catalog, this is an abstract, intaglio design composed of interlocking curves, fans and file sections. It was illustrated in the Brockwitz catalogs in three different sizes of epergne ranging from a single tiered version up to a full three tiered version. The pattern is all exterior.

Shapes: only the central section of the epergne is known to us at present
Color: marigold

MATTE FRUITS has a delightful combination of highly iridized marigold sides and a matte, frosted base. *Courtesy of Carol and Derek Sumpter.* NP.

Luise, 1 Teller

Brockwitz called this pattern *LUISE*—this illustration shows the epergne with just one plate (*teller*), but in fact it was produced in three different heights according to the catalogs: 15", 21", and 25". It is not known whether all three sizes were actually produced in Carnival.

MINIATURE HOBNAIL aka *KOH-I-NOOR* (Germany)

A familiar pattern based on the simple, regular hobnail design, Brockwitz gave it the catalog #12150. A great many shapes were made in this pattern but only the liqueur set (cordial or decanter set, known in Germany as a *likorsatz*) is reported in Carnival so far. Found in the USA, a liqueur set in this pattern was sold at auction in 1998 for $800.

Shapes: decanter and stemmed wines on a matching glass tray
Color: marigold

Service „Koh-i-noor"

Likörsatz, mit rundem oder ovalem Tablett

MATTE FRUITS

This pretty bowl features matte (acid etched or "sueded") fruit motifs on the base that contrast well with the rich marigold iridescence on the rest of the bowl. Our studies revealed that the pattern is *MATTE FRUITS* and it was made in an assortment of shapes and sizes. (Brockwitz referred to it as "Service mit mattierten Fruchten.") This rare example was found in the UK, another was found in Australia—who knows how many more examples there are? The bowl illustrated is the only shape currently documented in Carnival, but the Brockwitz catalog also showed a vase, tray, bowls, plate, ice cream dish, a handled basket, and a large stemmed fruit dish. Any of these may be found in Carnival.

Shape: bowl
Color: marigold with matte effect design on base

The delightful *MINIATURE HOBNAIL* liqueur or cordial set (pattern #12150) was called *KOH-I-NOOR* by Brockwitz. The catalog illustration notes that it came with either a round or an oval tray.

MOONPRINT aka GLOBUS (Germany)

A very wide range of utilitarian shapes was made by Brockwitz in this simple, yet effective, abstract design. Though in essence nothing more than a series of indented circles, the pattern reflects light incredibly well and provides a stunning Carnival effect. Some items in this pattern are quite easy to find in both the USA and UK, however, some rare shapes are very hard to find indeed. The MOONPRINT tumbler, as illustrated in the Brockwitz catalogs, has a plain wide band around the top and curves in at the base; also the circular "moonprints" decrease in size towards the base. Two versions of tumbler were shown—one with three bands of "moonprints" and one with two bands. The version with the three bands, standing just under 4" high, is the only one so far reported in Carnival Glass.

It has been erroneously suggested elsewhere in the past that Sowerby also made MOONPRINT and named it "Oxford." It is certainly true that there is a Sowerby pattern called "Oxford," however this is not currently known in iridized versions, and indeed, it is a totally different pattern to MOONPRINT. In the Brockwitz pattern the "moonprint" medallions are totally round and smooth, in "Oxford" the medallions have eight angular sides. Nor do the shapes that "Oxford" is illustrated in match the shapes that Carnival examples of MOONPRINT are known in. Sowerby did not make MOONPRINT.

Shapes: bowls, oval (jardinière or banana boat shaped) round and ruffled in various sizes, plates in various sizes, fruit stand (comprising upturned sugar and large bowl with shaped groove on marie), rectangular covered cheese stand, covered butter dish, cream jug, stemmed sugar basin (compote), stemmed ice cream dish, lidded biscuit (cookie) jar, covered bonbonniere, large salad bowl, lidded pickle jar, pitcher, tumbler (in two sizes), cordial or liqueur set (comprising wine glasses, decanter and under tray), carafe (larger than the cordial decanter), several sizes and shapes of wine glass/goblet, celery vase, candlestick, powder jar and flower vases in various shapes are all known in Carnival. Items depicted in the catalog but not yet known to us in Carnival are the tea container with a metal lid, ring tree, and pomade box. No doubt they will appear one day!

Color: marigold

A wide range of vase shapes was made in Brockwitz MOONPRINT pattern. Their values range from $200-400. *Courtesy of Mrs. Harry Habberley.*

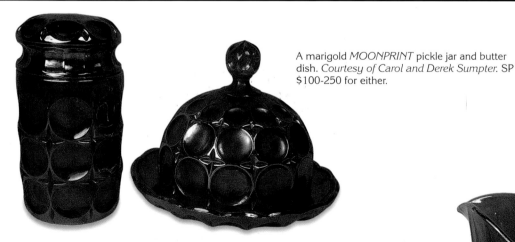

A marigold MOONPRINT pickle jar and butter dish. *Courtesy of Carol and Derek Sumpter.* SP $100-250 for either.

Two unusual shapes in MOONPRINT. On the left is the lidded bonbonniere: a chipped example sold in 1995 for $290. On the right is the pitcher, SP $300-450.

NIOBE see *TRIANDS*

NORTHERN LIGHTS aka *IMPERAT* (Germany) aka *OREBRO* (Sweden)

Though this geometric pattern is shown in the Swedish distributor (Oskar Hallberg's) catalog from 1914—and Carnival examples have been found in Scandinavia— *NORTHERN LIGHTS* was undoubtedly made in Carnival Glass by Brockwitz. A vast range of shapes, sizes, and variations on the same theme are depicted in the Brockwitz catalogs through the 1920s. The motifs within the complex main pattern are a distinctive star (also repeated on the base), a file segment, a cane segment, a fan, and a "rising sun" oval shape. On the variations, the "rising sun" may be omitted (see *TEXAS TUMBLER*) or both the "rising sun" and the distinctive star are omitted (see *STAR AND HOBS*). The motifs that remain constant are the file, the cane, and the fan, as well as the star base. The illustrations will make these variations clear. Examples have been found in the USA, UK, and Scandinavia.

Shapes: bowls in various sizes, rosebowl, celery vase (see *TEXAS TUMBLER*), flower bowl (see *STAR AND HOBS*), and jardinière (see *STAR AND HOBS*). An epergne is also known, on a metalwork base, though this is not illustrated in known Brockwitz catalogs. Other shapes were depicted in the Brockwitz catalogs but are not yet known in Carnival (for example, tumbler, pitcher, stemmed compote, and vase).

Colors: marigold and blue

NUTMEG GRATER aka *LONDON* (Germany)

A simple design that is very similar to Eda Glasbruk's *BOWMAN* pattern, *NUTMEG GRATER* can be identified by a wide encircling band of file with an arch topped, plain panel effect below. Bowls in

this pattern may also be found with *HEADDRESS* on the interior. Quite scarce—mainly found in the UK.

Shapes: bowls, creamer, stemmed sugar, and butter dish
Color: marigold

Zuckersatz

This splendid large, blue bowl in the *NORTHERN LIGHTS* pattern is shown here courtesy of Sue and Ray McLaren. A miniature rose bowl in this pattern sold at auction in the USA in 1999 for $400. This large bowl, SP $300-600.

At last, the maker of *NUTMEG GRATER* can be confirmed as Brockwitz. This illustration of the creamer and sugar bowl is taken from their 1928 catalog.

REGAL CANE aka *HAMMONIA* (Germany)

The *REGAL CANE* pattern comprises an all-over checkerboard or cane effect. Illustrated in Brockwitz catalogs from the 1920s in a wide variety of shapes, though only a handful are currently reported in Carnival. The Brockwitz name for the pattern was *HAMMONIA*. A fascinating and most unusual shape—a working clock—is known in this pattern. It was sold at the 1998 ICGA auction of the John and Lucile Britt collection for $800. Rare tumblers and water pitchers are also known. There is a 15-point star on the base of the tumbler. Found in Argentina, the USA, Scandinavia, and the UK.

    Shapes: water pitcher, tumbler, ashtray, and clock
    Color: marigold

REGAL CANE has an all-over pattern that reflects iridescence well—this marigold water pitcher is shown courtesy of Bob Smith. NP.

ROSE BAND aka *ARIADNE* (Germany)

This pattern is often confused with an Argentinean pattern by Cristalerias Piccardo that not only looks alike, but also has a similar name (*BAND OF ROSES*). Given the likely links between the two countries, it is possible that the similarities are more than just coincidental. A wide range of shapes was illustrated in the Brockwitz catalogs, indicating that shapes other than those currently known in Carnival may yet be found. Shapes illustrated but not yet known are: vase, jardinière, celery, stemmed sugar basin, creamer, bowl, plate, and tea container with metal lid. *ROSE BAND* has been found in the USA and the UK, but is rare.

    Shapes: water pitcher, tumbler and juice glass, decanter (with stopper), and stemmed wine glasses complete with matching, circular undertray
    Color: marigold

Service „Ariadne"

ARIADNE was the name that Brockwitz gave this pattern—collectors today call it *ROSE BAND*.

ROSE GARDEN aka *ROSE MARIE* aka *ROSEN* (Germany) aka *ROSOR* (Sweden)

A splendid intaglio design composed of exquisitely blended floral and geometric motifs. The uniqueness of the design is the interpretation of a naturalistic theme in an essentially stylized, intaglio manner. The result is a harmonious composition that blends near-cut precision with flowing, almost naturalistic lines. Marion Hartung wrote of the large oval vase in the *ROSE GARDEN* pattern back in 1965, saying "this is not only one of the most attractive pieces of intaglio glass we have ever seen in Carnival Glass, but is as well one of the most beautiful vases we have ever seen."[2] Rose Presznick named it *ROSE MARIE* and wrote about the pattern in a similar vein in 1967, saying "one of the most beautiful pieces of Carnival Glass I have ever seen."[3]

The pattern is illustrated in the catalogs of both Brockwitz and Eda Glasbruk (Sweden). In the Swedish catalogs, only one shape is shown—the splendid oval or fan shaped vase. In the Brockwitz catalogs through the 1920s, however, every known shape in the pattern is fully illustrated and documented by size. The likely explanation for the duplication of the oval vase is that Brockwitz either sold or leased the mould(s) to Eda and both companies produced the oval vase at some point (see Chapter Six on Sweden for more detail).

An amazing range of shapes are shown in the Brockwitz catalogs from the 1920s—all but a handful have now been found in Carnival—however, not all sizes have been found in all shapes. For example, five sizes of rose bowl (incurved) are noted, ranging from just under 5" in diameter to a full 9" across—yet only three of the middle sizes have so far been reported in Carnival. Four sizes of plate are noted, ranging from 8" in diameter to almost 13"—yet only one size (the 11.5") has so far been reported in Carnival. One of the few remaining elusive shapes is the tumbler. It is clearly illustrated in the catalog, yet none have so far been reported. The pitcher, however, is known (though exceptionally rare). All shapes in *ROSE GARDEN* are very hard to find.

    Shape: rose bowls (5.5", 6.5" and almost 8") pitcher, covered butter, oval fan vase (approximately 9", 7.5" and 5.5" high), cylinder vase in three sizes (approximately 7", 9" and 11" high) flower bowl with metal top, and chop plate
    Colors: marigold and blue

Service „Rosen"

Bowlenkanne		Blumenvase			Blumenvase		
Nr.	21350	Nr.	21906 1	21906 2	21906 3	Nr. 21141 19	21141 21	21141 28
Inh. Ltr.	8	cm	22½×19½	19×16	13½×10½	cm	19	23½	28
M	85.—	M	145	100.—	45.—	M	45.—	65.—	31.—
mattiert				mattiert			mattiert	
M	110.—	M	185.—	125	60	M	65.	90.—	50.—

From the Brockwitz 1928 catalog, three shapes of *ROSE GARDEN*: the pitcher, the oval vase, and the cylinder vase. For both vases, three size ranges are noted.

Two *ROSE GARDEN* pitchers from Brockwitz: in blue SP $800-1000; in marigold SP $500-900.

Bierbecher

Marmeladendose
nur mit Einschnitt

Two superb shapes of *ROSE GARDEN* were shown in the Brockwitz catalog, neither of which are currently known in Carnival. On the left, a tumbler and on the right, a covered marmalade (jelly) jar.

Two splendid cylinder shaped vases from Brockwitz in rich marigold. On the left is *SUNFLOWER AND DIAMOND*. $125-200. A sumptuous 11" high *ROSE GARDEN* vase is on the right. SP for this large size, $600-900 (a 9" high, marigold *ROSE GARDEN* cylinder vase sold for $575 in 1999).

ROSE MARIE see *ROSE GARDEN*

SAINT CANDLESTICK see *CHRIST* and *MARY*

SHOOTING STAR see *ANTIGONE*

SNOWSTORM

On a page in the Brockwitz catalog entitled "Diverse articles" there appeared a pretty, two-handled dish or small jardinière, pattern #9035. Its design is comprised of repeated, complex hobstars, reminiscent of large snowflakes. Just a few examples are known, found in the UK.

Shape: handled jardinière
Color: marigold

SNOWSTORM is a seldom seen Brockwitz pattern.

SQUARE DIAMOND aka COLUMN FLOWER

This vase was illustrated in the Brockwitz 1928 catalog, pattern #1062. The example shown was just over 8" high. An exquisite and complex geometric, it is also thought to be a product of the Riihimaki glassworks in Finland, and was illustrated in their catalog in 1939. See Chapter Seven for more detail. Possibly Riihimaki bought the mould from Brockwitz in the early 1930s (when Brockwitz were cutting back on production). It is quite possible that this rare vase was made by both manufacturers. Found in Scandinavia and the USA.

Shape: vase
Colors: marigold and blue

SQUARE DIAMOND is an exquisite vase that was shown in the Brockwitz catalogs through the 1920s.

STAR AND DRAPE

Long thought to be an Australian pattern from Crown Crystal, this was actually made by Brockwitz. So why the confusion? Crown Crystal were not only glass manufacturers, they were also wholesalers. They featured a great deal of glass in their catalogs that was not in fact made by them, but was instead simply other manufacturers' glass that they were selling. A great deal of Czech, Scandinavian, English, American, and German glass was illustrated in the Crown Crystal catalogs in the 1920s and early 1930s. The *STAR AND DRAPE* pattern was shown in one of the Australian catalogs, but it was simply an import from Brockwitz in Germany. Made by Brockwitz, it was shown in their catalogs from the 1920s. Found in Australia and the USA.

Shape: small pitcher
Color: marigold

Here's a surprise: *STAR AND DRAPE* was actually made by Brockwitz. Though the pitcher shape is not illustrated in the catalogs studied, the handled mug shown here was—and it clearly shows the pattern.

STAR AND HOBS

STAR AND HOBS is one of three variations on a theme that fall within the Brockwitz pattern range *NORTHERN LIGHTS* (called *IMPERAT* by Brockwitz). In the *STAR AND HOBS* version, only the file, cane, and fan motifs are present. See *NORTHERN LIGHTS* for full explanation.

Shapes: flower bowl with metal top and jardinières
Colors: marigold and blue

An unusual piece, a marigold *STAR AND HOBS* flower bowl complete with metal grille. *Courtesy of Carol and Derek Sumpter.* NP.

A splendid blue *STAR AND HOBS* jardinière. *Courtesy of Ann and David Brown.* NP.

SUNFLOWER AND DIAMOND

The intaglio pattern on this popular cylinder vase is a blend of stylized daisies and file-filled diamonds. Here is yet another instance where both Brockwitz and Eda are believed to have made versions of the same pattern. However, our studies suggest that there are clear differences. The commonly found Brockwitz version stands just over 9" high and has 36 petals in the daisy motif. There Is a high domed base in which is found a moulded, multi-petalled daisy. The Eda version has only 20 petals in the daisy motif—for greater detail on this version see the chapter on Sweden. The pattern is noted in the Brockwitz catalogs in three sizes: 16 cm., 20 cm., and 24 cm.—these measurements correspond very roughly to 6", 8", and 9".

The *SUNFLOWER AND DIAMOND* vase was actually part of Brockwitz' *ASTERS* pattern range. The overall concept is very similar indeed and it would appear that this tall cylinder vase was actually Brockwitz' interpretation of the pattern, slightly altered, to accommodate the elongated shape of the vase.

Shape: vase. The first reported 6" vase was found in June, 2000.

Color: marigold (a blue Brockwitz one is possible, but see Chapter Six on Sweden for details of the blue Eda version)

SUNGOLD FLORAL

This pattern is not typical of Brockwitz, but is clearly portrayed in their catalogs. The glass is thinner than usual for Brockwitz, the pattern is an exterior floral design and, unlike most Brockwitz, it is

cameo (albeit in low relief). It's a seldom seen pattern that is found mainly in the UK. The edges of the bowls and the epergne lily are ruffled and frilly in appearance.

Shapes: bowl and epergne

Color: marigold

A pretty, marigold bowl in the Brockwitz pattern *SUNGOLD FLORAL*. It is unlike most other Brockwitz Carnival in that the glass is quite thin and the edge is delicately crimped and ruffled. *Courtesy of Angie Thistlewood.* SP $75-100.

The delightful *SUNGOLD FLORAL* epergne was shown in this Brockwitz catalog illustration.

SUPERSTAR see CURVED STAR

The *SUPERSTAR* jardinière was illustrated in the Brockwitz 1928 catalog as part of the *CURVED STAR* range of shapes. The Brockwitz name for the pattern range was *ZURICH*. A deep intaglio, geometric pattern, all examples of this item that we have seen have been characterized by a superb, multi-colored iridescence. The *CURVED STAR* pattern was adapted to fit the shape of the low, oval boat. The file filled pointed claws of the *CURVED STAR* pattern appear on *SUPERSTAR* as file filled bands—furthermore, the fan shapes are omitted. Apart from that, the pattern is similar in overall concept. The shape may be referred to as a banana boat today, but it was actually termed a jardinière in the Brockwitz catalog—its purpose was to hold potted plants, probably displayed on a window ledge. The catalog number was #22323. *SUPERSTAR* has been found in the USA, UK, and Europe.

     Shape: jardinière
     Colors: marigold and blue

The *SUPERSTAR* jardinière is actually part of Brockwitz *CURVED STAR* range. In blue, SP $350-450.

TARTAN aka *DAISY AND CANE* aka *KOPENHAGEN* (Germany) aka *OLYMPIA* (Sweden)

The overall effect of *TARTAN* is of criss-crossed diamonds that are filled with flat buttons. Most items in *TARTAN* also have a very distinctive flat sectioned edge. There are two main variations of the pattern: on one variation alternate buttons have either a file pattern or a floral "daisy" pattern (the "daisy and cane" effect) while on the other main variation all the buttons are quite plain and smooth. A wide range of shapes in *TARTAN* was illustrated in Brockwitz' catalogs through the 1920s. The "daisy and cane" variation was shown in the 1921 catalog while the plain button variation was shown in the 1928 catalog—a full range of shapes was illustrated in each case. The likely explanation is that Brockwitz re-tooled the moulds, removing the "daisy and cane" effect and creating the flat, plain buttons. We cannot confirm that Carnival was made in 1921 at Brockwitz, but it seems likely that items with the "daisy and cane" effect are probably pre 1928.

This pattern may also have been made in Sweden (see Chapter Six), though probably most Carnival examples are from Brockwitz. The Brockwitz' name for the pattern was *KOPENHAGEN*, possibly indicative of export to Denmark and Scandinavia in general. A further variation was illustrated in a 1923 issue of the British *Pottery Gazette* in which all the buttons have the file pattern, however we cannot currently confirm this in Carnival. Examples of *TARTAN* have been found in the USA, the UK, Scandinavia, and Australia.

     Shapes: bowls in various sizes (included scroll footed bowls), epergne in two sizes (13" and 15"), vase, "cuspidor", celery, cake stand, tumbler, pitcher (8" high), rectangular plate or tray. A number of other shapes were illustrated in Brockwitz catalog but are not yet known in Carnival.

     Colors: marigold and blue (blue so far only known in the "cuspidor" shape)

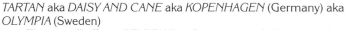

A magnificent table center: Brockwitz splendid marigold *TARTAN* epergne. *Courtesy of Frank and Shirley.* NP.

Found in the UK in 1998, this splendid cuspidor is the first blue item in *TARTAN* to be reported. (Brockwitz actually called the item a *blumenbowl*—or flower bowl—in their catalogs). *Courtesy of Carol and Derek Sumpter.* NP.

This small marigold creamer is the version of *TARTAN* where all the buttons are smooth. *Courtesy of Sue and Ray McLaren.* SP $80-150.

TEXAS TUMBLER aka TEXAS SHOT GLASS

Amusingly named a tumbler, this item is in fact a celery vase. It is part of the Brockwitz pattern range *NORTHERN LIGHTS* pattern (see above) and has the very distinctive star design on the base common to *NORTHERN LIGHTS* and *STAR AND HOBS*. The *TEXAS TUMBLER* was first reported in the USA, though several examples have also been found in the UK and Scandinavia.

   Shape: celery vase
   Colors: marigold and blue

An exquisite, small marigold creamer and stemmed sugar in Brockwitz *TRIANDS* pattern. Creamer SP $50-80; sugar SP $70-100.

The *TEXAS TUMBLER* is a magnificent item with intricate mouldwork—known in blue as shown here, and marigold. An example was sold at auction in the USA in 1998 for $450.

TRIANDS aka NIOBE (Germany)

Found in the USA, UK, Canada, South Africa, and Australia, this is a fairly straightforward design featuring concentric rings of parallel notches. The star design on the base of most items in the *TRIANDS* pattern is identical to the star in the main design of *BREMEN*. The Brockwitz catalog shows a wide range of shapes in this pattern (they called it *NIOBE)* several of which have not yet been reported in Carnival. *TRIANDS* is not too hard to find in the vase shape, but other shapes such as the butter dish or the stemmed sugar and creamer are scarcer. Covered pieces such as the stemmed and flat-based sugars, cheese stand, and the elaborate, high sided, honey or preserve dish (with a hole for the spoon to fit) would be a great discovery! None have been reported yet.

   Shapes: vase, plate, chop plate, bowl, creamer, open sugar (stemmed and flat based), covered butter dish, celery vase, and jardinière
   Color: marigold

TRIPLE ALLIANCE

Found in the UK and the USA, this is a magnificent item—a covered cookie jar (biscuit jar) in an intricate, intaglio design. The pattern features a stylized flower head that is identical to that on the *MARGUERITE* vase. Elsewhere, there is the familiar Brockwitz harmony of star, fan, and file motifs. Practical and functional, yet utterly exquisite—chocolate chip cookies served from this rarity would surely taste even better!

   Shape: cookie jar
   Colors: marigold and blue

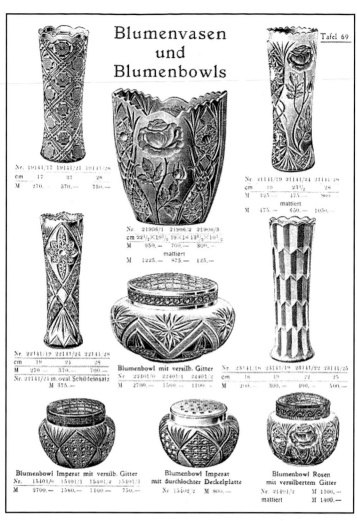

Blumenvasen und Blumenbowls

Nr. 19141/17 19141/21 19141/28
cm   17   21   28
M   270.-   370.--   750.--

Nr. 21141/19 21141/24 21141/28
cm   19   23½   28
M   325.-   475.-   800.-
          mattiert
M   475.-   650.--   1050.--

Nr. 21906/1 21906/2 21906/3
cm 23½×19½ 19×16 13½×10½
M   950.--   700.--   800.--
          mattiert
M   1225.--   875.-   825.--

Nr. 22141/19 22141/24 22141/28
cm   19   23   28
M   250.-   370.--   700.--
Nr. 22141/21 m. oval Schildeinsatz
          M 375.--

Blumenbowl mit versilb. Gitter
Nr. 22401/0 22401/1 22401/2
M   2700.--   1560.--   1100.--

Nr. 23141/19 23141/19 23141/22 23141/25
cm   16   19   22   25
M   250.-   300.-   400.--   500.--

Blumenbowl Imperat mit versilb. Gitter
Nr. 15401/0 15401/1 15401/2 15401/3
M   2700.--   1560.-- 1100.--   750.--

Blumenbowl Imperat
mit durchlochter Deckelplatte
Nr. 15402/2   M 800.--

Blumenbowl Rosen
mit versilbertem Gitter
Nr. 21401/2   M 1100.-
          mattiert   M 1400.--

A full page of patterns and shapes from the 1921 Brockwitz catalog (we cannot confirm that Carnival was produced at this time, but the patterns were certainly in the Brockwitz repertoire). Top row, from left: *TARTAN* cylinder vase (we cannot confirm this shape in Carnival), *ROSE GARDEN* oval or fan shaped vase, *ROSE GARDEN* cylinder vase. Middle row: *CURVED STAR* cylinder vase, *CURVED STAR FLOWER BOWL*, *BOND* vase. Bottom row: two *STAR AND HOBS* flower bowls (part of the *NORTHERN LIGHTS* pattern) and a *ROSE GARDEN* flower bowl.

WARDANCE see *ANTIGONE*

Possible Brockwitz Patterns in Carnival Glass

DIAMOND CUT

DIAMOND CUT is an interesting pattern that is known to have been produced by Josef Inwald in Czechoslovakia and in a similar design by Crown Crystal in Australia: it **may** also have been produced by Brockwitz. Inwald's Carnival is only known in marigold, Crown Crystal produced purple, marigold, and rarely, aqua. However, a **blue** jardinière was found in Argentina in 1998 in this pattern. In the Brockwitz catalogs are illustrations of a covered sugar basin in what appears to be the *DIAMOND CUT* pattern. The detail at the bottom appears to be slightly different to *DIAMOND CUT*, but as the illustrations were drawings and not photographs, it is hard to be certain. It is also known that Brockwitz Carnival is often found in Argen-

tina (there were firm trade links in the 1920s and early 1930s) and of course, Brockwitz made blue Carnival. It is quite possible, therefore, that they made the blue *DIAMOND CUT* jardinière. However, no proof has been found yet to determine the maker of this unusual item—indeed, it may even be Argentinean.

HEADDRESS

The main pattern motif on *HEADDRESS* is a feathered plume, repeated four times around a central stylized floral motif. Interestingly, there are several different variations of the pattern; the position of the curling tendrils and the presence (or lack) of stamens on the central flower may all vary.

Though this pattern does not, to our knowledge, appear in any Brockwitz catalog, circumstantial evidence points to it being used by them. *HEADDRESS* is found as the interior pattern on *CURVED STAR* items that have the file motif on the claws and *NUTMEG GRATER* bowls (both illustrated in the Brockwitz catalogs). It seems likely that *HEADDRESS* was used by several different manufacturers. The *EUROPEAN POPPY* design (which we strongly suspect to be a Riihimaki product on account of its appearance in the signature Riihimaki color of amber—see Chapter Seven) is also known with *HEADDRESS* on the interior. Just to further confuse, *HEADDRESS* is also found teamed with *COSMOS AND CANE* (made by the United States Glass Company). So how did U.S. Glass come into the situation? The answer would seem that the *HEADDRESS* pattern was simply copied by the European designers in much the same way that they copied several other patterns, such as Dugan's *FOUR FLOWERS*.

Shapes: bowls and compote (stemmed sugar)
Colors: marigold and blue

The interior *HEADDRESS* pattern is seen on this marigold bowl in conjunction with the exterior pattern, Brockwitz *NUTMEG GRATER*. $50-80.

Opposite page: Covered pieces have that extra "something" and this splendid, blue *TRIPLE ALLIANCE* cookie jar from Brockwitz is no exception. *Courtesy of Pat Thornton.* NP.

MARGUERITE

MARGUERITE is a rare vase, in fact only one marigold example is known so far. We believe that it was made by Brockwitz on account of the "house style"—in particular the mould work and typical shape of the vase. The marguerites featured in the pattern are identical to the floral motif found on the known Brockwitz pattern *TRIPLE ALLI-ANCE*. The base is ground flat. The sole reported example was found in Australia.

    Shape: vase
    Color: marigold

PLUME PANELS AND BOWS

Only a very few scarce examples of this pattern are currently known. The first reported tumbler was found in California and was reported in the HOACGA Bulletin, July 1993. The first reported water pitcher was sold by Ayers Auction Service in March 1999 (Item #150, it went unrecognized at the time, despite efforts by the auctioneers to identify it, and so was given the name "European Fleur-de-lis"). A water set comprising a pitcher and six stemmed goblets was then sold at auction by Ayers in November 1999. The pattern is all intaglio and features a plume motif surrounded by star motifs—it is an elegant design, delightfully accented by the notched handle. The manufacturer is currently not known, though both the pattern and the shape are very suggestive of Brockwitz.

    Shapes: water pitcher, tumbler, and goblet
    Color: marigold

[1]*Chronicle of Industry.* Pamphlet issued by the Municipal Museum of Industry, Coswig, Germany. 1998.

[2] Marion T. Hartung, *Carnival Glass. Books 1-10* (Emporia, Kansas: by author, 1960-73).

[3] Rose Presznick, *Carnival and Iridescent Glass. Books 1-4* (Lodi, Ohio: by author, 1974).

MARGUERITE is only known in this single, rare, marigold vase. The pattern echoes various other Brockwitz designs, but no maker has yet been attributed with certainty. NP.

Chapter Four

The Netherlands

Leerdam Glasfabriek, Leerdam

A British *Pottery Gazette* article in December 1931 stated that "iridised wares of considerable artistic interest were also being produced at the Leerdam Glassworks in Holland. Some of these pieces, covered first with selenium and then having the surface iridised, were particularly brilliant to transmitted light." It would appear, however, that only fairly limited amounts of Carnival were produced at Leerdam, mainly utilizing moulds that dated back to at least 1900.

Pressed glass making at the Leerdam factory, near Rotterdam, began in the eighteenth century, primarily for the production of bottles. Later, a whole range of shapes was introduced and by the beginning of the twentieth century, the factory was turning out tumblers, table sets, bowls, and many drinking vessels, often in matching suites—only a handful of patterns and shapes are known in Carnival, though. Most attributed Leerdam Carnival items are parts of table sets (creamers, stemmed sugar and butter dishes). Export was focused on England, South America, and Mexico. In 1953, the company became Royal Leerdam and now concentrates on fine crystal.

Signature Characteristics of Leerdam Carnival Glass

• Marigold was the main color produced, but amethyst is also known.

• Not the very best iridescence—weak and sometimes iridized on the inside only.
• Ground base (usually).
• Shapes are generally table set items.

Leerdam Catalogs

Two dated catalogs (1900 and 1910) as well as an undated one thought to be from the early 1920s have been used to confirm attribution of the following listed patterns to Leerdam Glassworks. Sincere thanks to Annet van der Kley-Blekxtoon, Curator of the Stichting National Glasmuseum, Leerdam, and Bob Smith for their assistance with sourcing these catalogs.

Leerdam Patterns Known in Carnival Glass

BEADS AND DIAMONDS see *BEADED SWIRL*

BEADED SWIRL aka *REMBRANDT* aka *BEADS AND DIAMONDS*
A detailed geometric design that contrasts plain panels with intricately patterned panels. The overall effect is rich and it reflects the light well.
Shapes: creamer, stemmed sugar, butter dish, stemmed fruit dish, and stemmed cake plate
Color: marigold

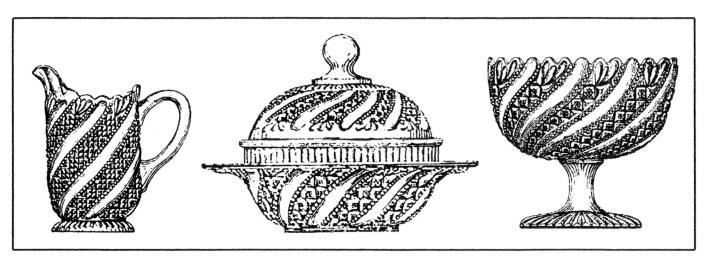

This trio of table set items in *BEADED SWIRL* was illustrated in an undated catalog for the Leerdam Glassworks—thought to be from the early 1920s.

BEADED OVALS

An elegant and classical design, a repeated pattern of large oval motifs. Simple yet effective.

Shape: bowl only known

Color: marigold

DUTCH STAR

Found in the UK (though rarely), this is one of Leerdam's older patterns. It was illustrated in their 1900 catalog and was maintained in production for at least thirty more years. A complex geometric design, its many years of use are borne out by the flatness of moulded detail on the finished Carnival items. The little creamer is only 4" high.

Shapes: creamer and small bowl. Other shapes were made but have not yet been found in Carnival.

Colors: marigold and amethyst

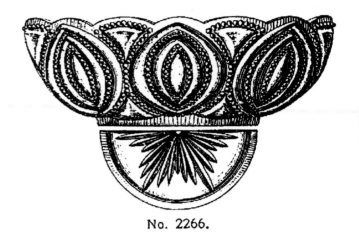

GEPERSTE SCHALEN. — RAVIERS MOULÉS MOULDED DISHES.

No. 2266.

Leerdam's *BEADED OVALS* bowl had the pattern #2266—this illustration is also from their 1920s catalog.

GEPERSTE MELKKANNEN. — CRÊMIERS MOULES. MOULDED CREAMS.

No. 1323.

No. 1408.

No. 1138.

No. 1315.

Clockwise from top left: creamers in *DUTCH STAR, HOLLAND, SQUARES AND QUILLS,* and *JEWELLED PILLAR FLUTE.* All were illustrated in the Leerdam catalog.

GRETA see MEYDAM

HOLLAND

This is a plain design that is easily overlooked, yet we only know of one recorded example, found in Australia back in the early 1980s. There are sure to be many more examples in existence, but perhaps because of their simple (uninteresting) design, no one bothers to record them. Nevertheless, this is a Leerdam item, known in Carnival, dating from the late 1920s or early 1930s. The shape known is a small creamer, almost 4" high, with a rich iridescence.

Shape: creamer is reported but a flat based sugar is also illustrated in the catalog

Color: marigold

JEWELLED PILLAR FLUTE

Not Leerdam's most interesting pattern, this is a utilitarian design that features plain panels and adjacent beaded ribs. Found in the UK.

Shapes: creamer, stemmed sugar, and flat based sugar

Color: marigold

MEYDAM aka GRETA

MEYDAM features interlocking tear-drop motifs in a complex geometric design. It must have been a best seller for Leerdam, as it appears in their catalog in two variations of the same basic pattern. Two versions of the table set comprising stemmed sugar, covered butter dish, and creamer were produced. The differences are fairly minor, yet distinct enough for Leerdam to illustrate and catalog them separately as 212/ no.1 and 212/ no.2. MEYDAM has been found in the USA, UK, Ireland, and also in Australia; indeed we thank Mary Hare from Virginia for details of her "find." Mary has the creamer, standing almost 4" high with a rich marigold iridescence and a ground base.

Shapes: creamer, stemmed sugar, butter dish (as mentioned above—in two variations as illustrated). Leerdam's catalogs illustrate several bowls in this pattern but we are not currently aware of them in Carnival.

Color: marigold

MEYDAM is an attractive little creamer that is only known in marigold. *Courtesy of John Kerr/Rob Innes.* SP $50-90.

REMBRANDT see BEADED SWIRL

SQUARES AND QUILLS

This one is an elusive pattern and has been reported in the UK only rarely. It's a simple square block and chevron design in a typical repeated pattern. Like DUTCH STAR, this pattern was also featured in Leerdam's 1900 catalog, so was probably in production for many years. First reported in 1986 in the newsletter of the now defunct Carnival Club of Great Britain.

Shapes: creamer and stemmed sugar

Color: marigold

SQUARES AND QUILLS is an unusual pattern, seen here in the shape of a diminutive, marigold creamer. SP $50-90.

Chapter Five

Czechoslovakia (Czech Republic)

"The only thing constant in life is change."
—Francois de la Rochefoucauld.

The political history of the region we now know as the Czech and Slovak Republics or Czechoslovakia is complex, however, it has significant bearings on the development of the glass industry, so a brief overview is needed here. The main glass producing area is that once known as Bohemia. It lay within the Austro-Hungarian (or Hapsburg) Empire of Middle Europe and in 1910 had a population of 51 million. With the collapse of the Empire after World War One, the newly born, independent Czechoslovakia inherited three-quarters of the former Hapsburg industry—and at a stroke, became the tenth most industrialized country in the world.

Significantly, Czechoslovakia had also inherited 92 percent of the Empire's glass industry. In the newly found freedom of the years immediately following 1918, the glass industry of Bohemia focused largely on exporting a great deal of its output. Export had always been a major feature of the glass industry in the region, indeed for years, the education system had been geared to schooling youngsters in up to six different languages with a view to careers in international sales. One school had even included glass manufacture in the teaching curriculum. In an essay written by Dr. Ing. V. Ctyroky, Director of the Glass Institute at Hradec Kralove in 1931, a delightful description of the early mode of export can be read:

> At first handcarts, and subsequently carrier's carts drawn by two to six horses were the means of transport for conveying Bohemian glass to Germany, Poland, Russia, Holland, Italy and even to Portugal and Spain. Some traders crossed over to London and others found their way to Riga, Constantinople and other more distant places.

By the end of the 1920s, exports had built up so much that Czechoslovakia could claim over 10 percent of the world glass market.[1] In the face of increasing international competition however, Czechoslovakia hung onto its position as a major exporter and indeed came through the Depression years of the following decade with renewed strength. Located in Middle Europe, the traders found that they could reach out in all directions: to the rest of Europe, the USA, and the Far East, especially India. By 1936 the region was producing 40 percent of the world's glass—even the Waldorf Astoria had Inwald glass tableware from Czechoslovakia! It was during this period that the production of Carnival Glass thrived in Czechoslovakia.

Fleur de Lis   Edward   Diamond Sugar

Telephone: Holborn 2358, 2359.   Telegrams: "Dornberger, Smith, London."

S. DORNBERGER & CO. L^{TD}.
GAMAGE BUILDING, HOLBORN, LONDON, E.C.1.
GLASS AND CHINA
FOR HOME TRADE AND EXPORT.
Large Stocks held at Home Ports.

Hard times were to follow; World War Two had a devastating effect on Czechoslovakia. War damage and subsequent political upheavals changed the face of the country's industry. Under Soviet domination the glass factories were collectivized and the era that produced Carnival Glass in Czechoslovakia was over. Near Teplice, (aka Teplitz, where Josef Inwald's main glass factory of Rudolfova Hut was situated) was the town of Terezin, originally named Theresienstadt, which housed a notorious concentration camp during World War Two. Eventually, on the first of January 1993, Czechoslovakia peacefully split into its two ethnic components, the Czech Republic (which contained Bohemia) and Slovakia. Tracking down documentation, catalogs, and records within the Czech Republic is a difficult task, as so much was destroyed. Finally we have been able to piece together the record of Carnival production that you read here.

The Heritage of Bohemia

The extensive forests found on the rolling plains, hills, and plateaus of Bohemia were home to the first centers of glass making in the area. Wood provided the fuel and the mountain streams gave motive power. The wood was also used as a raw material, as the glass itself was based on a potash-lime batch using ash from local beechwood (hence the name "forest glass" that is sometimes used). This type of glass did not lend itself to intricate work as it was thick and heavy. This accounts for the characteristic of much Inwald glass being based on simple lines and with a lack of complex intaglio mould work. Solid, more massive and simple in appearance and form, it is a harmony of aesthetic beauty and essential practicality. The simplicity of motif and pattern enhance the optical quality of the glass. Not only was it useful—it was also beautiful.

The glass of Bohemia (we now know it as Czechoslovakia) has a long standing reputation for outstanding beauty and quality. The industry dates back to the thirteenth century and includes the renowned Biedermeier period of glassmaking (a flourishing time in the early 1800s, when there were probably more glass craftsmen in Bohemia than anywhere else in the world) and the Wiener-Werkstatte, founded in Vienna in 1903. The latter produced art glass in the Art Nouveau style, indeed the iridized glass from the Loetz glassworks arguably rivaled that produced by Louis Comfort Tiffany himself. Bohemia had a reputation for being highly innovative in many kinds of glass technique; indeed, uranium glass (vaseline) was discovered and first made there.

The pressed glass output of Czechoslovakia is often overshadowed by the richly colored cut glass, the amazing iridized Art Nouveau glass and engraved glass that was produced and exported in quantity from this region during the nineteenth and early twentieth centuries. However, the glass-pressing technique had been carried out in the area since the 1830s and is still a major industry (AVIR is the main producer, linked to major plants in Italy and the rest of the world through their recent connections with Owens-Illinois Inc.)

Josef Inwald A. G., Teplice and other locations

It was a characteristic of Bohemian glassmaking that even factories devoted mainly to utility glassware also turned out a percentage of refined, luxury glass. This was particularly so in the case of the large concern of Josef Inwald. The company's head office was located in Vienna with factories at Grosspreisen, (now called Male Brezno), Prag-Slichov (Prague), Bad Podebrad (Podebrady), and Deutsch-Schutzendorf (Deutsch Gablonz after 1919). The main factory that produced Inwald's Carnival Glass, however, was located at Rudolfshutte-Teplitz (today known as Teplice). Lying to the northeast of Prague, only fifty miles or so away from the Brockwitz factory, this was known as a major glass "hut" (a facility for the production of hot glass). Also called Rudolfova Hut, this was the only Bohemian factory that made a major name for itself in the production of pressed glass. Founded in 1884 as a sheet metal factory, Josef Inwald had bought it in 1905 and converted it to glassmaking the following year. It was a huge success story and at its height over a thousand glassworkers were employed there.

Inwald had warehouses located at Budapest, Prague, London, Vienna, and Paris and a network of showrooms around the world. In London, England, several importers handled Inwald glass, though the main one was Clayton Mayers. Czech glass was also exported to Argentina and is illustrated in the catalogs of several South American companies. At its height, the fine Carnival Glass from Josef Inwald was exported to many countries, yet strangely enough, very little was retained for the home market and it is very hard to find in either the Czech Republic or Slovakia today. Collectors in the USA, Australia, and the UK probably have more chance of finding it on their "home turf."

Inwald's success story came to an end in 1938, when Hitler annexed the Sudetenland (a predominantly German speaking area of Czechoslovakia). As with Brockwitz, World War Two caused Inwald's downfall and all four Bohemian factories producing pressed glass were consolidated and placed under Sklo Union in Teplice, the location of Rudolfova Hut. During the 1950s, the state began replacing manual production with mechanization. Since then, Rudolfova Hut has oriented itself toward low cost, functional glass, especially bottles (such as Coca-Cola and Pepsi)[1]. From 1993, Rudolfova Hut has been selling pressed household glass under the brand name *Cristal* and still produces some of the elegant crystal glass that won it such acclaim in the 1920s and 1930s.

Josef Inwald's *JACOBEAN* pattern was produced in a very wide range of shapes and sizes—many of which are known in Carnival. This unusual ad is taken from the November 1926 British *Pottery Gazette*.

Opposite page:
Much Czech glass was imported into the UK and the USA during the 1920s and early 1930s. Clayton Mayers was one of the main importers in the UK, but was by no means the only one. This 1930 ad for the London glass importer, S. Dornberger & Co. Ltd., illustrates a range of items that were made in mainland Europe. The *FLEUR DE LIS* bowl (top left) and the *EDWARD* (aka *DIAMOND CUT*) vase alongside it, were produced by the Czech manufacturer, Josef Inwald, and are both known in Carnival Glass. The "Diamond" sugar (top right) and the tumbler with the triple roll base on the bottom row were very probably made by another Czech manufacturer, Josef Rindskopf—these two items are not known in Carnival. The remaining three items on the bottom row can't currently be attributed to a manufacturer.

Josef Inwald's Catalog

In William Heacock's *Collecting Glass. Volume 2* (Antique Publications, 1985) pages from Josef Inwald's catalog from circa the mid 1920s were printed. This is the only catalog source, so far, for this factory. Some pages are missing, but enough are present to paint a very full picture of Inwald's production.

Signature Characteristics of Inwald Carnival Glass

• High quality, refined glassware from a factory with a long and outstanding reputation.

• Ground base with a very distinctive polished finish that is mirror-shiny.

• Marigold is the only color known (though a blue *DIAMOND CUT* bowl is known, but this may well be an Argentinean or German item—it is not yet proven that Inwald made blue Carnival).

• Intaglio, "near-cut" designs with classically simple, geometric patterns or stylized florals. Little complex detail in the designs because of the nature of Czech pressed glass that was thick and heavy to work.

• The iridescence on much of Josef Inwald's glass is very dis-

tinctive and quite breathtaking. It varies from a deep, glowing pumpkin that has much red and purple tones in the iridescence to a breathtaking lighter peacock-marigold that flashes with lime, gold, pink, and purple; unsurpassable in electric hi-lites; astonishingly beautiful and ranking up with the very best.

• Full suites, water sets, and dinner services in single patterns: often many sizes in a single shape (for example the *JACOBEAN* tumblers).

Inwald Patterns Known in Carnival Glass

BANDED DIAMONDS AND BARS

A contrasting band of diamonds, bordered by plain panelled bands, gives this pattern its name. Almost thirty different shapes were illustrated in the Inwald catalog, yet *BANDED DIAMONDS AND BARS* is seldom seen in Carnival. Rare examples have been found, however, in the USA and the UK.

Shapes: tumblers in three sizes: shot glass, juice and regular size. A stemmed sherbert dish is also known. As the tumbler is known, it is very likely that a water pitcher exists.

Color: marigold

These two sherbets in Inwald's *BANDED DIAMONDS AND BARS* exhibit the stunning iridescence that is characteristic of Inwald's Carnival. *Courtesy of Carol and Derek Sumpter.* SP $75-125.

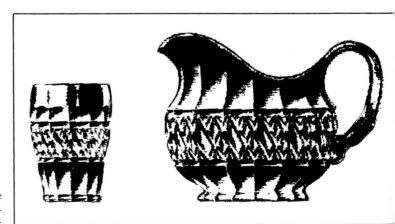

Inwald's *BANDED DIAMONDS AND BARS* is known in the tumbler shape (Illustrated), so it figures that a water pitcher must also exist in Carnival. This extract from Inwald's catalog shows how the pitcher would look.

BOHEMIAN PANELLED EIGHTS

This rare and lovely vase (named by Gale Eichorst and the authors), was purchased at auction in the USA in the mid 1990s—to date it is the only one reported. Clearly shown in the Inwald catalog, this delightful item stands almost 8" high on a pedestal base. As the name suggests, there are eight panels around the vase, eight sides to the base, eight ruffles at the flared top and eight vertical bands of varying width. To cap it off, the motifs on the central band look like the figure eight!

    Shape: vase
    Color: marigold

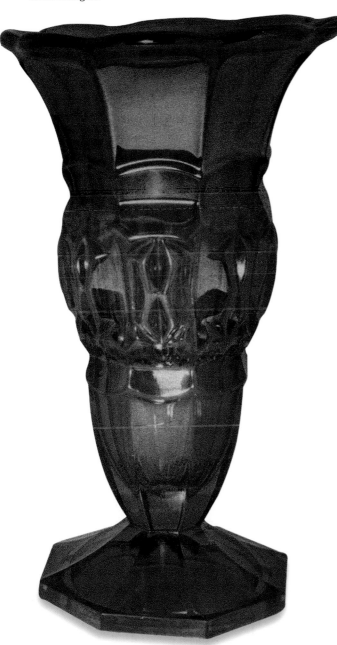

The iridescence on Inwald's marigold *BOHEMIAN PANELLED EIGHTS* vase is breathtakingly stunning and is typical of that factory's high quality. *Courtesy of Gale Eichorst.* SP $450-600.

The name is so apt—*DECORAMA* has an angular shape so typical of the Art Deco style. The Inwald catalog illustration shown here gives an indication of the diamond shape of the pitcher's base.

CORONET see PRINCETON

DANUBE

DANUBE is an elegant vase, typical of Czechoslovakian style. The pattern features deeply cut cross motifs and encircling bands. Almost forty individual vases were depicted in Inwald's catalog (not counting those included within suites/ranges of individual patterns such as *PINWHEEL* and *CORONET/PRINCETON*). Several of these have been found in Carnival; *DANUBE* is one of them. In David Doty's *A Field Guide to Carnival Glass*[2] he notes that an example of this vase was brought from Argentina to the HOACGA Convention in 1996. As noted below with reference to the *PRINCETON* range, Inwald almost certainly exported their glass to Argentina.

    Shape: vase
    Color: marigold

Bright marigold, reflecting blue, turquoise and magenta, this rather substantial (11.5" tall) *DANUBE* vase appears to be a taller version of the vase labeled 7871 in the Inwald catalog. SP $450-600.

DECORAMA

Aptly named (by the late William Heacock), *DECORAMA* is the very essence of an Art Deco design. The shape of items in this pattern (just four are shown in the Inwald catalog) is angular, as is the simple, yet effective, linear moulded design. The base on all four items is diamond shaped and the handle on the water pitcher is sharply angular, bearing strong similarities to the *NOLA* pattern also from Inwald and the *GRAND THISTLE* items from Riihimaki in Finland. Found in Canada and the USA.

    Shapes: tumbler and water pitcher
    Color: marigold

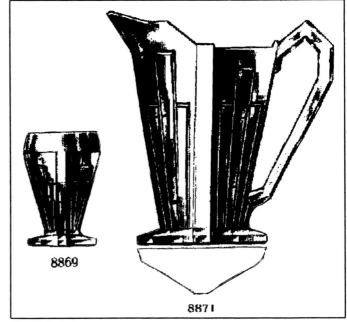

8869

8871

DIAMOND CUT aka EDWARD

The British *Pottery Gazette* in May 1929 had an ad for the London wholesaler, Shorter Brothers: illustrated in that ad was a footed bowl in the *DIAMOND CUT* pattern. A 1930 ad for another importer, S. Dornberger & Co., also of London, had an illustration of a *DIAMOND CUT* vase. However, the vase was given the name "Edward"—it might have been easier if the Carnival items in the pattern had taken that name, as a virtually identical pattern (also called *DIAMOND CUT*) was made by Crown Crystal in Australia. Nine items are shown in this pattern in the Inwald catalog. The vase, in several sizes, has been found in Carnival in the USA, UK, and Australia. A jardinière has been found in Argentina.

The intaglio design features a fan motif and cross or diamond shapes (the interpretation depends on how you view it)—so is it possible to tell the Czech and Australian patterns apart? Yes. Inwald Carnival is only known so far in marigold, so if the item is in amethyst, it would be a safe bet to assume it is the Australian version. Also there are differences in the pattern detail: the Inwald version has a fine file between the main motifs. The shapes and edging differ too—only Inwald made the vase shape, and the footed rose bowl is probably the only shape common to both manufacturers, though Inwald items in carnival in that shape cannot be confirmed. Crown Crystal often used a scallop and flute edge on this shape while the Inwald bowls have a regular fluted edge.

The real shock, however, came when a **blue** jardinière in this pattern was found in Argentina. Until that point, it was assumed that Inwald made no blue Carnival—only marigold. There still remains a substantial element of doubt. Was the blue bowl made by Inwald and exported to Argentina? A great deal of Inwald Carnival has been found there, along with many other European items. Or could it have been a copy that was actually manufactured in Argentina—or maybe Inwald sold the mould? There is the further possibility that it may actually have been made by Brockwitz (see Chapter Three). Research to determine the answer continues.

Shape: vase—two sizes are currently known, 12" and 8"

Color: marigold

DOUBLE DIAMOND

The name given to this pattern by Bob Smith echoes the main motif—an elongated oval enclosing two diamond shapes. A range of boudoir items is shown in this pattern in the Inwald catalog—all but the candlestick have been found in Carnival. Harry Barrett, a Carnival collector from London, England, found several *DOUBLE DIAMOND* items wrapped up in a Belgian newspaper at a London antique market. (Inwald, of course, had showrooms in Brussels, Belgium.) Other items in this pattern have been found both elsewhere in the UK and the USA. Indeed, *DOUBLE DIAMOND* was found back in the early 1980s in Oklahoma.

Shapes: lidded powder jars, cologne bottles, trays and perfumes in varying sizes, ring tree, atomizer, and tumble-up

Color: marigold

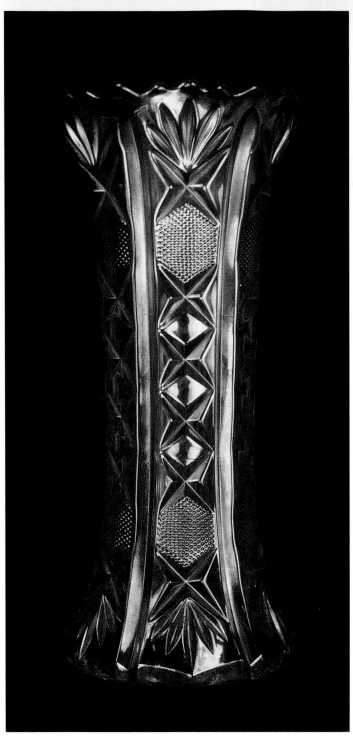

DIAMOND CUT is an impressive, statuesque vase that stands some 12" high and weighs a hefty two and a half pounds. Its 5" wide base is domed, the outer edge being highly polished and ground to a mirror shiny finish. Its iridescence, however—peacock marigold, shimmering with pink, turquoise and gold—is even more impressive than its massive size. Inwald Carnival at its best. SP $450-600.

A tumble-up was used in the bedroom—the upturned tumbler served as both a lid for the water carafe as well as a handy drinking vessel during the night. Inwald's *DOUBLE DIAMOND* was made in several shapes including the marigold tumble-up shown here as well as the perfume bottle. *Courtesy of Carol and Derek Sumpter.* SP $300-500 for the complete tumble-up, $100-200 for the perfume.

EDWARD see *DIAMOND CUT*

FINE RING

A simple pattern featuring plain panels and two bands of encircling concentric rings. Only known in the celery vase shape (pattern #8624), though other shapes including a bowl and water pitcher are shown in Inwald's catalog.

    Shape: celery vase

    Color: marigold

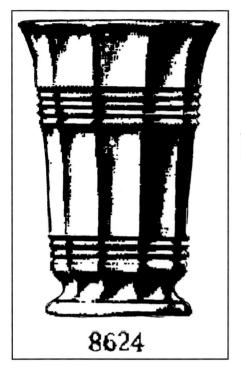

FINE RING is known in the celery vase shape only, as illustrated here.

FLEUR-DE-LIS

A simple, yet very elegant design, featuring the typical three pointed shape of the fleur-de-lis. This is a common, traditional form of ornament, best known as an emblem for the French monarchy. However, it is also considered to be a stylized portrayal of three white lilies or the white iris, ancient Egyptian and Indian symbols of life. Other schools of thought consider the motif to be representative of axe heads, spears, and similar weapons. *FLEUR-DE-LIS* appears in the Inwald catalog in a range of over forty shapes. Only a handful of these are currently known in Carnival. The splendid vases are typically very heavy and impressive items. On the polished, mirror shiny base is an unusual and characteristic whirling star that is only found on this pattern. Examples have been found in the USA, Canada, UK, Argentina, Australia and mainland Europe.

    Shapes: vase in several sizes, bowls, jardinières, and plates

    Color: marigold

Vases were certainly one of Inwald's specialties—here's another beauty, this time in the *FLEUR DE LIS* pattern. The iridescence on this 10" high vase is a rich pumpkin marigold. SP $300-500.

INTAGLIO STARS see *PINWHEEL*

JACOBEAN aka JACOBEAN RANGER

A familiar and very simple pattern that takes iridescence very well indeed, *JACOBEAN* is a square block type of pattern. Similar designs have been made by other manufacturers both before and after Inwald produced it, for example, *BLOCKS AND ARCHES* by Crown Crystal, Australia and *RANGER* by Cristales Mexicanos S.A. Inwald produced this pattern in a vast range of shapes and sizes. It is not currently known just how many of these were iridized. The *JACOBEAN* pattern has a fascinating history that reflects trade and politics in Europe during the 1920s and 1930s. It had one of the biggest and most impressive advertising campaigns ever devoted to glass. It was also one of the most widely distributed and sold crystal

glass patterns of its time. Examples have been found in the USA, UK, and Australia.

Hubert and Eric Mayers together traded as the British importing agent, Clayton Mayers. They had an excellent distribution organization, a large warehouse in Pentonville, London and one of the most comprehensive stocks of glassware in London. They also had firm trade links with Inwald. A study of the ads in the British *Pottery Gazette* over a ten year period from about 1923 to 1933 reveals a fascinating tale. Clayton Mayers were marketing the crystal *JACOBEAN* range strongly. They were undoubtedly publicity experts. Their advertising campaign was placed in all the top British magazines and by 1925 the *Pottery Gazette* reported that "Jacobean Glassware has spread all over the country like wild fire." The range of shapes was continually increasing, and by 1930 there were over 200 shapes in *JACOBEAN*. In 1931, they even produced a cinema film to sell their glass. Called *A Visit to Miss Madeleine Carroll's Flat*, it was intended to show "the beauty and utility of Jacobean Glassware in a modern home."

However, in 1932 a change took place. Tariffs on imported glass began to take their toll in Britain. Clayton Mayers announced that some (not all) of the *JACOBEAN* tumblers were to be made in Britain. Until that point, all the *JACOBEAN* items had been manufactured in Czechoslovakia. Within a few years, several more items in the range were also made in Britain by various firms that probably included Davidsons on Tyneside. However, the United Kingdom wasn't the only country to stock *JACOBEAN*. The United States, France, Sweden, and Argentina also advertised items in the crystal range. The pattern was known in France as "Milord." Later editions of the Inwald catalog call this pattern "Lord."

It is most likely that iridized articles in the *JACOBEAN* pattern were made and iridized in Czechoslovakia prior to 1932. All sizes of the iridized tumblers may have the registered design #702446 moulded into the glass. This was registered in the United Kingdom by the agent, Clayton Mayers, on December 17, 1923. On November 21, 1924, Clayton Mayers further registered a set of items in the *JACOBEAN* pattern with the number 709314. The copyright on this design was extended through to November 1934. A splendid, iridized decanter is known with this number moulded into it. Other items in the #709314 set were a sauce bottle, biscuit barrel (cookie jar), cress bowl with plate, hors d'oeuvre dish, and vinegar bottle. The copyright on #702446 expired on December 17, 1938. It was then replaced by the registered number 791409, which is only found on non-iridized crystal items. In the 1920s there was a certain *cachet* in having a British registration number on the glass. No doubt Josef Inwald, intent on marketing their glassware widely in the United Kingdom, believed that it would help them.

Shapes: tumblers in various sizes, water pitcher, decanter, and tumble-up. A full dressing table set including powder jars, perfume, atomiser and cologne bottles in various sizes, a large tray, small pintray, and a ring tree. Possibly many more items were iridized and have yet to be discovered by collectors

Color: marigold

Four *JACOBEAN* tumblers in gradually decreasing sizes. Note how the iridescence is a little different on each one, varying from Inwald's gorgeous peacock marigold to the deeper and more intense pumpkin shade. The Registered Design number 702446 is moulded into the side of the base of three of the four shown. Of the examples pictured here, the smallest is just 2" high, while the tallest is 3.5"—a larger tumbler is also known in Carnival. SP $80-150 for each.

NOLA aka *PANELLED TWIGS*

This pattern takes its name from the Oklahoma lady, Nola Schmoker, who first notified the collecting world of the pattern. The design is a panelled, intaglio zig zag effect—simple yet very effective, especially when iridized. Several shapes are shown in the Inwald catalog in this pattern, some of them having a very distinctive diamond shaped base. The British *Pottery Gazette* featured an ad for "International Glassware," which featured the *NOLA* tumbler (with the distinctive diamond shaped base) in 1929.

The pattern was first noticed in Carnival in the pitcher and tumbler shapes, though soon other shapes were found—indeed a complete boudoir set was found in an antique shop in Florida that dealt mainly in imported furniture from Europe. Various items in *NOLA* have also been found in the UK and mainland Europe.

Shapes: water set in which both pitcher and tumblers have the diamond shaped base. A full dressing table set, which includes colognes, perfume bottle, ring tree, tray, powder boxes, and a tumble-up. It is important to note that the tumbler in the tumble-up has a round base.

Color: marigold

A dresser set was produced by Inwald in the *NOLA* pattern—this is a powder jar. Note its distinctive square shape. *Courtesy of Frank and Shirley.* SP $100-200.

PINWHEEL

A complex design featuring stars and similar intaglio motifs, this pattern is very similar to one known in the output from Sowerby in England (where it was called *DERBY*). The identical suite of items in the same pattern appeared in the Markhbeinn catalog under the name of "Picadilly" (sic). However, a British *Pottery Gazette* ad from 1929 also showed the *PINWHEEL* items being imported into the United Kingdom via Hamburg and the British east coast ports by J.G. Wright, a London importer. Almost certainly these were coming via Hamburg from Czechoslovakia.

It is not too difficult to distinguish the Inwald items from the Sowerby ones. The Sowerby vases usually have a plain, domed base and any seen in amethyst are almost certainly from England. However, the most characterizing feature of the Inwald *PINWHEEL* items is the polished, mirror ground base with a complex star motif: this is found on the small 4.75" vase and some bowls. Vases in several sizes are the most frequently seen item in this pattern. The pattern is exterior on the bowls, with no interior design. A wide variety of tableware shapes was illustrated in *PINWHEEL* in the Inwald catalog, though only a handful of shapes are currently known in Carnival.

The tumbler in this pattern has been separately identified and called *INTAGLIO STARS*. It is simply the matching tumbler to the pitcher in the *PINWHEEL* pattern. An example of this tumbler was found in North Carolina in the late 1980s. Other shapes in the pattern have been found elsewhere in the USA, the UK, and Australia.

Shapes: vases (in several widths and sizes) and bowls
Color: marigold

The tumbler shown in this Inwald catalog illustration is known as *INTAGLIO STARS*, though it is, in fact, the tumbler from Inwald's *PINWHEEL* range. The plate also shown is not known in Carnival (only bowls have been reported so far as we know), however it is used here in order to illustrate the *PINWHEEL* pattern for ease of identification.

PRINCETON aka CORONET

At the HOACGA Convention in 1997, John Britt purchased a 10" high vase in this pattern from an Argentinean collector. The vase was unknown at the time and in his immediate quest for information, John showed the vase to Joan Doty, Bob Smith, and the authors (who were all present at the Convention). Fortunately, we were able to place it with Josef Inwald and John went on to name the pattern *PRINCETON*. However, a few months later, we came across contemporary advertising in the 1928 British *Pottery Gazette* for the pattern. The name apparently given to the range in that contemporary ad was *CORONET*.

PRINCETON is a simple "near-cut" effect pattern with elongated ovals and diamond facets; it was described in the *Pottery Gazette* ad as being a "deeply engraved pattern which catches and reflects the light a thousand times and conveys an irresistible impression of fine, hand cut glass." The pattern is also shown in the Inwald catalog— Clayton Mayers in England were acting as their agent and selling the range for them. Currently, the large and impressive vase (marked with a RD number) is only one of a handful of items known to us in this pattern. There may well be many more examples, as almost thirty different shapes were shown in the Inwald catalog. The *PRINCETON* vase was also illustrated in the Cristalerias Papini (Argentina) catalog. Interestingly, the example of this vase that we have seen was found in Argentina and the first Carnival bowl reported in this pattern was also found in Argentina. The likely explanation is that Inwald exported to Argentina. Other rare examples have also been found in the USA and Australia.

Shapes: vase and bowl
Color: marigold

This exquisite little marigold vase (just under 5" in height) is Inwald's *PINWHEEL* and was found in Australia. SP $400-600.

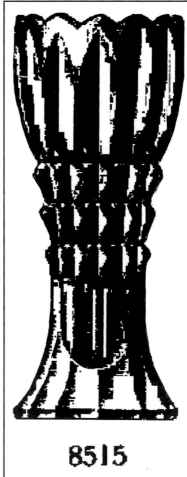

8515

PRINCETON or *CORONET*, call it what you will, this stately vase was shown in Inwald's catalog along with a range of other shapes. Only the vase and bowl have so far been found in Carnival.

Possible Inwald Patterns Known in Carnival Glass

JOSEF'S PLUMES (aka ACANTHUS)

An outstandingly beautiful vase, both in terms of its classic design and its breathtaking iridescence. The main pattern feature is a simple, stylized, intaglio plume motif, very characteristic of Czech production. The base is domed and has the polished, mirror-shiny, ground finish that is so typical of Josef Inwald's glass. The iridescence on the example we have studied is a truly superlative peacock marigold—quite breathtaking and showing scintillating highlights of pink and turquoise. This is surely an Inwald vase. JOSEF'S PLUMES has been found in Canada and the USA; only a handful of examples are known. A single example of a crystal example was found in the UK, standing alongside a crystal DIAMOND CUT vase—both had come from a house-clearance in the south of England.

Shape: vase
Color: marigold

Shades of lime, topaz, purple, and rose highlight the fabulous peacock marigold iridescence on this splendid vase. Named JOSEF'S PLUMES by the authors, it has a distinctive and elegant design. Found in the USA, this example was sold at the NECGA Convention auction in 1999 for $350; a similar vase in a mall for $800 was reported.

Josef Rindskopf A.G. (also called Riethof), Teplice

"Gotta leave you all behind and face the truth"
—Extract from lyrics of "Bohemian Rhapsody" by Freddie Mercury and Queen (1980s cult rock band)

It was a true "Bohemian Rhapsody" to finally open the pages of the Rindskopf catalogs and discover the truth. Nothing, however, could have prepared us for the sheer joy of finding a major manufacturer that was not previously known to have produced Carnival Glass. Our suspicions that the firm of Josef Rindskopf had been involved in producing Carnival were finally confirmed by the efforts of Bob Smith, who managed to finally locate two Rindskopf catalogs[3]. When we finally perused the catalogs (numbers 11 and 12A dating from the 1920s) we were amazed at the patterns that we were able to identify—patterns that had long been "mysteries." There were the CLASSIC ARTS and EGYPTIAN QUEEN patterns shown in detailed line drawings. Many other patterns that had previously been attributed to other manufacturers (or simply marked up as "unknown") are illustrated too. Indeed, Josef Rindskopf A.G. has emerged as being a major European producer of Carnival, equal to the other Czech manufacturer, Josef Inwald. A great deal of Rindskopf Carnival Glass was exported and is now being found in the USA, UK, and Australia as well as mainland Europe. In the UK, the International Bottle Company acted as both agent (registering patterns) and also as importer for a large volume of Czech glassware. Of course, there are sure to be more Rindskopf patterns that have not yet been reported. Hopefully many more will surface.

Josef Rindskopf Aktiengesellschaft (A.G.) was founded in 1878: the first factory built by Rindskopf (later known as Reithof) was in 1891 at Josefhutte, Kostany near Teplice. It was a large concern, employing 400 to 500 glass workers. Later the company expanded and iridized glass became a specialty during the Art Nouveau era, with dark purples and blues often predominating. However, according to Robert and Deborah Truitt[4] Rindskopf "experienced severe loss due to World War One. In 1920 it became a public corporation and concentrated on the production of pressed glass." Rindskopf's pressed glass was manufactured at Barbarahutte (also known as the Emina glass factory or Emina Hut), at Tischau (Mstisov) close to Kostany, and at Fannyhutte, Duchov. Sadly, further difficulties were experienced and the company declared bankruptcy in 1927.[4] Records suggest that there were connections between Rindskopf and Inwald and it is believed that the two concerns (what was left of Rindskopf) merged in the 1930s.

Signature Characteristics of Rindskopf Carnival Glass

• Lack of consistency in the finish and iridescence: some examples are high quality, refined glassware with outstanding iridescence that rivals the very best of Josef Inwald's glass, while other examples seem to be pale and inferior.

• Again a lack of consistency in the finish on the base. Some examples have a ground base that is quite shiny, while others are ground, but dull and are not as refined. Dainty scroll feet on some pieces.

• Some items are iridized on the base—this is particularly noticeable on some vases.

• Marigold is the main color known but rare examples of purple and blue are also thought to have been made by Rindskopf.

• Intaglio, "near-cut" designs with classically simple, geometric patterns. Certain motifs (in particular notches, circles, crosses, fans, and grooves) feature again and again, helping to identify Rindskopf's glass. Rindskopf also used typical Art Deco angular shapes on some items.

• Little complex detail in the designs because of the nature of Czech pressed glass which was thick and heavy to work.

• Table sets, water sets, bowls and vases predominate.

• Czechoslovakian origin may be marked on the glass (etched, enameled, or moulded) with various spellings.

Josef Rindskopf's Catalogs

Parts of two catalog of pressed glass produced by Rindskopf during the 1920s have been studied (catalogs 11 and 12A)[3]. There are many familiar shapes and patterns among the entries and the "house style" reveals typical Czech characteristics. Table sets, vases, bowls, and more: the patterns are geometric and essentially simple—free of cluttering detail. The majority of items are pressed glass, however several blow-moulded shapes are also illustrated. Patterns are not named, only assigned numbers.

Rindskopf Patterns Known in Carnival Glass

BANDED LAUREL WREATH see *LAUREL WREATH*

CANE PANELS aka *PANELLED CANE*

A tall, columnar, stately vase featuring alternate plain and geometric patterned panels, the manufacturer of this scarce pattern has long been a mystery—until now. Illustrated in the Rindskopf catalogs, this vase had the pattern #1082 and was made both slightly flared and straight sided. Three heights were produced: 13 cm., 21 cm., and 30 cm. These approximately equate to: 5", 8", and 12". Found in the USA and the UK.

Shape: vase (the 8" size is currently the only one reported in Carnival)

Color: marigold

CIRCLES AND GROOVES

One example only is documented, though there are sure to be others. Found in Belgium, the item known is a large, heavy vase. The pattern is shown in the Rindskopf catalog in several shapes—the distinctive circles and grooves seen on the vase are clearly illustrated. A master fruit bowl in the *CIRCLES AND GROOVES* pattern bears the pattern #8039, however, the bowl shape has not yet been reported in Carnival. Large heavy vases that have an almost identical shape to the *CIRCLES AND GROOVES* vase are also depicted in the Rindskopf catalog.

Shape: vase

Color: marigold

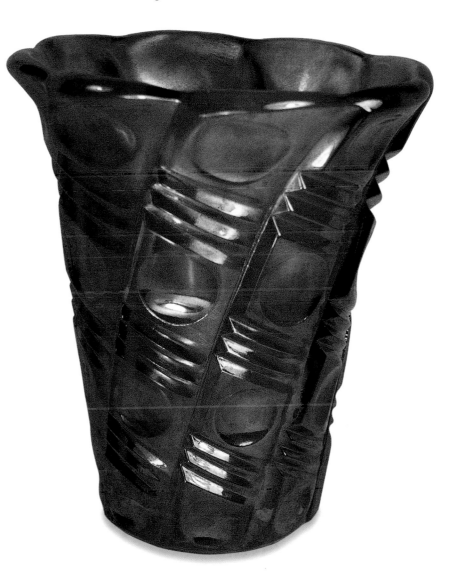

This is the only reported example (so far) of the *CIRCLES AND GROOVES* pattern. This heavy marigold vase was found in a street flea-market in Belgium. NP.

This rare *CANE PANELS* marigold vase was found in the UK—it has also been found in the USA. NP.

CLASSIC ARTS and *EGYPTIAN QUEEN*

The *CLASSIC ARTS* and *EGYPTIAN QUEEN* items are "sister" patterns, distinguished from all other Carnival Glass in that they have a kind of green (verdigris effect) staining as part of the decoration. Basically marigold items, they feature a decorated band of dancing figures that is picked out in the green effect. This gives an antique look and was almost certainly an attempt to evoke the 1920s Art Deco "King Tut" craze. (In 1922, the tomb of the Egyptian king Tutankhamen had been discovered.) Other items from Czech manufacturers such as Moser and Harrach featured similar decorated bands of dancing figures.

A splendid array of Rindskop's *CLASSIC ARTS* and *EGYPTIAN QUEEN* items, as shown in their catalog 12A. At the top are the open and covered sugars in the *CLASSIC ARTS* design; below are the three vases (the *CLASSIC ARTS* large vase or celery is on the left, the other two vases are *EGYPTIAN QUEEN*).

• *CLASSIC ARTS*

The *CLASSIC ARTS* pieces have a pattern band that features Roman type figures playing instruments and dancing. Examples have been found in the USA and UK. Previously, the *CLASSIC ARTS* range had been thought to consist of: celery vase, covered powder jar, and rose bowl. Now that we have the catalogs to study, it is possible to be precise as to the original nature and designated use of the items. The wide *CLASSIC ARTS* celery vase (7.5" high) was simply a vase, not specifically meant for celery (pattern #1658). The *CLASSIC ARTS* rose bowl was actually a finger bowl or open sugar bowl (pattern #1642). The *CLASSIC ARTS* covered powder jar is actually a covered sugar or marmalade bowl (pattern #1642 for the bowl and #1704 for the lid). Examples have been found in the USA, UK, and Australia.

Shapes: large vase, open sugar bowl (or finger bowl), and covered sugar bowl

Color: marigold with green stain band

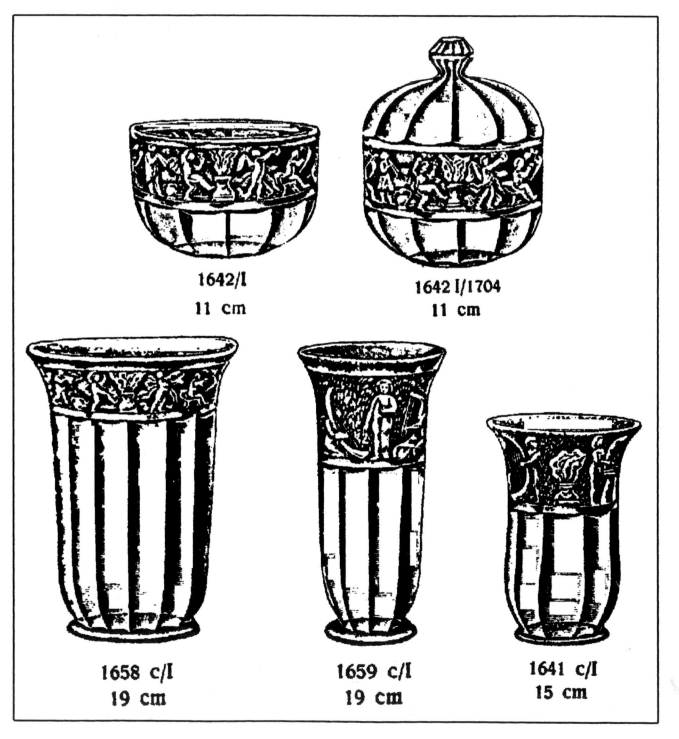

1642/I
11 cm

1642 I/1704
11 cm

1658 c/I
19 cm

1659 c/I
19 cm

1641 c/I
15 cm

CLASSIC ARTS and EGYPTIAN QUEEN vases in varying shapes and sizes from Josef Rindskopf. On the left is the tall and wide CLASSIC ARTS vase (or celery); center and right are two EGYPTIAN QUEEN vases in varying sizes. The smallest one (courtesy of Rita and Les Glennon) is just 6" high and is also collected as a tumbler. $250-500 each.

• EGYPTIAN QUEEN

The EGYPTIAN QUEEN items are "sister" pieces to CLASSIC ARTS but are distinguished by their green, pattern band with distinctly Egyptian looking figures playing harps and other instruments. It has been thought that the smaller of the two vases in this pattern (#1641) may have been a lemonade glass, but study of the catalog indicates that it was, in fact, simply a smaller version of the vase (the taller example has the pattern #1659). Examples have been found in the USA, UK, and Australia.

    Shape: vase in two sizes (6" and 7.5" high)
    Color: marigold with green stain band

CUT PRISMS

A simple pattern seen on bowls, featuring a series of prismatic diamond shapes. CUT PRISMS was previously thought by some to have been a Sowerby product, however it is clearly shown in the Rindskopf catalog 12A bearing the pattern #1463. Found in the USA and UK.

    Shape: bowl
    Color: marigold

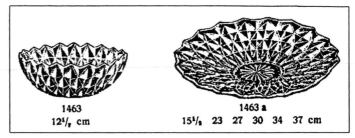

1463	1463 a
12½ cm	15½ 23 27 30 34 37 cm

Rindskopf's CUT PRISMS bowl was illustrated in their catalog 12A.

DIAMOND OVALS

In our first book we attributed manufacture of this pattern to Iittala in Finland, based on the appearance in that company's catalog of a sugar and creamer. However, comparison of known items in DIAMOND OVALS with the illustrations in the Rindskopf catalog 12A confirm that the true manufacturer was undoubtedly Rindskopf (see also Chapter Seven on Finland). Amend your books—DIAMOND OVALS is Czech and was made by Josef Rindskopf in a wide range of shapes and sizes.

The main pattern motif on DIAMOND OVALS is a diamond filled oval shape and alternate fans. The pattern was undoubtedly popular for a very wide range of shapes in this pattern were illustrated in Rindskopf's catalogs. A tumble-up (#1252), decanter with or without stopper (#1250, #1251), tumblers in two sizes (#1192 and #1235), round and oval bowls in several sizes (#1226, #1226a,b and c, #1243, #1243a and b), plates (#1255, #1256), large and small stemmed sugars in several sizes (without lids #1232, #1476 and with lid #1353), creamer (#1242), salver or cakestand (#1232a, b and c), covered sugar (#1236), covered butter (#1225), covered cheese dish (round #1241 and rectangular in two separate parts, #1276 and #1613), covered powder jars (#1238 and #1237), and perfume bottles in various sizes (#1260 and #1865).

Not all shapes are known in Carnival. The rare tumble-up was found in the USA and sold at a 1995 Seeck auction; other examples have been found in the USA, UK, Scandinavia, and mainland Europe. Almost certainly examples have also been found in Australia. In 1999, the first reported candlesticks (though not shown in the catalog) and the first reported perfume bottle with ground stopper (all with a light marigold iridescence) were found in the UK. The stopper is exquisitely moulded with a miniature version of the main pattern—the finial to the butter dish has the same repeated pattern.

    Shapes: creamer, stemmed sugar, butter dish, large and small bowls, tumble-up, stemmed cake plate or salver in various sizes, rare candlesticks, and perfume bottle
    Color: marigold

Rindskopf's DIAMOND OVALS pattern is seen to good effect on this marigold, three piece table set. Courtesy of Carol and Derek Sumpter. $40-50 each for sugar or creamer, $50-80 for the covered butter dish.

FANS

How wonderful to finally attribute this pattern to a definite manufacturer! A bold and simple geometric, *FANS* is only known in the pitcher and tumbler shapes. Oddly, the pitcher is fairly common in the UK and has either a very insipid iridescence or, rarely, a truly stunning pumpkin finish—typical of the widely varying standard of Rindskopf's iridescence. The tumblers are usually very well iridized and most attractive—they are also very hard to find. It is possible that the examples with the very good iridescence were early issues. When the factory entered troubled times, perhaps standards slipped and the quality of the iridescence was compromised. Found in the USA and UK.

Shapes: pitcher and tumbler
Color: marigold

Just a few of the wide range of shapes that was made in the *DIAMOND OVALS* pattern, as seen in these extracts from Rindskopf's catalog 12A. Their shapes can be identified by comparing the catalog numbers quoted in the text.

The *FANS* tumbler is a scarce item, yet the pitcher is found quite often in the U *Courtesy of Peter and Janet Rivers.* SP $200-300.

DIAMOND VANE see INVERTED PRISMS

EGYPTIAN QUEEN see CLASSIC ARTS

FALLING FRONDS

In 1998, UK collector Keith Langridge found a splendid, marigold jardinière in this pattern in Prague, Czechoslovakia. At the time, no one recognized the pattern, but we can now state with certainty that it is a product of Rindskopf. The design features a main motif comprising three hanging leaf fronds, each bearing three leaves. The pattern is repeated on the ground base. *FALLING FRONDS* is illustrated in bowl, plate, and jardinière shapes in Rindskopf's 12A catalog: the item found in Prague was designated pattern #1241.

Shape: jardinière
Color: marigold

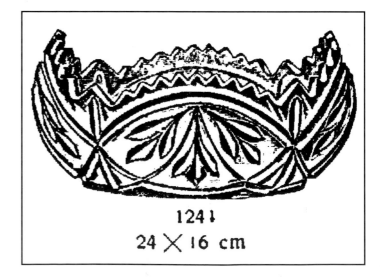

1241
24 × 16 cm

The *FALLING FRONDS* jardinière was a mystery until the discovery of the Rindskopf catalogs revealed the maker.

FORTY NINER VARIANT

So similar to the *FORTY NINER*, the *VARIANT* has three rows of diamonds, as opposed to the *FORTY NINER'S* four rows. According to Bob Smith's observations, there are also slight indentations extending from the bottom row of diamonds into the base rim on the outside. The base is similar to that found on the *FORTY NINER*.

Shapes: tumbler, decanter, juice glass, and tray
Color: marigold

Two tumblers that appeared side by side in Rindskopf's catalog 12A: left is the *FORTY NINER VARIANT* and right is *FANS*.

INVERTED PRISMS aka DIAMOND VANE

Fans and elongated prisms are the main pattern elements on this extensive range of shapes that features in Rindskopf's catalog 12A. There are round bowls in several sizes (#1739 b, c and d), oval bowls in several sizes (#1580), stemmed sugar or compote (#1575), stemmed sugar or compote with handles (without lid #1597 and with lid #1778), creamer (#1576), two shapes of pedestal footed sugar bowl (without lid #1585, #1946 and with lid #1951), covered butter (#1657), lidded cookie jar (#1653), and pedestal footed vase (upright #1590 and flared #1590c). Though only a few of these shapes are currently known to us in Carnival, it is very possible that any of the aforementioned items could be found in iridized glass. A similar pattern to *INVERTED PRISMS* can be seen in both the Inwald and the Karhula catalogs, but close study reveals minor differences in the actual pattern and a complete mis-match of shapes. Found in the USA and UK.

Shapes: creamer, lidded cookie jar and flared vase—almost certainly there are more shapes
Color: marigold

Lidded cookie jars are not easy to find. This example, in Rindskopf's *INVERTED PRISMS* pattern, has a rich marigold iridescence. *Courtesy of Don and Phyllis Atkinson.* NP.

LAUREL WREATH aka BANDED LAUREL WREATH

The distinctive pattern element here is an encircling band of stylized leaves around the upper edge of the item. Note that the band is split in the center by a deep notch; the leaf bands then circle in opposite directions, meeting again on the other side. Below the leaf band are further encircling, concentric rings. The pattern is shown in Rindskopf's catalog 11 in the form of an 8" bowl (pattern #8023). One of the two shapes currently reported in Carnival is the stemmed compote that was illustrated in the journal of the now defunct Carnival Club of Great Britain in 1985 (Journal #12). It was described as having been found in various shades of marigold that ranged from a pumpkin color with a "strong bright hue" to a pale "soft mellow, honey marigold." This wide variance in iridescence seems very typical of Rindskopf's production. The examples known have been found in the USA and UK.

Shapes: stemmed compote, tall stemmed goblet
Color: marigold

This bowl shape in the *LAUREL WREATH* pattern has not yet been reported in Carnival—the pattern is known in a stemmed compote and goblet shape only. However, only this shape was illustrated in Rindskopf's catalog 11, so it is used here as a pattern reference for identification.

95

MARIANNA

MARIANNA is a simple pattern combining notched bands and a simple fan shaped spray on a plain panelled background. Known in an 8" high, pedestal footed vase, it has the press moulded words on the base MADE IN CZECHOSLOVAKIA. Undoubtedly made for export, this example was found in England and is illustrated in the Rindskopf catalog 11 (pattern #1867). The similarities of the pattern to that on the *MARTHA* bowl are intriguing: surely *MARTHA* is also a Rindskopf product?

    Shape: vase
    Color: marigold

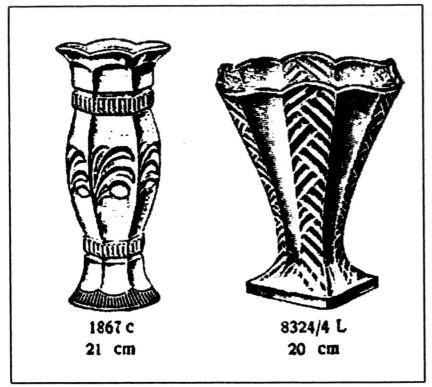

1867 c
21 cm

8324/4 L
20 cm

Two Rindskopf vases that are both marked with their country of origin. Left is the *MARIANNA* vase and right, the *SUMPTUOUS* vase—this illustration is from Rindskopf's catalog 11.

ORIGAMI

    Elongated geometric chevron shapes (like rectangles with pointed ends) are interlocked to form the pattern, the triangular pointed ends then become the jagged edge of the actual item. Illustrated in Rindskopf's catalog 12A (pattern #1471), the bowl in this pattern was first shown in the now defunct Carnival Club of Great Britain's journal #20 in 1988, where it was described as "heavy, thick glass" having 35 chevron or spear shapes around the bowl, a 48-rayed star on the base, and an iridescence that was "pinky rich marigold." Found in the UK.

    Shape: bowl
    Color: marigold

A plain design made a little more interesting by the way in which the top edge of the bowl echoes the pattern—this is *ORIGAMI* and the illustration is from Rindskopf's catalog 12A. It has a certain resemblance to Brockwitz *BOND* pattern.

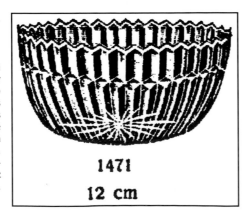

1471
12 cm

PANELLED CANE see CANE PANELS

STIPPLED DIAMOND SWAG

    A delightful pattern, reminiscent of drapery and pretty swagged ruching. The manufacturer has long been a puzzle—what a pleasure it is to finally attribute it with certainty. Two variations of stemmed sugar (compote) plus a covered version are shown in Rindskopf's catalog 12A (pattern # 1536 and #1538), as well as a covered sugar (#1596) and a dainty little creamer (#1486). Like other examples of Rindskopf's Carnival, the quality of iridescence is not consistent on reported examples, ranging from splendid, rich pink and gold tones to a very "washed out" marigold effect. Found in the UK.

    Shapes: creamer and stemmed compote
    Color: marigold

This dainty little creamer is in Rindskopf's *STIPPLED DIAMOND SWAG* pattern. *Courtesy of Rita and Les Glennon.* $50-80.

SUMPTUOUS

    Found in England by Carol Sumpter in early 1999, this unusual vase, just 6" high, was no doubt intended for export to France, as it is etched in gold on the base with the word "Tchecoslovaquie." It has a panelled pattern, each alternate panel featuring a series of interlocking grooves. The overall shape of the vase and the simple design concept are typical of Rindskopf's manufacture. Illustrated in their catalog 11, the vase has the pattern #8324.

    Shape: vase
    Color: marigold

WINGED DECO

    A truly splendid Art Deco style vase, this beauty (currently the only reported example in Carnival) was found in Paris by Liz and Tom Black. The pattern features a simple overall diamond pattern, but the shape is most distinctive and unusual. Pedestal footed, slightly flared and ruffled, the significant feature of this item is its "wings"—two glass filled, wing shaped "handles." A range of items in this pattern was shown in Rindskopf's catalogs 11 and 12A: this vase, a stemmed sugar or compote, plus two other variations of the vase were all shown "winged." Other shapes illustrated include bowls and more vases in extended ranges that appear to be "mixed and matched"—the diamond pattern being the constant linking factor. The *WINGED DECO* vase had the pattern #8331c. It was shown alone as well as "epergne style" atop a bowl and upturned stemmed sugar.

    Shape: vase
    Color: marigold

2 Flügelhenkel

8331 c
21 cm
8331 Z = Zapfen anstatt Fuß

8346 squ
22 cm

3 Flügelgriffe

8340 c
25 cm

8471
24 cm

This illustration is a composite of various Art Deco style vases shown in Rindskopf's catalog 11. The shapes are fantastic and imaginative, with a very distinctive style. The *WINGED DECO* vase is shown top left (#8331c)—it is also part of the epergne shown in the center. So far, none of the other vases illustrated are known in Carnival, but it is quite possible that they do exist in iridized form.

Possible Rindskopf Patterns Known in Carnival Glass

BALMORAL aka *HEAVY VINE*

A plain panelled pattern featuring an encircling band that has been loosely interpreted as a vine. *BALMORAL* was illustrated in the British *Pottery Gazette* in July 1930, with the words "Made in Czechoslovakia." Over seventy different shapes were offered in crystal, several of which are currently known in Carnival. The ad was placed in the *Pottery Gazette* by the National Glass Company of London—a British Registered Design number (RD 737581) was quoted in the ad. The National Glass Co. was acting on behalf of the Czech manufacturer and would have registered the design on their behalf. Some of the known items have superb marigold iridescence while others are very pale. Examples have been found in the USA, UK and the Czech Republic. In 1999, the first reported water pitcher and butter dish in the *BALMORAL* design were found by John and Frances Hodgson in France.

Shapes: water pitcher, tumbler, tumble-up, butter dish, plus a full range of boudoir items, including powder jar, perfumes, ring tree, tray etc.

Color: marigold

Called *BALMORAL* in the British Pottery Gazette in 1930, this pattern also goes by the name *HEAVY VINE*. This splendid marigold butter dish and water pitcher, both sourced in France, are the first *BALMORAL* items found in these specific shapes. *Photo courtesy of John and Frances Hodgson.* NP.

BARS AND CROSS BOX see PROVENCE

CHEVRONS

Undoubtedly inspired by Art Deco motifs and typical of Rindskop, this design features a panelled background on which is superimposed an angular zig-zag design. Most attractive and surely at its best in Carnival Glass where the iridescent effect gives depth to the unusual design. Scarce examples have been found in the USA (by Lance and Pat Hilkene) and the UK.

Shape: vase
Color: marigold

A trio of vases that are all of probable Rindskopf manufacture. On the left is a marigold, pedestal footed, *CIRCLE SQUARED* vase. In the center is *CHEVRONS*, an apt name for this marigold cylinder vase. On the right is the pedestal footed *RING OF STARS*, also in marigold. SP $100-200 each.

These *DOUBLE TULIP* vases have all the characteristics of Rindskopf's Carnival Glass—from their light, yet attractive marigold iridescence to their typically bold, Czech style. At 10" in height, the taller vase stands some 4" above its smaller "twin." Note the difference in the shaping of the vases' mouths. SP $100-250 each.

CIRCLE SQUARED

CIRCLE SQUARED is distinctive in that it is a square shaped, 8" high vase with an eight sided, domed pedestal base. The moulded pattern features five circles, decreasing in size downwards, on each of the four sides. The "house style" of thick glass and a distinctive pattern concept is strongly suggestive of Rindskopf. The only example reported was found in the UK.

Shape: vase
Color: marigold

DOUBLE TULIP

Only a handful of vases are known in this pattern, similar in many ways to Josef Inwald's *FLEUR-DE-LIS*. The iridescence on the examples we have studied is not typical of Inwald, being pale and light—much more suggestive of Rindskopf. The style of the vase in general, however, is typical of Czechoslovakian production: solid, heavy glass with bold, classical moulded intaglio designs. On the *DOUBLE TULIP*, the main motif is a stylized floral motif (the tulip) that appears as a mirror image. The base of the vase is ground and has a deeply-cut many rayed star. The top edge may be cupped in or waisted and flared. The only examples currently known to us have been found in the USA and Scandinavia.

Shape: vase in at least two sizes (heights of 6" and 10")
Color: marigold

EIGHT RINGS aka TCHECO

This is a blow moulded vase in purple Carnival Glass found by Clinton and Joanne Andrews in the USA. Significantly, the word THECO SLOVACIA is stamped on the vase with black ink, proving its country of origin. Rindskopf's catalogs feature a small amount of blow-moulded glassware including vases and it is thought that after their merger with Inwald in the mid 1930s they concentrated on blow moulded glass. Purple isn't a color in their repertoire for press moulded Carnival. However, it was a color that they specialized in during their Art Nouveau production of iridized ware. Other blow-moulded items (decanter sets and similar items, often trimmed with black enamel) marked with paper labels indicate Czechoslovakia as the country of manufacture. Again, it is very possible that Rindskopf was the manufacturer. For a photograph of the *EIGHT RINGS* vase see the HOACGA Pattern Notebook Vase section 2000.

Shape: vase
Color: purple

FACETS

A simple, deeply cut, geometric design, much like Rindskopf's *FANS* pattern, covers the exterior of these serviceable bowls. The glass is thick and heavy, characteristic of Czech pressed ware. The base is surprising—three exquisite little scroll feet, each perfectly ground flat—and serves to further suggest that this item is from Rindskopf. A number of similar, footed items (fairly unusual for European Carnival, most are flat based) are depicted in their catalogs. A pattern is also illustrated in Rindskopf's catalog 12A that is virtually identical, save for a few details, to *FACETS*. This is surely a Rindskopf item. Found in the UK.

Shape: bowls in various sizes
Color: marigold

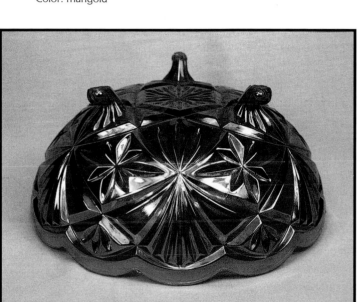

FACETS is a serviceable bowl with a "forgettable" geometric design! Though maybe not the most glamorous Carnival item, it must have brightened up many dinner tables with its brilliant iridescence. $30-60.

This cordial set in rich marigold is in the *FORTY NINER* pattern. Though the items were all purchased together in a Prague antique shop (in the Czech Republic), it seems likely that, although they are the same pattern, they are not an actual set. Probably a smaller cordial would have gone with the decanter and tray originally. *Courtesy of Bob Smith.* SP $350-500.

FORTY NINER

Concave diamonds in rows cover the exterior of items in the *FORTY NINER* pattern. On the ground base of the tumbler is a 24 point star. It is a seldom seen pattern, however a decanter set on a tray was found by Bob Smith in Prague, Czech Republic, in 1997. Everything about this pattern, especially the shapes in which it is found, is typical of Czech Carnival Glass. The candlesticks in this pattern have also been called *ORIGAMI* (however, please note that this is not the same pattern as the Rindskopf *ORIGAMI* design noted above). The strong similarity of this pattern to the *FORTY NINER VARIANT* (which is illustrated in Rindskopf's catalog) suggests that this pattern is almost certainly from Rindskopf, too. A very similar pattern called *DIAMONDS* aka *ROYAL DIAMONDS* is also known in a tumble-up and a tumbler. *FORTY NINER* has been found in the USA, UK, and the Czech Republic.

Shapes: pitcher and tumblers, stemmed wine glass, decanter and shot glasses (cordials) and tray. Dressing table items including powder jar, perfume, ring tree and candlesticks.

Color: marigold

ILLINOIS DAISY

Familiar to most collectors, this cookie jar features a stylized daisy motif and is usually found with a weak, pale iridescence. Rindskopf made a number of covered cookie jars in similar shapes to the *ILLINOIS DAISY* and though the pattern itself is not illustrated in the catalogs that we have had the privilege of studying, it seems very possible that this may well be a Rindskopf product. Found in the USA and UK.

Shape: cookie jar
Color: marigold

KING JAMES

Known in several sizes of pedestal footed vase, this pattern is a "look-alike" for Inwald's *JACOBEAN*. At first glance it could be mistaken for *JACOBEAN* (and no doubt has been): the difference is in the shape of the items and the way in which the pattern blocks (squares) interlock. A number of items are illustrated in Rindskopf's catalogs that have the same blocked pattern, however, the known Carnival vases are not shown. For this reason we are cautiously (rather than firmly) attributing the pattern to Rindskopf. Found in the UK and Belgium.

> Shape: vase (heights of 6" and 10" are known)
> Color: marigold

A pair of pedestal footed, marigold vases named *KING JAMES*—so similar to Inwald's *JACOBEAN*, yet with many differences. The large vase stands 10" high, its smaller counterpart is 6". SP $100-200 each.

MARTHA

At one time, this pattern could be found in almost every UK collection and at every UK antique fair. Known only in a deep and heavy pedestal footed bowl featuring a stylized frond pattern, *MARTHA* is not so easily found today. The pattern on *MARTHA* is a slightly altered version of that on the *MARIANNA* vase (see above), being a combination of notched bands and a simple fan shaped spray on a plain panelled background. As only the vase and not the bowl are shown in their catalogs, it is preferable to allow the Rindskopf attribution to be speculative at this time. Found in the USA, UK, and Australia.

> Shape: bowl
> Color: marigold

PETALS AND PRISMS

A simple intaglio design, this pattern bears all the hallmarks of Czech glass and could well be a product of Rindskopf. Found in the USA and UK.

> Shapes: bowls in several sizes. A stemmed sugar and creamer are also reported but we cannot confirm their existence.
> Color: marigold

PINEAPPLE CROWN

The pattern gets its name from the large pineapple like motif in the center of this stylized, simple geometric, seen only on various sizes of jardinières. The mouldwork is deep and the item chunky—characteristic of Rindskopf's production. The style of the jardinière is

Art Deco, another signature characteristic of that factory. Found in the USA and UK.

> Shape: jardinière
> Color: marigold

PROVENCE aka BARS AND CROSS BOX

This stunning pattern is known in the form of a single water pitcher (which was discovered in a street market in the south of France, hence the name *PROVENCE*) and a single, matching tumbler. The iridescence on these marigold items is quite incredible, with pinks, greens and blues flashing off the glass surface. The pattern is simple yet elegant: a combination of grooves and crosses (hence the alternative name *BARS AND CROSS BOX*), very suggestive of Rindskop's design. The iridescence on the two known items is of truly superior and exquisite quality.

> Shapes: water pitcher and tumbler
> Color: marigold

A truly magnificent iridescence adorns this marigold *PROVENCE* water pitcher. The only one currently known, its value is impossible to judge. The only known marigold tumbler in this pattern was sold at auction in the USA in 1998 for $800.

REGAL TULIP

The only example pictured of this vase is seen in Quintin-Baxendale's *Collecting Carnival Glass*[5]. The shape (with pedestal base) is typical of other Rindskopf vases and the tulip motif that appears in an encircling band is reminiscent of *DOUBLE TULIP.*

> Shape: vase
> Color: marigold

RING OF STARS

Currently known only in the vase shape, *RING OF STARS* features a six sided panelled design, encircled by a band of six intaglio star motifs. The band is known with both frosted and plain background. This elegant vase has a pedestal base and is strongly suggestive of Czech manufacture—quite possibly Rindskopf. Found in the UK.

> Shape: vase
> Color: marigold

RISING COMET aka COMET.

This classical, deeply intaglio pattern has been found in the USA, Czechoslovakia, and Australia. The overall style and heaviness of the glass is typically characteristic of Czechoslovakian Carnival. The shape of the vase is very similar to Josef Inwald's *FLEUR-DE-LIS* vase. The star motif, however, is seen on several Rindskopf items in the catalogs studied. Only known in a vase shape, rare examples of the *RISING COMET* have been found in the three different sizes currently known.

Shape: vase (heights of 6", 8" and 12")
Color: marigold

A pair of *RISING COMET* marigold vases. Each is a solid, heavy vase with motifs strongly characteristic of Rindskopf's manufacture. SP $200-400.

RISING COMET AND GROOVES

A decanter bearing a combination of both the *RISING COMET* and the *CIRCLES AND GROOVES* patterns was found in Argentina in late 1999 by collector Annie Rooks. Much Czech glass was imported into Argentina and Rindskopf seems the most likely manufacturer on account of the pattern design—which is highly suggestive of that factory's output.

Shape: decanter
Color: marigold

TOFFEE BLOCK

Known in the water pitcher shape, this pattern features broad blocks, separated by grooves. The style and overall look of the item indicates Rindskopf as the manufacturer. Further, several items bearing what appears to be this pattern (but not the pitcher) are shown in Rindskopf's catalogs. The iridescence on the items that we have studied is usually rather pale.

Shape: water pitcher
Color: marigold

VINING LEAF

This pattern is often confused with *BALMORAL* aka *HEAVY VINE*, however they are easily differentiated as *VINING LEAF* is the one that has an encircling (frosted) band with a sinuous scroll-like pattern. (*BALMORAL* aka *HEAVY VINE* has an encircling band featuring a

snaking line with little leaflets hanging from it.) Both patterns have a plain panelled background. A pedestal footed vase is known in this pattern, having characteristic features that suggest Rindskopf. The frosted, scroll like pattern band is shown on various other Rindskopf items in their catalogs. Found in the UK and Germany.

Shapes: pedestal footed vase, large, pedestal footed bowl (sometimes called a spittoon), large vase
Color: marigold

A pair of *VINING LEAF* vases with frosted band—in the snow! *Photo courtesy of Fiona Melville.* SP $100-200 each.

Coronet Trademark

This group of blow moulded vases all share the same, distinctive neck structure and design style and should be considered very scarce. One of the vases, the *GIANT LILY*, has an acid etched mark on the base that reads, CZECHOSLOVAKIA. The remnants of a paper label on the body of the same vase read *Trade Mark Coronet*. All four of the vases in this range (detailed below) that share the same distinct neck structure and design style, have been found in the USA. American legislation in 1921 required imported goods to be specific as to the country of origin. All these vases (with the exception of the *GIANT LILY*) have also been found in the United Kingdom in both iridized and non-iridized glass. Interestingly, they have also all (again except the *GIANT LILY*) been found in non-iridized vaseline glass that glows wildly under UV light. More vases are known with the Coronet label (reported by Alan Fullrich in the USA). They are blow moulded, tall and thin in shape, and have a light marigold iridescence. A further one in pale blue Carnival is also known as are non-iridized vaseline examples. Each has a moulded draped pattern.

The Coronet trademark found in the form of a paper label on some items of Carnival.

In the 1930s, the ailing Rindskopf concern merged with the flourishing Inwald business and their newly combined output focused on blown and blow moulded, rather than press moulded, glass. It is our tentative suggestion that Inwald (incorporating Rindskopf) may possibly have been the manufacturer of these splendid massive blow moulded vases. Inwald had used a trademark that was illustrated in the 1928 British *Pottery Gazette*—it was in the shape of a crown and the name was *Coronet*. The use of the word Coronet—the same as the trademark on the paper label— lends weight to the idea, but there is no further proof to substantiate the attribution at the present.

GIANT LILY

Standing 9" high and with a girth of 27", this bulbous vase has the identical neck structure of the other *Coronet* vases detailed below. The moulded pattern in high relief, depicts a stylized lily and a five budded spray, repeated three times around the vase. The style is pure Art Deco, boldly executed. The mould work is excellent. The lily buds are highly embossed, projecting out from the sides of the vase. Below them are curved wedge shapes in deep relief. Only one example of this vase is currently known to us; it was found in the USA and had obviously been imported there from Czechoslovakia.

Shape: vase
Color: marigold

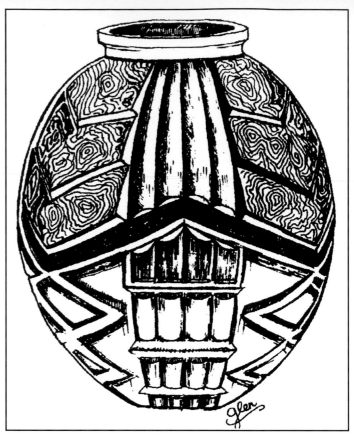

The *INCA* vase is an impressive, bulbous item with a typical Art Deco style.

This marigold *GIANT LILY* vase is currently the only example reported. NP.

INCA

Similar in height and girth to the *SEAGULLS* vase (see below), the *INCA* is a perfect example of Art Deco style with its broad sweeps of line and geometric "wrap-around" motifs. An impressive and striking item of glass that again shares the distinctive neck structure of the other massive bulbous vases. Very scarce indeed, a black amethyst *INCA* was found in Washington State, though it is possible that it came into the country via England. A non-iridized *INCA* in vaseline has been found in the UK.

Shape: vase
Colors: marigold and black amethyst

PEBBLE AND FAN

Similar in height to the *SEAGULLS* vase (see below), though not as large in girth, *PEBBLE AND FAN* measures 23" around its widest part. The style is again pure Art Deco, featuring broad sweeps of "wrap around" pattern, faceted angles and curves. The "pebble" in the pattern name refers to the hammered, textured effect that fills the large oval shapes. The "fan" refers to the broad, fan-like sweeps that divide the ovals. *PEBBLE AND FAN* has the same distinctive neck structure as the *SEAGULLS* vase. The vase is blow moulded and the glass is thick. Scarce examples have been found in England and the USA.

Shape: vase
Colors: marigold, blue, amber, and vaseline

The style is pure Art Deco on this blue *PEBBLE AND FAN* vase. SP $750-1250.

SEAGULLS

Though almost 11" in height, the most impressive measurement of this vase is its girth, which reaches an almost unbelievable 30" in circumference at its widest point. The interior seems cavernous, capturing sounds inside its vast emptiness. The *SEAGULLS* vase is blow moulded and is in high relief. Its design of seagulls, foaming waves, and clouds is clear and uncluttered, using simple, clean lines. Exuberant and bold, it is in the Art Deco style that was prevalent in the inter-war years. The glass itself is thick and the bulbous vase has a distinctive mould seam running horizontally around the neck. Found in the USA, though a non-iridized vaseline *SEAGULLS* has also been found in England.

Shape: vase

Colors: marigold, black amethyst. A single example of aqua base glass with marigold iridescence that reacts to UV light is known to us

Karl Palda, Haida

The company of Karl Palda was founded in 1888 in Novy Bor[4] (aka Haida), a town situated in the Elbe Valley in the northern region of the Czech Republic, the area once known as Bohemia. About fifty miles to the west, lay Josef Inwald's great factory at Teplice whilst a little over fifty miles to the northwest lay the Brockwitz glass works in Germany. Novy Bor had been an important center of the Bohemian glass industry since medieval times; indeed, by the mid eighteenth century, glass manufacture was even included in the curriculum of the local Piarist grammar school. In the late 1920s, there were over three hundred glass and decorating workshops in the area. Today the town— a two hour drive north from Prague—hosts a fine Glass Museum (the "Sklarske Muzeum") that was founded in 1892, as well as the current headquarters of two glass manufacturers.

Palda's output included a very wide range of novelty "colored glasses in fancy shapes and liqueur, wine and cocktail sets with nickel or silver plated frames"— the quotation is taken from Palda's own ad that proclaims them to be a "Glassworks and Metal Works." The Truitts[4] note that the firm Rachman had a foundry at Novy Bor that produced the metal parts for Palda's glass.

With these specific signature characteristics in mind—and having studied various catalog pages from a 50th anniversary Palda catalog [4, 6], several Carnival items, previously thought to be Czechoslovakian, can now be cautiously attributed to Palda. We urge caution, however, as the evidence is purely circumstantial at present.

The base color of this rare *SEAGULLS* vase is a pale aqua-blue. SP $1500-1750.

ENAMELED SHADES

Quite a variety of marigold lampshades enameled with typical central European scenes are known. Castles, churches, houses, rivers, flowers, snow capped mountains, and trees are all featured. The architectural style is very typical of middle Europe. Most examples have been found in the USA, though a few have also been discovered in the UK. Palda's catalogs from the 1930s illustrate a wide range of lampshades with scenes and paintwork identical to the enameled Carnival lampshades. Another Bohemian manufacturer, Ruckl, also produced similar enameled shades around the same time.

    Shape: lampshade

    Color: marigold with multi-colored enamel decoration

A trio of enameled lamp shades with a variety of painted scenes set against a rich marigold iridescent background. $75-100 each.

The painted scenes on Carnival lampshades often feature churches like this typical Bohemian example.

SHIP DECANTER SET

Named and found in the USA by Lance and Pat Hilkene, this is a fascinating set of Carnival items that is extremely scarce. The dealer from whom Lance purchased it informed him that it had been brought in by an elderly lady who had emigrated from Czechoslovakia to the USA in the 1920s. The *SHIP DECANTER SET* had been brought with the family and had originally been complete. The full set comprises a stoppered decanter and six matching cordial glasses, each a different base color—all fitting neatly into an amazing glass ship equipped with metalwork holders. A second set was reported and illustrated in the Lincoln-Land Carnival Glass Club News in January 2000. The photograph by Dave Doty shows the complete metalwork mast, rigging, and sail (bearing a cross). This set was all in light marigold.

Circumstantial evidence points to Palda as the manufacturer. Novelty decanter sets, featuring different colored glasses and metalwork frames were typical Palda products.

    Shapes: decanter, "ship," and cordials

    Colors: the ship itself is marigold, the glasses are clear, amethyst, smoke, lavender, light marigold, and deep marigold

The *SHIP DECANTER* set is almost certainly a Czech product.

Possible Czech Patterns in Carnival Glass

CZECHOSLOVAKIAN MAID

First reported and named by Rose Presznick back in the 1960s, the *CZECHOSLOVAKIAN MAID* is something of a mystery item. The shape is that of a syrup or milk pitcher, the blow moulded pattern, however, is most unusual: it features a lady in characteristic dress, possibly Czechoslovakian—certainly European in style. The base glass is clear and the color and iridescence (a blushed ruby with light golden marigold iridescence) appear to have been flashed on (flashing is a thin coating of colored glass that gives the appearance of a stain—also known as casing). It is reported that a crystal example of this pitcher has been seen with the moulded words *Made in Czechoslovakia*, thus we are cautiously attributing it to that country. A distinctive and exceptionally rare item that has so far only been found in the USA.

    Shape: pitcher

    Color: ruby (cranberry)

The *FOUR SIDED TREE TRUNK* vase is another cranberry "flashed" item that may well have been made in Czechoslovakia. Alongside it is a smaller version of the same pattern in marigold. *Courtesy of Rita and Les Glennon.* SP $60-100 each.

A most unusual item, this handled syrup jug or small pitcher is in cranberry "flashed" iridized glass. Known as the *CZECHOSLOVAKIAN MAID,* it was first illustrated in Rose Presznick's pioneering Carnival books dating from the 1960s. NP.

Bijouterie: Beads And Buttons From Gablonz

The name Porsche is familiar to most people, synonymous with fast cars. The Porsche family can trace their origins to Jablonec nad Nisou (aka Gablonz) in the area once known as Bohemia—but how many other names can the reader mention that are associated with that area? The fact is that the Czech costume jewelry (bijouterie)

FOUR SIDED TREE TRUNK
A square shaped vase with a contrasting pattern of smooth curves and tree trunk "knobbles," this rare item is thought to be Czech on account of its similarity of flashed ruby color and golden iridescence with that on the *CZECHOSLOVAKIAN MAID* pitcher. Only two examples of this vase are known—both were found in the UK.
Shape: square vase in two sizes
Color: marigold and ruby (cranberry)

A selection of buttons, beads, hatpins and related items, probably from Czechoslovakia. The splendid hatpins on the left are of recent make (courtesy of Harry Barrett) and are made using Carnival buttons.

industry was—indeed still is—concentrated in and around the area of Jablonec nad Nisou and Zelezny Brod (aka Eisenbrod). The area produced vast amounts of beads, hatpins, and buttons, many of them in iridized glass, around the latter part of the 1800s and the early 1900s. Despite that, not one of the names of either the craftsmen or the workshops that produced these items is likely to be known to the reader.

The production of beads, buttons, and hatpins was carried out in a series of stages, with one workshop producing the glass and yet another crafting and finishing the jewelry. It was essentially a cottage industry with a complex, supporting infrastructure. The numbers involved are quite staggering: for example, in around 1930, in Jablonec nad Nisou itself, the bijouterie trade was concentrated in 600 or so export houses. The raw glass for the industry was made in 18 glass works with 40 furnaces. Bars and rods of colored glass were supplied by them to the craftworkers, who then press moulded the glass beads, buttons, and hatpins heads. The bijouterie manufacture was carried on mainly in the surrounding villages by 3000 or so firms employing roughly 30,000 cottage workers. A contemporary account of life in the Gablonz area during the early 1900s noted that "full of busy life was every home; the cottages often being of two rooms only, and with windows all closed against the sharp mountain air. The rooms over-heated, and serving as workshops, living rooms and bedrooms, and yet smart and clean. Here we saw them making women's glass, dress ornaments and glass trinkets." [7]

A ladies handbag made up of iridized beads—probably from the Gablonz area of Czechoslovakia. SP $50-80.

A typical village scene in the area of Bohemia near Gablonz at the end of the 1800s.

Iridescent black beads were very popular in the late 1800s and early 1900s. Such beads were used not only for necklaces and other adornments, but also for making pretty bags and for embroidering on clothing. Butler Brothers catalogs show them clearly in the early 1920s. Hatpins and buttons were also made in iridized glass using innovative techniques that revolutionized the industry and ensured its success. Glass rods were re-heated in the press-moulding workshops till they were red hot. The glass was then squeezed with the help of moulding tongs into buttons and beads. Intricate patterns were impressed on the glass: flowers, animals, insects, and more. Button making in Czechoslovakia was (and indeed, is) a labor intensive operation, with many hands being involved and many stages in the process being necessary. [8]

The isolated nature of the area and its intensive working methods and infrastructure helped to build up a structure for trading and export. France, the USA, Australia, and India were the main overseas markets. Probably 90 percent or more of the output was for export. The industry suffered during the war years and the ensuing Communist regime. Development resumed in the 1960s and 1970s and is thriving again today. In 1991, the Association of Costume Jewelry Manufacturers (SVB) was founded to promote and protect the industry. There is a museum in Jablonec nad Nisou devoted to Glass and Costume Jewelry.

The *National Button Bulletin* (February 1999) reported that "the Czechoslovakian glass button makers are making buttons in the 1990s in the same manner that they did at the beginning of this century." In an article entitled "The Czech Glass Phenomenon," the *Bulletin* went on to say that button production today is being carried out by four main companies in the Jablonec nad Nisou area. "Two are factories and two are cottage based businesses." The two factories are "co-operatives with some salaried workers like managers, engravers and mouldmakers. Cottage workers like pressmoulders and painters do the production of buttons for piecework wages. Beautiful finishes like auroras and other lustres are produced in a factory specializing in that work." One of the factories produces jewelry and beads as well as buttons. Production in the area is on an international scale: the Ornela factory, for example, holds some 25 percent of the world's trade in glass beads. Some of the buttons being made today are from old Classic moulds as well as new moulds!

It is impossible to include a comprehensive look at the many, many buttons, hatpins, and beads that are documented in Carnival Glass. There are several books on the subject for the collector that detail all the known patterns. Particular thanks to Harry and Jean Barrett, collectors of Carnival Glass buttons, for their expertise and help.

[1] Diane E Foulds, *A Guide to Czech and Slovak Glass* (Prague, Czech Republic: European Community Imports, 1995).

[2] David Doty, *A Field Guide to Carnival Glass* (Marietta, Ohio: The Glass Press Inc., 1998).

[3] Rindskopf catalogs sourced courtesy of Robert Smith, Robert Truitt, the Corning Glass Museum and the City Archives at Teplice, Czechoslovakia.

[4] Robert and Deborah Truitt, *Collectible Bohemian Glass. 1880-1940* (Kensington, Maryland: B & D Glass, 1995).

[5] Marion Quintin-Baxendale, *Collecting Carnival Glass* (London, England: Francis Joseph, 1998).

[6] Robert and Deborah Truitt, *Collectible Bohemian Glass Volume 2. 1915-1945* (Kensington, Maryland: B & D Glass, 1998).

[7] James Baker, *Pictures From Bohemia* (England. The Religious Tract Society. No date, but circa early 1900s).

[8] Sibylle Jargstorf, *Baubles, Buttons and Beads. The Heritage of Bohemia* (Atglen, Pennsylvania: Schiffer Publishing Ltd., 1993).

Chapter Six

Sweden

"Masterpieces are made by artisans, not artists."
—Jean Renoir, French film director.

Glassmaking in Sweden dates back to the sixteenth century, when the first glassworks was established in Stockholm, the capital city. Workers were brought in from the European glass centers of Venice and Germany to establish the new industry: first window glass for the rich, then later, bottles and drinking vessels were produced. The main growth of Sweden's glass industry came in the last part of the nineteenth century when nearly eighty glassworks were founded, the majority of them in Smaland, which soon became known as "the kingdom of glass." Some of the names are familiar, for example, Kosta and Orrefors. Carnival Glass, however, was not made by the major companies—it was the smaller concerns, in particular Eda Glasbruk, that took up the mantle and produced some of the finest Carnival Glass—true masterpieces—ever made.

Eda Glasbruk, Charlottenberg

A land of enchanted forests on the "Road of Kings"

Eda Glasbruk is a small Swedish settlement that lies amongst richly forested countryside, a mere two minute's walk away from the border with Norway. The nearest Swedish town is Charlottenberg, today a bustling market town, in the heart of the Western Varmlands, a region that lies to the north west of Smaland. The area is simply beautiful; no visitor could fail to fall in love with it. Rolling hills, forests, and crystal clear lakes, the whole landscape dotted with colorful, timber clad farmhouses, painted red, brown, cream and white. Wildlife abounds, indeed the area around Eda is home to the world's only stock of white elk (moose).

The area is also rich in history. The name *"Ed"* or *"Eid"* means "the area between the lakes" and was in past ages, as now, the most important traffic artery between Norway and Sweden. Known as the "Road of Kings," everyone from king and warrior to pilgrim and pirate has traveled this highway. From St. Petersburg in Russia, the well-trodden route passed through Helsinki in Finland and Stockholm in Sweden, before finishing at Oslo in Norway. History continues to leaves its mark on the area. Countless wars have been fought in the border district between the two countries of Norway and Sweden in the past. But in 1914, they celebrated 100 years of peace by building a monument at the Morokulien border crossing, near Eda Glasbruk.

The Glassworks at Eda

The settlement at Eda Glasbruk was named after the actual glassworks. Driving into the area today, the traveler is greeted by a large, blue and white road sign, proudly bearing the name EDA GLASBRUK. Surely the only producer of Carnival Glass to actually have a settlement named after it? (With Millersburg it was the other way around—the factory was named after the town.) Around 1830-1835, the glassworks was first established there. It benefited from the fast flowing waters of the Vrangsalven (River Vrang)—it would later also benefit from its proximity to the main rail link to the Norwegian capital, Oslo (the closest major port), and the Swedish capital, Stockholm.

Could Eda Glasbruk be the only settlement to be named after a Carnival Glass factory? The name means "Eda Glassworks," but although the glassworks closed nearly fifty years ago, the settlement retains the name.

The countryside around Eda Glasbruk is full of lakes, sparkling in the summer months but frozen solid through the long winter—so thick that they can support the weight of a car. The name *Ed* (as in Eda) means the area between the lakes.

Glass for windows, bottles, and pharmaceutical use were the first products from Eda. Its close links with Norway are shown by the use of its window glass in the Royal Palace at Oslo, no less! However, increasing taxes imposed for using the port at Oslo caused the prudent Swedes to spawn a "daughter" glass factory in 1896 at Magnor, a five minute ride away, just over the international border in Norway.

Situated a short drive away from Eda Glasbruk—just over the border in Norway—was Eda's "sister," Magnor Glassverk. Today the factory is still working (producing mainly crystal tableware) and houses a small museum dedicated to glass making.

A cast iron mould in the *YORK* pattern—a crystal vase can be seen on top of the mould.

Eda produced a fine range of glassware, with minor interruptions, through to 1953. Press moulded glass began to be made at Eda in 1920. Five years later, Carnival Glass production began—it was to continue at Eda Glasbruk for barely four more years, ceasing around 1929 or perhaps 1930. A catalog called *Fargglas fran Eda Glasbruk* (Colored Glass from Eda Glass Works), considered to have been produced in 1925, illustrates the range of glass that was being iridized at that time. (This catalog, a superb piece of artistry itself, is detailed below.) Other patterns as depicted in the later 1929 catalog are also known in Carnival. Carnival at Eda was known as *lysterglas*— lustre glass.

Center right: This is the *kvarnhusen* or mould shop at Eda Glasbruk. Drawing by Sven Morfeldt, shown with permission from the Eda Glass Collectors Society.

Bottom right: Amongst the trees were the buildings that housed many of the workers from Eda Glasbruk. This group was called the *smaglasbyggn* and was specifically for the workers who produced the small pressed ware—Carnival Glass! Drawing by Sven Morfeldt, shown with permission from the Eda Glass Collectors Society.

Eda Glasbruk around the time that Carnival Glass was being made. *Photo courtesy of Eda Glass Collectors Society.*

In June 1931, the British *Pottery Gazette* reported that the Eda Glassworks was about to close. Six months later they reported that it had re-opened. It seems very likely that some of their moulds were sold to other European glassworks immediately after that period of likely re-organization. The company continued through good times and bad until its final closure in 1953. The factory at Magnor survived, however, and is still in production today.

Eda's Carnival is undoubtedly scarce: it was produced for barely four years. In 1927, a new management team, husband and wife Gerda and Edvard Stromberg, were installed at the plant. Within a year or two, Gerda, a designer, had markedly influenced the factory's output. The new look patterns and colors (in particular, pale browns and yellows in the fashionable minimalist shapes and patterns) became *de rigeur*; out went the rich patterns and colors of Eda's wonderful *lysterglas*. Carnival production soon ceased, leaving a legacy of scarce, yet superlatively beautiful items in Eda's magnificent *lysterglas* for today's collectors. In terms of quality, beauty, and rarity they are comparable in many ways to the short lived output of the Millersburg factory in Ohio that had been produced a decade or so earlier. Fleetingly beautiful and highly sought after, Eda's Carnival Glass features a combination of classic shape and pattern with outstanding iridescence and color.

Eda Carnival Glass has a ground base, which often exhibits tiny chips (a feature of this method of production). This is the grinding shop where this process was carried out. *Photo courtesy of Eda Glass Collectors Society.*

Links

There were undoubted links between the Swedes and the glass factories in the United States. The Imperial Glass Company in Ohio and the Fenton Art Glass Company of West Virginia had both hosted groups of visiting Swedish glassworkers in the early 1920s. Social contacts, too, had fostered the links. Furthermore, Gustav Kessmeier, a glass-master at Eda, had a son, Arthur, who is reported to have worked in one of the American Carnival glassworks. Stories are told that he sent the formula for the iridescent spray back to his father in Sweden. However, iridized glass had been made at Eda long before 1925! Indeed, their experiments with iridized blow moulded glass in around 1905 put Eda Glasbruks in line with the early production at the Fenton Art Glass Company. The early iridized Eda items were blow moulded in thin glass, not press moulded, and the iridescence was sprayed on, but note that a significant number of Classic Carnival pieces were made that way (bulbous pitchers and vases such as Imperial's *LOGANBERRY*). These early Eda items in marigold are scarce—but they are of great historical importance.

The catalogs of Riihimaki and Karhula in Finland, Elme in Sweden, and Brockwitz in Germany all illustrate items that are also shown in the Eda catalogs. Were the moulds traded (Eda almost certainly bought moulds from Brockwitz) or were the patterns simply copied? Probably both. Eda's Carnival was also exported to Iceland, Norway, the USA, South America, and the UK. The pattern names that Eda Glasbruks gave some of their items are intriguing and one wonders whether they possibly echo the export destination of the glass: *TOKIO, LONDON,* and *BERLIN* are three such pattern names.

Links with the Sowerby factory in the UK also exist. Factory catalogs from Sowerby are reported to have been found in Eda archives[1] and undoubtedly Sowerby's *WICKERWORK* was copied by Eda

Early attempts at Carnival Glass by Eda Glasbruk. It is thought that these intriguing vases were made around 1905. They were blown into moulds—probably wooden ones that were quickly and easily made and had simple patterns like the swirls on these vases. Note the hand finishing on the mouth of the small vase—Eda was one of the few European Carnival manufacturers that occasionally ruffled the edges of bowls and vases. The small vase stands some 5" high; the taller one is 9". NP.

Glasbruks, though not in Carnival Glass. The distinctive and quite exquisite bracket edge on Eda's *DESSIN* was an idea of J.G. Sowerby, indeed, his sketch book dated 1900 showed several items with this characteristic finish.[2] Other Sowerby patterns can also be seen in Eda's catalogs, though none of the Carnival items appear to have been copied.

Signature Characteristics of Eda Carnival Glass

• Exceptionally high quality glass in every way—a very sophisticated looking product.

• Ground base on all Eda Carnival.

• Marigold and blue were the main colors used and the Swedes referred to the Carnival shades as light (*ljus*) and dark (*mork*) lustre. However, Eda's production is characterized by their use of several other rare, base glass colors. There are very scarce examples of purple that range from a light, lilac shade (which the Swedes actually call lilac) to a deeper purple (which they called Oxblood). A dense iridized milk glass called pearl (*parlemorlystrad*) was also made, but is hard to find. Red was certainly produced and iridized examples are reported though we cannot confirm their existence.

• Intaglio, "near-cut" geometric designs or stylized florals—mainly exterior. These are often very intricate and detailed. Some items also known with an interior pattern (for example, *FOUR FLOWERS* aka *OHLSON*).

• A signature of Eda Carnival is the outstanding quality of their iridescence: the blue has multi-colored shades of pinks, purple, and green while the marigold is rich with deep pink and purple highlights.

• Some hand finishing and ruffling on a few items. Hand finishing in the form of crimped or ruffled edges on bowls, is not seen too often in European Carnival Glass. Some Eda bowls—in particular the *OHLSON* and the *TRE FOTTER*—are ruffled. Vases often have varied edge finishes.

Eda Catalogs

Several Eda catalogs were issued in the 1920s. The first, issued circa 1925, was produced under a joint sales consortium of several Swedish glass companies (called the *De Svenska Kristallglasbruken*) to which Eda Glasbruk belonged. It is entitled *Fargglas Fran Eda Glasbruk* (Colored Glass from Eda Glass Works). It is a work of art in itself, as it was printed in several different colorways to indicate the actual color of the glass. The pages illustrating Eda's Carnival Glass are amazing, giving the effect of iridized glass in both marigold and blue. Twenty-seven different items were illustrated, in eighteen different named patterns (several patterns were shown in a variety of different shapes). Illustrated in lustre-effect printing in 1925 were the following: *BERLIN, CHARLIE, CURVED STAR* (the *DAGNY* vase), *FOUR FLOWERS* (aka *OHLSON*), *HAMBURG, KULOR, MOLLER, PRISMA, ROSE GARDEN* (aka *ROSOR*), *SIX FASETT, STJARNA, SUNFLOWER AND DIAMOND* (aka *SOLROS*), *SUNK DAISY* (aka *AMERIKA*), *SVEA, THREE FOOTER* (aka *TRE FOTTER*), *TOKIO*, and *TRIO*. This time was the true "flowering" of Eda's Carnival production. Two further catalogs from 1929 and 1930 have also been used to attribute Eda Glasbruk's patterns, as well as a 1914 illustrated Eda price list for Oskar Hallberg in Orebro, Sweden.

Sincere thanks to Gerd and Lars Erik Olsson (Eda Collectors Society), Ann and David Brown, Gunnel Holmer at the Smalands Museum, Vaxjo, Sweden, and Bob Smith—all have helped us to source the Eda catalogs. Further thanks to Ann and David Brown, Gerd and Lars Erik Olsson, and Ann-Marie and Lennart Skoglands for their courteous provision of some splendid, rare Eda items for photographing.

The circa 1925 catalog *Fargglas Fran Eda Glasbruk* (Colored Glass from Eda Glass Works) had sophisticated color printing with effects of marigold and blue iridescence. This selection shows the following items in marigold (from left, top to bottom): *SIX FASETT* vase, *STJARNA* bonbon, *SUNFLOWER AND DIAMOND* aka *SOLROS* vase, *SVEA* ashtray, *SVEA* lidded powder jar, *PRISMA* jardinière, *SVEA* jar, *SVEA* oval tray, and *SVEA* perfume bottle.

Another page from the Eda colored glass catalog shows these blue pieces (from left, top to bottom): cupped in *SVEA* bowl, flared *SVEA* bowl, *ROSE GARDEN* aka *ROSOR* oval vase, *HAMBURG* jardinière, and *RANDEL* jardinière (the pattern of the last two is identical, the name denotes the specific shape).

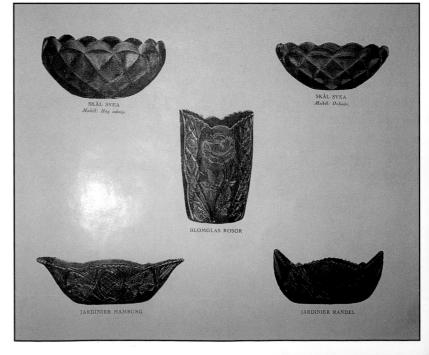

Eda Patterns Known in Carnival Glass

AMERIKA see *SUNK DAISY*

BERLIN

BERLIN is very similar to Imperial's *RANGER* pattern with its plain, squared blocked sides. No doubt it was a design brought back by the Swedish craftsmen who worked for Imperial during the early 1920s. Its simplicity is easy to copy, and of course, Eda weren't the only company to produce a *RANGER* look-alike. Josef Inwald's *JACOBEAN*, Crown Crystal's, *BLOCKS AND ARCHES* in Australia and *RANGER* by Cristales Mexicanos S.A.—all are very similar. *BERLIN* has so far only been found in Sweden.

Shapes: bowls, vase, and small plate (a wide range of shapes was depicted in the 1929 Eda catalog, but only a few of these have so far been found in Carnival)

Colors: marigold and blue

Eda Glasbruk's *BERLIN* pattern is reminiscent of Imperial's *RANGER*—the intense blue coloring and superb iridescence is typical of Eda production. *Courtesy of Ann and David Brown.* SP $150-200.

BOWMAN

A simple design that allows the smooth surfaces to show iridescence to great effect. *BOWMAN* is quite similar to the *NUTMEG GRATER* pattern, though there are differences. It appeared and was named in the 1929 Eda catalog and was made by them in lustre glass, the moulds then were transferred to Magnor in 1934. Found in Sweden.

Shape: bowl
Colors: marigold and blue

CARL (and CARLING)

Clearly shown and named in the 1929 catalog, *CARL* is similar to *CARLING* and both probably enjoyed a somewhat limited production in Carnival. Both patterns feature interlinked star and fan motifs and reflect Eda's superb, quality iridescence well. Found in Sweden.

Shapes: bowl and plate
Color: marigold

An interplay of star and fan motifs form the pattern on this marigold *CARL* bowl. *Courtesy of Ann and David Brown.* SP $150-300.

CHARLIE

To describe *CHARLIE* is easy: the pattern features contrasting bands of smooth glass and intaglio diamonds, both large and small. An essentially simple design that in reality translates into a stunning piece of Carnival Glass. The size, the weight, the astonishing quality of iridescence, and the optical brilliance of the contrasting diamond bands make *CHARLIE* a truly magnificent item. Found in both the USA and Sweden, the pattern was illustrated and named in both the 1925 and 1929 Eda catalogs.

Shapes: large bowl (base diameter almost 5") and small bowl
Colors: marigold and blue

Such a simple concept—contrasting bands of differently sized diamonds. Its elegant simplicity showcases the superb iridescence on this blue *CHARLIE* bowl. SP $150-300.

BOWMAN is a plain design with an encircling file band; this example has a rich marigold iridescence. SP $80-120.

CURVED STAR aka *LASSE* (Sweden)

A wonderfully complex geometric design featuring a variety of star, fan, and file motifs. If any pattern has the ability to confuse researchers and collectors, this one does! Who made it? What variations and colors can it be found in?

FACTS: to begin, let's examine the certainties, according to evidence from currently known company catalogs.

• **Eda**. *CURVED STAR* appears in the catalogs of Eda from 1925 and 1929. The 1925 catalog has color printing that illustrates iridized glass—the only item shown in that catalog in *CURVED STAR* was the *DAGNY* vase (*DAGNY* is a variation of the *CURVED STAR* pattern). In the 1929 catalog, a full range of 14 tableware items was illustrated and given the pattern name *LASSE*. Close inspection of the Eda illustrations from both dates shows that all items in the *CURVED STAR* design as illustrated (including the *DAGNY* vase) have **no file** pattern within the claw motifs.

• **Brockwitz**. *CURVED STAR* appears in the 1921, 1928, and 1931 Brockwitz catalogs in a wide range of shapes (see Chapter Three on Brockwitz for full details). The illustrations of all these items clearly shows that they **all have a file** pattern on the claw motifs.

• **Karhula**. *CURVED STAR* appears in the 1934 and 1938 Karhula (Finland) catalogs in the shape of bowls, large stemmed fruit dish or compote and stemmed cake plate or salver. All examples were clearly shown with **no file** pattern within the claw motifs and also **no star** within the diamond motif.

• **Papini**. *CURVED STAR* appears in the 1934 catalog of Cristalerias Papini of Argentina in the form of bowls. The illustrations show that there **is a file** pattern on the claw motifs. It was almost

This marigold cake stand or salver is an interesting shape that is in fact the first reported in the *CURVED STAR* aka *LASSE* pattern. The pattern is underneath, but can be seen through quite clearly. Note that there is no file on the claws. *Courtesy of Ann and David Brown.* SP $100-150.

certainly an import to South America from Europe—see Chapter Nine for details.

MORE FACTS: now let's consider further factual evidence that may help to establish provenance.

• **Color**. *CURVED STAR* is mainly found in marigold and blue, however rare examples are also known in purple.

• **Pattern**. *CURVED STAR* is mainly found with a file pattern on the claw motifs, however there are examples with no file on the claws. Furthermore, there is yet another variation where not only is there no file on the claws, but there is also no little star in the diamond shaped motif on the claws. These variations can be seen in the illustrations.

• **Interior pattern**. *CURVED STAR* is an exterior design. It is sometimes found on bowls and stemmed compotes (sugars) teamed with the *HEADDRESS* pattern inside. See Chapters Three (Brockwitz) and Seven (Karhula) for more on *HEADDRESS*.

• **Shaping**. Most shapes are "as moulded" with no shaping, but the stemmed compote (sugar) and some bowls can sometimes be found with ruffled edges.

• **Found**. *CURVED STAR* items **with the file** motif on the claws have been found in Scandinavia, the UK, USA, mainland Europe, South America, and Australia. *CURVED STAR* items **without the file** have so far only been reported in Scandinavia. Marigold and blue *CURVED STAR* examples have been found in all the locations noted. Purple examples have only been found in Scandinavia (one in Sweden and one in Norway).

This detail shows the *CURVED STAR* aka *LASSE* pattern as illustrated in the Eda catalog with no file on the claws. This marigold bowl is shown here courtesy of Ann and David Brown. SP $150-200.

Detail of the *CURVED STAR* design showing the version with the file motif on the claws—Brockwitz (A); the version with no file on the claws but with the star in the diamond motif—Eda (B); and the version with no file on the claws and no star in the diamond motif—probably Karhula (C).

SPECULATIONS: these may help to color in the blank spaces between the facts.

• When the Eda glass works went through a period of re-organization in early 1931 it appears that some moulds were sold. The likely result was that some of their *CURVED STAR* aka *LASSE* moulds (without the file pattern) were purchased by Karhula in Finland. These were probably re-tooled to remove the star motif in the diamond. They may also have simply copied the pattern. See Chapter Seven for possible production of *CURVED STAR* in Finland.

• Brockwitz were using the pattern in 1921, pre-dating Eda production. Brockwitz are known to have had a large and impressive mould shop and were very proud of their output from it. It seems quite possible that the Curved Star moulds used by Eda were sold to them by Brockwitz.

• In *Carnival Glass: The Magic and The Mystery,* the significance of slightly different stars on the maries of various *CURVED STAR* bowls was considered. No further evidence has emerged to substantiate the suggestion that these differences might help to determine manufacturer, thus it seems likely that they are simply variations on successive moulds.

• The production of Carnival Glass at Eda Glasbruks was fairly short-lived—it began to be phased out soon after the Strombergs took over the plant management in 1927. It had probably ceased altogether by late 1929-30. There was very possibly a market to be filled in Scandinavia as Eda's production of the popular *lysterglas* began to dwindle, and so Brockwitz almost certainly exported their Carnival into Sweden to fill the market gap. This undoubtedly explains the substantial amounts of Brockwitz Carnival Glass in Scandinavia.

CONCLUSIONS: taking into account the hard facts as well as the speculations.

• *CURVED STAR* in the *LASSE* variation with no file on the claws was made by Eda Glasbruks. Though fourteen shapes were illustrated in their 1929 catalog, only a handful are confirmed in Carnival in the *LASSE* variation: bowl, vase, oval dish, and stemmed cake stand or salver.

• Rare purple examples are from Eda, as they were the only one of the *CURVED STAR* manufacturers to use this color in their Carnival Glass repertoire.

• The vase in Eda's *LASSE* range was called *DAGNY* and is known in marigold and blue only. It is distinctive in that it has a plain panelled section on the lower two inches of the vase. *DAGNY* has been found in Sweden and the USA and is very scarce. There are at least two sizes of this cylinder vase, 5–6" and 8" high.

• The variation of the pattern that has no diamond and no file was almost certainly made only by Karhula in Finland.

• It is not possible to confirm with absolute certainty any examples of *CURVED STAR* with the file on the claws as being an Eda product. Maybe there are some—maybe there are not—it is impossible to say based on current knowledge. For Brockwitz and Karhula production of *CURVED STAR* see relevant chapters for details.

Shapes: bowl, oval dish, stemmed cake stand (salver), and *DAGNY* vase
Colors: marigold, blue, and purple

The vase in Eda's *CURVED STAR* range had its own name, *DAGNY*. A splendid item with a distinctive panelled lower section, this marigold example is SP $400-800.

DAGNY see CURVED STAR

DAISY SPRAY see FLORAL SUNBURST

DESSIN

This is a fairly simple pattern, yet the actual execution of the item—its shape, finishing, and iridescence— quite take the breath away. This is a stunning example of Carnival Glass that is almost certainly very scarce and has so far only been found in Sweden. The edge shaping is exquisite and very intricate—almost a "bracket" shape. (It is interesting to note that a distinctive edge identical to this was drawn by John Sowerby in his sketchbook dated 1900, possibly indicating a further connection between Eda and Sowerby.)

    Shape: bowl
    Color: blue

DESSIN is a simple pattern that has a distinctive edge shape. This blue bowl is cupped in like a rose bowl and has a rich iridescence. *Courtesy of Eda Glass Collectors Society.* NP.

1/2 DIAMANT

As the name suggests, the pattern features diamonds. It was illustrated in the Eda 1929 catalog in the form of a bowl, with the pattern name *1/2 DIAMANT* clearly written beneath it. A 10" vase is also known in the pattern.

A blue covered bonbon has been reported[1] with the Eda name *DIAMANT*. A "blueprint" of this bonbon is also depicted in the same source, however we have established with the help of glass researcher Karen MacIntyre, that it is identical to Fostoria's "American" pattern in the covered sugar shape. "American" was distributed in the UK as the "Georgian" range in the 1920s, then later copied by Jobling in England as "Icecube." It should be pointed out, however, that this pattern is not exactly the same as the *1/2 DIAMANT* design, thus we cannot confirm the existence of a Carnival covered bonbon by Eda Glasbruk.

    Shapes: bowl and vase (in at least two different sizes and shapes)
    Color: marigold

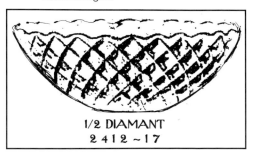

A simple diamond pattern characterizes Eda's *1/2 DIAMANT* design.

DIAMOND WEDGES see REKORD

EDLA

An essentially very simple vase design made up of blocked squares, *EDLA* is illustrated and named in the 1929 catalog.

    Shape: vase
    Color: marigold

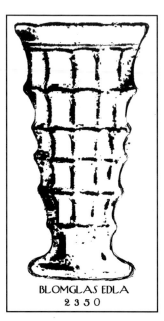

EDLA was shown in Eda's 1929 catalog—it is known in Carnival Glass in this vase shape.

EDSTRÖM

A pleasing, intaglio geometric design comprising large fan and file motifs. A highly complex hobstar fills the whole of the large marie. Found in Sweden.

    Shapes: bowl, plate, jardinière
    Color: blue

Fan and file motifs are the main design elements of Eda's *EDSTRÖM* pattern, while a complex hobstar covers the entire base. The rich iridescence on this lovely blue plate is shot with gold and pink. *Courtesy of Ann and David Brown.* SP $100-250.

FLORAL SUNBURST aka *TUSENSKONA* aka *DAISY SPRAY*

Here is a true gem amongst the intaglio, floral designs; *FLORAL SUNBURST* boasts a stylized yet flowing, intaglio interpretation. The Swedish name *TUSENSKONA* literally means "a thousand beauties"—the pattern is fittingly named, for it is an exquisitely lovely design. The vase has been found with at least four different hand finished shapes to the mouth: a simple flare, a flat topped flare,

incurved like a rose bowl, and tricorner shaped. Gunner Lersjo, Eda glass researcher and author of *Glas Fran Eda*[3], reports that the pattern is illustrated in the Eda 1928 catalog. Examples of this pattern have been found in the USA and Sweden.

Shapes: vase and small, deep jardinière

Colors: marigold, blue and pearl

Eda Glasbruk's *FLORAL SUNBURST* seen here in a pretty jardinière shape. *Courtesy of Ann and David Brown.* SP $250-600.

The mouth on this blue *FLORAL SUNBURST* vase has been shaped like a tricorn, pulled down in three corners. The iridescence is typical of Eda at its best—rich and multi-colored. *Courtesy of Eda Glass Collectors Society.* SP $800-1200.

The iridescence on this cupped in or incurved *FLORAL SUNBURST* vase is a rich pumpkin marigold, full of crimson highlights. A flared blue vase sold in 1995 at auction for $500. SP $500-900.

FOUR FLOWERS aka *OHLSON*

Tracing the history of this pattern is like chasing the wind. It would seem to be fairly safe to say that it has its origins in the Dugan/ Diamond pattern of the same name. However, whether the Eda version is a copy of the Dugan/Diamond pattern or from the same actual mould is virtually impossible to say. Close study of both Dugan and Scandinavian examples reveal almost no difference in the pattern detail. The basic size of the large bowls is also the same as the Dugan large bowls and chop plate. Both versions also share the same two-part mould structure. The differences lie in the color of the glass, the iridescence, and the edge finishing. Blue, marigold, and rare, delicate lavender are the three colors known in this pattern (note that the lavender is a light shade, very different to the deeper colors that Dugan/Diamond's *FOUR FLOWERS* or the *FOUR FLOWERS VARIANT* is found in). The iridescence on Eda's *FOUR FLOWERS* has a distinctive, lustrous, multi-hued effect with much bronzed gold—the overall effect is not unlike the best of Millersburg's radium—and is quite breathtaking. The edge finishing exhibits a characteristic 10-point ruffle, where the ruffles are tightly pinched dips rather than gentle curves. Note also that the Scandinavian version features a plain exterior and a ground base. Unusually for European glass, the main pattern (*FOUR FLOWERS*) is on the interior of the bowl.

The reader may note that we have carefully described this item as Scandinavian rather than simply Swedish. It is clearly depicted in Eda catalogs. It was also specifically shown in the small catalog called *Farrglas Fran Eda Glasbruk,* which actually shows the pattern in Carnival Glass and names it *OHLSON*. However, the *FOUR FLOWERS* pattern was also shown in the slightly later 1939 Riihimaki catalog—a Carnival example is also on display at the Suomen Lasimuseum at Riihimaki in Finland. The answer to this conundrum is almost certainly that both Scandinavian factories produced the pattern in Carnival; Riihimaki very likely purchased the mould from Eda early in the 1930s. Any rare lavender or purple examples, however, would be from Eda as they (and not Riihimaki) used that color for Carnival Glass. To date, we only know of this unusual item being found in Scandinavia, though examples sourced in Scandinavia have been sold at auction in other countries such as the UK and the USA.

Shapes: large 9-10" bowls only

Colors: marigold, blue, and lavender. Blue is probably the easiest to find, but all examples should be considered exceptionally scarce.

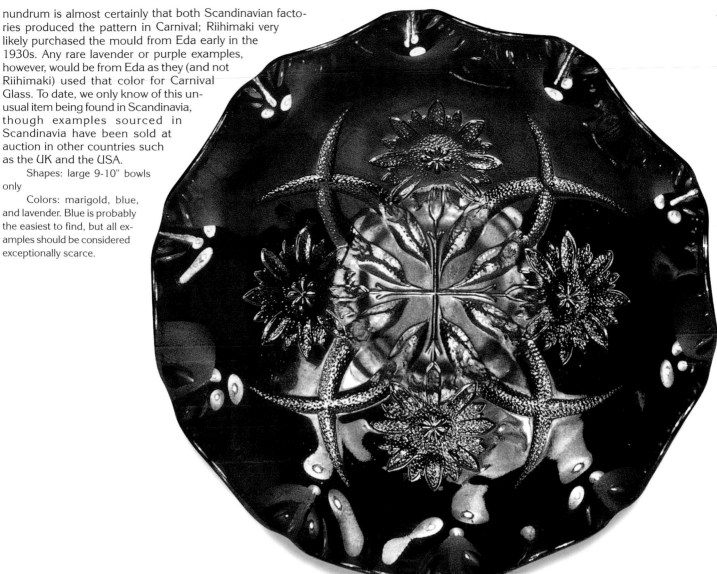

A radium iridescence on a *FOUR FLOWERS* blue bowl. Note that this design is one of the few European patterns that are cameo (proud) and not Intaglio. Also, the pattern is featured on the interior and not the exterior of the bowl, unlike most other European ones—furthermore, the edge is ruffled, again, not typical for Europe. Probably Eda: SP $400-600.

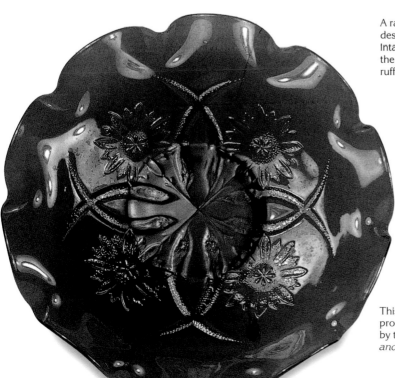

This *FOUR FLOWERS* bowl is undoubtedly an Eda product as it is in lilac Carnival, a rare color used only by that factory within Scandinavia. *Courtesy of Ann and David Brown.* SP $600-800.

GLADER see TORA

GRANKVIST (pronounced Grahn-kervist)
The delightful Swedish name GRANKVIST means "branches." Study of the pattern reveals how apt the name is: GRANKVIST is made up of six stylized "branch" type motifs, radiating from the base to the top of the pattern. Original "blueprints" of various moulds were discovered in the Eda archives by Gunner Lersjo, the Eda glass researcher. GRANKVIST was pictured, bearing the pattern number 1609. According to Lersjo, the mould was made in Germany. It is a scarce and elegant pattern that is not known to us outside of Sweden.
Shape: bowl
Color: marigold

Some splendid items of Eda's Carnival are on display at the Eda Glasbruk Museum: this is a rare GRANKVIST marigold bowl. *Courtesy of Eda Glass Collectors Society.* NP.

HAMBURG (and RANDEL)
An intaglio pattern of considerable complexity, HAMBURG was actually in production in crystal glass at Eda from 1912. A jardinière shaped somewhat like a banana boat is the only shape known in the pattern. Interestingly, when it is flared out at the sides, the pattern was called HAMBURG in the Eda catalogs, yet the identical pattern and shape when cupped in, was called RANDEL. Both shapes were depicted in the 1925 Eda catalog in *lysterglas*. Found in Sweden.
Shape: jardinière (flared out and cupped in)
Colors: marigold and blue

HAMBURG was the Eda name given to this large, flared jardinière. Also known in marigold, this blue example would possibly sell for $400-700.

KULOR
KULOR is essentially such a simple pattern—large, regular circles—yet when iridized, the effect is quite breathtaking. The circles reflect the light in such a way as to give a kaleidoscope of color over the surface of the glass. This is one of six different vase patterns shown and named in the 1925 Eda catalog. Examples have been found in the USA, Scandinavia, and Australia.
Shape: vase in two (possibly three) sizes— 6" and 8" are known
Colors: marigold, blue, pearl, and purple (rare)

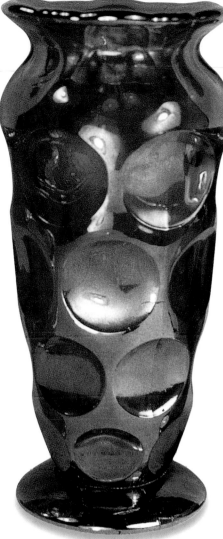

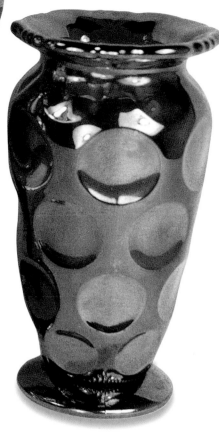

KULOR is a simple yet wonderfully effective vase that showcases Eda's magnificent iridescence. Note the flat topped, flare shape of the vase—all *KULOR* vases appear to have this characteristic mouth shape. At left is the 6" marigold vase (an example sold at auction in the USA in 1999 for $1600); center is an 8" blue vase (NP); right a 6" blue vase (an example sold at auction in the USA in 1999 for $3500).

Purple was a rare signature color of Eda's; this 6" purple *KULOR* is a true scarcity—a real treasure—and the only example currently known. *Courtesy of Ann and David Brown.* NP.

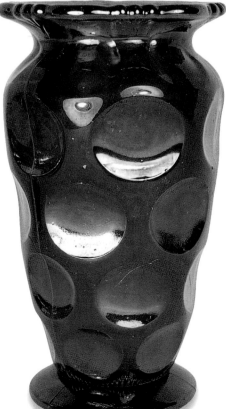

LAGERKRANS aka *LAUREL WREATH*

The Swedish name reflects the delightful, interlocking pattern that is found on the lid of this covered bonbon, which stands just 5" high. The lower part of the item features a ribbed design. A rarely found item that was illustrated in the 1929 Eda catalog. Found in Sweden.

Shape: covered bonbon
Colors: marigold and blue

LAGERKRANS was the Swedish name given to this beautiful item, only known in the lidded bonbon shape illustrated here. *Courtesy of Eda Glass Collectors Society.* NP.

LAUREL WREATH see *LAGERKRANS*

LONDON aka *SALAD PANELS*

This is a plain and simple design—a utilitarian piece with little adornment by way of pattern. A full range of *LONDON* tableware was shown in the Oskar Hallberg 1914 catalog of Eda glass. It was later depicted and named in the 1929 Eda catalog. Found in Sweden.

> Shape: bowl
> Colors: marigold and blue

MAUD

MAUD is quite unlike any other Eda pattern. It is a deep cut, boldly stylized grape design that covers the exterior and base. It was shown and named in the Eda 1929 catalog, but intriguingly it is also found in the 1926 catalog of another Swedish company, Elme Glasbruk. The iridescence and base color are typical of Eda, but what is not certain is whether the mould came to Eda after Elme finished production or whether both factories were producing the pattern at the same time from copied moulds. Found in Sweden.

> Shape: bowl
> Color: blue

MAUD is a deeply cut fruit design, known in Carnival Glass in the form of a blue bowl. This illustration is from Eda Glasbruk's 1929 catalog.

MÖLLER

A hard-to-find pattern, *MÖLLER* is a particularly beautiful, geometric design. The secret of its beauty lies in the way in which the fan like pattern (which forms a major feature of the *MÖLLER* bowls) utilizes the actual edge shaping of the item to echo the design. Quite exquisite. *MÖLLER* was illustrated and named in both the 1925 and 1929 Eda catalogs. Found in Sweden.

> Shape: large bowls with three basic shapes—flared out, straight up, and cupped in like a rose bowl
> Colors: marigold and blue

The way in which the shape of the bowl follows and accentuates the pattern on Eda's *MÖLLER* design is a stroke of genius. A truly exquisite piece of Carnival Glass, the iridescence on this blue bowl is multi-colored and high quality. SP $400-600.

NANNA

A wide range of named *NANNA* items was illustrated in this pattern in the 1929 Eda catalog, though only a few shapes are known to us in Carnival. *NANNA* is an intaglio design that features a blend of fan shapes, diamonds, and notches. Found in Sweden.

> Shapes: vase and small jardinière known. More shapes are likely in Carnival.
> Colors: marigold and blue

Eda's *NANNA* design is seen here on a delightful, small, blue jardinière *Courtesy of Ann and David Brown*. SP $250-600.

FOUR FLOWERS see *OHLSON*

PRISMA

A single shape in this pattern was illustrated in the Eda 1925 catalog, where it was noted as "jardinier *PRISMA*." It is a fairly unremarkable pattern that is made up of simple panelled facets. Found in Sweden.

> Shape: jardinière
> Colors: marigold and blue

REKORD aka *DIAMOND WEDGES*

Alternate plain and diamond cut panels are the main pattern motif. Gunner Lersjo reports that it was in Eda's range in 1929, where it was named *REKORD*. Found in Sweden.

> Shape: bowl
> Color: blue

Contrasting plain and diamond patterned panels serve to show the iridescence to good advantage on this blue *REKORD* bowl. *Courtesy of Ann and David Brown.* SP $200-300.

REX

REX, illustrated and named in the 1929 Eda catalog, is a variation on the "plain block" theme. However, the combination of top-notch iridescence that is usually found on Eda's Carnival along with the stately shape of the vase combine to make a most attractive item. Found in Sweden.

Shape: vase, with a variety of neck shaping. Probably in three sizes—the smallest being about 3" high.

Colors: marigold, blue, and pearl

A small *REX* vase in the dense iridized milk glass called pearl (*parlemorlystrad*). *Courtesy of Ann and David Brown.* NP.

Two splendid *REX* vases made by Eda Glasbruk are shown here courtesy of Ann and David Brown. The tall marigold vase at left has Eda's characteristic flat topped flare shaping as seen on the *KULOR* vases, while the smaller blue example has a simple, gentle flare. Either vase SP $300-600.

ROSE GARDEN aka ROSE MARIE aka ROSOR (Sweden) aka ROSEN (Germany)

The *ROSE GARDEN* oval vase was illustrated in blue and marigold Carnival in the Eda 1925 catalog. It is the only shape that was depicted in the *ROSE GARDEN* pattern in that catalog and is therefore the only shape in the pattern that can be attributed with certainty to Eda Glasbruk. The moulds were almost certainly either bought or leased from Brockwitz in Germany (see Chapter Three for more detail).

The oval vase, named *ROSOR* in Eda's catalog, is known in three sizes. The impressive large vase stands some 9" high, measures 8" from side to side and just over 3" from back to front. The middle sized version stands just over 7" high and measures 6.5" from side to side. The smaller version stands just over 5" high, measure 4" from side to side and is 2" from back to front. The small vase weighs in at a dainty 1 pound, while the large vase tops 4 pounds. All examples should be considered exceptionally rare. As noted in Chapter Three, the oval vase is also shown in the Brockwitz catalogs and was almost certainly produced by them in Carnival too. Rare examples of the oval vase have been found in the USA, UK, Sweden and Argentina.

Shapes: oval vase in three sizes
Colors: marigold and blue

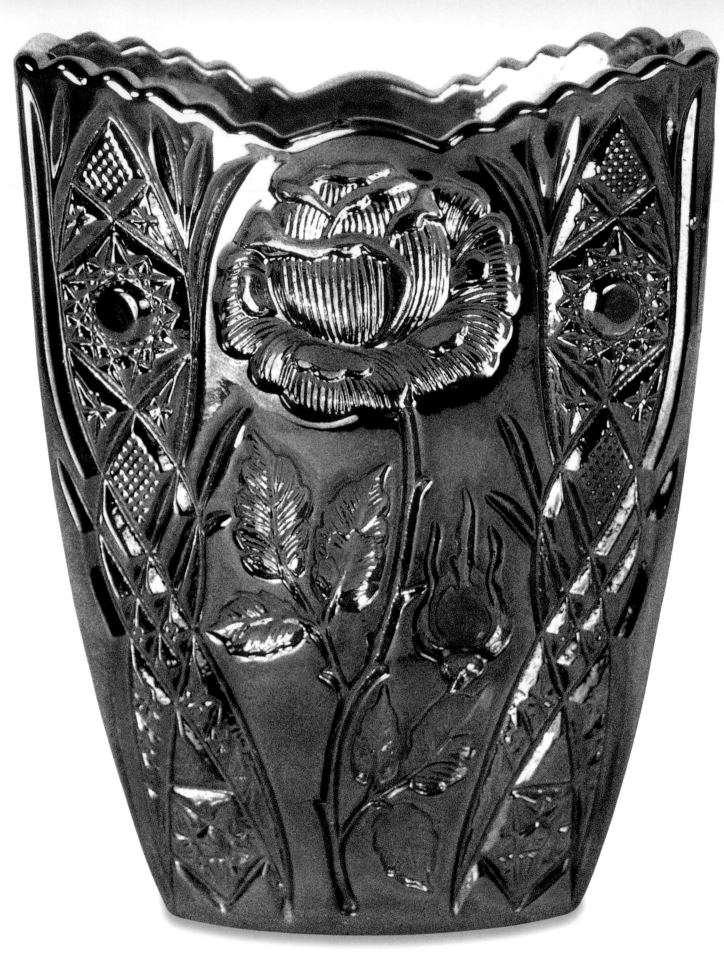

A magnificent *ROSE GARDEN* oval vase probably from Eda Glasbruk. This is the only item in *ROSE GARDEN* (called *ROSOR* by Eda) that was illustrated in their catalogs, however Brockwitz also made this shape—see Chapter Three for details. The vase shown here is the smallest of the three sizes known; this little beauty stands some 5" high (one sold at auction in 1999 for $2000).

ROSE MARIE see *ROSE GARDEN*

ROSOR see *ROSE GARDEN*

SALAD PANELS see *LONDON*

SIX FASETT

First shown in crystal in Oskar Hallberg's 1914 catalog of Eda glass, this simple, six sided vase was shown individually in Carnival Glass in the 1925 Eda catalog, and again later, where it was named *6 FASETT* as part of a range of Eda's *FASETT* items in their 1929 catalog. Found in Sweden.

    Shape: vase (more items possible)
    Colors: marigold and blue

A selection of iridized glass depicted in Eda Glasbruk's 1925 catalog: on the left is the *SIX FASETT* vase (*blomglas*); top right is the rare *STJARNA* covered bonbon and bottom right is a jardinière in the *PRISMA* pattern

BLOMGLAS 6 FASETT

BONBONIER STJÄRNA

JARDINIER PRISMA

SNIPA

A scarce "find" in Carnival Glass, *SNIPA* was illustrated and named in the 1929 Eda catalog. It was shown again in a catalog the following year in the form of a more detailed drawing. A simple design, the pattern's main interest comes in the form of a starred border. Found in Sweden.

    Shape: bowl
    Color: marigold

Eda's *SNIPA* design, as shown in the company's catalogs.

This marigold *STJARNA* bonbon, minus its lid, was found in a small antique shop in Stockholm, Sweden, in 1998. NP.

SOLROS see *SUNFLOWER AND DIAMOND*

STJARNA

A glance at the main pattern motif on *STJARNA* would undoubtedly suggest that the translation of that Swedish word is the English "star." Known in Carnival only in the form of a very rare covered bonbon, *STJARNA* was originally made at Eda in crystal glass in 1912, then again in Carnival in 1925. It is illustrated and named in the Eda catalog from that year. Very rare examples have been found in Scandinavia. Included in the small selection of Eda glass on display at the Morokulien border crossing between Norway and Sweden is a rare *STJARNA* bonbon.

    Shape: lidded bonbon
    Colors: marigold and blue

SUNFLOWER AND DIAMOND aka SOLROS

A sturdy looking columnar vase, *SUNFLOWER AND DIAMOND* combines file filled diamonds with "near-cut" floral motifs of stylized daisies. The non-iridized vase in crystal was shown in the 1914 Oskar Hallberg catalog that was advertising Eda's glass. It was also one of six vases depicted in Carnival and named *SOLROS* in Eda's 1925 catalog. It was also shown again in their 1929 catalog (with the pattern #2470) and noted to be a little over 7" (190 cm) in height. The way that pattern numbers are given in the Eda catalog suggests that items which came in several sizes had a spread of numbers. For example, the *SUNK DAISY* aka *AMERIKA* bowl that was made in four different sizes had the pattern number 2400-03. Vases which are known in several different heights are denoted similarly, for example *REX* (#2475-77) and *KULOR* (#2471-73). The *SUNFLOWER AND DIAMOND* vase has only one number, thus it is likely that it was only produced in the 7" high version.

The significance of this finding is that it indicates that the smaller, approximately 7" vases are from Eda, while the larger vases (9") are almost certainly the Brockwitz versions. Further differences can be found. The daisy motif has 20 petals on the smaller Eda version, while there are 36 on the taller, Brockwitz version. The Eda version may have a slightly pinched and flared top, while the Brockwitz examples are always straight with no hand finishing or flaring. Examples of Eda's *SOLROS* have been found in the USA (for example, in Nebraska in 1980) and, of course, Scandinavia.

    Shape: vase, just slightly over 7"
    Color: blue (marigold is unconfirmed in the 7" size)

SUNK DAISY aka AMERIKA

An exquisite blend of stylized floral motifs, with geometric fans and hobstars, *SUNK DAISY* presents a delightful and harmonic composition. Its most significant and characteristic feature, however, is its feet. All items in this pattern appear to stand on four, distinctive, squared-off feet. (Only the *VINLOV* jardinière has a similarity about the feet.) Another delightful feature of the *SUNK DAISY* items is the intaglio floral design on the base. The European designers can take no credit for this pattern, however, as it was originally conceived and produced in the United States by the Cambridge Glass Company.

Found in shapes that range from a diminutive rose bowl right up to a massive footed plate, Eda Glasbruk's *SUNK DAISY* was undoubtedly a popular design.. *Courtesy of Ann and David Brown.* Marigold rose bowl and plate: SP $150-750 (various sizes).

The design first appeared in the Butler Brothers catalogs from around 1910. It had the Cambridge pattern #2760 and was named "Red Sunflower" by Minnie Watson Kamm[4] as the items were finished in ruby glaze and gilt. The distinctive squared foot was patented by Cambridge Glass and most items were marked "NEAR-CUT." A few years after its appearance in Butler Brothers, the pattern was depicted in the Finnish Riihimaki 1915 crystal glass catalog (*Kristallien ja Talouslasien Kuvasto*). Named "Onerva," it was no doubt only produced in crystal and not in iridized glass. Later still, the 1925 Eda catalog featured the pattern again. Now called *AMERIKA* (which strongly suggests its origins) it was shown in Carnival Glass in a footed, open bowl shape. The subsequent Eda catalog of 1929 depicted *AMERIKA* again, its catalog number being 2400-03 indicating that it was made in four sizes.

Ten years later, the same pattern, but in a wider range of shapes that included jugs and bowls, appeared again in the Finnish Riihimaki catalog. No name appears to have been given the design in the Finnish catalogs at that time, but collectors today refer to it as *SUNK*

Eda's *SUNFLOWER AND DIAMOND* vase, at right, is slightly smaller than the Brockwitz version of the pattern. There are only 20 petals on the "sunflower" motif on the smaller, blue Eda version, while there are 36 on the marigold Brockwitz examples. Blue Eda vase shown courtesy of Ann and David Brown. SP $400-700. Marigold Brockwitz example, $100-200.

DAISY. The likely explanation is that Riihimaki retrieved the moulds back from Eda. But were the moulds original ones from Cambridge Glass or were they simply copied in Scandinavia and a fresh set of moulds made? Our feeling is that, given the complexity of the moulds and the unique foot design, at least some of them were probably purchased from Cambridge rather than copied. Possibly any extensions of the pattern (such as the flat based jardinière) would have been new Scandinavian moulds. It is not possible to be certain whether the blue and marigold examples of *SUNK DAISY* were made by Eda or Riihimaki—however, other colors will determine the manufacturer.

Pearl and rare purple examples are from Eda while any in amber are from Riihimaki. The *SUNK DAISY* pattern has been found in the USA and Scandinavia in a range of shapes and sizes. Crystal examples have been seen in the UK.

Shapes: bowls, plates and a jardinière in varying sizes. The bowls may be cupped in, upright, or flared out to varying degrees. Bowls and plates are footed and range from tiny diminutive examples right up to large, heavy items.

Colors: marigold, blue, pearl, and purple (very rare)

The *SUNK DAISY* pattern was made by both Eda Glasbruk in Sweden and Riihimaki in Finland. Blue and marigold examples could be from either manufacturer—but no problem with this purple bowl: this was a scarce color that Eda Glasbruks made. The astonishing iridescence on this splendid item would compare with Imperial's best—lime, gold, fuchsia, turquoise, and pink shimmer in contrast with the rich purple base color. This is currently the only purple example known. NP.

SVEA

This was probably one of the most popular patterns in Eda's Carnival at the time of manufacture, for a wide range of shapes is known. Not only was it popular, it was also very practical and usable. In the 1925 Eda catalog, no less than seven different shapes in *SVEA* were illustrated in Carnival Glass, including an ashtray, comb tray, powder box, and button or trinket box. The main pattern motif is a repeat of large, faceted diamond shapes—the glass is thick and the top of *SVEA* items is cleverly fashioned to achieve a distinctively shaped edge. The bowls may be cupped in as rose bowls or flared out as salad bowls.

SVEA's popularity didn't stop at Eda production. The moulds were sold to other factories and appear in the catalogs of both Riihimaki and Karhula in Finland. Interestingly, *SVEA* is also depicted in the 1926 catalog of Elme Glassbruk. Almost certainly the moulds were duplicated and were being used by more than one factory at a time. Production of *SVEA* in Carnival at Eda in 1925 is a certainty (evidence of *lysterglas* production is in their catalog). *SVEA* items have been found in the USA, UK, and Scandinavia.

There is a wide range and variety of shapes. The vase, for example, is known in both a large, flared trumpet shape in both marigold and blue as well as a diminutive cylinder shape that features a distinctive, wide plain band at the top.

Shapes: bowls of varying sizes from small 4-5" rose bowls to large salad dishes. Also known are the ashtray, several sizes of vase, comb tray, powder jar, cologne bottle, and button or trinket box.

Colors: marigold, blue, pearl, and purple

This small *SVEA* plate is actually blue, though the amazing colors of the iridescence make it almost impossible to discern the base shade. One example sold for $210 at a USA auction in January 2000. *Courtesy of Ann and David Brown.*

The *SVEA* lidded powder bowl was also illustrated in the 1925 Eda catalog—this example is blue and is on display at the Eda Glasbruks Museum. *Courtesy of Eda Glass Collectors Society.* NP.

SVEA was a popular pattern that was made in a range of sizes and shapes—this delightful small vase is one of several different shapes and styles made in the pattern. *Courtesy of Ann and David Brown.* SP $150-250.

THREE FOOTER aka TRE FOTTER

This shape simply shouts Dugan/Diamond! When one turned up in the USA in 1999 our immediate reaction was to assume it was a Dugan piece—the shape, and in particular, the three feet are exactly like Dugan's footed *CHERRIES* bowls. However, this item is clearly depicted in Eda catalogs and is known in Sweden. The geometric diamond design is only on the exterior. The *TRE FOTTER* was named and illustrated in Carnival in the Eda 1925 catalog. Examples have been found in the USA and Scandinavia.

    Shape: three footed bowl
    Colors: marigold, blue, and lilac

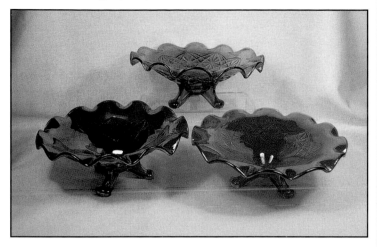

Three *THREE FOOTERS* in three different colors! Blue on the left, marigold on the right, and at the back, the scarce lilac shade. *Courtesy of Ann and David Brown.* SP $100-400 for marigold or blue. $400-600 for lilac.

TOKIO

A bowl and vase in the *TOKIO* pattern were named and illustrated in Carnival in the 1925 Eda catalog. *TOKIO*—an intriguing name, suggesting a Far Eastern connection, for a fascinating pattern. The main pattern motif is of overlapping squares in a waterfall effect, but the most intriguing aspect to *TOKIO* is the motif on the base, where an anti-clockwise (left facing) swastika fills the marie. The swastika has been identified as the Hammer of Thor, the Lord of Thunder and Lightning, the God of the Air—and amongst the Scandinavians was believed to have dominion over the Demons of the Air. However, it is quite possible that, given the Far Eastern sounding name of the pattern, the symbolism was that of China, where the swastika is believed to bestow great happiness and longevity. *TOKIO* is a scarce item that has been found in the USA and Sweden. The reported find in the USA is rather interesting: whilst en route to a Carnival Convention in June 1999, a couple of Carnival collectors spotted what they thought was a most unusual blue vase on the shelf of an antique shop—it turned out to be *TOKIO*. It seems that it had been there for several years, but no one knew what it was!

    Shapes: large and medium sized bowls and vase
    Colors: marigold, blue, and pearl

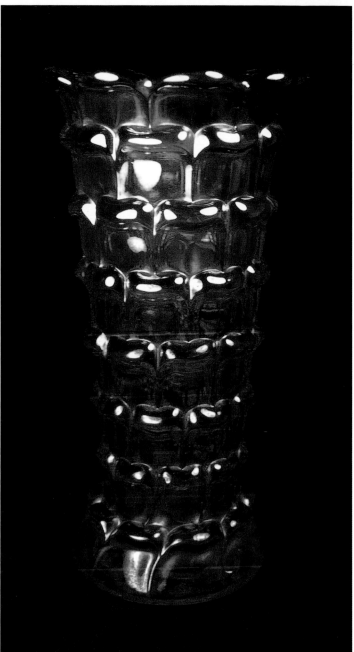

The *TOKIO* pattern was also used for a lovely cylinder vase—examples have been discovered as far afield as Sweden and Illinois, USA! This marigold example courtesy of Ann and David Brown. SP $500-1000.

Eda's *TOKIO* pattern has a rippling waterfall effect which, when combined with the magic of iridescence, creates a stunningly beautiful example of Carnival Glass. This blue bowl in the *TOKIO* pattern is hard to find. SP $400-600.

TORA aka GLADER

Simple star and fan motifs are the main features on this pattern. Named *TORA* and illustrated in four different tableware shapes in the Eda 1929 catalog, this pattern has also been illustrated and named "Glader" by Marion Quintin-Baxendale.[1] The other shapes illustrated in the 1929 catalog were a pitcher and a decanter, however, we are not currently aware of them in Carnival.

Shape: bowl
Color: blue

TORA features alternate simple star and fan motifs. The word *monster* in this extract from Eda's 1929 catalog simply means pattern suite.

TRE FOTTER see THREE FOOTER

TRIO

Illustrated in Carnival and named in the Eda 1925 catalog, *TRIO* is a simple panelled, exterior design that increases in complexity toward the base. Found in Sweden.

Shape: bowl
Color: blue

TRIO is seen here on a blue bowl that is displayed in the Eda Glasbruk's Museum. *Courtesy of Eda Glass Collectors Society.* SP $150-300.

TUSENSKONA see FLORAL SUNBURST

UNA

A simple, almost plain, exterior faceted design that displays iridescence very well. It was illustrated and named in the Eda 1929 catalog. Found in Sweden.

Shape: bowl
Color: blue

UNA, as shown in Eda's catalogs, had the pattern #2549.

VINLOV

Illustrated and named in the Eda 1929 catalog (pattern #2502), this is an interesting item that owes much to earlier Classic Carnival design. *VINLOV* is a magnificent jardinière or banana boat shape (6" high and 11" long) that was surely inspired by Northwood's *GRAPE AND CABLE* banana boat. A first glance at this magnificent rarity causes the onlooker to think that indeed, it is the Northwood item. A second look reveals the truth. This is a superb and impressive piece—the vines stand out massively in deep relief. Indeed, this is one of just a handful of Carnival patterns that were made by Eda in cameo (rather than intaglio) designs. The feet are unusual in that they are squared off, like those on the *AMERIKA* bowls. *VINLOV* is exceptionally rare, very beautiful and, so far, has only been found in Sweden.

Shape: jardinière
Colors: marigold and purple (also a version where only the grapes are iridized)

A magnificent, marigold jardinière (banana boat shape) in Eda's *VINLOV* pattern; note how the grapes stand out in high relief. An exceedingly rare and exceptionally elegant item. *Courtesy of Anne Marie and Lennart Skoglands.* NP

YORK

YORK was obviously a popular pattern when it was issued in the late 1920s, for a wide range of items was shown in the *YORK* pattern in the Eda 1929 catalog. Essentially it is a familiar drapery type of design. Some of the *YORK* moulds were later sold to other glass factories since items in the pattern appear in later Finnish catalogs. Some of the *YORK* moulds also went to Eda's "sister" factory Magnor, which was located only a mile or two away. The moulds of two *YORK* vases and a bowl are on display at the museum in the working factory at Magnor, in Norway. Examples have been found in Scandinavia and the UK.

    Shapes: vases, bowls, and jardinière
    Color: marigold

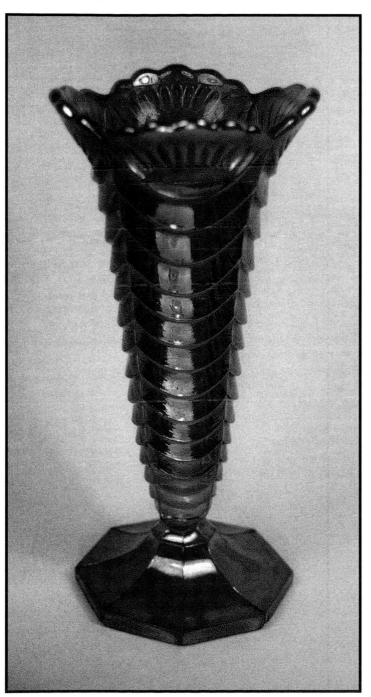

A wide range of shapes was made in the *YORK* pattern. This marigold vase was found in the UK and is shown courtesy of Frank and Shirley. SP $150-350.

ZEE-ONE aka WIDE FLUTES BANDED

This item had the Eda pattern name Z1—number one—in their 1929 catalog. A simple wide panel design, it would hardly warrant a second glance were it not for its splendid iridescence.

    Shape: bowl
    Color: marigold

ZEE-TWO aka CROWN/SWEDISH CROWN

An essentially simple pattern, but the overall concept, the shape, the edge finish, and the magnificent deep, dark iridescent finish combine to make this a truly startling (and memorable) example of Carnival Glass. Illustrated and named Z2—number two—in the Eda 1929 catalog, this item is known colloquially to the Swedish Eda collectors as *CROWN*. Its tall straight sides and overall concept, indeed, make it look exactly like a crown. We had the privilege to view this item (in a private collection) in a delightful Swedish country house. The owner took it out of the showcase and teasingly (but oh, so gently) pretended to place it on her head. A beautiful crown indeed! As far as we are aware, this rarity has only been found in Sweden.

    Shape: bowl
    Color: blue

ZEE-TWO was Eda's name for this delightful pattern that is known colloquially as *SWEDISH CROWN*. This blue bowl is shown here courtesy of Anne Marie and Lennart Skoglands. NP.

Possible Eda Patterns in Carnival Glass

TARTAN aka *DAISY AND CANE* aka *KOPENHAGEN* (Germany) aka *OLYMPIA* (Sweden)

The *TARTAN* pattern can be seen in the Swedish Oskar Hallberg 1914 catalog, which shows various known Eda pattern ranges—however, this was crystal glass, not Carnival. The range, called *OLYMPIA*, was illustrated in ten different tableware shapes: footed compotes, a footed cake plate, a vase, bowls, and a small creamer are all shown. The variation shown was the "daisy and cane" version (see Chapter Three on Brockwitz for further details) but with a distinctive central star on the marie that Brockwitz examples do not have. Examples of *TARTAN* also exist in the blue opalescent glass that was an Eda specialty. It seems very likely that Eda made crystal and blue opal examples of *TARTAN* but it is not possible to state with certainty that any Carnival examples were made.

Elme Glasbruk, Almhult

There was much competition in the Swedish glass industry in the 1920s and 1930s and the Elme glassworks at Almhult was located in the very heart of the country's "kingdom of glass"—Smaland. Today's visitors to Almhult, situated in the southern part of Sweden, would no doubt recognize the furniture giant, IKEA, whose headquarters are located nearby. There was, of course, much competition between the glass factories, and it appears that Elme had several items in production at the same time as Eda Glasbruk, including some Carnival lines. Ann and David Brown have found examples of Carnival Glass bearing paper labels marked Elme. A handful of patterns known in Carnival were shown in the Elme catalog (circa late 1920s)—interestingly, though, these were also shown in Eda's catalog. It is unlikely that Elme bought glass from Eda to sell as their own (and vice versa) so the obvious answer is that the moulds were simply copied. The item bearing the Elme label has a distinct coloring and iridescence—pale lilac that can look amber or even pink and an iridescence like light golden taffy—not at all like the richly colored and iridized glass produced by Eda Glasbruk, so it seems likely that Elme's Carnival can actually be identified by its very distinctive appearance.

AKTIEBOLAGET
ELME GLASBRUK
ÄLMHULT

Blomglas
Ranka

The Elme trademark as shown on the company's catalog. This illustration also shows "Blomglas Ranka"—the *SOPHIA* vase.

Elme Patterns Known in Carnival Glass

KAREN aka *POPULAR*

This item was found in Sweden by Ann and David Brown, bearing an Elme label. Illustrated in the Elme catalog in a range of shapes, it was given the pattern name, *POPULAR*. A plain and simple design, *KAREN* features a star base with large diamond shapes in panels around the sides. The color and iridescence, however, give the glass its distinctive appearance. The item found by the Browns has a pale marigold iridescence on a very pale lilac base glass that appears pink and even amber in certain lights! Most unusual.

Shape: bowl (other shapes are possible)

Colors: amber/pink as described above, also reported in a very pale blue

This *KAREN* bowl has a most distinctive light taffy colored iridescence and an odd lilac tint to the base glass. SP $80-150. *Courtesy of Ann and David Brown.*

QUATTRO

This pattern is also shown in the Elme catalog. A cake stand in this pattern with Elme's characteristic taffy-like iridescence and pale coloring was found in Sweden by Ann and David Brown—interestingly, it had an Elme label on it. QUATTRO is a fairly plain and simple design featuring fans and plain panels.

Shapes: cake stand and oval flat dish (other shapes are possible)

Color: pale lilac

Another Elme pattern is QUATTRO, seen here on a cake stand. *Courtesy of Ann and David Brown.* SP $80-150.

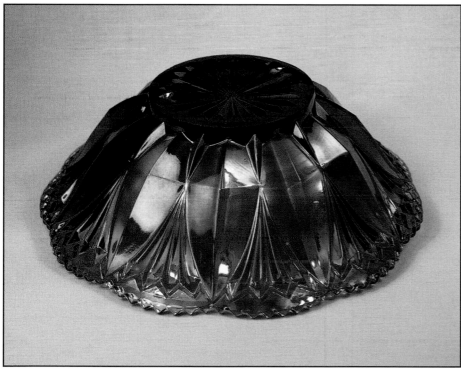

A QUATTRO bowl with the taffy-like iridescence that is a signature of this factory. *Courtesy of Ann and David Brown.* SP $100-200.

SOPHIA

Illustrated in the Elme catalog, SOPHIA is a pedestal footed vase with a square base and a simple fan like pattern. Again, the coloring and iridescence are typical of Elme. Found in Scandinavia, an example of this vase is on display at the Eda Museum in Charlottenberg.

Shape: vase

Color: pale amber-pink

SVEA aka ANANAS

Known to have been produced in Carnival by Eda Glasbruk and Riihimaki, SVEA also appeared in the Elme catalog though it had the name ANANAS (pineapple). A small bowl with a taffy-like iridescence is reported by Ann and David Brown—further, the Browns also have a small SVEA plate that bears an Elme label. It is possible that other shapes were made by Elme, but they would almost certainly be easily distinguished by their characteristic iridescence.

Shapes: small bowl and plate

Color: pale golden with taffy-like iridescence

[1] Marion Quintin-Baxendale, *Collecting Carnival Glass* (London, England: Francis Joseph, 1998).

[2] Simon Cottle, *Sowerby Gateshead Glass* (Gateshead, England: Tyne and Wear Museums Service, 1986).

[3] Gunner Lersjo, *Glas Fran Eda* (Arvika, Sweden: by author, 1997).

[4] Minnie Watson Kamm, *A Second Two Hundred Pattern Glass Book* (Grosse Pointe, Michigan: by author, 1950).

Chapter Seven

Finland

Almost one third of Finland lies within the Arctic Circle. Around 500 miles to the south is the Finnish capital, Helsinki. The line of latitude 60 degrees north passes almost through Helsinki, but follow that line of latitude around the world and see where it traverses the land mass of North America: Labrador and the southern tip of Baffin Island; across the Yukon and into Alaska, just brushing Anchorage. These are areas where winters are long and cold. The country itself is not vast, in fact it occupies an area slightly smaller than the state of Montana. Finland has seen various overlords. Sweden ruled the country for many centuries, then in 1809, Russia took complete control. Various changes of constitution followed, but since 1945 Finland has retained its independence and neutrality. Glass making is part of Finland's heritage and has its origins in the early eighteenth century; Nuutajarvi, the oldest surviving factory (which recently merged with one of the Finnish Carnival glassmakers, Iittala), was founded over 200 years ago. The Finns are rightly proud of their glass traditions, claiming that the two guiding principles of practicality and beauty characterize much of their output. Simple and sophisticated, Finnish Carnival Glass upholds the country's proud legacy.

Riihimaki

The town of Riihimaki lies about forty miles northeast of the capital, Helsinki. The glassworks in the town (and named after it) was established around 1910. A catalog from 1915 shows an extremely wide range of goods, many with elaborate "near-cut" designs. Many of them also seem familiar—American, Swedish, and even German. Possibly the most interesting pattern that appears in that 1915 catalog is the *SUNK DAISY* aka *AMERIKA*, for this was a pattern that was straight from the USA! The background to this puzzle is explained in the entry for *SUNK DAISY* above in the chapter on Eda production, but a brief résumé is appropriate here.

Cambridge Glass Company in the USA were the originators of this pattern and it was illustrated in Butler Brothers catalogs in around 1910. It was then either copied or the moulds were actually sold, for the identical pattern (called "Onerva" by the Finns) appeared in their 1915 catalog (at this stage, of course, it would have been produced in crystal glass). This much traveled pattern was subsequently used in Sweden at Eda between 1925 and 1929, where it was first made in Carnival Glass. Back again to Riihimaki for further production (almost certainly including Carnival) during the 1930s!

There were even more patterns in Riihimaki's repertoire that owe much to the USA. The *FOUR FLOWERS* aka *OHLSON* pattern, which also came to Riihimaki from Eda, had its origins with Dugan/Diamond. The *TIGER LILY* pattern that was made in Carnival by the Imperial Glass Company of Bellaire, Ohio was yet another copied pattern. Riihimaki also used patterns that look very like Imperial's *OPEN ROSE* and *IMPERIAL GRAPE*, though we do not believe that these items were made in Carnival in Finland. Bowls and plates,

even a tumbler, in a design identical to Fostoria's "American" pattern are also featured. Imitation is surely the most sincere form of flattery! There are also patterns that appear in the catalog of the German glass manufacturer, Brockwitz, as well as even more patterns that were featured in the catalogs of Eda Glasbruks, such as their popular *SVEA* pattern. Information from the Finnish Glass Museum confirms that Riihimaki bought in moulds; almost certainly some of these came from Germany and Sweden.

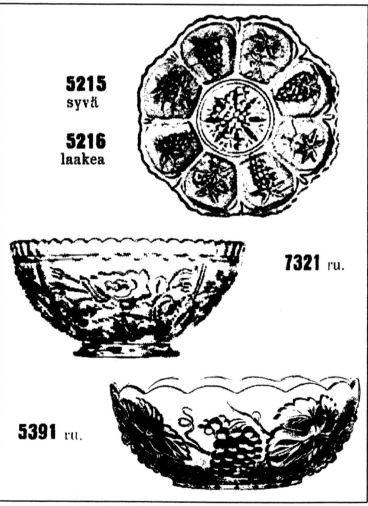

Featured in Riihimaki's 1939 catalog were several designs that seem very familiar, so very like *PEACOCK AND GRAPE, OPEN ROSE, IMPERIAL GRAPE,* or perhaps *VINTAGE*. None of these patterns illustrated, however, are thought to have been produced in Carnival by Riihimaki.

At Riihimaki today, occupying a renovated glass-blowing and crystal grinding plant that was originally built in 1914, is the Finnish Glass Museum, established in 1961 to provide a focus for Finnish glass design and history. The Finnish Glass Museum (Suomen Lasimuseo) is owned by the city of Riihimaki. The Museum is housed in a neat series of white and black buildings with a single chimney stack still standing—a reminder of its industrial past. On display within the Museum is a magnificent array of Riihimaki Carnival.

The Finnish Glass Museum (Suomen Lasimuseo) at Riihimaki near Helsinki, Finland.

The curator of the Suomen Lasimuseo is Kaisa Koivisto; she informed us that the glassworks at Riihimaki began to produce iridized Carnival Glass in 1929 for a grand Industrial Fair in the city of Turku. They invested in a major advertising campaign with a variety of designs that were made specifically for the Fair. Indeed, the *TURKU* souvenir ashtray was made in Carnival to commemorate the event. As well as being sold in Finland, the new iridized glass was exported. Shipments were sent out all over the world—England, the USA, Argentina, the Middle East, Germany, Estonia, Norway, and Denmark. (A few Carnival items were also produced in small quantities by Riihimaki for export at a later date—these may well be the ones that are marked RIIHIMAKI or have a paper label.)

Signature Characteristics of Riihimaki Carnival Glass

- High quality glassware—simple yet sophisticated.
- Ground base on all Riihimaki Carnival.
- Marigold and blue were the main colors used, however, Riihimaki's production is characterized by the occasional use of amber and pink as base colors. A smoky kind of blue was also sometimes used.
- Intaglio, "near-cut" geometric designs or stylized florals—all exterior. Some items also known with an interior pattern (for example, *FOUR FLOWERS* aka *OHLSON* purchased from Eda).
- Water sets, bowls (often jardinière shape), vases, and compotes are the usual shapes for Riihimaki. Occasional use of novelty items such as candlesticks and ashtrays.
- Superb iridescence, often with strong pink and purple highlights, seen on most of their Carnival Glass.
- Some hand finishing on a few items, in particular, the shaping of vases to give a variety of different shapes from the same basic model.

Riihimaki Catalogs

Those patterns which have been attributed to Riihimaki have been identified from the following editions of Riihimaki catalogs (by year of issue): 1915 catalog; 1939 catalog (Kuvasto-Hinnasto P).

Riihimaki Patterns Known in Carnival Glass

ALEXANDER FLORAL see *GRAND THISTLE*

BEADED DREAMS

This pattern is only known in the form of a candlestick, its pattern featuring panels, beads and notches. Only a few examples are currently known (one was found in Ireland), though there must be others in existence. The *BEADED DREAMS* candlestick stands about 6" high and has a most distinctive pink base color. It is illustrated in the Riihimaki 1939 catalog and has the pattern number 6739.
    Shape: candlestick
    Color: pink base glass with marigold iridescence

BEADED DREAMS (left) and *KULLERVO* candlesticks, as illustrated in Riihimaki's 1939 catalog.

BISHOP'S MITRE aka STIPPLE AND STAR

Only known in the shape of a vase, *BISHOP'S MITRE* is named for the New England collector, Bob Bishop, who first brought the pattern to our attention. Though Bob had never seen a Riihimaki catalog, he knew that the vase was made by that company. Why? Simple—on the base of the vase is the moulded trademark RIIHIMAKI. Moulded trademarks for the company are known but are rare.
    The pattern on the vase comprises four sets of pointed crossed arches, each containing a star. The vase is depicted in the 1939 Riihimaki catalog in one height only (8", pattern #5911/2) though the top may be flared out or be straight up. Examples have been found in the USA and Scandinavia. Wayne Delahoy found the first marigold one we were aware of in Australia in 1999. An example of the *BISHOP'S MITRE* vase is on display in the Suomen Lasimuseo.
    Shape: vase
    Colors: marigold and blue

COLUMN FLOWER see SQUARE DIAMOND

DRAPERY VARIANT

A familiar pattern, not unlike Northwood's *DRAPERY*. It differs mainly in that there are fewer lines in the drapes; the total concept however, is identical. On virtually every piece in this pattern that we have handled, the iridescence has been outstanding. An amazing marigold, shot through with pinks, limes, and gold—quite breathtaking. The *DRAPERY VARIANT* water pitcher has a most unusual shape unlike any other, being short and bulbous, its neck angled into a somewhat frilly effect. The pattern features in the Riihimaki 1915 catalog in the form of a covered butter dish; it is also depicted in the 1939 catalog in the tumbler shape. *DRAPERY VARIANT* has been found in the USA, UK, and Scandinavia. An illustration of the pitcher can be seen in the catalogs of the Argentinean company Cristalerias Papini. This is not at all surprising as Riihimaki exported much glass to South America.

Interestingly, there are variations to this pattern. A bowl with the drapes separated by ribs containing beaded diamonds was seen in an antique market in Paris, France and similar examples have been found in the UK, but we cannot confirm that the pattern is from Riihimaki. A tumbler that is very similar to the *DRAPERY VARIANT*, but has only part of the same pattern (the owner has called it *REGAL DRAPE*—see the Carnival Glass Society UK Newsletter #92), has been sourced in the UK. A similar bowl to the Parisian one has been reported in Washington State—but this one also has intaglio fruits on the base. See *YAKIMA* below for details. The basic pattern concept for these items appears to have been the *DRAPERY VARIANT*.

Shapes: pitcher, tumbler, plate, bowl, juice glass, shot glass, and decanter

Color: marigold

ELEKTRA aka SHOOTING STAR aka HOBSTAR WHIRL aka WHIRLIGIG

Such a proliferation of alternate names gives an indication of how confused collectors have been by some of the European patterns over the years. However, the name *ELEKTRA* was given to the pattern back in the 1920s when it appeared in the Brockwitz catalogs in a whole range of items. Several years later it also appeared in Riihimaki's catalog. It seems logical to assume then, that the appearance of vases, plates, bowls, and various sugars and creamers in the 1939 Riihimaki catalog indicate that the moulds were sold by Brockwitz to Riihimaki between 1931 and 1939. As both companies are known to have produced marigold and blue Carnival Glass of good quality, it is virtually impossible to state with certainty which items were made by which company—unless of course, the item is **amber**, in which case it will be from Riihimaki! Found in the USA, UK, and Scandinavia. Examples of this pattern are on display in the Suomen Lasimuseo.

Shapes: creamer and stemmed sugar (compote)
Colors: marigold and amber

ELEKTRA was shown in the Riihimaki catalog in several shapes.

Riihimaki's iridescence was high quality, their marigold frequently showing pink, blue, and lime highlights. *DRAPERY VARIANT* items often have this superb iridescence—seen here are the water pitcher (SP $200-350) and tumbler ($100-200).

FIREFLY aka MOTH

This splendid candlestick was an old pattern for Riihimaki, as it is shown in their 1915 catalog. No doubt it was brought out for service when the company decided to venture into Carnival production during the late 1920s. It is also depicted in the Riihimaki 1939 catalog (bearing the pattern number 5850) and a blue example is on display at the Suomen Lasimuseo. The design features a flying insect motif, repeated around the base and up the column of the candlestick. Examples have been found in the USA, UK, and Scandinavia.

> Shape: candlestick
> Colors: marigold and smoky blue

FIREFLY was illustrated in Riihimaki's 1939 catalog. This example is one of a pair found in England—the color is an unusual shade of smoky aqua-blue. SP $150-250 each.

FLASHING STARS

A rarity amongst tumblers, this splendid pattern is deceptive in its simplicity. A bold, 15-point star is repeated either side of both water pitcher and tumbler—the only items illustrated in this pattern in the 1939 Riihimaki catalog. Of course, what makes it stand out is the fine quality of iridescence that is typical of most Scandinavian Carnival. Found in Finland.

> Shape: tumbler
> Colors: marigold and blue

FOUR FLOWERS

The reader is referred to the chapter on Sweden for the detailed information and background history on this pattern. Suffice it to say here that Riihimaki were not the first glass manufacturer to use this design. Bowls and plates in the pattern were illustrated in the 1939 Riihimaki catalog and an example is on display at the Suomen Lasimuseo. Owing to the similarity between the Carnival output of Eda Glasbruk and Riihimaki, it is not possible to state with certainty who made the blue and marigold examples of this pattern, though any lilac examples are from Eda in Sweden. Examples found in Scandinavia.

> Shape: large 9-10" bowls only
> Colors: marigold and blue

GARLAND AND BOWS

A delightful interpretation of a ribbon swag motif, GARLAND AND BOWS features six bows linked by draped garlands, joined around the design by a checkered band. Several shapes including a cream jug and sugar bowls were illustrated in the 1939 Riihimaki catalog, but only the compote is currently reported in Carnival. Found in the USA, Argentina, and Scandinavia.

> Shape: compote
> Color: marigold

6636

Riihimaki's GARLAND AND BOWS has so far only been found in the stemmed sugar or compote shape. Illustrated here is a creamer in the pattern—surely they were made in Carnival Glass too.

GRAND THISTLE aka *ALEXANDER FLORAL* aka *WIDE PANELLED THISTLE*

A magnificent, bold, intaglio design featuring stylized flower heads, *GRAND THISTLE* bears many similarities to its "sister" pattern, *WESTERN THISTLE*. The two differ greatly, however, in their shape and form. A most distinctive, angular shape characterizes this pattern. The base of the pitcher is an elongated diamond, whilst the tumbler has a square base (these are the only two shapes known in this pattern so far). The body of both shapes echoes these forms while the pitcher handle is very similar to the "Etruscan" shape that the Cambridge Glass Company used. *GRAND THISTLE* first became known to Carnival collectors when several tumblers were discovered in Northbrook, Illinois. Though scarce, they have since been reported again in the USA, UK, Australia, and, of course, Scandinavia.

Shapes: pitcher and tumbler
Colors: marigold, blue and amber

Riihimaki's *GRAND THISTLE* water pitcher and tumbler are shown here in rare amber. Pitcher SP $400-600; tumbler $250-350.

HOBSTAR WHIRL see *ELEKTRA*

JET BLACK BEAUTY

Illustrated in Riihimaki's 1939 catalog (pattern #6266), just one example of this unusual item is currently known. An almost flat plate, it has very distinctive open-work handles. This item is currently the only example of iridized jet black glass from Riihimaki that the authors have handled. Found in the UK.

> Shape: handled plate
> Color: jet black

JET BLACK BEAUTY is named for its distinctive black coloring. *Courtesy of Frank and Shirley.* NP.

JULIANA

A sturdy, simple vase—just the one shape and size was depicted in the Riihimaki 1939 catalog, bearing the pattern #5907. The pattern comprises a plain, six panelled design, set off with six star motifs around the top edge.

> Shape: vase
> Color: blue

KORONA

Found and named by Jim Nicholls, this is only the second confirmed ashtray to have been produced by Riihimaki (the first was the *TURKU* ashtray). Clearly shown in their 1939 catalog as #5706, this round, heavy ashtray features an interlocking, complex geometric design all around its sides, while the ground base has a large and intricate star motif cut deeply into it. The iridescence on the only example reported (discovered in Scandinavia) is a splendid, rich, electric blue.

> Shape: ashtray
> Color: blue

KULLERVO

A sturdy looking candlestick, the moulded pattern featuring upright ribs, *KULLERVO* can be found in Riihimaki's 1939 catalog bearing the pattern #5861. Examples have been found in the USA, UK, Ireland, and Scandinavia.

> Shape: candlestick
> Color: pale pink base glass with weak marigold iridescence

MOTH see *FIREFLY*

RIIHIMAKI TUMBLER

An uninspired geometric pattern consisting mainly of crossed lines is the main feature on this tumbler. Depicted in the Riihimaki 1939 catalog in tumbler form only (#5034), no matching pitcher was shown. An interesting feature of the tumbler is that it has been found bearing the word RIIHIMAKI moulded onto the base, in the same fashion as on an example of the *BISHOP'S MITRE* vase. Unconfirmed reports suggest that items bearing the moulded trademark of the factory are later items, dating from the 1950s. Found in Scandinavia.

> Shape: tumbler (barrel shaped or upright)
> Color: blue

5034

The *RIIHIMAKI* tumbler is so called as it has the factory name "Riihimaki" moulded on the base. The straight sided tumbler had the pattern #5034.

5907   **5908**   **5911**   **5938**

Four vases all known in blue Carnival and featured in Riihimaki's 1939 catalog. From left: *JULIANA, SQUARE DIAMOND* (aka *COLUMN FLOWER*), *BISHOP'S MITRE,* and the *STARBURST AND DIAMONDS* (see also *VICTORIA*).

SHOOTING STAR see *ELEKTRA*

SQUARE DIAMOND aka COLUMN FLOWER

An exquisite geometric, a stunning work of the mouldmaker's art, this rare vase is on display at the Suomen Lasimuseum at Riihimaki in marigold Carnival. Don Moore, writing in the early 1980s, reported two examples that had been found in the USA: one in marigold and one in blue. Its name indicates the unusual nature of its shape, for the vase is quite square. It was depicted in Riihimaki's 1939 catalog bearing the pattern #5908/9—however, it was also illustrated in the Brockwitz catalog of 1928. Possibly Riihimaki bought the mould from Brockwitz in the early 1930s, when they were forced to cut back on production. It is quite possible that this rare vase was made by both manufacturers.

Shape: vase
Colors: marigold and blue

STARBURST

This pattern can be distinguished by its alternate whirling buzz stars and 8-pointed stars within oval medallions—between the ovals are geometric motifs. The pattern changes slightly to accommodate the shape on which it appears. For example, tall *STARBURST* vases have a double row of alternate stars, one above the other, whilst small, squat vases have only a single row. A wide range of *STARBURST* items was depicted in the 1939 Riihimaki catalog; several pieces are on display at the Suomen Lasimuseo. Linked to *STARBURST* is another pattern, *VICTORIA* (see below for details)—the link being the pedestal footed vase called *STARBURST AND DIAMONDS*. *STARBURST* pieces have been found in the USA, UK, and Scandinavia.

Shapes: vases in several shapes and sizes, creamer, sugar, rose bowl, cuspidor, and tumbler
Colors: marigold, blue and amber

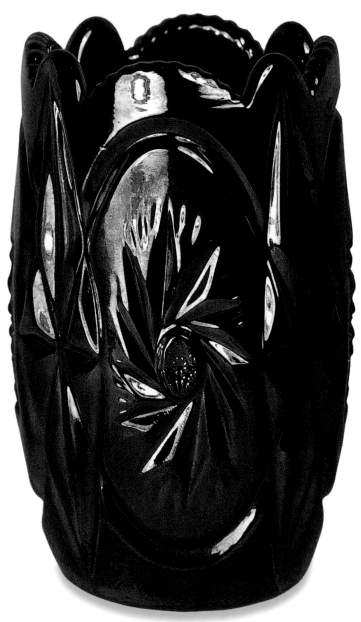

A *STARBURST* vase in blue with a splendid iridescence, found in England. *Courtesy of Brian and Doreen Lapthorne.* SP $400-650.

The same vase—Riihimaki's *STARBURST*—but moved a quarter turn to view a different aspect and see a different star. *Courtesy of Brian and Doreen Lapthorne.*

STARBURST AND DIAMONDS

This is the pedestal footed vase that connects the two patterns *STARBURST* and *VICTORIA* (see these two patterns for details). Found in the USA.

    Shape: vase
    Color: blue

STARBURST AND CROWN

The main pattern elements of *STARBURST AND CROWN* are a large whirling buzz star plus an elegant, elongated fan shape (the "crown" in the pattern name) atop a small hobstar. Although a wide range of items were depicted in the Riihimaki 1939 catalog, only a few shapes are currently known in Carnival. Examples have been found in Scandinavia and the UK. Very similar to the Brockwitz pattern *ANTIGONE*, but there are significant differences.

    Shapes: compote and tumbler
    Color: marigold

5152

STARBURST AND CROWN is known in the tumbler shape, but no pitcher has yet been reported. The Riihimaki catalog illustration of the tumbler did not show the pattern well, so here is the pitcher for the purpose of identification.

STIPPLE AND STAR see *BISHOP'S MITRE*

SUNK DAISY

The full story of the much travelled *SUNK DAISY* pattern is detailed in the chapter on Eda Glasbruk's production and the reader is urged to study it. This pattern—an exquisite blend of geometric motif and intaglio flowers—is illustrated in the Riihimaki 1939 catalog in a range of footed shapes. Owing to the similarity between the Carnival output of Eda Glasbruk and Riihimaki, it is not generally possible to state which examples of *SUNK DAISY* bowls were made by which manufacturer, however, not all the shapes are duplicated. The plate and jardinière shape were possibly only made at Eda, while the sugar and creamer were possibly only made at Riihimaki. Examples in pearl and purple Carnival are from Eda while the rare examples in amber are from Riihimaki. *SUNK DAISY* has been found in the USA and Scandinavia. See Chapter Six for illustrations of this pattern.

    Shapes: bowls in varying shapes and sizes, sugar and creamer
    Colors: marigold, blue and amber

SVEA

We know that *SVEA* was produced in Carnival at Eda Glasbruk circa 1925 to 1929, however, it also appears in the Riihimaki 1939 catalog in the form of a small bowl and plate. Almost certainly, the moulds were sold by Eda to Riihimaki in the early 1930s. Other *SVEA* moulds appear to have gone to Karhula, also located in Finland. It is impossible to be certain as to whether Riihimaki actually produced *SVEA* in Carnival. Just to confuse, *SVEA* also appears in the Elme catalog (see Chapter Six on Sweden for more detail).

    Shapes: small bowl and plate
    Colors: amber (possibly marigold and blue)

TENNESSEE STAR

The first item in this pattern to come to our attention was found by Mike Cain in Tennessee in 1997—a beautiful blue vase, brilliantly iridized, showing pink, purple, and lime green highlights. The pattern is an intricate geometric featuring hobstars and intersecting arches. It would appear that Riihimaki made only vases in this pattern, in fact there were eight different vase shapes shown in their 1939 catalog. The appearance of the pattern changes markedly according to the shape of the vase. This can cause the collector to suspect that different shapes may be different patterns—not so! The Suomen Lasimuseo has an example on display. Other scarce vases in this pattern have been found in Scandinavia and the USA.

    Shape: vase (in different shapes)
    Colors: marigold, blue and amber

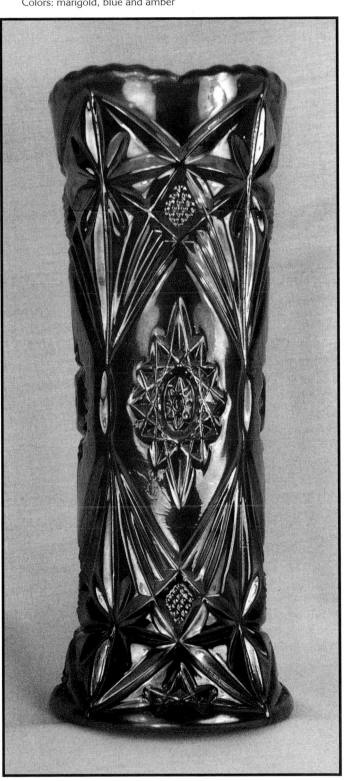

TENNESSEE STAR vases have been found as far afield as the Pacific Northwest, Tennessee, and Sweden (where this 7.5" high amber example was discovered). SP $400-650.

TIGER LILY VARIANT

At first glance you would believe this to be the Imperial version of the *TIGER LILY* pattern, so alike is this Riihimaki copy. Only found in pitcher and tumbler shapes, the Finnish items can be easily distinguished by the complex hobstar on their ground bases. (The Imperial tumbler has a 24-point star on its base while the water pitcher has a pattern of four stylized flower heads and leaf fronds on its base.) There are many more small differences. The Riihimaki tumbler is smaller than the Imperial version. The more frequently found Riihimaki pitcher has a larger diameter and bells out more around its middle.

The rare, small sized pitcher has a different profile altogether (see the photograph caption for comparative details). There are also several subtle pattern differences. The pattern was illustrated in the Riihimaki 1939 catalog, where the tumbler was actually shown in two slightly different shapes—one straight sided and one slightly flared. *TIGER LILY VARIANT* has been found in the USA, Australia, Uruguay, and Scandinavia.

Shapes: water pitcher in two sizes and tumbler
Colors: marigold and blue

Two different sizes of Riihimaki's *TIGER LILY VARIANT* water pitcher were made. On the left is the rare, small size pitcher (only one reported) that stands 7.5" high, SP $500-700. Tumbler $125-250; full size pitcher SP $450-600. All are in blue.

TULIP AND CORD

A distinctive and unusual design: the stylized tulips are seen in cameo relief, contrasted against a horizontal ribbed background. Just two shapes in this scarce pattern are depicted in the 1939 Riihimaki catalog. Found in Scandinavia and on display at the Suomen Lasimuseo.

Shapes: creamer and handled mug
Colors: marigold and blue

TURKU ashtray

A marigold *TURKU* ashtray is on display at the Suomen Lasimuseo. A souvenir or commemorative item, it depicts buildings in the city of Turku. The moulded inscription on the ashtray reads "Jubilee of 1229-1929 of the city of Turku. As a souvenir made by O.Y. Riihimaki."[1] The date of 1929 is very interesting as it provides evidence that Riihimaki were making Carnival at that time. There was a major Industrial Fair in the city of Turku in 1929 and, of course, this was one of the factors that caused Riihimaki to begin producing iridized Carnival Glass in 1929.

Shape: ashtray
Color: marigold

5610   **5150**

TULIP AND CORD is known in both these shapes, as depicted in Riihimaki's 1939 catalog.

VICTORIA

Three particularly interesting vases were shown in the Riihimaki 1939 catalog—each is pedestal footed and, until now, they have been considered only as part of the *STARBURST* range of vases. They have the familiar alternate whirling buzz stars and 8-pointed stars within oval medallions. However, they also have a diamond band above a pedestal base and a plain panelled band at the top of the vase. This pedestal footed vase is also depicted in the catalog of the South American glass company, Cristalerias Papini, where it is shown as part of a full range of items named *VICTORIA*, all sharing the same diamond band at the base and plain panelled band at the top (some shapes also have a pedestal foot). The water pitcher illustrated is known in marigold Carnival and the pedestal footed vase (*STARBURST AND DIAMONDS*) is known in blue Carnival. It is very likely that all the other shapes were also produced in iridized glass.

Despite the appearance of this pattern in Papini's catalog, we feel sure that this is a Riihimaki item. Much of the glass illustrated in Papini's catalogs is, in fact, of European manufacture. The trade links between Argentina and European were very strong during the 1930s and indeed, a surprisingly large amount of European Carnival Glass has been found in South America. The *VICTORIA* range was described in Papini's ad as being of high quality lustre and brilliance with the impression of a much more expensive product.

Shapes: water pitcher and pedestal footed vase (actually *STARBURST AND DIAMONDS*). Other items not yet known in Carnival, but illustrated in the above mentioned catalog are: tumbler, plate, jardinière, stemmed compote, stemmed fruit dish, bowl, and handled bonbon.

Colors: marigold and blue

WIDE PANELLED THISTLE see *GRAND THISTLE*

WESTERN THISTLE

A distinctive pattern that has many similarities with *GRAND THISTLE*, though the shapes of the items in the two patterns are

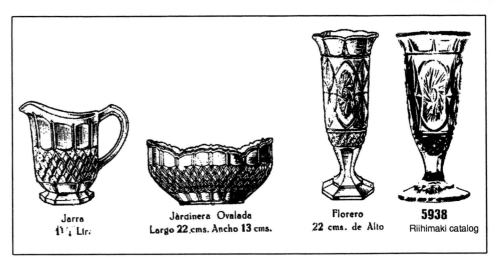

Jarra
1¼ Ltr.

Jardinera Ovalada
Largo 22 cms. Ancho 13 cms.

Florero
22 cms. de Alto

5938
Riihimaki catalog

VICTORIA, as shown in Cristalerias Papini's 1932 catalog—it seems likely that this range was actually made by Riihimaki. From left: pitcher and jardinière in the *VICTORIA* pattern and a *STARBURST AND DIAMONDS* vase—all three as illustrated by Papini. On the right is the *STARBURST AND DIAMONDS* vase as shown in the 1939 Riihimaki catalog (pattern #5938).

very different. The *WESTERN THISTLE* pitcher is quite short and bulbous; the design is deeply incised and gives a dramatic effect. The small vase has a very distinctive, waisted shape. At first glance, one might think that it has been swung from the tumbler shape; close inspection, however, indicates that this is not so. A band of diamonds near the base of the pattern is seen on the vase, pitcher, and tumbler shapes, however others, such as the bowls and the compote, don't have the diamonds. The first tumblers in this pattern were reported in the USA in 1977—the owner said that he had bought them from a collector who had found them in a St. Louis antique shop back in 1969. Other items have since been discovered both in the USA and Scandinavia.

Shapes: pitcher, tumbler, bowls, compote, and vase
Colors: marigold, blue, pink, smoky blue, and amber

Riihimaki's *WESTERN THISTLE* in three different colors. From left: blue tumbler ($250-500), amber pitcher ($500-900), marigold vase ($450-650). Note that these amber and marigold examples have a similar iridescence and overall look—it is only when you hold the item to the light that the amber base color is clearly seen.

Possible Riihimaki Patterns in Carnival Glass

FIR CONES

A design of contrast. The twelve, smooth, angular panels that make up the top and bottom sections of this pattern set off the intricate detail of the fir cone band that encircles the middle section. *FIR CONES* is not illustrated in the 1939 Riihimaki catalog but it is on display at the Suomen Lasimuseo, Riihimaki. Marion Quintin-Baxendale[1] attributes the pattern to Riihimaki and quotes a pattern number; scrutiny of the 1939 Riihimaki catalog, however, reveals that the number quoted (5161) is quite definitely not *FIRCONES*, though the shape of the item is very similar. Therefore, we include the pattern in this section with some reservations as to firm attribution. Found in the USA, Argentina, Australia, and Scandinavia.

Shapes: water pitcher and tumbler

Color: blue

The splendid *FIR CONES* tumbler in blue. *Courtesy of Bob Smith.* SP $450-550.

YAKIMA

This is a variation of Riihimaki's*DRAPERY VARIANT* (see above). Enough of "variations"! This pattern has been called *YAKIMA* after the location in Washington State where it was found by Jeri Sue Lucas. Essentially the same concept as *DRAPERY VARIANT*, there are two main differences. The first is the beading on the ribs between the drapes. The second and most significant, is the intaglio fruit pattern on the base, which is similar in style to the*GOLDEN CUPID* and others. (Note, though, that they are iridized on the intaglio base design yet clear elsewhere, whilst the *YAKIMA* bowl is the reverse— it is marigold on the sides of the bowl but clear on the base.)

Shape: bowl

Color: marigold

Found in Yakima, Washington State, this is the *YAKIMA* bowl. *Courtesy of Jeri Sue Lucas.* NP.

Karhula and Iittala

The glassworks at Iittala was founded in 1881, the glassworks at Karhula was founded eighteen years later in 1899. A few years later, in 1915, the two companies merged to forge a company that was to produce much award-winning glassware. In more recent years (1987) they merged with Nuutajarvi. It is thought that they began producing Carnival Glass during the 1920s.

Signature Characteristics of Both Karhula and Iittala Carnival Glass

- High quality glassware—simple yet sophisticated.
- Ground base on all Karhula and Iittala Carnival.
- Marigold and blue were the main colors used, however, Karhula and Iittala production is characterized by the occasional use of a pink or pinkish lilac shade as a base color.
- Intaglio, "near-cut" geometric designs or stylized florals—all exterior.
- Small output in the form of tumblers, candlesticks, bowls, and vases.
- The quality of iridescence can vary from superb (as seen on most of their Carnival Glass) to some, possibly early examples, where the quality is not quite as good.
- Very small amount of hand finishing on vases to give a variety of different shapes from the same basic model.

Karhula and Iittala Catalogs

The catalogs that contain illustrations of patterns and items known in Carnival Glass are dated 1922, 1932, 1934, and 1938. Though Karhula and Iittala merged in 1915, the catalogs still attribute the glassware to one or the other of the two companies, thus the Carnival Glass listings below follow these attributions. The glass museum at Karhula (Karhula Lasimuseo) has Carnival Glass on display.[1]

Karhula Patterns Known in Carnival Glass

BORDERED PENDANT

BORDERED PENDANT is known only in the tumbler shape that was illustrated in the Karhula catalog dated 1922, where it was given the catalog #4016 (though it was almost certainly not made in Carnival Glass until several years later). It is essentially a very simple design comprising a patterned border from which is "suspended" a simple pendant, all against a smooth, plain background. The tumbler is on display at the Karhula Lasimuseo.

Shape: tumbler
Color: blue

BRITT

Clearly illustrated in the Karhula 1934 catalog are a tumbler and water pitcher in the *BRITT* pattern. The catalog #4041 was given to the tumbler, the tall tankard shaped pitcher was #4642. The pattern is a complex and rather distinctive geometric, based on interlocking, pierced medallions, which fills the shapes on which it is portrayed. The name *BRITT* was given to the tumbler in honor of the late John Britt, well known Carnival Glass researcher and writer. The single example known to date was found in the USA.

Shape: tumbler
Color: blue

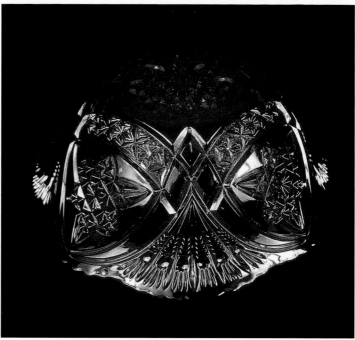

CURVED STAR in yet another variation from Karhula. Note carefully: this marigold bowl has no file on the claws and no stars in the diamond shapes. *Courtesy of Ann and David Brown.* SP $300-500.

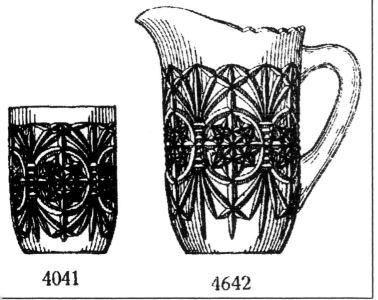

4041   **4642**

The *BRITT* pattern was illustrated in Karhula's 1934 catalog in the shape of both pitcher and tumbler; only the tumbler, however, has so far been reported in Carnival Glass.

CURVED STAR

The 1934 and 1938 Karhula catalogs clearly show bowls, plates, and footed dishes in the *CURVED STAR* pattern very similar to those seen in the Eda Glasbruk's catalogs—however, the Karhula items all have no file pattern within the claw motifs and also no star within the diamond motif. The illustrations clearly show this variation. See Chapter Six on Sweden for full detail in *CURVED STAR*.

Shape: bowl
Color: marigold

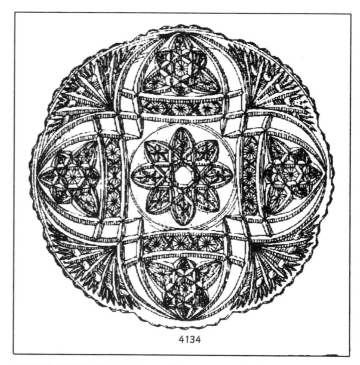

4134

CURVED STAR by Karhula has no file or stars on the claws, as shown in this catalog illustration.

DAVANN

Named after the two British collectors, David and Ann Brown, who reported the first vase in this pattern, *DAVANN* boasts a stylish blend of floral motif and large "cut" diamonds. The flower (possibly a rose) in the pattern is unusual in that at its very center is a perfect square—it draws the eye and captures the attention. The vase that we have studied has pink/amethyst base glass known as lilac, and light amber iridescence—very delicate and very pretty. The metal ware on the *DAVANN* basket, also found by the Browns, is nickel plated and typical of the metal ware used by the Finns (it is known to keep its silver color well and show little signs of age). The pattern is illustrated in the Karhula 1934 catalog. Found in Sweden.

Shapes: vase and small handled basket

Color: lilac (pink/amethyst)

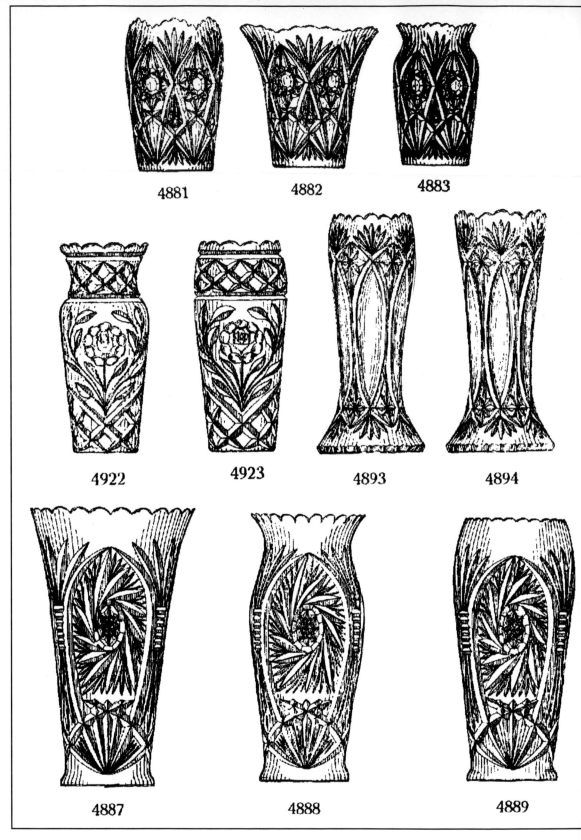

4881   4882   4883

4922   4923   4893   4894

4887   4888   4889

Karhula made several superb vases in Carnival Glass. Top row: three shapes in the *STARLIGHT* pattern. Middle row, left: two shapes in the *DAVANN* pattern; right: two shapes in the *NORA* pattern. Bottom row: three shapes in the *SPINNING STAR* pattern.

A metal ware basket from Finland, this pattern has been named *DAVANN* after the British collectors who reported the first examples: Ann and David Brown. SP $100-150.

KARHULA PEAKS

This pattern (un-named) was reported in the Carnival Glass Society (UK) Newsletter in February 1996. At the time, it was un-known and the maker of the oval bowl that had been found was not determined. However, the pattern is illustrated in the Karhula 1934 catalog in the form of a sugar bowl, creamer. and a metal ware handled basket.

> Shape: oval bowl
> Color: marigold

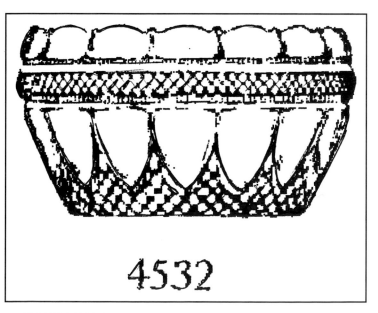

4532

KARHULA PEAKS was featured in Karhula's 1934 catalog—an oval bowl is known in this pattern.

HOBSTAR AND SHIELD

This is a distinctive and scarce pattern that is only known in the water pitcher and tumbler shape. Examples have been found as far apart as France, the USA, Australia, and Argentina—yet what un-doubtedly appears to be the same pattern is shown on bowls that are illustrated in the Karhula 1934 catalog.

> Shapes: water pitcher and tumbler
> Colors: marigold and blue

NORA

Clearly depicted in the Karhula 1934 catalog (pattern #4893/4) are two variations of the *NORA* vase. The pattern is distinctive owing to the elongated ovals that form the greater part of the pattern. Fan and star motifs occupy the remainder of the de-sign.

> Shape: vase
> Color: marigold

ORNATE BEADS

Karhula made sev-eral candlestick patterns, at least one of which was iridized. This item was shown in the 1922 and the 1934 catalogs as #4863. A pair of *ORNATE BEADS* candlesticks are on display at the Karhula Lasimuseo.

> Shape: candlestick
> Color: blue

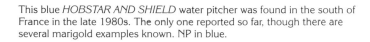

This blue *HOBSTAR AND SHIELD* water pitcher was found in the south of France in the late 1980s. The only one reported so far, though there are several marigold examples known. NP in blue.

QUILTED PANELS

QUILTED PANELS is known only in the tumbler shape illus-trated in the 1922 Karhula catalog (#4020), though it was probably not made in Carnival Glass until several years later. The pattern is rather distinctive—adjacent oval panels have a crossed effect, above them is a scrolled border. An example is on display at the Karhula Lasimuseo.

> Shape: tumbler
> Color: marigold

SPINNING STAR

A dramatic, large spinning buzz star is the main design motif on this intaglio pattern. Contained within a large oval, the stars are flanked by fans. Known in the vase shape only, as depicted in the 1934 Karhula cata-log. There are three shape variations reported (catalog #4887, #4888, #4889)—the tops may be flared, waisted, or incurved. All three ex-amples are on display at the Karhula Lasimuseo. A single example is on display at the Suomen Lasimuseo at Riihimaki. Found in Scandinavia.

> Shape: vase
> Color: blue

Karhula's *ORNATE BEADS* candlestick.

4863

STARBURST MEDALLIONS

A wonderfully impressive intaglio design, the main motif is a huge spinning star, flanked by intricate hobstars. Three *STARBURST MEDALLION* bowls were depicted in the Karhula catalog from 1934 (#4363, #4364, and # 4365). Examples have been found in Finland and Sweden.

    Shape: bowl
    Color: blue

This splendid *STARBURST MEDALLIONS* bowl has been identified through its appearance in the Karhula 1934 catalog. *Courtesy of Ann and David Brown.* SP $150-400.

STARLIGHT

It really is difficult to keep track of all the "Star" patterns. If only those who named them had been a little more inventive! Here is another vase with a very distinctive intaglio, geometric pattern. As with the *SPINNING STAR* vase, Karhula made three different vase shapes—incurving, flared, and waisted (catalog #4881, #4882, and #4883)—that are depicted in the Karhula 1934 catalog.

    Shape: vase
    Color: marigold

SVEA – see previous entries for Riihimaki and Eda Glasbruk

VERTICAL STAR PANELS

Illustrated in the Karhula catalogs of 1922 and 1934 and bearing the number 4670, this pattern features upright panels each separated by a line of star motifs. A lidded bonbon in this pattern is on display at the Karhula Lasimuseo.

    Shape: lidded bonbon
    Color: blue

Iittala Patterns Known in Carnival Glass

DIAMOND OVALS

This is a simple geometric design composed of fans and large, distinctive ovals (the latter filled with a diamond file motif). Shown in the 1922 Iittala catalog only in the shape of a small creamer (#4535) and stemmed open sugar (#4534). However, a very wide range of shapes in this pattern (all known in Carnival) were also illustrated in the Rindskopf catalog dating around the same time and, based on other characteristics, it seems most likely that the Carnival Glass examples of this pattern were all produced by Rindskopf. Indeed the upright stem of the sugar bowl (compote) on the Iittala illustration does not have the curving shape that the known Carnival items possess. See Chapter Five on Czechoslovakia for full information on this pattern.

4670

The lidded bonbon *VERTICAL STAR PANELS* depicted in Karhula's catalog.

IITTALA PEACOCK aka *SLEWED HORSESHOE*

Here is another pattern that has a fascinating connection between the USA and Scandinavia. Illustrated in the United States Glass 1919 Export catalog was a range of bowls plus a table set called the "Peacock Pattern," catalog #15111. In Iittala's 1922 catalog, a large and a small bowl were illustrated in exactly the same pattern (catalog #4333). As this is such an intricate intaglio design, featuring fans, complex star motifs and more, it is unlikely that Iittala would have made a new mould. It is far more likely that some of the moulds were sold by the United States Glass Company to Iittala. In 1996, a blue Carnival bowl in this pattern and made by Iittala appeared at the Air Capital Convention. Some examples are known with the word IITTALA marked on the interior.

Shape: bowl
Color: blue

QUILTED FANS

An open candy dish in a geometric design composed of fan shapes and diamond file, this piece is on display at the Suomen Lasimuseo at Riihimaki. *QUILTED FANS* is depicted in the 1922 Iittala catalog, #1820. The item has the letters IITTALA moulded into it.

Shape: candy dish
Color: blue

YORK

It is important to note that the 1938 Iittala catalog clearly shows vases in the *YORK* pattern identical to those seen in the Eda Glasbruk's catalogs. We know that *YORK* was produced in Carnival at Eda Glasbruk circa 1925 to 1929. Almost certainly the moulds were sold by Eda to Iittala during the 1930s. It is impossible to say with certainty that the pattern was produced by Iittala in Carnival.

IITTALA PEACOCK was originally a United States Glass pattern—however, this illustration is from the Iittala 1922 catalog. The bowl was made in blue Carnival by the Finns.

1820

This *QUILTED FANS* dish was one of three sizes illustrated in Iittala's 1922 catalog.

Possible Finnish Carnival Glass Patterns

The "GOLDEN" Designs

There are a number of reasons why the following patterns are included in the Finnish section. Although we cannot be certain as to the manufacturer of the following items, we feel that they may well be Scandinavian. We know that the mould for *DIANA THE HUNTRESS* was in the hands of Eda Glasbruks in 1914, but we can find no record of that factory's production of the item at a later date. It is known that moulds changed hands between the Scandinavian manufacturers on several occasions and thus it is highly probable that the *DIANA* mould was bought from Eda by a Finnish concern. Also, similar items with what appear to be intaglio bases are depicted in the Finnish Karhula-Iittala catalogs from the 1920s and 1930s. However the main reason for our current suggestion that they are probably Finnish, is the reported discovery of a *GOLDEN PANSY* in pink base glass with marigold iridized pansies in 1980. Finland was the main European country to manufacture iridized pink base glass.

Finally, scarce examples of the grouping listed below have been found primarily in two areas—Australia and the UK, with other examples turning up in the USA—all are known to have imported other items of Finnish Carnival.

The mouldwork on this *DIANA THE HUNTRESS* bowl
indicates high quality craftsmanship. SP $800-1000.

• *DIANA THE HUNTRESS* and the *GOLDEN CUPID*

DIANA THE HUNTRESS is found on scarce bowls only and is a truly magnificent example of mouldmaking. The main part of the piece is clear crystal of high quality and polish, with a moulded geometric panelled motif around the sides. The main design features Diana the huntress, the Roman goddess of the woods and mother of creatures. She is portrayed in the traditional manner, accompanied by a stag and equipped with bow and arrow, for she is the archer whose arrow never fails. The design is intaglio on the base of the bowl, in relief, and moulded to different depths. Thus, the golden

GOLDEN CUPID is found on a smaller bowl than *DIANA THE HUNT-RESS*—it has the same high quality. SP $275-325.

iridescence takes on many shades and nuances of pink and gold when viewed from the top side of the bowl. The effect is breathtaking, the detail of the figure and the drapes of her robe are quite superb.

This pattern was illustrated in the Oskar Hallberg catalog in 1914, where other Eda Glasbruks items were shown: however, it is impossible to state with certainty that it was made in the iridized form at Eda. Since *DIANA* has been found in Scandinavia, it does give weight to the supposition that the item is from that area. To add to the inconclusiveness, though, a non-iridized *GOLDEN CUPID* has been found bearing a paper sticker that states "Made in Poland."

DIANA has been found along with several small "matching" crystal bowls known as *GOLDEN CUPID*. These smaller bowls were part of a full berry set and are fashioned in the same manner as *DIANA THE HUNTRESS*. They feature winged creatures armed with bows and arrows and are probably not actually "cupids" but are more likely acolytes of the hunting goddess. Other variations of the cupids have been found—a lute playing version is also known as well as one chasing butterflies. Similar patterns abound. In Australia, several full sets in cardboard boxes, consisting of the large *DIANA* bowl and six or more small *CUPIDS* have been discovered over the past twenty-some years. Partial sets have also been found in the UK and the USA.

Shape: master bowl and small berry bowls
Color: marigold and crystal combination.

• *GOLDEN CARP*

In the style of the *GOLDEN CUPID* and similar items, this delightful item features a large carp—intaglio and iridized—on the base of a crystal bowl. It is quite possible that these are Eda items, as suggested in the chapter on Swedish production, though they do not feature in any of that company's catalogs, yet similar items are also shown in Finnish catalogs. A range of similar items, with iridized, intaglio patterns on the base, is documented. All have very detailed and skillful intaglio mould work. A wide variety of examples have been found in the USA, the UK, and Australia.

Shape: oval dish
Color: marigold and crystal combination.

The *GOLDEN CARP* is found on the oval dish shape, which fits the fish perfectly. *Courtesy of Carolyn and Paul Walkden.* SP $275-325.

• *GOLDEN PANSY* (and *EUREKA CROSS*)

There are two variations on this theme. One features a single pansy on the intaglio design, the other features a stylized grouping of four pansies in a "wheel" formation, their stems meeting in the very center—this latter has also been called *EUREKA CROSS*. Found in Australia and the UK.

Shapes: small plates, large and small bowls, and a flat dresser tray
Colors: marigold and crystal combination as well as marigold and pink base glass (rare).

GOLDEN PANSY is shown here on a small plate. SP $75-125.

• *GOLDEN PINEAPPLE AND BLACKBERRIES*

A grouping of fruits is the pattern feature on these "golden" items. Found in Australia and the UK.

Shapes: bowls and plates in various shapes and sizes
Color: marigold and crystal

• *GOLDEN THISTLE*

As with the *PANSY* items, these are found with a single (two flowered) thistle sprig as well as in a stylized grouping. Found in Australia and the UK.

Shapes: small bowls, plates, and large oval tray
Color: marigold and crystal

• *LEDA AND THE SWAN* aka *GOOSE GIRL/BOY*

Another delightful variation, this time featuring a classical figure. Found in Australia, UK, and the USA.

Shape: small bowl
Colors: marigold and crystal

EUROPEAN POPPY

This pattern is currently known in scarce examples of small and large bowls as well as a butter dish. The design is a combination of hobstars and intaglio flowers, but its most unusual feature is the repeated "Star of David" 6-sided, geometrical shape that is found on its base and within the pattern itself. The pattern is exterior on the bowls, the interior having the *HEADDRESS* pattern (see below). On the butter dish, the pattern is inside the lid and around the outside of the base. The butter dish has a distinctive, 6-sided knob top. A significant fact is that the butter dish is known in amber, a typical (though scarce) color used by Riihimaki. Thus we strongly suspect that Riihimaki could have been the manufacturer. Note that the floral motif is a poppy, a flower native to northern latitudes (Iceland Poppy). *EUROPEAN POPPY* has been found in the UK, Ireland, and Australia.

Shapes: bowls and butter dish
Colors: marigold, blue, light honey amber, and deep amber

HEADDRESS

This pattern is the interior design on the *EUROPEAN POPPY* bowls. It is one of several variations of the pattern, which is also found on Brockwitz *CURVED STAR* items. Very possibly it was utilized by several different manufacturers, indeed, it was originally used in the USA on Classic Carnival by the United States Glass Company. See Chapter Three on Brockwitz for more detail.

Shape; bowl
Colors: blue and light honey-amber

KARVE

A tulip pattern, stylized and deeply incised on the smooth glass, is the main feature of this design. Two examples of this unusual vase were found in Sweden by Ann and David Brown in 1999. The base glass is a delicate, pale, pinky lilac with a most distinctive, light brown, taffy-like iridescence. The overall effect is very similar to both the iridescence and the style of the *DAVANN* items that are shown in the Karhula catalog, so we are cautiously attributing it to Finland.

Shape: vase
Color: pale lilac

WESTERN SUNFLOWER

First illustrated in the HOACGA Pattern sheets on vases (issued in 2000), this cylinder vase with a distinctive high-waisted shape has many similarities with the *KARVE* and *DAVANN* items. The base color is a pale pinky, amber and the iridescence has the same shiny toffee effect. The deep intaglio pattern features a stylized daisy (sunflower) and is similar in style to both the aforementioned patterns. Indeed, it also has a diamond effect around the lower part of the vase that is similar to the diamonds on *DAVANN*.

Shape: vase
Color: pale amber-lilac

[1] Marion Quintin-Baxendale, *Collecting Carnival Glass* (London, England: Francis Joseph, 1998).

EUROPEAN POPPY has an intriguing blend of stylized floral and geometric motifs. This example is blue—also known is a pale, almost honey-amber example that is not quite marigold yet not quite amber, found in England by Sue and Ray McLaren. A deeper amber butter dish is known in this pattern. *Courtesy of Carol and Derek Sumpter.* SP $150-300.

The base glass is a pale pinkish amethyst and the iridescence is a taffy-like gold on this scarce *KARVE* vase. SP $200-400.

Chapter Eight

Puzzles

Many puzzles remain. The very nature of Europe in particular, with its recent political upheavals, has caused many records to be lost or destroyed. Some of the puzzling Carnival items will probably never be attributed to a maker. Some of the makers can be guessed at, based on common characteristics, but some items defy attribution. Below are listed most of the remaining patterns that we are aware of—most of them are almost certainly European. For this reason, we have placed this listing immediately following the chapters on Europe. However, the reader should be aware that the origins of the following "puzzle" patterns are still not proven and thus some could be from outside Europe—indeed, several items are listed that are quite possibly of Argentinean manufacture.

ARCHES AND WHIRLING STAR

Only one example of this attractive 6" high vase has so far been recorded. Found (and named) by Steve and Trudy Auty in the UK, *ARCHES AND WHIRLING STAR* is an Intaglio pattern bearing a most striking design. Four large, deeply incised arches form the main motif, bordered by whirling stars. The base is ground. The style and overall concept of the vase suggests that it is either a Brockwitz or a Scandinavian product (possibly Finnish).

Shape: vase
Color: marigold

ARCHES AND WHIRLING STAR is only known in the form of this marigold vase. No doubt other examples will one day appear. *Courtesy of Trudy and Steve Auty.* SP $150-400.

ART DECO

Not a very apt name for this rather plain pattern with a small, scroll motif on a plain background. It is of great interest, however, that a creamer in this pattern bearing a paper label with a trademark was found by Wayne Delahoy in Australia. The label clearly stated that the item was made in Germany; the other information was simply JRIS. This is currently under investigation; should any reader have any information that might help, we would be delighted to hear from them. Found in the USA, UK, and Australia.

Shapes: bowls and creamer
Color: marigold

AUCKLAND see SPEARS AND DIAMONDS

CHARIOT

A stemmed compote or sugar is known in this pattern. The design is an intaglio geometric on the exterior, very typical of European Carnival. Mainly found in the UK.

Shape: stemmed sugar
Color: marigold

CHECKERBOARD PANELS aka ZIPPER ROUND

An interesting exterior geometric that is not often found, this is almost certainly a European item. Examples have been found in the UK.

Shape: oval bowl
Color: marigold

DAISY AND SCROLL

A stylized pattern featuring a flower and a flowing scroll motif inset with beads, this intriguing design has not yet been attributed with certainty to a manufacturer. Found in Argentina and Australia, the shape of the small glasses in this pattern echo the Art Deco shape of those in the Finnish pattern *GRAND THISTLE*. However, it is likely that this style was simply copied, as the circumstantial evidence and the signature characteristics of the glass actually suggest Argentinean manufacture.

Shapes: decanter and glasses
Color: marigold

FINE CUT RINGS

FINE CUT RINGS is a scarce Carnival pattern that is found (mainly in the UK) in a footed celery vase and a cake stand or salver. The pattern is fairly plain—an encircling band of medallions (plain or file patterned) above vertical plain and beaded panels; its significance lies in the fact that all examples we have studied bear the moulded UK registration number 704493. According to the British Patent Office records researched by Janet Mollison in the UK, this was registered on the 25th of March, 1924 by M & J Guggenheim Ltd., of London. A full range of shapes was shown, but only one or two are known in Carnival. The question remains, however: did Guggenheim manufacture the glass? Notley states in his *Shire Album*[1] that although the

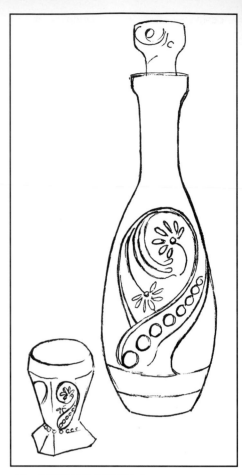

The *DAISY AND SCROLL* decanter and tiny shot glass may well have been made in Argentina.

FINE CUT RINGS was illustrated in the British *Pottery Gazette* in 1928 in a variant of the design where the rings are plain and not filled with the "fine cut" motif. Clearly seen on the illustration was the Registered Number, proudly written on the side of the celery vase—RD 704493. M & J Guggenheim were the promoters of the glass shown, but did they make it or merely market it? The latter seems the likely answer.

design was registered by Guggenheim, the *FINE CUT RINGS* items were made for them by Leerdam in Holland. However, 1928 British *Pottery Gazette* ads for Guggenheim illustrate the *FINE CUT RINGS* celery vase and state "M & J Guggenheim Ltd., Manufacturers of Table Glass"—it also states that they were agents too. So who made it? Study of the Leerdam catalogs did not reveal the pattern, in fact it has many of the characteristics of Rindskopf's Carnival Glass. For now, however, the maker must remain uncertain.

Shapes: celery vase, footed cake stand (salver)
Color: marigold

FIRCONE

This is a particularly spectacular and rare vase. Words which look like "COTY" and "FRANCE" are moulded into its base. It is an impressive item, large and heavy, patterned with deeply moulded fircones and foliage. Research continues into the identity of the manufacturer.

Shape: vase.
Color: marigold.

The *FIRCONE* vase is still a mystery. France is the likely country of origin, but who made it? Various other small Carnival items marked "Made in France" have surfaced, though none possess the imposing beauty of this vase. *Courtesy of Charles and Jeanette Echols.* NP.

FLORAL FROST

A single example of this splendid pattern, found in the UK, is known in the form of a large chop plate. The pattern is all exterior though, owing to the clever design, can be seen to best advantage from the front of the plate. A stylized motif, featuring various different flowers, is found on the center of the base—it is ground flat and frosted. Encircling it is a wide marigold band that features a moulded design bearing a resemblance to Brockwitz *MOONPRINT*.

Shape: chop plate
Color: marigold and frosted

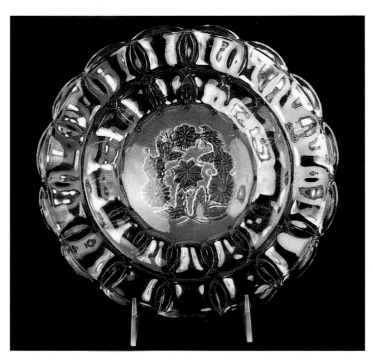

A delightful contrast of rich marigold iridescence and white, acid etched "frosting" appears on this *FLORAL FROST* chop plate. Manufacturer unknown. NP.

The "GODDESS" EPERGNES

These are impressive Art Nouveau style epergnes that share a common style and similar iridized glass. These epergnes have been found as far apart as the United States and Australia. All have in common the same *PEACOCK TAIL* style pattern on the glass.

• GODDESS OF ATHENA

"Breathtaking" is the only word to describe this magnificent, statuesque item—a blend of metalwork and iridized glassware. The goddess is fashioned in metal, and perched above her head is a large, shallow, glass bowl out of which rises the epergne lily. At the bottom of the figure are two smaller glass bowls. The glass is beautifully iridized with a *PEACOCK TAIL* pattern. The peacock tail motif and moulded beadwork, both interior and exterior, match perfectly. Few examples are known and all have been found in the USA. The late Rose Presznick sketched this beauty for her books and later auctioned it in March 1973, when it sold for $1250. At that time it was believed that only three examples were known.

A fascinating "story to be told" lies behind the wonderful *GODDESS OF ATHENA* that is illustrated. Collectors Elaine and Fred Blair had been collecting for only a few years when they saw an ad in the

Antique Trader for an old issue of *Woman's Day* magazine that had a good Carnival Glass article. Elaine called about purchasing the magazine and struck up a conversation with the seller, Ted Parent. She reports that "He was so enthusiastic about Carnival Glass. He had been a long-time collector. He'd known Carnival Glass pioneer, Rose Presznick, well and was the last 'distributor' of her books. When all the pieces in her museum were auctioned March of 1973, he purchased what she told him was her 'favorite' piece, the *GODDESS OF ATHENA* epergne. (The auction brochure stated that there were only three known at that time.) Ted was in the process of selling his collection, and the *GODDESS* was one of his last pieces to part with. He had carried it with him to display at conventions for years. By the end of our conversation, he offered to sell the *GODDESS*. Because we were fairly new collectors, he knew we would treasure such a special piece as the shining-star of our beginning collection! Presznick's museum sticker is still on the piece, number 262."

Shape: epergne
Colors: amber and green

The amazing *GODDESS OF ATHENA* epergne. Exquisitely detailed and magnificent in her symmetry, this fabulous blend of metalwork and iridized glass is shown here courtesy of Elaine and Fred Blair. Note the Presznick auction sticker from 1973 still on the lily. *Photo Copyright Rick McDaniel.*

• DESERT GODDESS

The *DESERT GODDESS* is a magnificent Art Nouveau style centerpiece, This rare epergne is marked *WMF* for Württembergische Metallwarenfabrik of Geislingen, Germany, founded in 1883 and known for its fine silver plated metal and glassware. The centerpiece was found in Nevada, and has thus been aptly named *DESERT GODDESS* by April and Ron Duncan. It stands almost 22" tall and is 19" long and 7" wide. It features a classical female figure standing on a pedestal in front of a palm tree. The figure is executed in silver plated pewter and has great detail, right down to her hands with fingers and thumbs separated. The branches and leaves of the tree fan out over the figure, and rising above it all is the iridized green *PEACOCK TAIL* style bowl and epergne lily.

WMF report that the centerpiece was called "Tilly" and was featured in their catalogs in 1898. All the company's metal ware was stamped WMF. According to their representative, Thomas Dix, customers could choose between various different glass inserts. The company produced most of their own glassware, though they cannot be certain that the *"PEACOCK TAIL"* glass featured in the Duncan's "Tilly" was made by them, as it is not the glass depicted in WMF'S 1898 catalog Illustration. Currently, therefore, though the provenance of the metal centerpiece is fully documented, the manufacturer of the glass remains uncertain.

Shape: epergne
Color: green

• GRECIAN GODDESS

The same green *PEACOCK TAIL* glassware links this delightful item with the two previous examples. The *GRECIAN GODDESS* glass bowl is supported by an Art Nouveau style female figure in metalware.

Shape: epergne
Color: green

GOLDFISH

This is an unusual item, which is seldom seen. A large, stylized fish, surrounded by waves and bubbles, is intaglio on the wide base of this bowl. The only shape in which it is known is a 7" bowl that was made from a one-piece mould. This was quite possibly intended for serving sardines and similar small fish. Found in the UK.

Shape: bowl
Color: marigold

The *GOLDFISH* bowl would not win prizes for being the prettiest piece of Carnival Glass—however, it certainly is an unusual item. SP $30-60.

LUCILE

This splendid intaglio geometric was named in honor of Lucile Britt, long time collector and wife of the late John Britt. The pattern was originally produced by the Indiana Glass Company of Dunkirk, Indiana. They called it "Prosperity" (Kamm also named it "Ferris Wheel") and advertised it in the Butler Brothers catalogs circa 1909 in crystal and ruby flashed crystal. It is very unlikely that Indiana produced Carnival Glass at that time—a much more likely eventuality is that the moulds were sold. But to whom? The maker of this rare and lovely pattern in Carnival Glass is still a mystery. It could be European or it could be Argentinean. (For further information, see Chapter Nine on Argentina.) Examples have been found in the USA, Argentina, and Australia.

Shapes: water pitcher and tumbler
Colors: blue and marigold

MY LADY'S POWDER BOWL

This is known in marigold and in this delightful boudoir item only. The style is pure Art Deco—a female figurine with flowing tresses and gown forms the finial handle. The maker has not yet been determined. Examples have been found in the USA, UK, and Australia.

Shape: powder bowl
Color: marigold

LUCILE is a geometric design of great complexity. Equally complex is its history—who made it? $175-275.

A splendid example of Art Deco style, the figure that forms the finial on *MY LADY'S POWDER BOWL* is shown here both from the back and the front.

PINEAPPLE AND FAN

The "pineapple" in the pattern is a diamond checkered effect that looks akin to the outer peel of the pineapple fruit: the fan is an old favorite, a simple, intaglio fan motif. Rare examples of this pattern have been found in the USA, though by its appearance and shape, it would appear to be of European or Argentinean manufacture. The late Don Moore featured it in a "Carnival Cameo"[2] in 1983 and suggested that it was European, since a complete cordial set had been found in a US shop that specialized in European imports. However, a virtually identical pattern was shown in the United States Glass Company's Domestic catalog in 1909,[3] where it was given the number 15041 and was described as a "Strawberry and Fan" design. Several patterns that were illustrated in that 1909 catalog have been found in Carnival Glass in Argentina: the *STATES, REGAL, MANHATTAN* to name just a few. So, was *PINEAPPLE AND FAN* a U. S. Glass Co. product, or did one of the Argentinean glass companies perhaps buy the mould or copy the design and make it themselves? For more information, see Chapter Nine on Argentina.

Shapes: tumble-up with under plate, wine decanter, and wine glass
Color: marigold

ROSE AND DRAPE.

Currently known in the vase shape only; we are aware of only two or three examples. One is a superb marigold vase, standing 7.5" high, with a 3" diameter base—another is a diminutive treasure standing only 3.5" high (with a 2" diameter base). The vase is panelled with a central, draped band containing roses. These are exquisite

vases; their quality of manufacture is very apparent. Who actually made them is currently unknown, though we feel they may well be Czechoslovakian. Found in the UK and Australia.

Shape: vase
Color: marigold

ROSE PANELS

This large, heavy compote is fairly easily found in the UK, yet the manufacturer has not yet been determined. The simple and rather plain exterior pattern features rose and star motifs in adjacent panels.

Shape: compote
Color: marigold

SPEARS AND DIAMONDS aka AUCKLAND

A geometric patterned vase that features spear-like notches and deep grooves. Found in New Zealand (hence its name), though almost certainly of European manufacture. Also found in the UK.

Shape: vase
Color: marigold

STAR AND FAN

A decanter and cordials have been found in Argentina in this pattern. The maker has been suggested to be European, though Argentinean manufacturers also produced several decanter sets in similar styles to this one. Note that the *CURVED STAR* vase has been termed *STAR AND FAN* in the past.

Shapes: decanter, cordials, and undertray
Color: marigold

STAR MEDALLION AND FAN

Another puzzle pattern that has all the characteristics of European manufacture, yet has not yet been traced in a catalog. An exterior, intaglio star pattern found in the UK.

Shape: bowl
Color: marigold

STARSTRUCK

Known in the shape of a small bowl with a plain interior and exterior, relieved only by several small stars at intervals around the outer rim. Possibly European.

Shape: bowl
Color: blue

This rich blue *STARSTRUCK* bowl is surely the product of a European Carnival manufacturer. *Courtesy of Frank and Shirley.* NP

A high quality product with a classically simple design, *ROSE AND DRAPE* is only known in the form of rare marigold vases. This example stands some 7.5" high. SP. $200-400.

WIDE PANEL AND DIAMOND

WIDE PANEL AND DIAMOND is currently known in a single example of a black amethyst vase, standing 6.25" high. It bears a striking similarity to the *SOWERBY DRAPE* vase both in color and design style. Found in the UK.

    Shape: vase
    Color: black amethyst

ZIPPER STITCH

Back in 1983 this set was featured by the late Don Moore[2]. At the time he suggested that it was Czechoslovakian. Indeed, this is quite likely though another possibility is that it was made in Argentina. The pattern is very distinctive and bold—each item is panelled and the zigzags of the zipper motif are diagonal across each of the panels. Two different stoppers have been reported paired with the decanter: one short, the other taller and pointed. The matching undertray to the set is 12-sided and has a 24-point star on its base. Complete *ZIPPER STITCH* cordial sets have been found in Argentina and the USA.

    Shapes: decanter, cordials, and undertray
    Color: marigold

[1] Raymond Notley, *Carnival Glass* (Princes Risborough, England: Shire Publications, 1990).

[2] Donald Moore, *Carnival Glass, A Collection of Writings* (Alameda, California: by author, 1983).

[3] William Heacock and Fred Bickenheuser, *Encyclopedia of Victorian Colored Pattern Glass Book 5, U.S. Glass From A to Z* (Marietta, Ohio: Antique Publications, 1978).

Currently the only reported example of *WIDE PANEL AND DIAMOND*— there must surely be others—this vase stands a little over 6" high. The maker is a mystery. NP.

ZIPPER STITCH is a splendidly effective geometric design.

Chapter Nine

Argentina

Argentina, under Spanish rule until the early 1800s, began to witness large scale European immigration and British investment from around the 1880s. This helped to develop a flourishing economy, though the years of the Depression ended that prosperity, in common with the rest of the World. The links with Europe, however, remained strong. Argentina's capital city of Buenos Aires was the location of the country's Carnival Glass manufacturers, most of who had originally been founded as glass bottle and container manufacturers. The European connections were a strong influence on the way in which Carnival Glass production developed in Argentina. The country had imported much glassware from Europe but as the Depression began to bite, the glass companies cut back on their imports and began to produce their own glass. Carnival from Europe had been imported during the latter part of the 1920s and early 1930s; in an effort to save costs, however, the glassworks in Argentina tried their hand at producing the glass (including Carnival) themselves. It is interesting to note that the main colors used for Carnival produced in Argentina are the same colors used for Finnish Carnival—mari-

gold, blue, and amber. Other colors used by the Argentinean manufacturers, though very rarely, were purple and green.

Firms in the United States, Germany, Czechoslovakia, and Scandinavia all had offices in Argentina. One London agent, R. Johnston and Co. Ltd., imported glassware from Sweden and Bohemia into England and then exported it on to Argentina. As well as importing actual glassware from Scandinavia and mainland Europe, the Argentinean factories also brought in moulds and glass from the USA. The United States Glass Company in particular, had catalogs specifically for the South American market. Many rare and beautiful examples of European Carnival have been found in Argentina, side by side with Carnival actually manufactured in Argentina itself. Some scarce United States Glass Company Carnival has also been found in Argentina, though the possibility remains that some of it may actually have been made in Argentina using old U.S. Glass moulds. It is very likely that many more Carnival items will be discovered in Argentina; collecting is in its infancy there, but as interest grows, many more patterns are sure to be found.

Some agents imported glassware from the European mainland into England and then exported it on to South America. This British *Pottery Gazette* ad from the 1920s shows one of the ferry services that would probably have been used.

Argentinean Catalogs

Catalogs used to attribute Carnival Glass patterns to Cristalerias Papini and Cristalerias Piccardo were sourced by Bob Smith. The Cristalerias Papini catalogs are dated 1932-33 and 1933-34. Cristalerias Piccardo is dated 1934. Iridized items are described as *Articulos Anacarados O Irisados* (iridescent or "mother of pearl" items); articles also described as *prensados* (lustrous) and *iris* (rainbow) were probably also iridized.

Cristalerias Rigolleau S.A.

This company was located in Berazategui, Buenos Aires and was founded around the turn of the twentieth century by a Frenchman, Leon Rigolleau. They did not produce a large amount of Carnival Glass, but their items are distinctive and attractive.

Signature Characteristics of Cristalerias Rigolleau Carnival Glass

- Quality of glass and iridescence varies.
- Carnival colors were blue, marigold, amber, and rare green.
- Novelty designs often with lettering (commemorative or advertising).
- Individual items (ashtrays), possibly for commercial customers as promotional lines.

Cristalerias Rigolleau Patterns Known in Carnival Glass

BEETLE ASHTRAY

This is a round, 5.5" diameter ashtray with eight beetle shapes arranged in a ring around the center. The words "Cristalerias Rigolleau. Buenos Aires" surround the very center, where "Sociedad Anonima Usinas En Berazategui F.C.S." is written (Note: the lettering translates to mean "Limited Liability Company of Berazategui," the location of Rigolleau's factory.) All the words are moulded in the design. Wily Adis found an example of this ashtray in an antique shop in Columbus, Ohio, in 1968. His subsequent research[1] and correspondence with Cristalerias Rigolleau gave rise to the following note from Carlos Righetti, the General Manager of the factory at the time: "This company did in fact make this piece of glass strictly as a souvenir piece that was given to special customers." Examples of this rare ashtray have been found in the USA and Argentina.
   Shape: novelty ashtray
   Colors: blue and amber

The splendid amber *BEETLE ASHTRAY* was made by Cristalerias Rigolleau in Argentina. NP.

"C.R." ASHTRAY

A most unusual novelty in Carnival Glass, this splendid item is fashioned into the shape of the letters C and R (representing the Cristalerias Rigolleau company). This must be the only Carnival Glass piece that is actually in the shape of the initial letters of the company who made it! On the "C" part the words "Cristalerias Rigolleau S. A." are moulded. The "R" has "Paseo Colon 800 Buenos Aires" on it. Found in the USA and Argentina.

Shape: novelty ashtray
Colors: marigold, amber, blue, and rare green

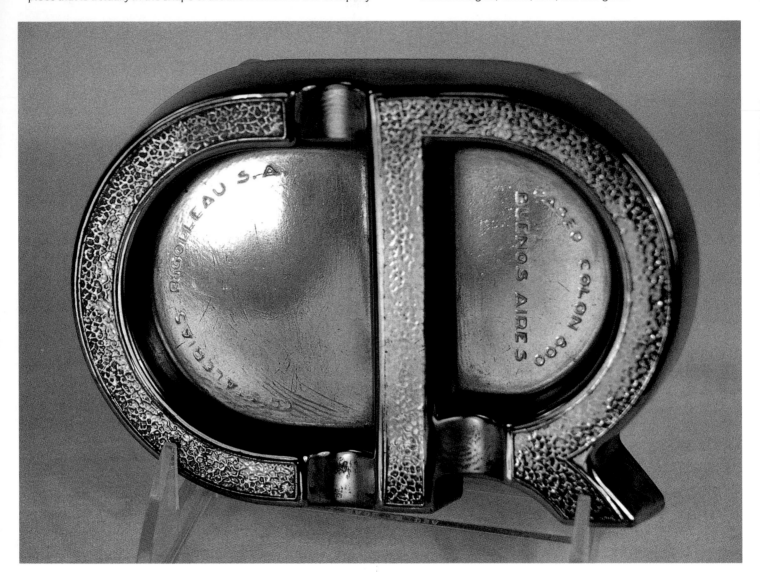

Surely the only Carnival Glass item that is actually in the shape of the initial letters of the company that made it? This is the green *C.R. ASHTRAY* by Cristalerias Rigolleau—the first reported in this color. The iridescence is deep and rich, showing purples and dark green shades and the lettering can be clearly read (see text for details). SP $350-500.

The back view of the green *C.R. ASHTRAY* clearly shows its unusual base color.

Cristalerias Papini (also called Cristalux S. A.)

This factory was located in Buenos Aires and, according to their catalogs, was founded in 1896. Their trademark was Cristalux and they used the phrase INDUSTRIA ARGENTINA on their advertising. Cristalerias Papini imported glass from Europe. In the introduction to their 1933-34 catalog, Papini explained to their customers that as the price of imported glassware was increasing, they were therefore starting to increase their range of homemade goods. However, a good number of European articles remained. On the cover of their 1933-34 catalog is a *JACOBEAN (RANGER)* vase that is identical to that produced by Inwald of Czechoslovakia. Other items also appear to be from Inwald; in particular, the *CORONET* (aka *PRINCETON*) vase is depicted in the catalog. A stemmed compote in the Brockwitz *TARTAN* pattern is also evident. A range of Riihimaki items in the *VICTORIA* (see *STARBURST* and *STARBURST AND DIAMONDS*) pattern was also depicted. A massive compote and a smaller bowl in the *CURVED STAR* pattern are illustrated too. There is no evidence to suggest that Papini made these patterns and, given the vast amount of known European items illustrated in their catalogs, we believe that the *CURVED STAR, JACOBEAN, TARTAN, VICTORIA, STARBURST AND DIAMONDS*, and *CORONET* items illustrated were almost certainly European imports. However, Cristalerias Papini did make some of its own Carnival Glass. Today the company is known as Cristalux S.A., and their main office is still in Buenos Aires. They are a primary glass manufacturer producing mainly domestic glassware, barware, bottles, and containers.

Signature Characteristics of Cristalerias Papini Carnival Glass

- Quality of glass and iridescence varies.
- Carnival colors were marigold and blue.
- Much European Carnival imported and sold by this company.

Cristalerias Papini Patterns Known in Carnival Glass

CANE PANEL aka CANE AND PANELS
CANE PANELS is an all-over checkerboard pattern, interspersed with upright panels or ribs. Known in a three part set comprising tumble-up and under plate, which is illustrated in the Cristalerias Papini catalog as Modelo No.2. Not to be confused with the Rindskopf vase of the same name.

Shapes: tumble-up and under plate; smaller glasses are also reported
Color: marigold

INDUSTRIA ARGENTINA STAR
An intaglio star, evocative of a similar Brockwitz pattern, is repeated around the exterior of this pattern. There is a star base. The most distinctive feature is the wording moulded on the base, which reads "INDUSTRIA ARGENTINA," the phrase used in Papini's advertising. Found in the USA and Argentina.

Shape: small bowl, plate, and vase
Color: marigold

GOOD YEAR ASHTRAY (and FIRESTONE ASHTRAY)
These must be amongst the oddest and most unusual ashtrays ever reported. The center section is a marigold disk with the wording "INDUSTRIA ARGENTINA" encircling the words "GOOD YEAR." In between the wording is the Good Year logo, the flaming torch. Around the outside of the central disk is a miniature Good Year automobile tire. There are reports that the date 1928 is inscribed on some examples of the tire. The *FIRESTONE* ashtray is similar, but with different wording. Found in the USA and Argentina.

Shape: ashtray
Color: marigold (*FIRESTONE* in blue and marigold)

An unlikely marriage between Carnival Glass and a rubber tire is seen here on Cristalerias Rigolleau's *GOOD YEAR* ashtray. $90-125.

TRIPLE DIAMOND aka THREE DIAMONDS
A tumble-up in this pattern is illustrated in Papini's catalog, called Modelo No. 8—the difficulty is establishing with certainty that the item was made by Papini and not simply imported by them from one of the European Carnival manufacturers. The pattern is a simple geometric featuring diamond bands. There is a 16-point star on the base. Found in Argentina and the USA.

Shape: tumble-up
Color: marigold

The *TRIPLE DIAMOND* tumble-up was illustrated in Papini's catalog where it was called Modelo No. 8. *Courtesy of Bob Smith.* SP $350-450.

CRISTALERIAS PAPINI - SOC. ANON - FUNDADA EN 1896
— BUENOS AIRES - ROSARIO —

Juegos Mesa de Luz, Labrados

| Modelo No. 1 Blanco | Modelo No. 2 Blanco | Modelo No. 6 Blanco | Modelo No. 8 Blanco, Verde Nilo Azul y Rosalin |

A group of four tumble-ups as illustrated in Cristalerias Papini's 1933/4 catalog. Modelo No.2 is what collectors know as *CANE PANELS*, while Modelo #8 is the *TRIPLE DIAMOND* pattern.

Cristalerias Piccardo

Cristalerias Piccardo was another glass manufacturer located in Buenos Aires. Some amazing Carnival items are depicted within the pages of their 1934 catalog. Undoubtedly, Piccardo was an Argentinean manufacturer that actually produced quite a wide range of its own Carnival lines. Several distinct and intriguing patterns are featured in their 1934 catalog. Further, it would seem that they traded with Riihimaki in Finland, since what appears to be the very distinctive Riihimaki *DRAPERY VARIANT* water pitcher is illustrated. Czechoslovakia was also one of Piccardo's trade links, as Josef Inwald's *JACOBEAN* pitcher is clearly illustrated.

Cristalerias Piccardo produced a wide range of splendid boxed presentation sets in Carnival Glass; these included items in the patterns *BAND OF ROSES* as well as the *JEWELLED PEACOCK TAIL* vase. Various other Carnival pieces (such as the *ACANTHUS LEAF* plate) were offered as promotional items—*Articulos para propaganda*. The catalog ads noted that inscriptions could be added to promote goods or companies.

Signature Characteristics of Cristalerias Piccardo Carnival Glass

- Quality of glass and iridescence varies.
- Carnival colors were marigold and blue, though rare purple is also known.
- Full pattern suites in various types of tableware, wine sets are typical.

Cristalerias Piccardo Patterns Known in Carnival Glass

ACANTHUS LEAF aka OAK LEAF LUSTRE

Illustrated and named in the HOACGA Bulletin of September 1999, a covered butter dish and larger cheese dish in this pattern were found in the USA. The pattern had, however, already been named "Acanto" (which translates to 'acanthus') by the manufacturers, Cristalerias Piccardo, in their 1934 catalog, where several shapes in this pattern were shown. The main pattern motif is the acanthus leaf, which is repeated around the items. The base is very distinctive, featuring a 16-point star—the points being alternately short and long. Also illustrated in the catalog, but not yet reported in Carnival were the tumbler, decanter, salt dip, and advertising plate.
Shapes: cheese dish and butter dish
Colors: marigold and purple

ACANTO

ACANTHUS LEAF (aka *OAK LEAF LUSTRE*) was called "Acanto" by Cristalerias Piccardo in their 1934 catalog. Of the items shown here, only the covered butter dish (bottom right) is known in Carnival—it is quite possible that the other shapes may well be seen in iridized glass too.

BERRY BAND AND RIBS

Similar in concept to the *BAND OF ROSES* pattern, here the pattern band features leaves and berries. Several shapes were illustrated in this pattern in the Cristalerias Piccardo 1934 catalog—denoted as No. 3. There may well be several variations on this berry band theme. Found in the USA and Argentina.
Shapes: decanter set with stemmed glasses, water set with barrel shaped tumblers, stemmed compote
Color: marigold and blue

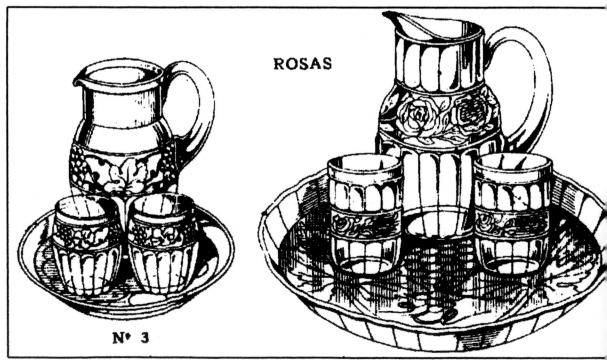

ROSAS

N° 3

Water sets in *BERRY BAND AND RIBS* (left) and *BAND OF ROSES* (aka *ROSAS*), as depicted in Piccardo's 1934 catalog

Nᵒ 3

Piccardo's No. 3 was the *BERRY BAND AND RIBS* pattern. On the left is the decanter, which had matching, stemmed glasses—another shape of decanter is also known with a longer, narrower body. On the right is the barrel shaped tumbler.

A marigold tumbler from Cristalerias Papini in the *BAND OF ROSES* aka *ROSAS* pattern. SP $150-250.

BULLSEYE AND DIAMONDS

In the HOACGA Bulletin from September 1994, John Britt reported an unusual mug in this pattern, stating that he felt it could be European; indeed, it did look as if it could be—surprisingly, however, it features In the 1934 Piccardo catalog, denoted as pattern #11641. Indeed, a full suite of items was illustrated including various covered dishes, a decanter, wines, and bowls. Note the similarity to Imperial's *THREE IN ONE* pattern. Other items in the catalog also show that Piccardo was not afraid of borrowing ideas and design inspirations from other glass companies.

Shape: handled mug
Color: marigold

BAND OF ROSES aka *ROSAS*

The name is very apt and descriptive. This is a panelled design with a simple horizontal band of roses. In the Cristalerias Piccardo 1933-34 catalog, a whole range of items, including water pitcher and handled mug, were shown, though it isn't certain whether all were iridized. A decanter with stopper was listed as *irisado* (iridized) in two different sizes: a larger one for port and a smaller one for liqueurs. A water pitcher was also depicted in the catalog as *irisado*. This pattern is very similar to a Brockwitz design called *ROSE BAND (ARIADNE)*. Found in the USA and Argentina.

Shapes: tumbler, water pitcher, decanter, and stemmed compote. Other shapes are depicted in the 1933 catalog and may well be found in Carnival Glass.

Color: marigold

11641

BULLSEYE AND DIAMONDS is known in the shape of a handled mug (illustrated) but other items were also shown in Piccardo's catalog, such as this stemmed wine glass and water pitcher.

GRACEFUL aka FANTASIA

A full set of *GRACEFUL* items—water pitcher and six tumblers on a glass tray—is depicted in the Cristalerias Piccardo catalog. Single tumblers were also offered. Note that the name given to the design by Piccardo was *FANTASIA*. The pattern is a curling scroll design that repeats around the tumbler. The shape of the tumbler is different from most Classic Carnival examples, being somewhat belled out at the bottom. A 12-point star is pressed into the base. Found in the USA and Argentina.

Shapes: tumbler and water pitcher

Colors: blue and amber

FANTASIA

The water set in *GRACEFUL* aka *FANTASIA* as illustrated in Piccardo's 1934 catalog.

IMPERIAL

A stunning water pitcher turned up in this pattern in England in 1996. It was quite a surprise. The design is geometric and the catalog illustration gives the impression that it is all intaglio—oddly that is not the case. The design is cameo. Consequently it doesn't have the clear-cut edges and feel of a "near-cut" design. Instead, the pattern has a softness to it; the hobstars and file effect blur into one another. It is a startling and splendid example of Carnival Glass. The name *IMPERIAL* was given this pattern by Cristalerias Piccardo. It's an interesting choice, suggesting that they were imitating the geometric style of the Imperial Glass Company. The stemmed goblet is very reminiscent of Imperial's *OCTAGON* pattern. Found in Argentina and the UK.

Shapes: pitcher (in two different sizes) and stemmed goblet
Color: marigold

JEWELLED PEACOCK TAIL

The first *JEWELLED PEACOCK TAIL* vase known in Carnival collecting circles was sold at auction (Burns) in 1998 for $700 (interestingly, it was actually found in Australia). In the 1934 Cristalerias Piccardo catalog, this item is illustrated in several shapes and sizes as well as a boxed presentation item. It is a superb amphora shaped vase, 8" high, featuring a peacock tail pattern. The color is most interesting, as there are very few purple items from Argentina.

Shape: vase
Color: purple

IMPERIAL was the pattern name given by Cristalerias Papini to this superb water pitcher, which was found in the UK. *Courtesy of Jim Nicholls.* An example sold for $890 at auction in early 2000.

The *JEWELLED PEACOCK TAIL* vase was offered in various shapes.

LULES was offered in a wide range of shapes, but only the plate (right) and bowl have so far been found in Carnival Glass.

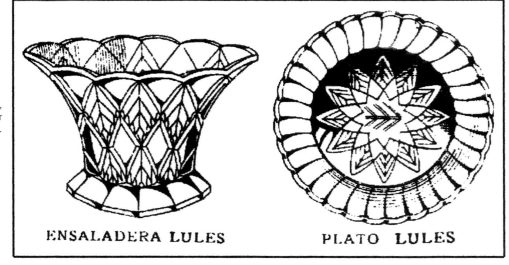

ENSALADERA LULES   PLATO LULES

LULES

A feathered diamond effect is the main motif on this pattern. Single examples of both plate and bowl have been reported in Argentina, though undoubtedly more exist. *LULES* was illustrated in the 1934 Piccardo catalog. Also shown in the catalog but not yet reported in Carnival were the water set and decanter set.

Shapes: bowl and plate
Color: marigold

OAK LEAF LUSTRE see *ACANTHUS LEAF*

ROSAS see *BAND OF ROSES*

Other Cristalerias Piccardo Patterns

Several more iridized items are illustrated in the Cristalerias Piccardo catalogs. So far, these are not documented by Carnival collectors. *PRINCESA* is a water set comprising a bulbous water pitcher and barrel shaped tumblers. The pattern features a large grape bunch and leaf design. *IVONNE* is a geometric pattern that was offered in iridized fruit sets and salad bowls; *FLOR DE LIS* (a stylized fleur de lys pattern) was also shown as iridized. It seems very possible that these items will be found in Carnival some day.

ENSALADERA PRINCESA

BANDEJA PRINCESA

BANDEJA ROSAS
Irisada, 31 cms.   Docena $ 18.-

CRISTALERIAS PICCARDO

ENSALADERA IVONNE
Irisada . . . . Docena $ 12.-

PLATO IVONNE
Irisado, 14 cms. . . . . . Docena $ 4.—

AZUCARERA FLOR DE LIS
Irisada . . . . Docena $ 12.—

ARTICULOS ANACARADOS O IRISADOS

Of the four different patterns shown in this composite ad from Piccardo, only one (*ROSAS*) has so far been reported in Carnival, yet look at the description of the goods: irisado (iridized)—Carnival Glass! On the top row is *PRINCESA* in the shape of both bowl and tray. On the bottom row is a bowl and a plate in *IVONNE* and a handled sugar in *FLOR DE LIS*.

United States Glass Company's Carnival Found in Argentina

There were established and proven links between the United States Glass Company and South America. In 1915, U.S. Glass produced a catalog specifically aimed at the export market of Mexico and South America. The *OMNIBUS* pattern was featured in that particular document. Another U. S. Glass catalog from 1919 was aimed at a more general export market. Both catalogs were written in English and Spanish. Many interesting Carnival items originally in the U. S. Glass Company's catalogs have been found in Argentina and other South American countries. *THE STATES, OMNIBUS, REGAL,* and *RISING SUN* have all been found in Argentina, sometimes in shapes and colors not considered to have been used by the U. S. Glass Company. *OMNIBUS*, for example, has been found in the form of a green pitcher and tumbler—the top of the pitcher is flattened and there are subtle pattern differences—it is surely not a U. S. Glass product. But who made it and why have these items been found in Argentina? Were these undocumented iridized items exported from the United States to Argentina? Or were the moulds sold by the U. S. Glass Company to glass manufacturers in South America, who then slightly altered them and subsequently put them into iridized production? The answer is not yet certain, but this does appear to have been the case.

Further, the Indiana Glass Company of Dunkirk, Indiana, is known to have bought moulds from the U. S. Glass Company. They also sold moulds to Argentina. An Indiana Glass pattern, *LUCILE,* has been found in the form of iridized water sets in Argentina. There is no documentary evidence to show that Indiana Glass made *LUCILE* in Carnival. So was it made in Argentina? It's very possible.

Evidence supporting the theory that some of these original U.S. Glass patterns were actually made in Argentina is provided by the recent discovery of a *C. R. ASHTRAY* (made by Cristalerias Rigolleau) in green. The color is very similar to the aforementioned green *OM-NIBUS* items also found in Argentina—quite possibly Rigolleau either purchased some U.S. Glass moulds or copied the patterns.

[1] Wily Adis. "What's Behind Old Carnival," circa 1970s, Ohil, by author.

Two *OMNIBUS* tumblers: a marigold version is on the left (credited to the United States Glass Company), but who made the unusual green tumbler on the right? Could it have been a copy, made by one of the Argentinean manufacturers? Cristalerias Rigolleau is known to have made the *C.R. ASHTRAY* in green Carnival—its iridescence and base color are similar indeed to the green *OMNIBUS* items. A green pitcher sold for $600 while two green tumblers sold for $350 and $375 at auctions in 1999. An olive green tumbler sold for $550 the same year; marigold tumblers are $100-250. In June 2000, a green *OMNIBUS* tumbler sold for $100.

166

Chapter Ten

Mexico and Peru

Owing to the small amount of Carnival made in these two South American countries, we have grouped them together for the purpose of considering their contribution to the Carnival Glass legacy. Both countries have experienced strong Spanish influence throughout their history and indeed, Spanish is the principal official language of both Mexico and Peru. Inca traditions have also left their legacy on Carnival Glass, as shown by the fascinating examples that were made in Peru. The history of Mexican glass goes back to pre-Hispanic times with a "flowering" represented by a variety of glass vessels used in the "pulquerias" period of the late nineteenth century. However, it is with the first mass produced bottles and pieces made during the early twentieth century, that the source of Mexican and Peruvian Carnival Glass is found.

Cristales Mexicanos S.A. (now part of Grupo Vitro), Monterrey, Mexico

The Mexican Glass group, Vitro S.A., was founded back in 1909. Its main product in those early days was beer bottles. Mexico's growing beer industry demanded growing numbers of bottles and by satisfying that demand in the home market, Mexico was able to cut down its imports of glassware. The company grew and expanded, at all times being aware of the need to keep up with the latest technology. In 1934, Grupo Vitro created Vidriera Mexico S.A. in Mexico City to satisfy the increasing demand for glassware.

In 1957, the glassmaker Cristales Mexicanos S.A., who were also located in Monterrey, was purchased by Grupo Vitro. Cristales Mexicanos were known as producers of dinnerware and household glass. The trademark M inside a larger C, as found on several items of Carnival Glass, was their logo. Iridized glass was produced by Cristales Mexicanos; most likely before its incorporation into the Vitro S.A. group. Any items marked with the CM trademark date from before the 1957 amalgamation. The *Catalogo General de Cristales Mexicanos S.A.* (dating from just before 1957) shows many bottles (some of them in novelty form) and similar containers in a whole range of shapes and sizes. A number of iridized bottles and jars are known and it is very likely that some of these were made by Cristales Mexicanos.

Grupo Vitro is now Mexico's largest glass manufacturer and indeed has recently (January 2000) bought the United States company Harding Glass, a subsidiary of Sunsource Inc. Today, Grupo Vitro exports glassware to more than seventy countries worldwide.

OKLAHOMA

The *OKLAHOMA* tumbler is a scarce and sought after item. The pattern is geometric, consisting of large diamond shapes set amongst smaller diamonds. It is unusual in that the top of the tumbler bells in, making the top diameter narrower than that of the collar base. In the center of the rayed star on the base is the CM trademark. Lois Langdon, a Carnival collector, took several vacations with her husband in Guadalajara, which lies about three hundred miles from

Mexico City (and about five hundred miles from Monterrey). At a flea market in Guadalajara, some years ago, they found a box that contained six *OKLAHOMA* tumblers and four *RANGER* tumblers. On the box there was a large printed label that read "Cristales de Mexico—Monterrey." This pattern is very similar to an Imperial design #281 as seen in the Imperial 1909 catalog. The shape of the tumbler is very different, however, as the Imperial version has straight sides and a ground base. It would seem that the Mexican version could well be a copy of the Imperial design. Scarce examples have also been found in the USA.

Shapes: tumbler and carafe (decanter)
Color: marigold

The marigold *OKLAHOMA* tumbler from Cristales Mexicanos. A similar example sold in 1998 at auction for $335.

MEXICALI

This pattern was also found by Lois Langdon on her Mexican trip—a pair of 8" high, pedestal footed vases that have now been named *MEXICALI*, they feature a rather plain, panelled design.

> Shape: vase
> Color: marigold

RANGER

A familiar blocked design, so like many others, yet distinct in that this one has a star base with the CM trademark moulded in the very center. Tumblers in this pattern were found at a flea market in Guadalajara. Scarce examples have also been found in the USA.

> Shapes: pitcher and tumbler
> Color: marigold

Cristales Mexicanos made this *RANGER* tumbler in marigold. It is easily identified by the CM trademark on the base. SP $100-150.

VOTIVE LIGHT

At first glance, the shape is like that of a small celery or a vase, but this item undoubtedly has religious connections and is possibly a candleholder. The pattern on one side is of a "bleeding heart." On the other side there is a cross. The familiar CM trademark is on the base. Lois Langdon found two of these items in a Mexico City shop on one of her vacations. A shot glass depicted in the 1957 catalog from Cristaleria S.A. is decorated with a cross that is very reminiscent of the design on the *VOTIVE LIGHT*.

> Shape: chalice or vase
> Color: marigold

P. and J. Hartinger S.A., Lima, Peru

All credit in discovering the manufacturer responsible for Carnival Glass in Peru goes to Bob Smith, whose determined research and enquiries identified Hartinger as the manufacturer of the Carnival Glass *INCA* bottles. The company was founded by Senor Pio Hartinger Machalek in 1939. Their trademark has the appearance of a four-leafed clover, but in fact is four stylized hearts (Hartinger) with a central circle that contains the letter *H*. The company ceased to trade in the mid 1990s when the owner, Mr. Hartinger, died and all the company assets were disposed of. Bob had originally thought that Peru must have been the source of the *INCA* bottles, owing to the wording on a small label attached to one of the bottles that read: *Huaco d'oro Peruano*. Bob explains that *Huaco* is a strictly Peruvian word for the small, ancient Inca statues with huge heads and tiny bodies that were carved out centuries ago by the Inca Indians—of course, this is the shape of the *INCA* bottles. Sincere thanks also to Clinton Arsenault for his excellent information regarding the *INCA BOTTLES*.

INCA BOTTLES

There are several variations of these splendidly quixotic novelties; a wonderful collection of which has been assembled by Clint Arsenault and illustrates their variety. His research has shown that some of these bottles were actually sold in a specially designed, plastic carrying case. The case has a moulded insert that fits the bottles precisely to ensure their safety in transit. Labels and moulded text found on the bottles and the case indicate that they were made for Santa Josefa Vina, probably a wine or liqueur producer. The original content of the bottles was known as *pisco*, which appears to be a grape distillate (like brandy) that notches up a rather high alcohol content of 43.9 percent. The label on the front of the case states that the contents are *3 PARRAS*—which translates to mean three guys or fellows—in other words, the three *INCA BOTTLES* that were contained within the carrying case.

Four different versions of the *INCA BOTTLES* are currently recorded. Each has in common a grotesque appearance: three feature just a face, the other is shaped like a squat figure with a disproportionately large face and neck. Small wine glasses have also been found with one example of this bottle. *INCA BOTTLES* are scarce and unusual items in collecting circles. Examples have been found in Argentina and the USA. According to the text on the bottle labels, they were distributed to Bogota, Colombia, and Buenos Aires, Argentina.

> Shape: bottle
> Colors: marigold and blue

The intriguing label attached to the case that was made for transporting the *INCA BOTTLES*.

Chapter Eleven

India and China

"India . . . with the Seven Seas to the south and the white-swan Himalaya to the north . . .
the land of the elephant and the monkey-world, of parakeets and peacocks."
—Raja Rao, Indian writer

This splendid group of Indian Carnival includes both vases and tumblers. At the top is a rare Jain blue
DIAMANTE STARS vase, SP $150-350. The remainder, from left: *BEADED SPEARS VARIANT* in rare Jain blue,
SP $200-250; marigold *BEADED SPEARS* tumbler, SP $75-100; small *HAND* vase (*LEFT HAND STOLEN
WATCH* version), SP $150-400; *ELEPHANT* vase (small size), SP $300-600; *FROSTED FISH* vase—one sold at
auction in the USA in 1999 for $500; group of three tumblers—at the back *BRIDE'S BOUQUET* (SP $150-200),
front *SHALIMAR* ($125-175), and *GRAPEVINE AND SPIKES* (SP $125-175).

Of all the countries known to have produced Carnival Glass, India is probably the one that surprises most. Yet the known output of that country continues to be documented as more and more exotic items are reported and sold at auction. Vases and tumblers dominate the Indian Carnival scene. Frequently their designs feature symbolism and motifs that have meaning unfamiliar to Western culture. Much Indian Carnival was exported to Australia, sold there by travelling salesmen during the 1950s and 1960s. In more recent years, collectors report containers from India full of antiques and bizarre ornaments arriving from the sub-continent. Indian Carnival also continues to be found in the UK and in the USA as well as in India itself. The only documented manufacturer of Indian Carnival is the Jain Glass Works (P) Limited, who were based in Firozabad, the main glass making area in northern India. The company is no longer trading. Its 1986 closure, in the words of director, Mahavir Jain, was due to "unavoidable conditions." There may have been other manufacturers, but communication with India is hard; documentation and archives do not exist. The faithful recording of actual items is the only way forward. Bob Smith has possibly the greatest collection of Indian Carnival tumblers in existence. His detailed records and photographic evidence allow us to present a listing of all Indian tumblers known in Carnival Glass (see below). Credit must also go to Bob for "discovering" the existence of the Jain Glass Works and indeed, for establishing India as a major manufacturer of Carnival Glass. Carnival Glass from China is still being researched and very little is currently known. At the end of this chapter we present several Chinese tumblers that have been identified by Bob Smith.

Jain Glass Works (Private) Limited

In the wide floodplain of the sacred River Ganges in northern India lies the industrial town of Firozabad, the country's main location for the manufacture of glass articles. Bangles, beads, drinking glasses, and general household goods were produced. There, in Firozabad, at the factory of the Jain Glass Works (P) Ltd., they made Carnival Glass—a fact confirmed by a director of the company, Mahavir Jain. The Jain Glass Works was founded by the late Shri Chhadamilal Jain in 1928. It was one of the first companies to bring the (then) latest technology in glass manufacturing and decoration into India. As seen on their factory letterhead, the company's logo is a *sathya* (swastika), which in India is an auspicious, traditional, and sacred symbol. This emblem is a very old, auspicious good luck symbol, almost certainly first used in India in the first and second centuries. In Sanskrit it is *Svasti*, meaning fortune or happiness.

Iridized glass was first made at the Jain factory in 1935. Vases and drinking glasses were the main items that Jain produced in iridized glass. Pitchers (sometimes with a frosted design) and tumble-ups are also known. The designs and styles are quite wonderful and exotic, reflecting the rich culture and history of the Indian sub-continent. The founder's son, the late Bimal Kumar Jain, added his own style of manufacturing the glass and called it "Lustre Glass." The company name JAIN can sometimes be found moulded or acid etched into the glass—even initials such as "CB" and "UMM" are known moulded into the glass. The swastika logo is also seen on some items of Jain Carnival.

Signature Characteristics of Indian Carnival Glass

• The quality of the glassware is very variable. The quality of iridescence can vary from superb to poor. The mould work varies in the same way. Poor quality control at the factory is evident.

• Often the glass is very thin, especially on the tumblers (there are one or two exceptions), but some items, especially the vases such as *DIAMANTE STARS*, are made of thicker, sturdier glass.

• The method of manufacture meant that the tops of articles were ground smooth and in the case of vases, often ruffled and shaped or pinched, while the base is often iridized.

• Marigold and a pale aqua blue were the main colors used. The very distinct pale blue color has been termed Jain blue to distinguish it from other shades of the color. Frosting was also used.

• Exotic figural designs and abstract patterns (probably symbolic for the Indian culture), all exterior.

• Tumblers in several sizes and shapes, vases in many variations and shapes, pitchers, and tumble-ups are all typical of the Indian output.

Two splendid marigold Indian tumblers in slightly thicker glass than most—this allows for much greater depth of moulded detail. On the left is the *SHALIMAR* tumbler (SP $125-175), a kissing cousin to the *DIAMANTE STAR* vase. On the right is *BRIDE'S BOUQUET*, quite a tall tumbler that stands a full 6" high. SP $150-200.

Indian water pitchers are not found too often; this one is in Jain's *BEADED SPEARS VARIANT* pattern and was found in Scotland. *Photo courtesy of Fiona Melville.* NP

Indian Tumblers

In *Carnival Glass: The Magic and the Mystery,* we presented a glossary (courtesy of Bob Smith) of all Indian tumblers that were known at the time. Bob Smith's extensive research and cataloging has now produced the following listing of Indian tumblers, inclusive of size and pattern variations. Most tumblers are found in two basic sizes: regular (from just over 4" to 5" high) and large (over 5"). Juice glasses are known and stand around 4" high—even smaller are the tiny shot glasses. Where the JAIN trademark is known to exist on the item, this is noted in the text. It is impossible to state with certainty the manufacturer(s) of unmarked tumblers. The majority of Indian tumblers photographed here are shown courtesy of Bob Smith. Sincere thanks to Michael Whitten for the use of his copyrighted photographs of Bob Smith's rare tumblers.

The Jain trademark is moulded into the base of several Indian items. On other pieces, such as the *FROSTED FISH VASE,* the trademark is etched on.

AUSTRALIAN DAISY

The pattern features four panels, each containing a stylized daisy type of flower, complete with leaves and buds. The tumbler is pinched in near the bottom with a ribbed band and there is a 6-pointed star on the base.
>   Shape: belled (4.25")
>   Color: marigold

This marigold *AUSTRALIAN DAISY* tumbler has a distinctive and unusual shape. *Photo © Michael Whitten.* SP $125-175

BANDED MOON AND STARS

A ribbed band near the rim contains the moon and star motifs. The greater part of the pattern is taken up with a repeated pattern of stylized flowers on stems. A diamond pattern near the bottom has stylistic similarities with the *BEADED SPEARS* design.
>   Shape: straight (5.25")
>   Color: marigold

BANDED MOON AND STARS is only known in marigold. *Photo © Michael Whitten.* SP $125-175.s

BEADED MIRRORS

The background pattern is a hatched diamond effect, broken up by large mirror-like medallions.
>   Shape: straight (4.25")
>   Color: marigold

The *BEADED MIRRORS* tumbler is on the left while the variation *BEADED MIRRORS WITH ETCHED FLOWERS* is shown on the right. *Photo © Michael Whitten.* SP $125-175.

BEADED MIRRORS WITH ETCHED FLOWERS

The pattern is as above, but in the medallion is a rose-like etched flower.
>   Shape: straight (4.5" and 5.25")
>   Color: marigold

BEADED PANELS AND GRAPES aka TRAILING BERRIES AND BEADED PANELS

Manufacturer unconfirmed, though similar to another Jain tumbler. *BEADED PANELS AND GRAPES* features grapes and plain panels. It differs from *MUSCADINE* in that it also has a pattern band near the rim that features grapes and leaves.
>   Shape: straight (4.5" and 5.25")
>   Color: marigold

BEADED PANELS AND GRAPES is seen here on two sizes of tumbler; the one on the left stands at a little over 5", the one on the right is 4.5". *Photo © Michael Whitten.* SP $75-100 each

BEADED SPEARS

The overall effect given by this pattern is jewel like. Beaded panels and diamond spears interlock, the whole jewel like effect being enhanced by the iridescence. The upward pointing triangle within the design is an auspicious talisman symbolizing goodness and aspiration. As with the vases, there are several variations. A water pitcher is known in this pattern, which, in its original state, would have had a metal cover.

Shape: straight (4.5" and 5.5") and flared (4.5" and 5.5")
Color: marigold.

Shapes: various sizes and shapes as detailed below—also a juice size with a pedestal base has been found by the McGraths in Australia.
- straight (5.5") – marigold
- straight (5.5") – blue
- juice, collared, straight (4") – marigold and blue
- regular size, collared, straight (4.75") – marigold and blue

Colors: marigold and blue—ice blue and amber have also been reported

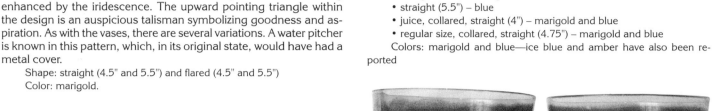

Two marigold *BEADED SPEARS* tumblers (one flared and one straight sided) in the smaller 4.5" size. *Photo © Michael Whitten.* SP $75-100 each.

BEADED SPEARS VARIANT is seen here in Jain blue on the left (SP $200-250) and marigold (SP $150-175). *Photo © Michael Whitten.*

The larger size of *BEADED SPEARS* tumblers (also one flared and one straight sided)—these stand at 5.5" high. *Photo © Michael Whitten.* SP $75-100 each.

BEADED SPEARS VARIANT

Similar to *BEADED SPEARS*, this pattern differs in that part of the pattern is plain. There is also a collar based variation to the pattern. (Just to complicate matters, there is a further variation that does not have the lattice band around the top, nor is there a lattice next to the spears.)

A further variation to the *BEADED SPEARS VARIANT* design is in the addition of a collar base. The juice size is shown on the left in marigold while the regular size is shown in Jain blue on the right. *Photo © Michael Whitten.* SP $100-200 each.

BRIDE'S BOUQUET

Features a hand holding a bunch of flowers against a horizontal ribbed background. Delightful and exotic.

Shape: flared (6")
Color: marigold

CANARY TREE

An exquisite harmony of marigold iridescence and acid frosting, this tumbler features four repeats of birds on a branch. The birds are picked out in rich marigold, the background is white frosted. On the base is JAIN in half inch high moulded letters.

Shape: belled (4.5")
Color: marigold and acid etched

CANARY TREE is a delightful tumbler. Marked JAIN on the base in moulded letters, it also features a blend of frosting and marigold iridescence. *Photo © Michael Whitten.* SP $150-200.

CELEBRATION

This unusual design features an amusing figure of a small boy and the words "Good Luck" in script. Scattered across the face of the tumbler are flower petals.

Shape: straight (5.5")
Color: marigold

CELEBRATION has the words "Good Luck" written on it in script. A rare item, this is the only one reported so far. *Photo © Michael Whitten.* SP $175-200.

CIRCLED STAR AND VINE

A vine-like cable is at the top of the tumbler, hanging from it are three clusters of grapes and three leaves, evenly spaced. At the bottom of the leaves is a circle enclosing a 5-pointed star. Moulded on the base are the initials PGW.

Shape: straight (4.75")
Color: marigold

CIRCLED STAR AND VINE has the moulded letters "PGW" on the base. *Photo © Michael Whitten.* SP $125-175.

CROWN OF INDIA

This is a most impressive tumbler featuring several different interpretations of the crown motif—quite possibly reflecting the period of the British Raj in India.

Shape: straight (4.25")
Color: marigold

The CROWN OF INDIA is a splendid tumbler that unsurprisingly features a variety of crown motifs. *Photo © Michael Whitten.* SP $175-200.

EMBROIDERED FLOWERS has a similar pattern band to BEADED SPEARS VARIANT around the top—but there the similarities end, as EMBROIDERED FLOWERS also features a delightful floral motif. The word JAIN is moulded on the base. *Photo © Michael Whitten.* SP $125-175.

EMBROIDERED FLOWERS aka POTTED FLOWERS

A pattern band around the top features medallions containing floral motifs. The body of the design has elegant alternate panels that feature a stylized and typically Indian looking tall, stemmed flower (possibly a lotus) in a vase. Alternate panels have smaller flowers. Both the vase and the flower motifs are Indian talismans. Known examples have the moulded trademark JAIN on the base.

Shape: straight (5.5")
Color: marigold

EMBROIDERED PANELS

This is a variant on the EMBROIDERED FLOWERS that does not have the floral panels. There may well be other sizes (probably a larger flared shape).

Shape: straight (4.5" and 5.25") and flared (4.5")
Color: marigold

EMBROIDERED PANELS tumblers in three slight variations: from left, the 4.5" high flared tumbler then the straight sided tumbler in two sizes. *Photo © Michael Whitten.* SP $125-175 each.

FOUR SUITS

Crosshatched fine lines fill the greater part of this tumbler, much like the *MIRROR AND CROSSBARS*. Three large plain oval medallions are evenly spaced around the design. Over this are circles in which the playing card symbols of the four suits are found.

> Shape: straight (5.5")
> Color: marigold

FOUR SUITS is the apt name for this marigold tumbler. *Photo © Michael Whitten. SP $125-175.*

GRAPE AND PALISADE see *GRAPE-VINE AND SPIKES*

GRAPEVINE AND SPIKES aka *GRAPE AND PALISADE*

Grapes and vine leaves curve around the top part of this tumbler. A vertical ribbed pattern is the feature around the base. JAIN is found on the bottom of the tumbler.

> Shape: straight (4.5" and 5.5")
> Color: marigold

GRAPEVINE AND SPIKES has the word JAIN moulded on the base of the tumbler. *Photo © Michael Whitten. SP $125-175.*

INDIAN SUMMER

An intricate floral design in three bands (widest band at the top). Many varieties of flowers are depicted in a stylized manner that is very typical of Indian design.

> Shape: straight (5.5")
> Color: marigold

INDIAN SUMMER has a very intricate floral design. SP $125-175.

JASMINE JAIN

Encircling narrow bands at top and bottom feature flowers and leaves. The central motif has four repeats of a jasmine-like flower.

> Shape: straight, juice (4")
> Color: marigold

MAHARAJAH

A simple design composed of nine circles and nine plain panels

> Shape: flared shot glass (2.75")
> Color: marigold

MAHARAJAH (left) and MAHARANEE (right) are similar patterns found on diminutive shot glasses. They differ in the encircling pattern band at the top—the MAHARAJAH has nine circle motifs repeated around the circle while the MAHARANEE has only six. *Photo © Michael Whitten. SP $150-200 each.*

MAHARANEE

A variation of the *MAHARAJAH*, with six circles and twelve panels.

> Shape: flared shot glass (2.75")
> Color: marigold

MIRRORED PEACOCKS

The peacock is the national symbol of India and the motif can be seen on the walls of many government

The *MIRRORED PEACOCKS* tumbler is proof that the peacock symbol was truly international.

buildings. The stylized peacocks on the tumbler face each other. An example was found in California.

> Shape: straight (4.5")
> Color: marigold

MIRRORS AND CROSSBARS

Cross hatched fine lines fill almost all the tumbler. Three large oval plain medallions are evenly spaced around the design.

> Shape: straight (5.5")
> Color: marigold

The *MIRRORS AND CROSSBARS* tumbler in marigold. *Photo © Michael Whitten. SP $100-150.*

MUSCADINE

Three alternate panels containing grapes and vine leaves are the main feature. Around the rim is a pattern band featuring interlocking un-beaded rectangles and diamonds.

Shape: straight (5.25")
Color: marigold

MUSCADINE features a familiar grape motif. *Photo © Michael Whitten.* SP $100-150.

MUSCADINE VARIANT

Similar to *MUSCADINE,* but this has beaded rectangles and diamonds in the pattern band.

Shape: straight (4.75")
Color: marigold

The *MUSCADINE VARIANT* is different from the regular pattern by virtue of the encircling pattern band around the rim. *Photo © Michael Whitten.* SP $100-150.

OLYMPIC TUDOR AND BEADS

Featuring a floral spray and bud, very similar to that on the *HERBAL MEDICINE* vase, this tumbler also has an encircling band of beads at the bottom. Around the top edge is a band of overlapping circles.

Shape: straight (4.75")
Color: marigold

OLYMPIC TUDOR AND BEADS features a floral motif that is reminiscent of the *HERBAL MEDICINE* vase. SP $125-175.

PALACE GATES

The "gates" are arched motifs. Grapes hang down from the top in four bunches.

Shape: straight (4.75")
Color: marigold

Although the detail is a little indistinct on this light marigold *PALACE GATES* tumbler, the arches of the gates can be clearly seen. *Photo © Michael Whitten.* SP $125-175.

PINNACLE

A very fine and beautifully made tumbler with a pattern quite similar, yet with a much stronger interpretation, to *BEADED SPEARS.*

Shape: straight (5.5")
Color: marigold

PINNACLE is a splendid marigold tumbler with a strong pattern and excellent moulded detail. *Photo © Michael Whitten.* SP $150-200.

POTTED FLOWERS see *EMBROIDERED FLOWERS*

PUNJAB FLOWER

A stylized flower, as the name suggests, is the main pattern motif. There is a further pattern band encircling the top and the bottom of the design. JAIN is moulded on the base.

Shape: straight, juice (4")
Color: marigold

PUNJAB FLOWER features delightful floral motifs and also has JAIN moulded on the base. *Photo © Michael Whitten.* SP $125-175.

ROYAL GARLAND

An ornate tumbler, with a stylized, abstract motif.

Shape: straight (4.5")
Color: marigold

ROYAL GARLAND has a pretty and intricate beaded design. *Photo © Michael Whitten.* SP $125-175.

SHALIMAR

The pattern on this tumbler is very reminiscent of the *DIAMANTE STARS* and *DIAMANTES* vases (see below). The glass is thicker than most Indian tumblers, indeed it is more like the vases.

Shape: belled (4.25")
Color: marigold

STARS OVER INDIA

A full moon and star motif are the main features in a band around the top. The rest of the tumbler has a stepped design and on the base there is a very unusual motif—alternate tear drop and rounded triangles (eight in all).

Shape: straight (5.5")

This *STARS OVER INDIA* tumbler has a light marigold iridescence and detailed mouldwork. *Photo © Michael Whitten.* SP $125-175.
Color: marigold

TWISTER is aptly described by its pattern name. *Photo © Michael Whitten.* SP $75-100.

SWANS AND FLOWERS

Four elongated fan shapes at the bottom of this pretty tumbler frame the alternate motifs of swans and flowers. The only known example has JAIN on the base and the etched letters UMM near the bottom. The tumbler is a delightful combination of white acid etching (as the background) and rich marigold iridescence (on the swans, flowers, and fans). The only known example was found in Ohio.

Shape: belled (4.5")
Color: marigold and acid etched

TRAILING BERRIES AND BEADED PANELS see *BEADED PANELS AND GRAPES*

TWISTER

The pattern name says it all—slanted continuous lines encircle the tumbler.

Shape: juice (3.75")
Color: marigold

VINEYARD HARVEST

Another variation on the grape theme, the main feature of this pattern is the large, pendulous bunch of grapes—there are horizontal bands at the top and bottom of the design.

Shape: straight (5.5")
Color: marigold

WHIRLSAWAY

A *whirling and* continuous spiral threads around the whole tumbler.

Shapes: straight (4.5") and flared (4.5" and 5.5")—other sizes than those are thought to exist
Color: marigold

WHIRLSAWAY seen here in three different tumblers, two flared in different heights and one straight sided. *Photo © Michael Whitten.* SP $100-125 each.

Indian Vases

"As we bought the vase, we could see the blue of the Arabian Ocean beyond the gently swaying palms."
—Jose Ordish, UK Carnival Glass collector, on her return from the island of Goa

Indian Carnival Glass vases must be amongst the most exotic and bizarre items ever to be found in Carnival Glass. Their shapes reflect the religion and rich culture of the area in which they were made. Each is highly individual and there are many variations to be found. The thickness of the glass varies: the thickest are the *DIAMANTE STARS* and similar vases, the thinnest are the *GOA* style vases. Collectors have come across Indian vases in most parts of the world, including the USA and the UK, although Australia has perhaps the highest number of "finds." Possibly the most memorable was Goa, where a family of English collectors on vacation found all manner of wonderful Indian Carnival laid out on blankets under palm trees at a flea market!

FISH VASE

A weird and quite wonderful piece of glass. The fish twists around the vase, its head being at the base and its tail coiling, first left then right, around and upward. There is great detail in the mould work, the scales on the fish's body being very distinct. Why a fish? In Hindu legend, the god Vishnu reincarnates into a horned, golden scaled fish called Matsya. The golden fish then saved all mankind from destruction during a terrible flood. The image on the vase may well represent this legend. The vase is frequently found bearing the moulded letters JAIN to the left of the fish's mouth. JAIN is also found acid etched onto the underside of the base of the vase. Standing at around 9" to 10", these are the tallest of the Indian vases. Examples of the *FISH* vase have been found in the USA, UK, Australia, and India.

• *SERPENT.* There are several variations to the basic *FISH*, though the oddest is a vase called the *SERPENT* vase. This is, in fact, a re-modelled *FISH* vase. On this variant, the fish/serpent winds the other way around the vase. It does not have the JAIN trademark and it is not yet confirmed whether the *SERPENT* is a product of the Jain works.

• *FISH VARIANT.* Another variant to the regular *FISH* was discovered in Australia by Peter Phillips in 1999. It is exactly the same as the *FISH* vase in mould detail; although it doesn't have all the re-modelling of the *SERPENT*, it winds the opposite way to the regular *FISH* (that is, the same way as the *SERPENT*).

• *FROSTED FISH.* Marigold on the fish but white acid etching on the body of the vase.

Shape: vase
Color: known in marigold and acid etched version

Indian vases are amongst the most exotic you could ever hope to find. Here a *FROSTED FISH* vase is flanked by a marigold *DIAMANTE STARS* on the left (SP $100-150) and a Jain blue *DIAMANTE STARS* on the right (SP $150-350). Note that a *FROSTED FISH* vase was sold at auction in the USA in 1999 for $500.

A trio of *HAND* vases: on the left is the diminutive *LEFT HAND STOLEN WATCH*, in the center is the *LEFT HAND FLOWER VARIANT,* and on the right is the *RIGHT HAND REGULAR*. SP $150-400 each.

HAND VASE

The *HAND* vase Is captivating and fascinating. It depicts a hand, complete with details such as rings and round wristwatch, holding a flared cone shape that is the body of the vase. In Hindu iconography, the lifted hand protects both the conscious and unconscious order of the creation. Many Hindu gods are multi-limbed and have several hands that are frequently placed in divine gestures (*mudras*) very similar to the *HAND* vase. The vases come in left and right hand versions, both with wristwatch and ring. There are two main sizes: 8" to 9" high and around 5" to 6" high. The moulded JAIN trademark may or may not be present. The neck of the vase is usually crimped and has a beaded band near the top. There is a distinctive, thick circular base. *HAND VASES* have been found in Australia, the USA, the UK, India, and Ceylon. There are several further variations to the *HAND* vase. Indeed, difference in size and significant details alter the piece tremendously. Some of these variations are:

• *LEFT HAND NO ARCHES*: time reads 9:00, beads but no arches on cone. 9" and 6" versions.

• *LEFT HAND FLORAL*: bracelet type watch, flower spray on cone and semi circles around base. Just over 8" high.

• *LEFT HAND FLOWER VARIANT*: a little smaller than the regular version. No watch or ring. Flower spray moulded on cone. Half moons and circles around the base. No beaded band at top.

• *LEFT HAND STOLEN WATCH*: no beads or arches around the neck (also a variant with arches) and no watch. A fraction over 5" high.

• *LEFT HAND MINI*: round watch, beads, and arches on cone. Only just over 5" high.

• *RIGHT HAND REGULAR*: round watch, beads and arches around cone, and semi-circles on base. 9" high.

• *RIGHT HAND UPRIGHT*: oblong shaped watch. The cone shape is not flared. Beaded band at the top. 6" high

• *RIGHT HAND MINIATURE*: no time shown on the watch. Beads and arches in band round the neck. 5" high.

• *RIGHT HAND STOLEN WATCH:* no beads or arches around the neck and no watch. Under 5" high.

We cannot be certain if all these variations were made by the Jain Glass Works. There may well be more variations.

Shape: vase
Color: marigold

ELEPHANT VASE

The *ELEPHANT* vase is a rare and exotic piece of Carnival Glass. The head of the elephant is seen as if looking upwards, his trunk curling around the vase. The elephant is a symbol long associated with India and its iconography. The elephant headed Lord Ganesh is a popular and auspicious deity, believed to guard the threshold of home and sanctuary. He is worshipped before the commencement of any new work or ceremony. All the examples of the *ELEPHANT* vase known to us have a swastika motif moulded on the back of the vase, some also have the letters CB. The swastika was, of course, the trademark of the Jain Glass Works. As with the *HAND* and *FISH* vases, there are variations on the theme. Two sizes are known: 7" and almost 9". The trunk may wind to the left or the right. Some vases have the letters JAIN, some have a jewel design, and others bear the letters CB. Found in Australia, the USA, the UK, and India.

Shape: vase

Color: marigold

Two exotic *ELEPHANT* vases, both marked JAIN. SP $300-600 each.

GODDESS VASE

As with the other vases, there are two main variations to the *GODDESS*, but both share the basic characteristics. The vase features an ornate and richly decorated (presumably) female figure, arms held upwards, undoubtedly representing a deity or similar figure. It stands around 8" high. These splendid items have been found in Australia, the USA, and India—probably the most surprising was the one that turned up in an antique mall in the middle of Chicago! It only goes to prove that you never know where Carnival Glass might be found.

    Shape: vase
    Color: marigold

DIAMANTE STARS and similarly styled vases

The main characteristic of these vases is that they are made of glass that is substantially thicker than the other Indian vases and they share a very distinctive bulbous shape with a long, ribbed neck and a ruffled top. The patterns are stylized and feature abstract geometrics and/or floral motifs. Examples have been found in Australia, the USA, the UK, Czechoslovakia, Afghanistan, and India. Five different patterns are currently known in this style of vase:

• *DIAMANTE STARS* has a geometric sort of pattern that is all cameo; the effect is of small and large diamond effect stars over the body of the piece. Two sizes are known: 6.5" high (most frequently seen) and 8.5" high.

• *DIAMANTES* has a similar kind of pattern but is a little smaller than *DIAMANTE STARS*.

• *DIAMANTE LEAVES* is similar yet again, but the diamond shapes are formed instead like pointed leaves. Two examples are known (found as a pair in the UK) and are both Jain blue. They are both the large 8.5" size.

• *DIAMOND HEART* has a stylized, upside down, heart shape as the main motif and little flower motifs scattered over the design.

• *DAISY DRAPE* features a large stylized flower as well as diamond shapes and a draped border.

    Shape: bulbous vase

    Colors: marigold and Jain blue (for *DIAMANTE STARS* and *DIAMANTE LEAVES* only)

The only two *DIAMANTE LEAVES* vases so far known are both 8.5" high and have a splendid iridescence on Jain blue base glass. *Courtesy of Pat and Alex Chalmers. Photo © Susan Brewer.* SP $200-400 each.

DIAMANTES (left) is very similar to *DIAMANTE STARS*, but note that it is a little smaller, as well as having a slightly different interpretation of the diamond pattern. *Courtesy of Alan Henderson.* SP $100-350.

The *DIAMOND HEART* vase in a rich marigold. One sold at auction for $350 in 1998.

The *HERBAL MEDICINE* vase (center) has the "*GOA* style" shaping (hour glass). It features floral and grass-like motifs. SP $150-300. Note that the *OLYMPIC TUDOR AND BEADS* tumbler (at left) has a very similar floral motif to the vase. The tumbler at right is *INDIAN SUMMER*.

GOA style vases

This group of Indian vases with a distinctive, classic hourglass shape are named for the island of Goa where the first examples were found. Five different patterns are currently known in this style of vase. These vases are usually made of quite thin glass.

• *CB VASE*—this was first seen at the ICGA Convention in Schaumburg, 1999 and is unusual in that the actual pattern of the vase features a flower branch with the letters CB clearly incorporated within the design.

• *GOA* is a most exotic vase that features a lightly moulded, repeated design that echoes that found on the headdress seen on the *ELEPHANT* vase.

• *HERBAL MEDICINE* features two repeated motifs—a floral spray, complete with bud, and a tall sheaf of grass.

• *POTTED FLOWERS* is an easy one to describe—simply as it sounds.

• *TRIBAL* was given its name to represent the strange mixture of motifs that it features.

Shape: hourglass shaped vase

Color: marigold

The *TRIBAL* vase has a blend of exotic symbols.

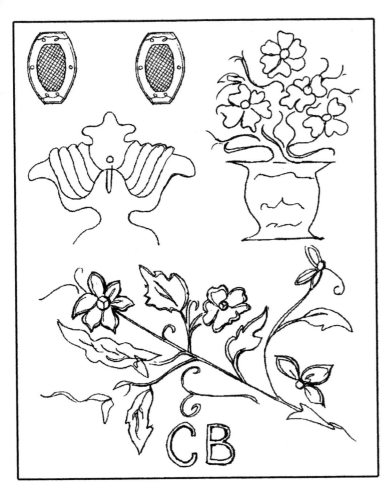

GOA style vases feature various motifs. The strange shield shapes and the odd figure below them at top left are seen on the *GOA* vase itself. Top right is the motif on *POTTED FLOWERS* and across the bottom is the floral motif as seen on the *CB* vase

ETCHED style vases

This group of Indian vases shares a blend of acid etched frost effect and rich marigold iridescence. They have been found in Australia, the USA, and India.

• *SWANS AND FLOWERS*—very similar to the *SWANS AND FLOWERS* tumbler described earlier. The vases are a mixture of a white acid etched background with intense marigold colored decoration. A water pitcher is also known in this pattern.

• *MISTY MORN* takes its name from the vase's frosted effect, which John and Margaret McGrath from Australia (who found the first vase in this pattern) said gave the vase the impression of a misty morning. The marigold pattern features floral motifs.

Shapes: vases and water pitcher
Color: marigold and acid etched (frosted)

In the epilogue to *Carnival Glass: The Magic and the Mystery*, we noted that Bob Smith had sent us a "Stop Press" reporting Carnival tumblers from China. At the time, he had catalogued three patterns that originated in China. Now Bob reports there are six patterns known (plus one other that may or may not be Chinese). The date of manufacture is still a matter of conjecture, but based on Bob's own experience with glass, he suggests that use of the words *Made In China* and *Shanghai China* seen on the tumblers should put the time frame for these Chinese examples in the Late Carnival period—anywhere from the 1930s through the 50s, most likely the late 30s or late 40s, though recent information from Ray and Jean Rogers in Australia suggests that production may have continued to more recent years. Possibly then, these items fall within the time frame of Part Three, which deals with Late Carnival, however they neatly form a bridge from the main section of the book into the next one.

All the Chinese tumblers reported so far share a prominent feature, a common trademark—it is a small triangle (about an eighth of an inch long) on the base of each tumbler, which very possibly links them to one factory. Their bases are non-iridized and all are marigold. Six different Chinese patterns are currently known (plus the *GOLDEN DIAMOND*, which we cannot currently be sure is Chinese—see below). No pitcher has yet been found to go with any of these tumblers, though a vase is known (see *SHANGHAI* below).

All these items are probably barware and thus made for places like hotels, restaurants, or bars. The numbers on the base point to a special order made particularly for such places. The fact that they have been found in one and twos, and in places as far apart as the USA and Australia, suggests that it might be a case of tourists bringing back souvenirs!

In Bob Smith's opinion "There's no doubt that they were made in China, and further were made in Shanghai in particular—else why would Shanghai China be moulded into the base? If it was a souvenir it would be on the face of the glass, not hidden on the bottom. Being made in Shanghai presents a problem however, in terms of further research. The Communist government changed all the names of the glass factories from proper names into mundane names such as Glass Factory #3 and Glass Factory #12, etc. That is how all factories were described in the 1980s Chinese Business Directory—about a dozen glass factories in the Directory were located in Shanghai."

Confirmation of this came when Ray Rogers supplied us with details of a business trip to Shanghai when he and his wife, Jean, were entertained in the apartment of a Chinese colleague. The Rogers were amazed to find themselves sipping orange juice from *SNOW CHRYSANTHEMUM* glasses! They were even more amazed and somewhat nervous when another Chinese business associate filled one of the glasses with hot water to make Chinese tea! The Rogers explained that their Chinese associates had been given a set of six glasses in the 1980s by a friend in Shanghai. Ray studied the set of six tumblers and noted that "the design is ground, not etched. Comparing the tumblers side by side the design is the same but each was ground by hand as the size of the leaves and flowers vary." Sincere thanks to the Rogers for this information.

A selection of Chinese tumblers, courtesy of Bob Smith. From left: *SHANGHAI, GOLDEN TRIANGLE, CHINESE GRAPE, SNOW CHRYSANTHEMUM,* and *CHINA SUN. Photo © Michael Whitten.* SP $15-40 each.

BAMBOO SPIKES

This tumbler has a triangle moulded on the base—the number 4 is above it and the number 2 is below. There are twelve "spikes" around the base. Two examples have been found in the USA.

> Shape: regular sized tumbler (4") for mixed drinks
> Color: marigold

CHINESE GRAPE

This tumbler features a grape pattern ground into the glass. It has a triangle moulded on the base—the number 1409 is above it and the number 36 is below. The triangle is at the center of many narrow spikes, radiating outward like a star. Three of these are known, of which one was found in Tennessee and one in Louisiana. All these have at least one different smaller number on their bases.

> Shape: regular sized tumbler (4") for mixed drinks
> Color: marigold

CHINA SUN

This tumbler has a ground pattern and also features *Made in China* moulded on the base. It has the triangle, but no top number—below the triangle there is a 0. Three examples are known, all have been found in the USA.

> Shape: shot glass (3")
> Color: marigold

GOLDEN TRIANGLE

Eight elongated thumbprint-like indentations are found around the tumbler, just over an inch up from the base. On the base is the moulded triangle with the number 1408 above it. Below, three different numbers are reported—14, 36, and 37. These three examples have all been found in Australia.

> Shape: regular sized tumbler (4") for mixed drinks
> Color: marigold

SHANGHAI

A pattern of ovals or floral motifs goes around this tumbler. On the base above the moulded triangle is 2106 and underneath the triangle is the number 21. It also has *Shanghai China* moulded on the base. Two examples are known, both found in the USA. Ray and Jean Rogers report a vase in similar marigold with flower and leaf design ground through the iridescence. It is 9" high with a flared top, below which are two urn like scrolls. The neck diameter is 1.5", body diameter is 4" and base diameter is a little over 1.5". There is no code on the bottom. The iridescence on the vase is identical to that on the tumblers.

> Shapes: shot glass (3") and vase
> Color: marigold

SNOW CHRYSANTHEMUM

A white etched chrysanthemum and a string of leaves are found about half way up the tumbler. On the base above the moulded triangle is 27H9 while underneath the triangle is a number that differs from tumbler to tumbler (21, 24, 28, 30, 34, and 36 are currently known).

Shape: regular sized tumbler (a little over 4").
Color: marigold

GOLDEN DIAMOND

Finally, six examples of one other pattern have also been found in the USA. Bob Smith has named them GOLDEN DIAMOND, as there is a diamond and the number 29 moulded into the base. The color and all other characteristics are the same as the triangle ones except for the fact that these have the diamond and not a triangle.

Also there is just the one number on the base, but this is also a characteristic of the CHINA SUN tumbler.

Shape: whiskey glass.
Color: marigold

Finally, a brief mention of a number of other items recently found in the Far East (by Ray and Jean Rogers) and New Zealand (by Galen and Kathi Johnson). Several bowls and a stemmed compote were found by the Johnsons in broad geometric designs that are unlike any other known patterns. Intriguingly, a delightful covered jar matching the identical pattern of one of the bowls was found in Shanghai by the Rogers. The pattern on the body of the jar is of buzz stars and file-filled circles. The finial on the covered lid is in the shape of a little rabbit. Research continues into these fascinating items that quite possibly were made in the Far East.

Opposite page:
A composite drawing of mystery patterns that may well have been made in the Far East. Center is the BUNNY JAR found by Ray and Jean Rogers in Shanghai—its pattern of buzz stars and file-filled circles is identical to that on a bowl found by the Johnsons in New Zealand. The three "lacy-pattern" details across the bottom are from two other bowls also found by the Johnsons. From left: the marie on the LATTICE HOOK bowl, detail from the flowing S pattern on the LATTICE HOOK bowl, and detail from the LOTS O'DOTS bowl. Could they all have been made in Malaysia? Jane Dinkins reported (Texas Carnival Glass News January, 1997) a covered jar with a similar "lacy pattern." Jane noted that on the base was written MALAYSIA in raised letters, with KIG opposite. More mysteries? Research continues.

Part Three

The Second Movement

Late Carnival Glass: The Legacy in America

It's not easy to date the period of Carnival Glass production that collectors call Late Carnival. It followed on from the years of Classic production, which loosely covered the period from around 1907 to 1925 or even later. Some Classic patterns that had been introduced in the early years of Carnival manufacture were still in production up to the late 1920s, according to illustrations in the Butler Brothers catalogs. The popular Fenton patterns *ORANGE TREE* and *HOLLY* as well as the Imperial favorites *HEAVY GRAPE* and *OPEN ROSE* spanned the years from around 1911/1912 right up to 1929.

There was an overlap in production, as Late Carnival is frequently said to date from around 1925 or 1930—running on into the 1950s. Indeed, a study of the Butler Brothers catalogs from the 1920s shows that that is exactly what happened. The Late Carnival patterns were introduced just as the Classic patterns were being phased out. Sometimes Carnival from this era is termed Depression Carnival Glass, though the years of Late Carnival production cover the pre-Depression, Depression, war and post-war years. Bob Smith, who has an astonishing collection of Late Carnival tumblers, says:

> Surprisingly, the years of production of Late Carnival are greater than the production of the old glass. . . In spite of the huge amounts that were made, it is surprising to learn that there is not really much that survived to the present time. I would venture to say that most is already in shards in the landfills and town dumps across America. You might say that you see it all the time in flea markets, shops and thrift shops, but look closely—there really is not that much about—you just think there is. Late water sets were meant to be used daily and were made to be as expendable as razor blades. Old (Classic) Glass was also meant to be used, but it also had a decorative use which helped to preserve it. (Reference: *The Late News*. Premier Newsletter edition. Oppenlander, Kansas).

Note that of the original main five producers of Classic Carnival Glass, those who were still in business in the 1920s continued to put out iridescent lines. Diamond, Fenton, and Imperial all produced some form of Carnival during all or part of the era that covers Late Carnival. Fenton continued such patterns as *BUTTERFLY AND BERRY* and many others, as well as introducing several new patterns in less "busy" designs and shapes. The iridescent Stretch Glass was popular at this time too. A similar shift took place at Diamond (formerly Dugan). Though the Northwood factory had declined following the death of Harry Northwood in 1919, some Iridized glass was still produced at the factory in the 1920s before its final closure in 1925. Imperial's Late Carnival production is looked at in more detail below.

As a matter of fact, the main producers of Late Carnival Glass were an altogether different set of glass manufacturers from those that produced the earlier Classic Carnival. Jeanette and Federal were almost certainly the main producers of Late Carnival in terms of output; Bartlett-Collins plus a few others such as Hazel-Atlas (who produced the peach iridized milk glass "Egg Nog" sets and "Tom and Jerry" punch sets that visitors to antique malls are no doubt familiar with) also produced smaller amounts.

Our aim here, however, is not to present a detailed inventory of Late Carnival, but rather an overview of the characteristics, the main producers, and examples of some of the patterns. Sincere thanks to Michael Whitten for the use of his copyrighted photographs of Bob Smith's Late Carnival tumblers.

Characteristics of Late Carnival

- Machine made in entirety.
- Moulded pattern, flatter and less prominent and in low relief.
- Exterior pattern.
- Pale iridescence with a lighter, airier feel.
- Uniform iridescence.
- Stenciled designs.
- Acid etched designs
- Unusual colors including pale lilac and yellow, though popular colors were green and pink.
- Simple utilitarian shapes—luncheon sets, dinner sets, water sets, and stemware. Often very full ranges with lots of shapes.
- Novelty giftware including banks, powder jars, and ashtrays.

Opposite page:
Butler Brothers catalogs from the late 1920s were carrying Carnival Glass selections that overlapped both the original Classic designs as well as the newer patterns that we now call Late Carnival. This composite ad is from April 1929 and shows, on the left, United States Glass pattern *CHERRY SMASH* (aka *CHERRY BERRY*)—note that the ad mentions Iridescent. On the right are two Imperial patterns: *HEAVY GRAPE* at top and *IMPERIAL ROSE* (aka *OPEN ROSE* or *LUSTRE ROSE*) at bottom.

The Main Manufacturers of Late Carnival Glass

Bartlett-Collins, Sapulpa, Oklahoma

Bartlett-Collins was founded in 1903 in Coffeyville, Kentucky, moving to Sapulpa, Oklahoma in 1912. The location was unusual in that it was west of the Mississippi—the plant had been established there owing to good local fuel supplies. Though its beginnings were small, the company soon made its name by producing attractive, decorated tableware. Lustre treatments were in full swing during the late 1920s, with marigold, cranberry and blue being key colors. Two tumblers, *HAWAIIAN MOON* and *LATE WATERLILY* are detailed below, but a third known as *ENCRUSTED VINE* is also known. All came in the same colors mentioned below.

A selection of Late Carnival tumblers from Bartlett-Collins. From left: *LATE WATERLILY* in marigold, *HAWAIIAN MOON* in cranberry, and *ENCRUSTED VINE* in blue. $15-35 each. *Photo © Michael Whitten.*

HAWAIIAN MOON

Illustrated in the Bartlett-Collins 1943 catalog,[1] *HAWAIIAN MOON* is a decorated pattern featuring a Hawaiian dancer and palm trees against a moonlit sky. The decorating process was a screen and lustre combination, typical of its era, utilizing the silk-screen method of decoration. Found in the USA.
  Shape: tumbler
  Colors: marigold, cranberry and blue

LATE WATERLILY

Illustrated in the Bartlett-Collins 1943 catalog,[1] *LATE WATERLILY* is a decorated pattern featuring a lily pad and cattails. As with

HAWAIIAN MOON, the decorating process was a screen and lustre combination. Found in the USA.
  Shape: tumbler
  Colors: marigold, cranberry, and blue

Belmont, Bellaire, Ohio

In her book *Colored Glassware of the Depression Era,*[2] Hazel Marie Weatherman reports that little is known of this Bellaire company. It seems that a fire razed it to the ground in 1952 and few clues to the factory remain. Iridescent glass was one of the company's lines, however, and at least two items of Late Carnival are credited to Belmont.

SHIP PLATE

A crackle effect rim surrounds the central section of this plate, where a sailing ship in full glory is featured. Weatherman[2] indicates that this item was made by Belmont in iridescent amber (marigold). Mainly seen in the USA.
  Shape: plate
  Color: marigold

STORK ABC PLATE

A delightful gift for a new-born baby, something to treasure; this deep sided child's plate features a stork in the center, surrounded by numbers, while around the rim are the letters of the alphabet. A delightful, whimsical item that is mainly found in the USA but has been discovered in the UK and Australia.
  Shape: plate
  Color: marigold

Dunbar Flint Glass Corporation (later Dunbar Glass Corporation), Dunbar, West Virginia

The Dunbar Flint Glass Corporation began in 1913, making lamp chimneys; its expansion came during the 1920s as it widened its range to produce tableware. Iridescent glass was a staple product at Dunbar, but the iridescence was applied at room temperature rather than onto hot glass, as is usual with Carnival, and then left in a decorating lehr or kiln. Measell and Wiggins[3] explain that this procedure "allows the decorator to coat areas of the piece with the lustre treatment while other portions remain untreated." Lustre colors used by Dunbar include rose, yellow, green, blue, and amethyst. The company ceased operating in 1953.

ARAMIS

A typical style for Dunbar, featuring a series of encircling, horizontal rolls. The pattern was part of a range of water sets produced during the 1930s bearing the names of Alexander Dumas' literary characters. *D'ARTAGNAN* (a smooth and very plain water set) was similarly produced in six different lustre treatments at the same time ("Porthos" and "Athos," the other two Musketeers, were not made in iridized glass). Mainly found in the USA.

Shapes: water set in several different size and shape variations. Tumblers are known in five different sizes; the pitcher is known in a tall shape, a smaller, squatty shape, plus one further size/shape.

Colors: several different lustre treatments: clear, light marigold, dark marigold, light blue, light green, cranberry, and light cranberry. Rare cobalt blue is also known.

ARAMIS by Dunbar, showing the whole range of colors made—courtesy of Bob Smith. *Photo © Michael Whitten. SP $75-100 for set.*

A selection of tumblers from Dunbar, courtesy of Bob Smith. From left: *KEW GARDENS* (marigold), *DUTCHESS* (clear, but is also known in marigold), *PARAMOUNT* (marigold), *ARAMIS* (marigold with gold rings), *TOREDOR* (blue), and *EL PRADO* (marigold). $10-$20 each. *Photo © Michael Whitten.*

Federal Glass Company, Columbus, Ohio.

Federal began producing glass in 1900 and by the 1920s had become "one of the biggest suppliers of machine-made tumblers and jugs."[2] They began their iridescent and lustre treatments during the 20s.

BOUQUET AND LATTICE aka NORMANDIE

Produced by Federal around 1933 to 1940, *BOUQUET AND LATTICE* features a combination of floral and netted motifs. In common with most other examples of its time, the pattern is in low relief. Federal called their iridized marigold "Sunburst." Found in the USA, UK, and Australia.

Shapes: bowls, plates, cup and saucer, sugar
Color: marigold

FRUIT LUSTRE aka LATE EMBOSSED FRUIT

Illustrated in Federal's catalog from 1936 to 1939, *FRUIT LUSTRE* is a familiar tumbler to many collectors. A pattern band featur-

ing a variety of fruits encircles the top of the tumbler while a cluster of grapes (or cherries) is found on the base.

Shape: tumbler
Color: marigold

PIONEER

This pattern was in Federal's line during the 1940s in crystal. Iridized versions of this pattern are known, though it is uncertain as to when they were actually manufactured. The fruit pattern is intaglio on the base. Found in the USA and Australia.

Shapes: bowls and plate
Color: smoke

The Fostoria Glass Company, Moundsville, West Virginia

The company began at Fostoria, Ohio in 1887, but moved to Moundsville, West Virginia when the fuel supplies at the Fostoria location ran out. They are known for their iridescent Mother of Pearl, Taffeta Lustre ware, and iridized Brocaded patterns. The Brocaded designs are especially distinctive with their acid cut-back patterns and unusual colors. Pink, ice green, and ice blue often with gold edges, were typical of Fostoria's iridized colors. According to Weatherman,[2] " In 1925 Fostoria became the first glasshouse to introduce all glass dinnerware in color. These elements fused beautifully and in no time the Fostoria name was known to brides and homemakers everywhere." The company finally folded in the 1980s. Carnival collectors are divided as to whether Fostoria's iridized ranges are "true" Carnival. The patterning on the glassware is achieved not by the press moulding process, but by acid cut-back. However, we feel it is right to mention some of their range in this context.

Fostoria's Brocaded patterns are probably the most easily recognized of the company's iridescent glassware. The patterns all feature stylized floral motifs (*BROCADED ACORNS*, *BROCADED DAFFODILS*, *BROCADED PALMS*, to mention a few of the most popular ones). The pastel colors are easily recognizable: ice green, ice blue, pink, rare lavender (known as "orchid"), and white. The shapes in which the glassware was made are also fairly typical of Fostoria: handled plates and trays, console sets and even ice buckets. Mainly found in the USA.

Hocking Glass Company / Anchor-Hocking, Lancaster, Ohio

The Hocking Glass Company began in Lancaster in 1905 in a small way, producing decorated milk glass products,[3] but by the mid 1920s they had grown substantially and were incorporated in 1937 within the Anchor Cap and Closure Corporation (a container manufacturer) to become the Anchor-Hocking Glass Corporation, a leader in machine-made glass tableware and containers. In the 1957-58 Anchor-Hocking catalog, large and small *PIG* money banks as well as the *LIBERTY BELL* bank are listed. Quite likely they had been in production for some years prior to that date. Very possibly the *WORLD* and *RABBIT* money banks were also Anchor-Hocking items. A number of tumblers in light marigold were produced by them, and can be identified by the anchor trademark on the base.

FIREKING PEACH LUSTRE

Included here for information purposes, as most Carnival collectors would not include this tableware in their collection, yet it **is** iridized and press moulded with a pattern! Introduced in the 1950s and used sporadically through to the 1970s, this tableware had the added attraction of being heat-resistant! The peach iridized examples are on milk glass. "Peach Lustre" was used for the color and not just the pattern range. Moulded patterns featuring either a laurel design or a swirled effect are both known.

A cup and saucer in *FIREKING PEACH LUSTRE*. *Courtesy of Pauline and Duncan Rowlinson.* $10-15.

SORENO

Hocking's name for this pattern was *SORENO* and today's collectors have retained it. The pattern is similar to a *TREEBARK* design except the bark goes around the tumbler instead of up and down.

Shapes: regular water set and juice
Colors: white, green, and cranberry

Imperial Glass Corporation, Wheeling, Ohio

Familiar to every Carnival collector as one of the "Big Five" manufacturers from the Classic era of Carnival production, Imperial also produced several iridized lines through the Late Carnival period.

FROSTED BLOCK

This pattern and its "sister," *BEADED BLOCK,* were introduced in the mid 1920s and appear to have been produced in fairly large quantities; indeed, F.W. Woolworth & Co. advertised and marketed the range. Examples are often found that were presumably intended for export, with the moulded wording "Made in USA." The pattern is basically a squared block design, the edges to the squares being beaded. The *FROSTED BLOCK* variation has stippling ("frosting") within the squares and was made in Carnival Glass in the 1920s. *BEADED BLOCK* was made in pink Carnival in the 1970s when Imperial re-issued this line (items are marked IG). Imperial called the color—a shimmering light purplish pink—"Princess Pink." Only a vase and bowl were issued in the *BEADED BLOCK* pattern in Carnival at that time.

FROSTED BLOCK items were produced in the distinct clambroth shade (a delicate, multi-hued, golden color) that was called "Rainbow" by Imperial at the time of issue. Later in the 1920s a deeper shade called "Rubigold" (marigold) was made[4]. Examples of *FROSTED BLOCK* have been found in the USA, UK, and Australia.

Shapes: bowls, plates, milk pitcher, creamer, sugar, rose bowl, pickle dish, handled nappy, stemmed sherbert, and vase
Colors: marigold, clambroth, white, and smoke

Jeanette Glass Company, Jeanette, Pennsylvania

Jeanette was one of the major manufacturers of Late Carnival Glass, "a pioneer in bringing automation together with color."[2] In common with many other glass producers, Jeanette began as a bottle plant in the late 1800s (probably around 1898[3]). As time went on, however, table glassware (very occasionally marked with their early trademark J-in-triangle) became the company's staple output. They introduced iridized lines in around 1920 and continued them over a long period of time. Automation took over and by 1927 the company had announced the cessation of all hand operations in favor of mechanical ones. By 1928, they were turning out over fifty tons of glass a day. The company grew and expanded; in 1961, Jeanette bought the old McKee factory and moved the premises to their site. Glass from that period is often referred to as Jeanette McKee. In 1982, it was reported that the Fenton Art Glass Company purchased over a thousand moulds from Jeanette McKee.

The *SOUVENIR OF BUFFALO* juice glass was made by Jeanette.

Golden Iridescent

IC1884—7 piece set, fine pressed glass, rustic effect, fired golden iridescent finish, tall tankard shape jug, six 9 oz. bell tumblers. ⅓ doz. sets in case, 50 lbs.
Doz sets $8.25

TREE BARK is variously thought to be Imperial, Jeanette, or possibly even Diamond—this ad was shown in Butler Brothers catalogs through the late 1920s.

BEEHIVE HONEYPOT

An attractive covered honeypot that features a little bee on the lid. This distinctive item has been found in the USA and UK.

Shape: honeypot
Colors: marigold and pale teal blue

BUTTERFLY

Familiar to many as pintrays or party dishes, the *BUTTERFLY* items were also issued as ashtrays, being part of a cigarette set that also included a butterfly-adorned cigarette box! The actual dishes were made in the shape of a butterfly with outstretched wings. The "5 piece Party Set," containing dishes for bonbons or the like, was "presentation boxed" and comprised one large butterfly and four small, matching ones. Found in the USA, UK, and Australia, they were made between 1940 and 1960 and were undoubtedly popular items.

Shapes: ashtray, pintray, dish
Colors: marigold, aqua, pink, and smoke

CORNUCOPIA aka HORN OF PLENTY

The *CORNUCOPIA* vase was featured in Jeanette's advertising over a number of years. A most attractive and unusual little vase. Found mainly in the USA.

Shape: vase
Color: marigold

CRACKLE

A familiar, flat crackled design. The automobile vase in this pattern was being advertised in 1925 and has a metal holder to attach it to a car's interior. All shapes of *CRACKLE* are found in the USA, though only the bowls are found in any quantity in the UK.

Shapes: bowls, plates, covered candy jar, pitcher, tumbler, vase, and automobile vase

Colors: marigold. Other reported shades are pale blue, lavender, and green but we cannot confirm these colors.

GONDOLA

This is a large fruit bowl or planter, according to Jeanette's advertising, and was sold gift-boxed. It is distinctive by virtue of its size (it's almost 18" long, yet only 5" wide) and its Rococo style pattern. Often mistaken for Classic, older Carnival, this splendid item was actually made in the 1950s and is found mainly in the USA, but also the UK and occasionally Australia.

Shape: banana boat shaped fruit bowl
Color: marigold

IRIS AND HERRINGBONE

Possibly the most familiar pattern in Late Carnival that has been found all over the world (though the greatest quantities have naturally been found in the USA). The pattern was introduced in crystal in 1928, though iridized production was later, from the 1950s through the 1970s. Characterized by the horizontal herringbone ribs or stripes in the background, against which is set the stylized iris blossoms, this pattern is known in a very wide range of shapes and colors. There are sought after rarities in this pattern: at the top of the list would be the water goblet and the demitasse cup. There is also a variation to this pattern where the iris is replaced by chrysanthemums (*HERRINGBONE AND MUMS*)—only rare marigold tumblers are known in this variation. Interestingly, the *IRIS AND HERRINGBONE* tumbler is the only one that was also used as a food container (filled with cottage cheese and sealed with a brass colored lid).

Shapes: bowls, plates, butterdish, candlestick, cup and saucer, demitasse cup and saucer, goblet, pitcher and tumbler, covered sugar, sherbet, and vase

Colors: marigold and rare shades of lavender, blue, and rose pink

IRIS AND HERRINGBONE is probably one of the most well known patterns from the Jeanette Glass Company. This is a splendid marigold plate that really shows the pattern well. *Courtesy of Rita and Les Glennon.* $15-25.

LATE SUNFLOWER

Originally called "Cosmos" or "All White Cosmos" in Jeanette's own advertising from 1949, this water set was decorated in white—known as "Decoration No. 58." The water pitcher has a distinctive ice lip, to trap ice cubes. The white enameled decoration depicts a stylized cosmos flower and encircling leaves. Found in the USA and UK.

Shapes: pitcher in two sizes and tumbler in three sizes
Color: marigold (Jeanette called it "Golden iridescent") with white decal decoration

LOMBARDI

Advertised as a "4 Toe LOMBARDI bowl" back in the 1950s, this large Rococo style, banana boat shaped dish (almost 11" in length) is often mistaken for much older glass. Found in the USA, UK, and Australia.

Shape: banana boat shaped fruit bowl
Color: marigold and possibly other colors including light blue

LOUISA or FLORAGOLD tumblers usually have a distinctive, light iridescence. $2-5. This is the easily found small example—the larger lemonade size has a value around $85-100 and is exceptionally scarce.

The large, marigold LOMBARDI fruit bowl from Jeanette Glass. *Courtesy of Rita and Les Glennon.* $20-50.

LOUISA aka FLORAGOLD

In Classic Carnival, this pattern was made by Westmoreland (the footed rose bowl is probably the most frequently seen item) but it was also made in the 1950s through the early 1970s by Jeanette. The pattern features a lacy, stylized floral motif; the shapes have a squared off effect. The tumbler is known in two sizes, the large one being highly sought after by collectors, as it was in production for a very short time before being re-issued as a vase shape. Examples of LOUISA aka FLORAGOLD have been found in the USA, UK, and Australia.

Shapes: bowls, plates, butterdish, candlestick, candy dish, cheese dish, creamer, cup and saucer, pitcher, ashtray, salt and pepper, sherbet, sugar, tumbler (in two sizes), and vase
Color: marigold

TREEBARK VARIANT

Another familiar pattern often seen on water sets and vases, TREEBARK VARIANT is a fairly simple pattern that quite simply imitates the texture and appearance of tree bark. Found mainly in the USA, but also (though infrequently) in the UK and Australia. A similar pattern, TREEBARK, has not been attributed with certainty to a manufacturer.

Shapes: bowls, water pitcher, tumbler, covered candy jar, candlestick, and vase
Color: marigold

D. C. Jenkins Glass Company (formerly Kokomo Glass Co.), Kokomo, Indiana

The glass plant at Kokomo began back in 1901 and lasted through till only 1932. Tumblers, kitchenware, and some tableware were the main products. Weatherman reports that green was the company's main color, but "during its later years, doped ware, in which pieces of crystal glass were given a golden iridescent bath to yield a Carnival-like effect" was made.[2]

STORK VASE

Standing on one leg in the traditional pose, a stork is the main pattern motif on this Depression era vase—in the background are the typical rushes. The pattern is on one side only. Butler Brothers catalogs carried ads for the STORK VASE during the late 1920s. Found mainly in the USA.

Shape: vase
Color: marigold

IC1154—2 colors, crystal and amber iridescent, 7¾ in., floral and stork embossed patterns. 3 doz. in carton.. Doz 92c

Jenkins *STORK* vase was advertised in the Butler Brothers catalogs in the late 1920s

Morgantown Glass Works / Economy Glass Company, Morgantown, West Virginia

Tumblers and stemware were the staple outputs of the Morgantown Glass Works (later successively named the Economy Tumbler Company, the Economy Glass Works, and then again Morgantown Glass Works). Iridescent glass was one of the new color lines brought in during the 1920s during a period of expansion, as a wide variety of tableware was added to the company's range.

ROUND ROBIN
Though the pattern is a simple pillar flute, the shape of the creamer and sugar is most distinct, being tightly waisted above the stem. Found mainly in the USA.
Shapes: bowl, plate, cup and saucer, creamer, sugar, and sherbet
Color: marigold

United States Glass Company, Pittsburgh, Ohio (and other locations)

The United States Glass Company was formed in 1891 from an association of fifteen separate glass manufacturers. Company headquarters was in Pittsburgh, Pennsylvania. In the early 1920s the company was boasting 30,000 pieces of glassware, on display at its Pittsburgh showrooms. From 1924, however, the conglomerate began to suffer heavy financial losses and in 1938 only two of the original companies remained: the Tiffin plant and the head office at Pittsburgh. Operations finally dwindled during the 1960s and 70s.

AUNT POLLY
Here is another pattern whose manufacturing origins frustrated Weatherman. This rather simple pattern, made in the late 1920s, features plain panels and diamonds. Another version simply has the panels. Found mainly in the USA.
Shapes: bowls, butterdish, sugar, creamer, plate, candy dish, and vase
Color: marigold

CHERRY SMASH aka *CHERRY BERRY*
CHERRY SMASH and its "sister" pattern, *STIPPLED STRAW-BERRY*, were un-attributed to a manufacturer for a long time. The frustration of Weatherman can be felt when she lists both patterns as a riddle she had been trying to solve for years, stating "If I could just find out who made that #@*% STRAWBERRY."[2] Thanks to the research of Fred Bickenheuser and William Heacock, the U.S. Glass Company was finally proved to have been the elusive manufacturer. All examples are very hard to find and often have very light marigold iridescence. The notched band around the top is common to all shapes. Found mainly in the USA.
Shapes: bowls, tumbler, and pitcher in both patterns
Color: marigold.

DIAMOND AND DAISY CUT aka *FLORAL AND DIAMOND BAND* aka *MAYFLOWER*

A combination of a stylized intaglio floral motif and a band of double diamonds. Catalog ads from 1928 illustrate the pattern in the water set. As with *CHERRY SMASH*, this pattern was un-attributed for many years. Found mainly in the USA.

Shapes: tumbler and pitcher
Color: marigold

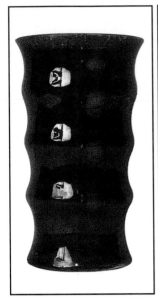

A selection of Late Carnival tumblers to give an idea of their variety, all shown courtesy of Bob Smith. This one is *BEAUTY QUEEN*. Unknown maker. $20. *Photo © Michael Whitten.*

BLUMS DEPARTMENT STORE. Unknown maker. $100-125. *Photo © Michael Whitten.*

CIRCLES. Anchor Hocking. $10. *Photo © Michael Whitten.*

FEDERAL JUICE. With trademark (rare), $30. Without trademark, $15. *Photo © Michael Whitten.*

LATE PEACOCK. Jeanette Glass Co. Rare. $40-50. *Photo © Michael Whitten.*

LATE MORNING GLORY. Jeanette Glass Co. $20-25. *Photo © Michael Whitten.*

LATE POINSETTIA. Jeanette Glass Co. $20. *Photo © Michael Whitten.*

MEADOW FLOWERS. Jeanette Glass Co. $20-25. *Photo © Michael Whitten.*

MERRY GO ROUND. Unknown maker. $15. *Photo © Michael Whitten.*

MINUET. Jeanette Glass Co. Known in three sizes. Rare. $50-100. *Photo © Michael Whitten.*

SCHLITZ BEER and *HAMM'S BEER* advertising tumblers made by Libbey. Each $35. *Photo © Michael Whitten.*

Postscript

Various enameled tumblers are known that were almost certainly produced in Czechoslovakia and Germany. Various theories put the date of these tumblers from the late 1800s through the 1940s. It seems quite possible that they were, in fact, produced at the same time as Carnival in Czechoslovakia or possibly even earlier. However, some of them may have been from the Late Carnival era and so fit within this section of the book. Made of thin glass and with carefully applied enamel work, they are very hard to find.

[1] Hazel Marie Weatherman, *The Decorated Tumbler* (Springfield, Missouri: Glassbooks Inc., 1978).

[2] Hazel Marie Weatherman, *Colored Glassware of the Depression Era 2* (Ozark, Missouri: Weatherman Glass Books, 1974).

[3] James Measell and Berry Wiggins, *Great American Glass of the Roaring 20s and Depression Era* (Marietta, Ohio: The Glass Press, 1998).

[4] National Imperial Glass Collectors' Society, *Imperial Glass Encyclopedia. Volume 1. A-Cane* (Marietta, Ohio: The Glass Press, 1995).

Czech *ENAMELED LITTLE GIRL* large tumbler in marigold, age uncertain. *Photo ©️ Michael Whitten.* NP.

Czech light blue liqueur set, age uncertain. *Photo ©️ Michael Whitten.* NP.

Czech *ENAMELED MELON RIBBED DAISY* large tumbler in marigold, age uncertain. *Photo ©️ Michael Whitten.* NP.

REINDEER tumbler, possibly from Germany, age uncertain. *Photo ©️ Michael Whitten.* NP.

Part Four

The Encore

We offer no apologies for using the same name as Dorothy Taylor's books[1] and journals [2] on Contemporary Carnival for the title of Part Four—in fact we use it here as a tribute to her phenomenal contribution and pioneering work. Dorothy's *Encore* journal was issued every two months over a period of nearly twenty years that began in 1975. Within it are contemporary ads and reports on factories as well as contributions from subscribers—all of these help to paint a picture of the Carnival scene in those early years of Contemporary Carnival Glass collecting (from around the late 1960s and 1970s) that is truly invaluable. Also of great importance are O.J. Olson's *Carnival News and Views* and *Tumbler Reviews*[3] for similar contemporary reports. Our sincere thanks go to Ray and Judy Steele for sourcing the Olson newsletters. Fellow long-time Carnival collector John Resnik also assisted greatly by loaning an archive file of Contemporary Carnival ads assembled by the late Don Moore. Our thanks to him and all the other collectors who have provided information and allowed their glass to be photographed—we are indebted to them all. Further information on Contemporary Carnival can be obtained via collectors' clubs such as the Collectible Carnival Glass Association. As the production of Contemporary Carnival is ongoing, we strongly recommend to all readers with Internet access, John Valentine's excellent and very comprehensive, subscription access website, which is constantly updated. Full details of how to access it are given in the footnote at the end of Chapter Four.

It is difficult to be totally precise with regard to the phenomenal range of Contemporary Carnival Glass that is available. Indeed, many moulds are still in production, so colors and shapes as noted in the text below cannot be taken as finite and conclusive. Glass is still being produced and moulds are still changing hands. New patterns, new colors, and new shapes will continue to emerge. Confusingly, some old trademarks remain on some examples of Carnival glass that is still being made today. Fortunately this is not widespread and most manufacturers take pride in trademarking their current production.

Notes on Price Bands. Assigning values to Contemporary Carnival is a very difficult task indeed. Prices vary enormously and little information beyond simple observation is available. For this reason it was decided to use value ranges for photographed glass in this book. Four main price bands have been used: A for items below $25, B for items in the $25-50 range, and C for items between $50 and $100. For items that are rare and/or likely to exceed $100, the price band is D. Where an item overlaps the groups, AB or BC is noted instead. As with other value estimates in this book, we emphasize that this is a guide only and neither the authors nor the publishers can be liable for any losses incurred when using the values attributed within this book as the basis for any transaction.

Chapter One

The Impetus

With the passage of time, iridized glass, particularly that from the Classic era, began to be seen as a collectible in its own right. As we noted in our book *Carnival Glass: The Magic and the Mystery*, the turning point probably came with the first authoritative article on Carnival Glass, written by Gertrude L. Conboy and published in *The Spinning Wheel* on January 10, 1952. Mrs. Conboy had fallen under the spell of Carnival ten years earlier, when she had come upon a furniture store sale and discovered a table full of the glass. She had purchased a deep purple, Northwood *ORIENTAL POPPY* tumbler, which had become the impetus for her subsequent research into its background. Her article was a milestone for Carnival—and the glass began to acquire an identity. Soon Marion T. Hartung and Rose M. Presznick fuelled the development of Carnival's rise to fame through the 1960s. Both writers issued pattern books on the glass based on their own research and collecting experiences. Writers and Carnival researchers such as Don Moore and Sherman Hand fuelled the boom. Carnival Glass continued from strength to strength, boosted by the continuing formation of collectors' clubs and associations on an international basis.

The first such club was the Society of Carnival Glass Collectors (SCGC), based in Kansas City and founded by O. Joe Olson in 1964. Within four weeks there were one hundred and fifty charter members. Joe was the founder and editor-secretary, publishing the very first newsletter on August 10, 1964. The world's first Carnival Glass convention was organized under the aegis of the newly formed club. The first president was the Reverend Leslie Wolfe, who later went on to jointly found the International Carnival Glass Association (ICGA), while another of the early SCGC pioneers, E. Ward Russell, was later instrumental in organizing the American Carnival Glass Association (ACGA). Then came the Heart of America Carnival Glass Association (HOACGA)—these clubs were all primarily devoted to the older, Classic Carnival.

At around the same time, several glass manufacturers realized there was a niche in the market for contemporary versions of the old, Classic Carnival. The Imperial Glass Company in Ohio and Joe St. Clair in Ellwood, Indiana were two of the first manufacturers to introduce Carnival—as a collectible—to their line in the 1960s. Imperial re-issued their *IMPERIAL GRAPE* goblets in marigold in 1961, following up with a major line of seventy different items in 1965.

One club in particular was also established—Carnival Glass *Encore*. It was the inspiration of Dorothy Taylor and was based entirely around new Carnival Glass. Established in 1975 and based in Kansas City, it grew and thrived; indeed, the club and its newsletter[2] inspired a generation of collectors to acquire the new glass. It was a passion for Taylor. She continued to write the newsletter for almost twenty years, mailing it all over the USA and even further afield; *Encore* also had its annual conventions and even its own Carnival Glass commemorative souvenirs. A trio of ring bound books was also published by Taylor, solely devoted to modern Carnival Glass[1].

From these beginnings in the 1960s and 70s, other glass manufacturers soon joined in: Mosser, Westmoreland, Viking, Boyd, L.E. Smith, Summit, and more. Most recent is the Northwood Glass Company, established in 1998. The accolade, however, must be given to the Fenton Art Glass Company, who manufactured their first Carnival Glass around 1907. Of all the original manufacturers, Fenton is the only who has continued in production to this very day. Carnival Glass of the highest quality, sought after by collectors world-wide, is still made at Williamstown, on the original site where Frank L. Fenton oversaw the first Carnival items taking shape so many years ago.

Contemporary Carnival is not simply Reproduction Carnival. Though quite a number of Classic Carnival patterns have been re-issued, they are often trademarked (Fenton and Imperial virtually always is) and are usually in different colors or shapes from the original Classic examples. There are exceptions, of course, and it behooves the collector to read as much as possible to gain information on the re-issues. There are also the fakes (see relevant section in Part Four, Chapter Five). However, the majority of Contemporary Carnival is comprised of new issues: new moulds, fresh patterns, inventive shapes and designs, wonderful and exotic colors. Many of the new items have been made in limited quantities, affordable at the time of release but rapidly increasing in value as time goes by. The location of items "found" has not been noted in this section on Contemporary Carnival Glass, as owing to modern marketing, it is frequently distributed worldwide and can be found all over the world.

A whole sub-section of Contemporary Carnival centered around the collectors' clubs has also grown up. Souvenirs for conventions, table favors, and other commemoratives have been commissioned by internationally known clubs such as HOACGA, ICGA, and ACGA. Almost all the smaller, regional clubs have done likewise, resulting in some beautiful and unique items being produced over the years. Similarly, collectors' clubs in the UK, Canada, and Australia have also commissioned some fine examples of commemorative Carnival Glass. Most recently, the Internet based club, Woodsland World Wide (www.cga) has had its own Commemorative plunger and mould produced (in the *WOODSLAND PINE* pattern, exterior design *FLOWERS OF THE WORLD*). More on all these items is presented below: see also *Carnival Glass Club Commemoratives, An Informative Guide* for comprehensive information[4].

[1] Dorothy Taylor, *Encore by Dorothy. Books 1 to 3* (Kansas City, Missouri: by author, 1984-1986).

[2] Dorothy Taylor, *Encore* journals (Club newsletters).

[3] O. Joe Olson, *Carnival Glass News and Views* and *Carnival Glass News* journals and newsletters (Kansas City, Missouri: by author).

[4] Diane C. Rosington, *Carnival Glass Club Commemoratives, An Informative Guide* (Rochester, New York: by author, 2000).

The Major Manufacturers (and Wholesaler Distributors) of Contemporary Carnival Glass

Boyd's Crystal Art Glass, Cambridge, Ohio

The Boyd family's connections with glass go back to Zackary Thomas Boyd, who began work at Cambridge Glass Company in 1901 at the tender age of thirteen. His marriage to Erma Hollet in 1907 cemented the tradition, as she was also a Cambridge employee. Zack's work took him to over twenty-five other glass producers and he worked for such notable concerns as Imperial, Kemple, and Degenhart during his career. Zack and Erma's only son, Bernard C. Boyd, followed in Zack's footsteps and at age sixteen, became apprenticed to his father. Bernard C.'s growing interest in glass chemistry and its processes led him to get further involved with his father's glassmaking at the Degenhart Glass factory.

A delightful collection of Boyd novelties shown here courtesy of Rita and Les Glennon and Angie and Andrew Thistlewood. Top row, left to right: *TRACTOR* (royal plum), *VIRGIL, SAD & HAPPY FACE CLOWN* (royal plum), *"J.B." SCOTTIE DOG* (cobalt). Middle row: *ARTIE, PENGUIN* (cardinal red), *ZACK, ELEPHANT* (cardinal red), *PATRICK, BALLOON BEAR* (classic black). Bottom row: *WILLIE, THE MOUSE* (cardinal red), *JEREMY FROG* (sunkiste), and *SKIPPY* (cardinal red). All price band A.

Bernard C.'s son, Bernard Franklin—and in turn, the fourth generation, Bernard Franklin's son, John—all had a passion for glassmaking: it was "in the blood." With the passing of Elizabeth Degenhart, the Boyds, in accordance with her will, purchased her business in Cambridge. Their first task was to have the "D" in a heart logo removed from the moulds and be replaced with the Boyd "B" in a diamond. On October 10, 1978, production began at the newly established Boyd's Crystal Art Glass (formerly Degenhart Glass). Glass production at Boyd's is labor intensive and hand pressing is the norm; it's also still very much a family business. In their own words, "Boyd's Glass still manufactures collectibles the old-fashioned way, to the delight of visitors and collectors, with a man and a mould and not with an automated machine." John Boyd gave us the following insight, written by his father, Bernard Franklin, on how Boyd's produce their Carnival Glass.

We use titanium spray to give the glass the Carnival look. We use the same spray on all the colors and the base color makes the different looks. If you hold the glass to the light, you can see the base color. The problems of the Carnival Glass are the mixture is very flammable, and if we have a build up of this white power, this build up can cause a fire. The titanium liquid is light yellow, but when sprayed on hot glass it will become a white powder residue. Another problem is the titanium will freeze, or get solid at 60 degrees F., and our factory gets cold in the winter. That is why most of our Carnival is done in the warm weather, or if we have an unusually mild winter. To make Carnival Glass, you need another man to spray the glass. Our normal shop is made up of just 4 men: gatherer, presser, turning-out man, and carrying-in man. We carnivalize the glass when it is hot. The turning-out man takes the glass to the spray area, and the hot glass is sprayed, and given to the carrying-in man who puts the glass in the lehr to be slowly cooled to the proper temperature. This normally slows down the production of the glass, because of this extra process, and the using of another man to make Carnival Glass. That is why Carnival Glass is a little more expensive to produce than regular glass.

Experimentation with color has always been a characteristic of the factory's work and the tradition continues to this day; indeed over three hundred colors are listed. Many items are offered in Carnival finish. Boyd's first Carnival color was "Mint Green Carnival"—an iridescent opaque green; it was to be the first of many iridized colors that would make Boyd's a favorite with the collectors. John Boyd kindly provided the authors with a complete listing of every Carnival color made by Boyd—complete with dates. This list, reproduced in Appendix 2, will be a great asset to all Boyd collectors. Sincere thanks to the Boyd family for their assistance.

The shapes that are particularly characteristic of the factory are the small whimsical, novelty shapes: colonial ladies and men, mice, owls, ducks, teddy bears, horse, dogs, and the splendid airplane, tractor, taxi, tugboat and train set—and more. They have over two hundred moulds! A number of old Imperial moulds were purchased at that company's liquidation in 1985. Boyd's glass is always marked with their trademark: the B in a diamond. The position and number of lines around the diamond indicate the year of manufacture (see Appendix 3).

A Selection of Boyd's Contemporary Carnival Glass

BOYD SPECIAL TRAIN

This is a splendid miniature train set in glass that comprises engine, tender, box car, tanker, hopper, and caboose. The concept was decided upon in 1984 and the moulds were made by the Laurel Mould Shop in Jeanette, Pennsylvania. A wide range of Carnival colors has been used for the *SPECIAL TRAIN*, including such delicious sounding names as banana cream Carnival (1994), mint julep Carnival (1995), and sunkiste Carnival (1995).

Shape: novelty train set
Colors: to date, 20 Carnival colors have been used for the train set. The first was cobalt blue Carnival completed in 1989.

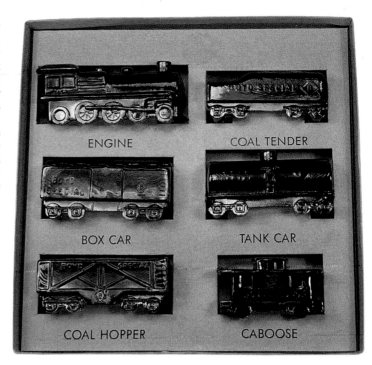

ENGINE   COAL TENDER

BOX CAR   TANK CAR

COAL HOPPER   CABOOSE

The delightful *BOYD SPECIAL TRAIN* in mulberry purple—neatly set out in its box. *Courtesy of Rita and Les Glennon*. Price band C.

COLONIAL MAN

Striking an elegant figure in his long top-coat, stylish cravat, knee breeches, and buckle shoes, *COLONIAL MAN* was introduced in 1986 as a companion to another Boyd favorite, the *COLONIAL DOLLS*. Over four years, twenty-six individual *COLONIAL MAN* figurines were issued in as many different colors, each bearing a different name, tagged with descriptions, and issued alphabetically—thus, the first was Adam in 1986. The named dolls were limited to a production run of only 500 each. Only three of the named *COLONIAL MAN* figures have been issued in Carnival: Stephen (cobalt Carnival), Ulysses (milk white Carnival), and Zachary (grape parfait Carnival), all in 1989. Further un-named and un-tagged *COLONIAL MAN* novelties were issued between 1990 and 1995 in six further Carnival Glass colors.

Shape: novelty figurine
Colors: named dolls in cobalt blue, milk white, and grape parfait Carnival. Un-named dolls in the following Carnival colors—sunkiste, chocolate, classic black, lime, crown Tuscan, and alexandrite.

This cobalt blue *COLONIAL MAN* is named "Stephen" on the accompanying label. Price band AB.

ELI AND SARAH

An Amish couple, *ELI AND SARAH* were first made in 1996. Delightful novelty miniatures in full Amish dress, Boyd has so far made them in just two Carnival colors, both in 1997.

    Shape: pair of novelty figurines
    Colors: cobalt blue and purple

ELI AND SARAH were made in cobalt blue Carnival by Boyd in 1997. *Courtesy of Rita and Les Glennon.* Price band AB.

LOUISE

Introduced to Boyd's range in 1979, the *LOUISE* Colonial Lady figurine was designed in the style of a Lornetta Glass mould that had been made by Bernard C. Boyd. It was altered a little by a local artist and made daintier and was named *LOUISE* after Bernard's wife, Louise Helen Boyd. The company reports that, although it was re-

tired from the general line in 1984, it is still produced twice a year: once as a doll bell and once as a hand-painted doll.

    Shape: novelty doll
    Colors: before retirement *LOUISE* was made in the Carnival colors of olympic white and purple, both in 1984. Carnival colors since then include vaseline, mint julep, classic black, pale orchid, cardinal red, crown Tuscan, holiday, Windsor blue, lemon custard, and alexandrite.

ZACK

As a tribute to Boyd's first glassmaker, an elephant named *ZACK* was introduced on January 20, 1981. Boyd's promotional literature states that "this item was patterned after another New Martinsville mould" and goes on to relate the delightful story that on a Barbara Walters' television special with President and Mrs. Reagan, a Boyd *ZACK* elephant "could be seen on a shelf in the background." No carnival examples were made in *ZACK*'s first year of production, but in 1984, white and cobalt Carnival were produced. The mould was retired from the general line in 1985 but has since been brought into use just once each year, on a date close to the late Zack Boyd's birthday, November 8th.

    Shape: novelty elephant figurine
    Colors: cobalt blue (1984), crown Tuscan (1990), classic black (1991), cardinal red (1992), alexandrite (1993), and sunkiste (1995). (*ZACK* was also made in 1994, but not in Carnival Glass.)

Crider Art Glass, Wapakoneta, Ohio

Terry Crider's family background was in antiquing and collecting—and this is what fostered his love of glass. Terry's glass knowledge was self-taught: his chemistry background led him to experiment with glass formulas and iridescence. He first began to make Carnival around 1967. Between then and the spring of 1974, he used a process of applying metallic lustres to cold glass and firing them in a kiln. Back in those early days, before 1974, everything took two applications and two separate firings—indeed some took three applications and three separate firings. In the spring of 1974, however, Crider started using thermo-lustres that were sprayed onto hot glass—these were the same lustres that Fenton and other factories were using at the time. The glass was re-heated in the kiln, taken out of the kiln, sprayed quickly, and put back in the kiln. The Criders report that "there was a lot of breakage this way."

Terry and Donna Crider working together to make a "Heart and Vine" cuspidor (not Carnival). In this shot, Donna is applying the white milk glass to be used for the hearts. *Photo courtesy of Terry and Donna Crider.*

Boyd's *LOUISE* bell in delicious lemon custard Carnival. Price band B.

In conversation with the authors, Terry told of his association with L.G. Wright in the late 1970s and early 1980s, when he bought glass from Wright's and then iridized it. Wright's version of the "Pulled Husk Corn Vase" and the "Town Pump" were both iridized by Crider, who also re-shaped sugar bowls into spittoons and iridized them. These Wright items iridized by Crider were made in very limited quantities—usually no more than twelve of any one item. Terry Crider usually signs his glass "Crider" or "Terry Crider"—even simply "TC" if there is only a little available space (originally he signed with a diamond-point pen, today he uses an electric engraver); on the limited L.G. Wright pieces, he numbered as well as signed them. Many of those limited items were wholesaled to dealers by the Criders. By the mid 1970s, Crider had begun to iridize items as large as water pitchers. He also took individual commissions (indeed still does) from customers to iridize their glass.

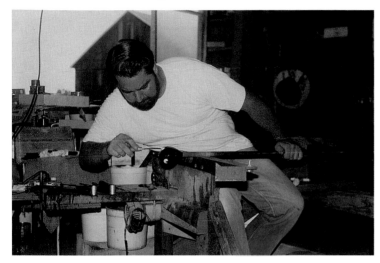

Here Terry Crider is "pulling" the applied hearts on the cuspidor. *Photo courtesy of Terry and Donna Crider.*

After the Criders built their own furnaces, they were able to alter the whole process somewhat. First the "blank" (the uniridized item to be treated) is re-heated in a ceramic kiln to about 1000 degrees F. Whilst hot, it is attached to a punty (pontil) rod and heated further in the glory hole, then sprayed with the metallic salts that provide the iridescent effect. The item may or may not receive further re-heating; the spray may be applied several times between returns to the glory hole in order to achieve the final desired effect. Due to various re-heatings in the glory hole and spray techniques, most of the time the result would be the satiny "Tiffany" Carnival finish rather than the shiny Carnival.

Re-shaping is also possible following re-heating, though breakage is a risk that needs to be borne in mind when carrying out such a procedure. The older the glass, the more likely it is to break on re-heating and re-shaping. Though today Terry mostly makes paperweights and will "custom iridize" glass to order, over the past twenty or more years he has created some splendid and wonderful limited editions of modern Carnival. Sincere thanks to Terry and Donna Crider for their information and photographs.

A Selection of Crider's Contemporary Carnival Glass

EYE WINKER
Crider iridized a number of L.G. Wright blanks in this pattern. W.C. "Red" Roetteis and James Measell note[1] that the moulds were "probably made by Al Botson's Machine and Mould Company in Cambridge, Ohio" and the design was based on "an 1800s motif popularized by the Dalzell, Gilmore and Leighton Company of Findlay, Ohio." Hansen also iridized this pattern (see relevant section), so check signature for correct attribution.
Shape: water set
Colors: red, white, ice blue, pastel green, amber, and marigold.

A red *EYE WINKER* water set, custom iridized by Terry Crider. *Photo courtesy of Terry and Donna Crider.* Price band D.

MAPLE LEAF
Again, Crider iridized L.G. Wright blanks that were made (probably by Westmoreland for L.G. Wright) using the original Dugan/Diamond moulds. Crider's examples will bear his trademark signature.
Shape: water set
Colors: cobalt blue and white

A blue *MAPLE LEAF* water set, custom iridized by Terry Crider. *Photo courtesy of Terry and Donna Crider.* Price band D.

A marigold *CAPE COD* tumbler custom iridized by Crider, shown here courtesy of Bob Smith. *Photo © Michael Whitten.* Price band C.

Crider's *ROSE SPRIG* tumbler in vaseline Carnival, shown here courtesy of Bob Smith. *Photo © Michael Whitten.* Price band C.

Fenton Art Glass Company, Williamstown, West Virginia

It is quite impossible to do justice to the contribution which the Fenton Art Glass Company has made to Contemporary Carnival Glass in the small amount of space we have here. The reader is referred to the various books written about Fenton for greater detail[2]. However, this is possibly one of the first attempts, in print, to look solely at Fenton's production of Contemporary Carnival Glass.

Back in 1905, Frank Leslie Fenton, along with his elder brothers John and Charles, founded the Fenton Art Glass Company at Martin's Ferry, Ohio. The first glass at the Martin's Ferry location was primarily "blanks"— the brothers bought in other companies' glass and decorated it themselves. Soon they moved to Williamstown where they established their own glass plant and introduced Carnival Glass to the world. Fenton continued to produce Carnival throughout the years of Classic pro-

An aerial view of the Fenton factory (center of picture) in Williamstown, West Virginia, on the banks of the beautiful Ohio River. Just across the river is the historic town of Marietta, Ohio.

duction; indeed, from 1907 to 1920 Carnival was the company's major line. Butler Brothers catalogs even carried some Fenton ads through the early 1930s, overlapping with the Depression era. In the late 1960s, however, everything changed. Fenton was approached by Rose Presznick, one of the pioneering Carnival Glass author/researchers, to make Carnival Glass for her that she could sell in her museum at Lodi, Ohio. Imperial had also just begun to reissue their Carnival lines, which encouraged Fenton to look again at the market. So, prompted by Mrs. Presznick's request and the general market situation, Fenton began to revive its Carnival Glass lines.

Issued in 1980 and marked "Number 1 in a series of four," this splendid purple Carnival plate was called *THE OLD GRIST MILL* and was the first in a run of *CURRIER AND IVES* plates. Its color and iridescence are truly gorgeous. Price band B.

Fenton's Carnival Encore

January 1970 saw Fenton's catalog supplement proudly proclaiming "Famous Fenton Carnival Glass from the Original Fenton Formula." Ten pieces were illustrated in that first ad: two sizes of covered hen, the *FISH* paperweight, a souvenir plate, *DAISY AND BUTTON* boot, *WILD STRAWBERRY* covered candy box, *PANELLED DAISY* covered candy box, a large *CHRYSANTHEMUM* planter bowl, and the *POPPY* pickle dish (a reproduction of an early Northwood piece). One of the first ten items in purple Carnival Glass was the premier *CRAFTSMAN* plate—the *GLASSMAKER*. Through 1981, eleven more followed, all in purple Carnival. Also in 1970 came the *CHRISTMAS IN AMERICA* series; again eleven more followed. Fenton determined that, in order to make these special editions more collectible, the moulds were to be destroyed. Other series, such as the *MOTHERS DAY* and later *CURRIER AND IVES*, proved equally popular. One important fact is that Fenton decided to trademark all their new Carnival with the company's logo: "Fenton" in script within an oval. Through the 1970s the logo was simply that; then, during the 1980s, an "8" was added; for the 1990s, a "9." Only a few items have different marks (see following paragraphs) or, rarely, none at all (see Appendix 3 for trademarks).

1985 also saw the issue of Fenton's wonderful *GARDEN OF EDEN* plate in cobalt blue ("Cobalt Marigold Carnival")—the fine detail of the mouldwork is breathtaking. Price band B.

Fenton's *CURRIER AND IVES* series Included this splendid "Cobalt Marigold Carnival" *WINTER PASTIME* plate ("Number 4 in a series of four," issued in 1985 and limited to 3,500). In terms of its outstanding iridescence and detailed mouldwork, this is a masterpiece. Price band B.

In 1971 Fenton launched their *MOTHER'S DAY* series of nine plates based on the Madonna and Child theme. This contemporary 1971 ad notes that the plate was "hand made in original formula" which was, of course, Carnival Glass. The design of the first plate was based on Michelozzo's "Madonna with Sleeping Child" painting. The moulds were created by Anthony Rosena and were subsequently destroyed to preserve the value and collectibility of the series.

Back in the 1950s, Fenton had marketed a non-Carnival line through catalog houses such as General Merchandise Company that was not shown in their own catalogs: *DAISY AND BUTTON, THUMB-PRINT,* and *FINE CUT AND BLOCK* were some of the patterns used in this range that was finally dropped twenty some years later when the catalog method of distribution lost favor. Around 1960 the range acquired the name *OLDE VIRGINIA* and, in 1971, the glass was marked OVG, though it had not born the Fenton mark. A range of purple Carnival was added to the line then: the shapes were novelties such as shoes and a top hat toothpick, as well as various stemmed items in *FINE CUT AND BLOCK* and a swung vase.

As well as using original moulds and designs, such as the *CRAFTSMAN* series, for their newly found Carnival output, Fenton embarked upon putting their own moulds (and other companies' old moulds) into service. A Carnival "renaissance" followed, as many patterns that hadn't been used since the days of Classic Carnival production made a fresh appearance—graced with the new Fenton trademark. Just one year after they had reintroduced Carnival, Fenton followed up in January 1971 with a catalog announcement proclaiming more "Original Formula Carnival Glass." This time they illustrated more items—several were from the original ten, but new patterns included *PERSIAN MEDALLION* plate, *OPEN EDGE BASKETWEAVE* bowl, and one using an original Imperial pattern, the *HEAVY GRAPE* bowl.

In the 1970s Fenton issued the *HEAVY GRAPE* pattern. It was a new mould and this example in rich purple still has its paper Fenton label attached. *Courtesy of Rita and Les Glennon.* Price band B.

In 1977, Fenton's catalog announced that the Carnival items depicted would be "available just for the life of this catalog." In Frank M. Fenton's words, "that's the year when we started to limit the items to just one year for that particular color, shape and pattern." By limiting the output, collectibility was enhanced and moreover, it aided the dating and identification of pieces. This trend has continued with the lines that Fenton specifically refers to as "Carnival Glass."

In 1982, Fenton purchased many (between 1,100 and 2,000) old McKee/Jeanette moulds. An "F" in an oval trademark was added when other moulds, such as the McKee ones, were used by Fenton. The company has also purchased many old United States Glass Company moulds (their most recent purchases in 1999 were various L.G. Wright moulds.) Through the 1980s Fenton continued with their Carnival lines, often producing items in the same patterns as those launched a decade earlier, but in different Carnival colors or shapes.

An ad from Fenton's 1983/4 Catalog Supplement (shown here with the kind permission of the Fenton Art Glass Company) illustrates a wonderful range of what Fenton called "Cobalt Marigold Carnival"—a rich and glowing iridescent effect on cobalt blue base glass. Clockwise from top right: handled nut bowl in COSMOS AND HOBSTAR pattern; handled basket made from the POPPY pickle dish; three novelty items—miniature LOVEBIRD bell, FABERGE bell, and an elephant; 3-toed nut dish with BUTTERFLY interior and LEAF TIERS exterior; Fenton #8654 NK PINWHEEL vase; BEAR CUB novelty; CURRIER AND IVES WINTER PASTIME limited edition plate; PERSIAN MEDALLION compote; covered candy dish with butterfly finial; ORANGE TREE bowl and candleholder.

1986

FENTON
Carnival

Iridescent glass, the original name for Carnival glass, was The Fenton Art Glass Company's major product from its inception in 1907 until 1920. This unique glass was first introduced nationally by Louis Comfort Tiffany in the 1890's. It is produced by spraying various shades of glass with a metallic salt mixture while the glass is still very hot, creating a permanent rainbow across the surface of each piece.

Carnival glass authorities have acclaimed Fenton's reproduction of this treatment as the best representation of the antique iridescent formula ever produced. Most people would be unable to distinguish the difference were it not for the Fenton hallmark identifying the current pieces. Fenton Carnival—another example of superb handcraftsmanship for those who look for the unusual in fine glass. Your customer will recognize it as an investment in "the antiques of tomorrow."

——— Carnival ———

39

A 1986 catalog ad from Fenton (shown here with the kind permission of the Fenton Art Glass Company), which features more "Cobalt Marigold Carnival"—few of which were in any of the familiar Fenton Classic Carnival pattern reproductions. The top picture shows a *SYDENHAM* bell, *QUINTEC* pitcher, and *BUTTON AND ARCH* toothpicks. Bottom picture shows (top row, from left) *DOGWOOD* vase, *MARQUETTE* compote, *BUTTERFLY AND BERRY* handled basket, and *INNOVATION* compote; (bottom row, from left) *FABERGE* rose bowl, mouse and kitten novelties, bowl with *ORANGE TREE* exterior and *CHERRY CHAIN* interior, *BARRED OVAL* bell.

Fenton's 1987 catalog (ad extract shown here with the kind permission of the Fenton Art Glass Company) contained more "Cobalt Marigold Carnival." At top is the *PLYTEC* pitcher. Main picture shows (top row, from left) *ROSE* footed covered candy, *ACANTHUS* handled basket, *WAVE HOBNAIL* (aka *HOBNAIL SWIRL*) bell, *WAVE HOBNAIL* (aka *HOBNAIL SWIRL*) rose bowl, *FAMOUS WOMEN* bell; (bottom row, from left) *PRAYING BOY AND GIRL* novelties, *OPEN EDGE* handled basket, *PUPPY*, *FOX* and *PIG* novelties, *ACANTHUS* ruffled bowl, *FAMOUS WOMEN* bell (showing different aspect).

Handmade in the age old manner . . . and right here in our good old U.S.A.

1987

FENTON
Carnival

Iridescent glass, the original name for Carnival glass, was one of The Fenton Art Glass Company's major products from its inception in 1907 until 1920. This unique glass was first introduced nationally by Louis Comfort Tiffany in the 1890's. It is produced by spraying various shades of glass with a metallic salt mixture while the glass is still very hot, creating a permanent rainbow across the surface of each piece.

Carnival glass authorities have acclaimed Fenton's reproduction of this treatment as the best representation of the antique iridescent formula ever produced. Most people would be unable to distinguish the difference were it not for the Fenton hallmark identifying the current pieces. Fenton Carnival—another example of superb handcraftsmanship for those who look for the unusual in fine glass. Your customer will recognize it as an investment in "the antiques of tomorrow."

——— Carnival ———

FENTON

Teal Marigold

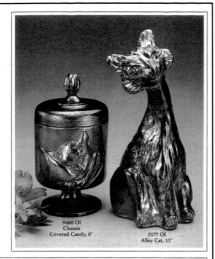

The appeal broadens to a whole new group of consumers! Not only will this new color capture the dyed in the wool carnival collector, it will also have a broad appeal to those who appreciate beautiful colorations in unusual designs and decorative patterns.

Iridescent glass, the original name for Carnival glass, was one of The Fenton Glass Company's major products from its inception in 1907 until 1920. This unique glass was first introduced nationally by Louis Comfort Tiffany in the 1890's. It is produced by spraying various shades of glass with a metallic salt mixture while the glass is still very hot, creating a permanent rainbow across the surface of each piece. Another example of superb handcraftsmanship for those who look for the unusual in fine glass. Your customer will recognize it as an investment in "the antiques of tomorrow."

Handmade in the age old manner. By Fenton, of course.

9480 OI
Chessie
Covered Candy, 8"

5177 OI
Alley Cat, 11"

1988 saw "Teal Marigold" in Fenton's catalog (ad extract shown here with the kind permission of the Fenton Art Glass Company). The top picture shows the CHESSIE covered candy and the ALLEY CAT. Main picture shows (top row, from left) OPEN EDGE handled basket, DAISY AND BUTTON slipper, PERSIAN MEDALLION compote, BIRD novelty, ORANGE TREE rose bowl (aka FENTON'S FLOWERS); (bottom row, from left) PANELLED DAISY covered candy, OPEN EDGE ruffled bowl, SITTING BEAR CUB novelty, footed bowl with FANTAIL interior and BUTTERFLY AND BERRY exterior, FABERGE bell.

8335 OI
Basket, Open
Edge, 7¾" h.

1995 OI
Slipper, Daisy and
Button, 6"

8234 OI
Comport,
Persian Medallion,
6½"

8223 OI
Rose Bowl, Leaf
and
Orange
Tree,
5¼"

5163 OI
Bird, 4"

9185 OI
Covered Candy,
Panelled Daisy, 8½"

8323 OI
Bowl, Open Edge, 6½"

5151 OI
Bear Cub,
Sitting, 3½"

8428 OI
Bowl, Butterfly and Berry, 9"

8466 OI
Bell, Fabergé, 6"

———— *Teal Marigold* ————

Fenton does not strictly consider this "Shell Pink" part of their mainstream Carnival lines, but it is iridized and very popular with collectors. Described in this 1988 ad (extract shown here with the kind permission of the Fenton Art Glass Company) as having "iridescent accents" the items shown in the top right picture are (from left) FABERGE bell, ROSE vase, SWAN novelty, ROSE compote. The bottom right picture shows (top row, from left) HURRICANE candle lamp, ROSE basket, ROSE trinket box, PANELLED DAISY covered candy, PANELLED DAISY votive; (bottom row, from left) FENTON LOGO sign, ROSE bud vase, SMALL BIRD novelty, ROSE handled basket, DAISY AND BUTTON slipper, FAIRY LIGHT. The picture at left shows a ROSE student lamp.

FENTON

Shell Pink

Shell Pink . . .
Soft opal glass with a pearl finish. Iridescent accents for the bedroom or bath, but at home in most country and victorian settings.

0350 AS
20 Pc. Assortment
Combines shell pink with handpainted Hearts & Flowers shown on page 11. Displays and sells beautifully together.

For those discriminating people who like the unusual in fine American handmade glass.

8466 PE
Bell, Fabergé, 6½"

5750 PE
Vase, Rose, 9"

5161 PE
Swan, 4"

9223 PE
Comport, Rose, 6½"

8376 PE
Hurricane Candle, 11"
w/candle

5783 PE
Oval Trinket
Box, Rose, 4½"

8294 PE
Votive,
Panelled
Daisy, 3½"
(with
candle)

9185 PE
Covered Candy,
Panelled Daisy, 8½"

5730 PE
Basket, Rose, 7" h.

9256 PE
Bud Vase, Rose, 11"

9790 PE
Fenton Logo

5113 PE
Small Bird, 3½"

9240 PE
Basket, Rose, 6½" h.

1995 PE
Slipper, Daisy & Button

8406 PE
Fairy Light,
Heart, 7"

Shell Pink . . . destined
for the "Best Sellers" list!

9208 PE
Student
Lamp, Rose,
19"

Build your display or room setting around this lovely handmade Fenton Lamp. Provides a warm romantic glow that will attract sales and loving thoughts.

———— *Shell Pink* ————

Fenton's Classic Re-Issues

Since Fenton's re-introduction of Carnival in 1970, they have used a number of old moulds that were previously used for the production of Classic Carnival. All these items were trademarked with Fenton's logo, so it is very easy to recognize them. The colors of Fenton's contemporary production and the shapes in which the patterns were made also frequently differ greatly from their Classic counterparts. The following list of patterns used in Classic Carnival production as well as modern Fenton Carnival production, may prove of interest to collectors. We can't be certain that it is exhaustive: there may be patterns that we have overlooked, and of course, there may well be patterns produced in the future. However, it is interesting to study. Please refer to the key below the list to determine which company previously used the pattern for the original production of Classic Carnival Glass.

Two *APPLE TREE* tumblers in red and blue, a Classic Fenton pattern that was re-introduced in Contemporary Carnival. All modern examples are marked with Fenton's logo. *Courtesy of Rita and Les Glennon.* Price band A.

ACANTHUS *I
APPLE TREE *F
BUTTERFLY *N
BUTTERFLIES BONBON *F (currently called "Butterfly Bonbon")
BUTTERFLY AND BERRY *F
CAROLINA DOGWOOD *W
CHERRY CHAIN *F
CHERRIES SUGAR AND CREAMER *M
CHRISTMAS COMPOTE *DD (now owned by Richardson)
DIAMOND AND RIB VASE *F
DIAMOND POINT COLUMNS VASE *F
DRAPERY *N
FANTAIL *F
FARMYARD *DD (new mould—items are currently made for Singleton Bailey. See entry under Mi Mi Inc. and Singleton Bailey for more detail)
FINE RIB VASE *F
FISHERMAN'S MUG *DD (made from a new mould owned by the Pacific North West Carnival Glass Club—taller and thinner than the original)
FRUIT AND FLOWERS *N
HEARTS AND FLOWERS *N
GRAPE AND CABLE *F
HEART AND VINE *F
HEAVY GRAPE *I (new mould cut by Fenton)
HOBNAIL SWIRL *M (now called "Wave Hobnail")
HOLLY *F

LEAF CHAIN *F (currently called "Daisy Pinwheel and Cable")
LEAF TIERS *F
LIONS *F
MILADY PITCHER *F
OPEN EDGE BASKET *F
OPEN ROSE exterior *I
ORANGE TREE (FENTON'S FLOWERS) *F
PEACOCK AND DAHLIA *F
PERSIAN MEDALLION *F
POPPY PICKLE DISH *N (new mould made by Fenton)
POPPY SHOW VASE *I (made for Singleton Bailey)
ROSALIND *M (currently called "Drape and Tie")
SUNFLOWER pintray *M
SWAN SALT *F

Also, the "3 toed grape" which is very similar to Northwood's *FINE CUT AND ROSE* rose bowl

Key to above list:

F = Fenton
N = Northwood
DD = Dugan/Diamond
M = Millersburg
W = Westmoreland
I = Imperial

Fenton doesn't just make Carnival Glass for itself: for many years now they have manufactured iridized ware for a variety of marketing companies, distributors, and Carnival Glass clubs. The Levay Glass Company (run by Gary Levi). Singleton Bailey, Gracious Touch, and Richardson, to name a few, have all had glass manufactured for them by Fenton. Beginning in the late 1990s, the Northwood Art Glass Company has also appointed Fenton to produce their glass. Details can be seen under the relevant companies within Part Four.

Once Carnival had been fully reintroduced, Fenton concentrated on producing specific Carnival lines each year. Particular colors, such as red or plum Carnival, have been used for just a few years each. A cobalt blue Carnival color called "Independence Blue" was produced in 1975-76 as one of the Bicentennial colors. The patterns and shapes of Carnival pieces have been kept to a small number, with certain shapes in certain patterns being produced in specific years and denoted in their catalogs with the word "Carnival." This helps to date Fenton's Carnival items. The patterns used for the Carnival ranges typically have strong designs, often featuring figures or flora and fauna. Alongside this, in more recent years, has been the development of more widespread use of iridescence on other lines that Fenton doesn't specifically call "Carnival." Examples are seen on some items in the pastel pink shade known as "Shell Pink," or the vaseline-like "Topaz Opalescent," as well as various examples of their "Collectible Eggs," "Secret Slippers," and "Heavenly Angel" series. Some items in their 1997 ranges in champagne satin and misty blue were iridized too—this is a fairly typical and popular use of iridescence by Fenton and is done on a regular basis as it has proved to be both attractive and popular with collectors.

Fenton's red Carnival in a beautiful *HOBNAIL* vase with a jack-in-the-pulpit shaped top. Price band C.

It would be impossible to do justice to Fenton's contribution to Carnival Glass without mentioning the roles played by various key members of the Fenton family and their employees. Frank Muhleman Fenton, eldest son of the founder of the factory, Frank Leslie Fenton, has been instrumental in ensuring the continued appreciation of Carnival and its history for many, many collectors. His brother Wilmer C. (Bill), his son George, and many other members of the Fenton family play significant parts in ensuring the continued success and inventiveness of the firm. Employees past and present have made their marks. Anthony Rosena designed all but one of the original *CRAFTSMAN* plates. Louise Piper presided over the Decorating Department for many years, not only designing and applying the decorations but also training a growing team of decorators—her work on some Carnival items is highly sought after. Howard Seufer, now retired from Fenton but still maintaining close contact with the factory, educates and entertains Carnival clubs and collectors on the more technical aspects of pressed glass manufacture. Other names stand out: Jon Saffell (designer); Bob Hill (mould shop); decorators Martha Reynolds, Kim Plauche, Frances Burton, and Robin Spindler; as well as chemist Wayne King, to name just a few. Fenton is more than a family business, it's an extended family business, where everyone contributes. Their continued success is a result of quality, skill, and dedication.

A Selection of Fenton's Contemporary Carnival Glass

ALLEY CAT

Collectors seem to either love or detest this novelty creature! He measures a little over 10" high and sits, his head on one side, wearing a grotesque, yet winningly affectionate, grin. The mould for this item was purchased from the United States Glass Company. In 1924, that company had illustrated the novelty cat on the cover of their brochure (*The Glass Outlook*) and described it thus: "This weird feline holding down a front cover position on the *Outlook* team this month has been christened 'Sassie Susie.' . . . Makes a very efficient door stop. Brightens a dull corner. Sits pretty under a Christmas tree. Never fails to arouse comment when seen for the first time. Strong enough to be used as a means of defense . . . All in all, 'Sassy Susie' has a real job in life cut out for her."

In 1963, U. S. Glass Co. were declared bankrupt—later that same year a tornado destroyed the factory premises at Glassport. Frank M. Fenton tells[3] of wading around in the flooded basement of the building after the roof had been ripped off. He was able to purchase some of the U.S. Glass moulds, including the *ALLEY CAT*.[2] Fenton first made it in Carnival Glass in 1970 to 1972—the mould is still in production.

HAPPY CAT, a smaller and slightly different version of the *ALLEY CAT*, is also made by Fenton, using a mould owned by the Fenton Art Glass Collectors of America that was made by the Island Mould and Machine Company (in the style of another U. S. Glass mould). *HAPPY CAT* is just a little over 6" high and was first made in stiegel green Carnival in 1993: a very limited number of black Carnival ones were also made at that time and the mould is still in production.

Shape: cat novelty figurine

Colors: purple, teal marigold (teal base glass), Favrene, spruce green, and various other colors

Fenton's amusing *ALLEY CAT* in deep purple on the right (price band C), and smaller friend the *HAPPY CAT* in blue on the left (price band B).

The *CRAFTSMAN* Series and other Collector plates

The *CRAFTSMAN* series was part of the original Fenton Contemporary Carnival launch in 1970: the very first plate was the *GLASSMAKER*—the image depicted on it is familiar to all who visit the Fenton factory in Williamstown, as the figure is mounted prominently on the façade of the Fenton factory. A mistake was made on the first run of the plate: the word "craftsman" had no "s" and read "craftman"—the fault was recognized only after a number of plates were released.

The *CRAFTSMAN* series of plates ran for eleven years with all but the first plate being designed by Anthony Rosena. On December 31 of each year, the moulds of that year's plate were destroyed in order to safeguard the collectibility of the items.

Other collector series followed in which Carnival examples can be found: *CHRISTMAS IN AMERICA*, the *MOTHER'S DAY* plates, and the magnificent *CURRIER AND IVES* series.

Shapes: plate, note also that a stein was made in the *CRAFTSMAN* design in 1979

Colors: purple for the *CRAFTSMAN* series. Other colors including blue and red were used variously for the others (often the color corresponded to that which Fenton specified for Carnival production in the year that the specific plate would have been produced).

The figure on Fenton's first *CRAFTSMAN PLATE* is a visual symbol of the factory. The color is purple. Price band B.

LOVEBIRD VASE and other Verlys vases/planters

In the late 1960s, Fenton purchased sixty-five moulds belonging to the Holophane Company, some of which had originally been made in France during the 1930s by Verlys[2]. The style of the items was typical of French design from the Art Deco era and when Fenton used some of the vase and planter moulds for Carnival Glass in the 1970s, they were instantly successful. In 1974 only—and never since— the delightful *LOVEBIRD* vase was produced in purple Carnival using a Verlys mould. The deeply moulded pattern is sheer delight: two little birds nestle toward the base of this fan shaped vase. A canopy of leaves fills the remainder of the pattern—the leaves were added by Fenton.

Other Verlys moulds that have been made in Carnival are the *MERMAID* planter (a breathtaking design, produced from 1970 through 1972 in purple) and the more recently produced *SEASONS* vase.

Shapes: vase and planter (jardinière)

Colors: purple (1970s). *SEASONS* was produced in 1998 in decorated Favrene and acid cut-back on cobalt blue base glass. A small number of experimental *SEASONS* vases were also produced in 1998 in all-over Favrene on cobalt. Silver is included in the Favrene iridescence to create an exquisite, vivid iridescence.

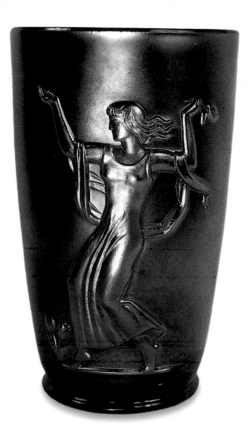

The delightful and scarce purple Carnival *LOVEBIRD* vase was only produced by Fenton in 1974. Price band CD.

The *SEASONS* vase is shown here in Favrene—a Fenton specialty with a truly stunning iridescent effect. The figure depicted represents Spring. Fenton's information leaflet on their Favrene color notes that "Favrene was first developed by L.C. Tiffany as Blue Favrile. The formula contains pure silver which is coaxed to the surface through a series of cooling and reheating steps." Price band D.

The other side of the *SEASONS* vase features a female figure carrying a sheaf of wheat, representing Fall.

Made in purple Carnival in the early 1970s, this splendid *MERMAID* planter is a sought after item. Price band D.

PERSIAN MEDALLION

Used by Fenton in their Classic Carnival production, the popular *PERSIAN MEDALLION* design was re-introduced in the 1970s in the form of an 8" ruffled bowl. The exterior bears a slightly altered version of Fenton's *BEARDED BERRY* pattern. A contemporary version of *PERSIAN MEDALLION* has been adapted onto an extended range of shapes not made previously in Classic Carnival.

Shapes: bowl, plate, compote, fairy light, spittoon, and chalice
Colors: lavender, red, marigold, peach opalescent, "cobalt marigold," and possibly various other colors

A delightful fairy light in the *PERSIAN MEDALLION* pattern in white and pink opal Carnival. Price band C.

A stunning effect on this lavender *PERSIAN MEDALLION* chop plate from Fenton. *Courtesy of Rita and Les Glennon.* Price band BC.

POPPY

One of the original ten Carnival pieces re-introduced by Fenton in 1970, the *POPPY* pickle dish was simply described as "9125 CN Oval Dish." The pattern was, in fact, a copy of the original Northwood one that had been used in the oval pickle dish shape in Classic Carnival. The interior design (poppies) and the exterior (ribs) are very similar to the Northwood original. Present in the center of the marie is the Fenton trademark in an oval.

Shape: oval dish
Color: purple

The purple *POPPY PICKLE DISH* was issued by Fenton in 1970. Price band B.

PRESZNICK OIL LAMP

Produced by Fenton for the grandchildren of Rose Presznick in 1984, this superb oil lamp features a deeply moulded pattern of poppies: the color is a rich rose red. On the base an engraved inscription reads "In memory of Rose Presznick." Collector Nigel Gamble has researched this item and has the lamp in four other experimental colors, produced for Eileen Von Myers and her husband (who was Rose Presznick's grandson). It would appear that none of the other four experimental shades were liked by the Von Myers, whose preference for the red lamp led to the decision to produce six hundred of them. According to Nigel, less than two hundred were actually made, at least four of which were broken early on and a significant number of others that didn't sell immediately were left in a cold barn (following which they broke or cracked). The surviving perfect lamps are now few and far between.

Shape: oil lamp comprising base, bowl, and clear glass chimney

Colors: red. Experimental colors known for the lamp bowls are: plum opal (the first experimental color made, only three examples were produced), marigold on milk glass with a light iridescence, white, pale marigold on clear, and lemon yellow. All have a milk glass base.

Fenton's *ATLANTIS* vase is an old U. S. Glass mould that was purchased by Fenton in 1964. It has been made in a wide range of Carnival colors including peach opal made for Dorothy Taylor's *Encore* in the early 1980s. The illustrated example is in purple. Price band CD.

Two delightful novelties in rich cobalt blue: both have the Fenton logo moulded into their sides. Price band B.

A much sought-after item, the *PRESZNICK OIL LAMP* is a beautiful example of Contemporary Carnival Glass. Price band D.

Hansen Brothers, Bridgeport and Mackinaw City, Michigan

The three Hansen brothers, Ronald, Robert, and Richard all worked with glass—however Ronald and Robert are the two whose work with Carnival is legendary. Chemistry had always interested Ronald and he and his wife, Dorothy, began experimenting with iridescence on glass in the 1950s. His work and methods were passed on to his brother Robert and in 1960, both brothers began iridizing glass to sell. According to Scott Ackerman (writing in *Carnival Glass Encore*, December 1983) AA Importing was the first buyer of Ronald's Carnival Glass in the early 1960s.

Most of the Hansen glass is new, though some old items were also iridized by the brothers. Their method of "custom iridizing" was similar to that later used by Terry Crider—the glass "blanks" were heated up to the required temperature then sprayed with the metallic salts that create the iridescence. Often, items were re-fired and sprayed several times to intensify the effect. Ackerman also reported that the Hansens used a method called "soaking the glass." It seems that they would "turn a piece of glass in the glory hole when it was very hot—this would burn off the skin of the glass making it velvety smooth."

The Hansens bought their glass "blanks" from various companies including L.E. Smith, Degenhart, Guernsey, St. Clair, Mosser, L.G. Wright, and Imperial. It is interesting to note that Lucile Kennedy of Imperial is believed to have informed Ronald Hansen that his production of iridized glass caused Imperial to re-introduce their Carnival lines somewhat earlier than they had originally intended. The Hansens limited the amount produced to around three hundred maximum per item, though many items were limited to as few as from six to twenty-four pieces. Most of their glass is signed or bears their initials, however some items were not signed and most "seconds" certainly escaped the Hansen trademark. Some items of Hansen iridescent art glass were signed with the name "Zanadu."

Items iridized by the Hansens include the recognizable *EYEWINKER* tumbler (which was also iridized by Crider), the *PUMP AND TROUGH* (also some iridized by Crider), and the splendid novelties such as the *VIOLIN* and *BANJO* bottles and the fabulous *SANTA CLAUS* fairy lamp (which in red Carnival, has sold for $1000).

CHERRIES

This is the Dugan/Diamond pattern known as *WREATHED CHERRIES*. The original Dugan/Diamond moulds were owned by L.G. Wright who had glass pressed for them by various manufacturers. The red example illustrated was custom iridized and signed by Robert Hansen.

Shapes: spooner and creamer (and possibly other shapes)
Color: red

A red *CHERRIES* spooner, custom iridized by Robert Hansen. Price band D

MOON AND STARS tumbler iridized by Hansen, courtesy of Bob Smith. *Photo © Michael Whitten*. Price band D.

Imperial Glass Corporation / Lennox Imperial Glass, Bellaire, Ohio

The Background to Imperial

The Imperial Glass Company was founded in 1901 and first produced glass in 1904. It was to continue, in one form or another for eighty more years, through 1984. In its early years, pressed glass tableware and lamps were the staple lines, but in 1909 the company added a note to their General Catalog stating that they were currently producing "Rubigold-Iridescent ware"—Carnival Glass! They subsequently became one of the five major Carnival Glass manufacturers, finally stopping production around the same time as Fenton and Dugan/Diamond in the late 1920s. When Carnival enjoyed a revival of popularity in the early 1960s, Imperial decided that the time had come for production to begin again, and their first items were marigold (rubigold) *IMPERIAL GRAPE* goblets. This time, production was for a very different market—it was for collectors—and the company cleverly utilized the new name "Carnival" that the glass had recently begun to be called by the ever growing band of collectors. Their ads in 1962 read "Genuine and authentic 'Carnival Glass' American Handmade by Imperial USA. From moulds used 60 years ago."

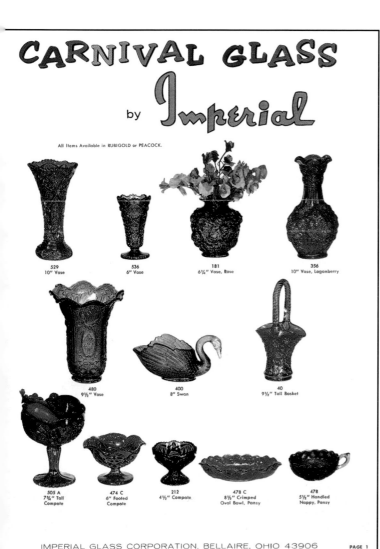

This original ad shows Imperial's Sunset Ruby—a rich red Carnival—that was in production for just a few years from the late 1960s into the early 1970s. Top row, from left: *ACANTHUS* sugar and cream set, *IMPERIAL LACE* toothpick, *ROBIN* mug, *FIELDFLOWER* tumbler and pitcher. Next row, from left: *IMPERIAL LACE* 8" vase, *474* vase, *474* compote, *ACANTHUS* compote. Next row, from left: *DIAMOND LACE* bowl, *ROSE* bowl, *ACANTHUS* bowl, *ACANTHUS* covered box. Bottom row, from left: *IMPERIAL LACE* bowl, *ACANTHUS* candleholders and bowl.

An original Imperial ad from the 1960s offering "all items available in RUBIGOLD or PEACOCK"—marigold and smoke. Top row, from left: *HOBSTAR AND FAN* vase, *IMPERIAL LACE* 6" vase, *LA BELLA ROSA* vase, *LOGANBERRY* vase. Middle row, from left: *SCROLL AND FLOWER PANEL* vase, *MASTER SWAN*, *DAISY* basket. Bottom row, from left: *IMPERIAL LACE* compote, *474* compote, 4.5" compote #212, *PANSY* pickle dish, *PANSY* handled nappy.

Pink Carnival was made in 1978 and 1979 by Lennox Imperial Glass. Very top: *ROSE* footed bowl. Top row, from left: *TIGER LILY* tumbler, *LOGAN-BERRY* vase, *IMPERIAL LACE* toothpick, *ROSE* vase, *HATTIE* bowl, *SUZANNE BELLE* novelty bell, candleholder, *TIGER LILY* water pitcher, *ROBIN* mug. Middle row, from left: *ROSE* butter dish, *PANSY* handled nappy, *SCROLL EMBOSSED* bowl. Bottom row, from left: *BEADED JEWEL* covered box, Imperial's #42563 bowl (unnamed), *FROSTED BLOCK VARIANT* bowl, *SWAN* salt.

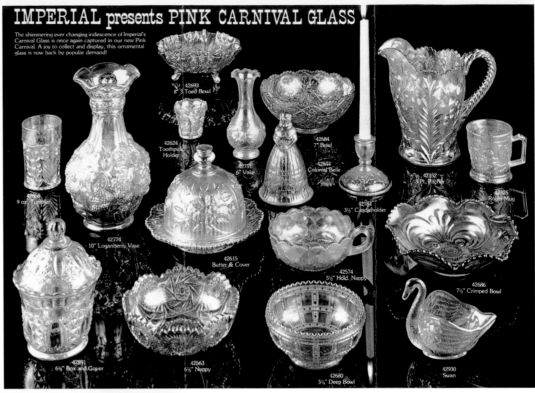

IMPERIAL presents PINK CARNIVAL GLASS

The shimmering ever changing iridescence of Imperial's Carnival Glass is once again captured in our new Pink Carnival. A joy to collect and display, this ornamental glass is now back by popular demand!

aurora jewels in cobalt blue by Imperial

A delightful contemporary ad for Imperial's Aurora Jewels range (deep, rich blue). Here, the *THREE SWANS* vase is shown in use.

The new phase had begun, though it didn't have the sales success that Imperial might have hoped for and another four years passed before Imperial attempted Carnival again. In 1965, a major line of fifty or so items were offered by Imperial in rubigold (marigold) and peacock (smoke) Carnival Glass, including *WIND-MILL* and *OPEN ROSE* from the original moulds. To identify the new glass it was marked with an "I" superimposed over a letter "G"; further, a stipple finish was sometimes added to parts of the pattern (usually the base) that wasn't present on the originals. In 1966, more lines were added, including the *NU-ART CHRYSAN-THEMUM* and *HOMESTEAD* plates and the *ZIPPER LOOP* lamp. Imperial's Classic patterns that were re-issued include: the *POPPY SHOW VASE*, the *LOGANBERRY VASE* (reproductions can be identified by having a ruffled top), *ACANTHUS, HATTIE, HOBSTAR, RIPPLE* vase, *PANSY* (pickle dish), bowls in *SCROLL EMBOSSED* and *HEAVY GRAPE*, and water sets in *HEAVY GRAPE, ROBIN*, and *FIELDFLOWER*. New moulds were produced too, such as the *AMERICA THE BEAUTIFUL* limited series of collector plates, made from 1964 through 1974 (conceived, commissioned, and distributed by E. Ward Russell), and the set of twelve annual *CHRISTMAS PLATES* (see below)

During the early 1970s Imperial began to experience financial problems. Badly in need of capital, they worked out a deal with Lennox in 1972 to become a wholly owned subsidiary of Lennox Inc. Carnival Glass from this era bears the trademark of intertwined letters LIG for Lennox Imperial Glass. In 1981, Lennox sold the company to Arthur Lorch (items from this era are marked ALIG for Arthur Lorch Imperial Glass). Further complicated wranglings took place when Lorch failed to meet his financial commitments, and in December 1982, Imperial acquired a new owner, Robert Stahl of Minnesota. Attempts were made to keep the plant alive but late in 1984 it was clear that they had failed. The company was ordered to liquidate under Chapter 7—Bankruptcy. Production ceased, shipments to wholesalers stopped, and the two gift shops closed their doors. Despite efforts from a local Bellaire group called "Save Imperial Committee," all the company's assets were sold and the moulds purchased by various glass companies including Fenton, L.E. Smith, Boyd, and Summit. The Heisey Club, the Cambridge Collectors Club, and a marketing company called "Mirror Images" also purchased several moulds. In 1995, Maroon Enterprises announced that the factory buildings would be torn down to make way for a shopping mall. Imperial was no more.

Imperial's Carnival Colors

Imperial used different colors during different years for their Contemporary Carnival Glass. The first two colors that were utilized were the familiar marigold and smoke. These were new times, however, and the company wanted to distinguish its product as being fresh—hence new names were given to the colors that were in use primarily between 1965 and 1972: marigold was known as "Rubigold" and the smoke (a gray iridescence, shot with multi-colors on a clear base glass) was called "Peacock." The next color introduced was "Helios Green"—virtually identical to the Classic Carnival color, it did not prove to be very popular; consequently, examples of Contemporary Helios are quite scarce. "Sunset Ruby"—a red Carnival glass—was produced from around 1968 to 1973. "Azure Blue," a light ice blue, was only used for a very short time: examples can be identified by having the IG trademark (a similar color, "Horizon Blue," was made later by Lennox and has the LIG trademark). "Aurora Jewels," a stunning deep, electric, cobalt, was produced around 1970 to 1972, followed by amber and white in the early 1970s. "Pink and "Horizon Blue" (ice blue), made in 1978 and 1979 and marked LIG, were very popular and were sold through Hallmark gift shops. "Meadow Green" (light and bright in color, produced in 1980-81 and marked LIG, described by Imperial as "the fresh spring hues of a Vermont meadow"), amethyst/purple (LIG), and "Sunburst" (yellow, made in 1982 and marked ALIG) were the final main color lines. There were experimental colors too, not in the regular line, that only appear on select items. "Ultra Blue" is one such example that was employed mainly on the 474 water sets for Joan Westerfield. An unusual combination of frosted or sueded panels combined with rubigold (marigold) are also known on the WINDMILL water sets.

A Selection of Imperial's Contemporary Carnival Glass

CHRISTMAS PLATES

New moulds were made for this set of twelve plates, each issued for Christmas over the twelve year span from 1970 through 1981. The theme for all twelve was "The Twelve Days of Christmas," the carol written by Helliwell in 1842. The designs were interpreted for Imperial by Robert P. Robinson, a local art teacher. Each of the limited edition plates was issued in its own presentation box, complete with an information leaflet. The twelve patterns and Carnival colors are listed below (the set was also issued in sueded crystal)[4].

Shape: plate
Colors:
- blue 1970 "Partridge in a Pear Tree"
- dark green 1971 "Two Turtle Doves"
- amber 1972 "Three French Hens"
- white 1973 "Four Colly Birds"
- verde 1974 "Five Golden Rings"
- yellow 1975 "Six Geese-a-Laying"
- ultra blue 1976 "Seven Swans-a-Swimming"
- brown 1977 "Eight Maids-a-Milking"
- pink 1978 "Nine Drummers Drumming"
- horizon blue 1979 "Ten Pipers Piping"
- light green 1980 "Eleven Ladies Dancing"
- ruby amberina 1981 "Twelve Lords-a-Leaping"

FIELDFLOWER

An old Imperial mould was used for the re-issue of this water set in 1970; the color at the time was a rich red. All examples should be trademarked IG. Though the pattern looks virtually identical, it is possible to distinguish the old tumblers from the new by checking the moulded scalloped line near the rim of the tumbler. On the old tumbler the top line is a double scallop that matches the double scallop below it. On the new tumblers, the top line is a single scallop that does not match the double scallop below. Though identifying the items as new is not hard when the trademark is present, it should be noted that the moulds are now owned by Summit Art Glass, who have produced some beautiful purple water sets that do not bear the IG trademark.

Shape: water set
Colors: red and ice blue (the latter for Levay in 1978)

Imperial's Classic Carnival *FIELDFLOWER* tumbler in marigold (left), and their reproduction red tumbler (right). Price band B for each.

Imperial's *CHRISTMAS PLATE—NINE DRUMMERS DRUMMING* in pink Carnival, made by Lennox Imperial Glass in 1978. Price band C.

FOUR SEVENTY FOUR (474)

A stylized, geometric floral design featuring a stemmed daisy-like flower surrounded by hobstars. During the 1970s, Imperial re-issued the old *474* pattern, though the colors were not the same as the Classic output and some new shapes were made. The new vase, for example, sits on a domed base unlike the Classic vase, which has a pedestal base. All Contemporary examples should be trademarked IG (look **inside** the vase for the trademark). An interesting limited edition of 250 water sets were issued in 1977 by Imperial for Joan Westerfield. Made in ultra blue (a vivid mid-blue with a superb iridescence), these items are distinguished by having a peanut motif on the base and the words "A New Spirit '77"—President Jimmy Carter's well known phrase. The *474* pattern is sometimes confused with Imperial's *MAYFLOWER*. Though both are stylized floral designs, only *474* has hobstars.

Shapes: water set, vase, mug, compote, covered box, and various table set items such as salt and pepper shaker

Colors: red, green, horizon blue, and amber

HOMESTEAD

The *HOMESTEAD* chop plate and its "sister," the *CHRYSANTHEMUM*, were both re-issued by Imperial, Lennox Imperial, and Arthur Lorch in the 1960s and 1970s. The trademark altered on the plates from IG to LIG to ALIG by simple and convenient additions. Some colors were exceptionally limited and unusual. Some of the white Carnival examples were marked in error "No.5 America the Beautiful." The pink *HOMESTEAD* plates were never actually in the Lennox Imperial line, but were instead given to dealers if they purchased a fixed amount of pink glass in other patterns and were accompanied with a certificate of authenticity signed by H. J. Opperman, president of Lennox Imperial Glass. The azure plates were also never in the Imperial line and were possibly only issued as samples to dealers. Note that on the marigold and smoke examples, the collar base is stippled but the remainder of the exterior is smooth. The entire back surface is stippled (including the collar base) on the white and pink examples.

Shape: chop plate

Colors: rubigold (marigold), peacock (smoke), azure blue, white, and pink

IMPERIAL GRAPE

As with *474*, some of the shapes re-issued are from the old, original moulds while other shapes (such as the salt and pepper shakers and the oblong butter dish) were made fresh at the time of the pattern's re-issue. Where old moulds were used, the final finishing and shaping of the item sometimes differed, too. The goblet in this pattern was the first item that launched Imperial's new Carnival lines in 1962. These are easily distinguished from the old goblets in the *IMPERIAL GRAPE* pattern as they have a smooth interior, whereas the old ones had a grape pattern inside as well as outside the goblet.

Shapes: water set (several sizes of pitcher and tumbler), goblet, wine, juice, covered jar, compote, sherbert, cruet, sugar, creamer as well as various other shapes[4]

Colors: rubigold (marigold), peacock (smoke), helios, white, amber, and meadow green

Sunset ruby was the color used to make this *474* vase. Note the paper label that reads "Hand Crafted Imperial USA"—it is marked IG at the bottom of the inside of the vase. Price band BC.

Marigold salt and pepper shakers in *IMPERIAL GRAPE*. Price band BC.

LA BELLA ROSA

Deeply moulded roses stand out all over this delightful vase that was made in 1966. It stands some 6" high and at its widest is a full 5". The base of the vase is stippled and has the IG trademark.

Shape: vase
Colors: rubigold (marigold) and peacock (smoke)

STORYBOOK MUG

Originally a Heisey Glass mould (their #1591 "Baby cup," which they produced in crystal only, in 1947) this delightful child's mug features a handle shaped like an elephant's head and trunk. The panelled pattern around the mug is of nursery rhyme characters: "Puss in Boots," "Jack be nimble," "Bo Peep," and so on. Imperial produced the mug in a wide range of Carnival colors including special editions for E. Ward Russell. The Ward Russell examples are marked E.W.R. on the base and some amber ones also have the moulded words "NIXON AGNEW"—one of the few items of Carnival Glass that are also examples of political memorabilia! In 1985, the Heisey Collectors of America obtained the mould and have used Fenton and Viking to produce it for them—examples are marked "HCA."

Shape: child's novelty mug
Colors: blue (Aurora Jewels), amber, helios, smoke, red, green, and horizon blue. Ice blue and ice green examples with the LIG mark. A few scarce examples in crystal, rose pink, milk glass, and other unusual shades were also iridized by Terry Crider for Madonna Woodward.

LA BELLE ROSA in smoke. Price band BC.

Imperial's delightful STORYBOOK mug in rich amber. Price band BC.

THREE SWANS

A truly breathtaking example of the mould maker's craftsmanship, this astonishing item features three swans' heads, their elegant necks curving out from their bodies to form the distinctive top to the vase. The maximum height of the vase is 9": at its widest point the vase extends to 8". Made in 1970 only, this scarce item is one of the true "jewels" of Contemporary Carnival Glass. Fitting, then, that the only color in which Imperial made it was their stunning cobalt Carnival—called "Aurora Jewels." We believe that the mould was an original Cambridge item.

Shape: vase
Color: "Aurora Jewels" (blue)

Imperial's swans came in various guises—the magnificent THREE SWANS vase in rich blue Aurora Jewels (price band D) is flanked by red (left) and amber (right) SWAN salts (price band BC).

Imperial's *SUZANNE BELLE* novelty bell was made in a variety of colors—this example is in the Aurora Jewels deep, rich blue. Price band C.

Indiana's *WINDSOR* candy is still in its box. Note that the pattern is very similar to the *ENGLISH HOB AND BUTTON* aka *CHUNKY* made by Sowerby (see Part Two, Chapter Two). The regal sounding name *WINDSOR* reflects the English connection. Price band A.

Windsor Candy Box
Bonbonnière
Caja para Dulces

Indiana Glass Company, Dunkirk, Indiana

The Indiana Glass Company was formally created in 1907, though its origins are in the National Glass Company combine. During the Depression years they produced a great deal of tableware and later, car headlights. In 1963, the company became part of the large Lancaster Colony Corporation—a position which they are still in to this day.

During the 1970s, Indiana launched their Carnival Glass ranges in distinctive colors, patterns, and shapes that are familiar to most collectors. A report from California, written for *Carnival Glass Encore* in 1984, noted that Indiana Carnival Glass first appeared in local Safeway stores in 1970: "at that time it was really cheap, all the major drugstores had a big line." In the 1980s it was being sold in Thriftway grocery stores in colorful Indiana boxes. The first color Indiana introduced was "Iridescent Blue" in 1971. This was followed by "Iridescent Gold" (a golden yellow-amber shade), "Iridescent Sunset" (red to amberina), "Iridescent Green," and finally, in 1974, "Iridescent Amethyst." Purple and rare black were also used by Indiana—the *HEIRLOOM* series includes items in these colors.

Indiana also made glass for Tiara Co. in 1971. Tiara was an independent sales and merchandising company based in Dunkirk, Indiana and used the house party plan for selling. Quite scarce examples of the light green Carnival *ECLIPSE* (a geometric pattern often simply called *TIARA*) water set, which comprised a pitcher and four stemmed goblets, were made for Tiara in the early 1970s by Indiana. This was actually made using an old Indiana glass mould known originally as "Eclipse" (as well as "Flower Medallion" by Pattern Glass collectors). Other Tiara items included a *DIAMOND POINT* covered candy box, compote and chalice in marigold, as well as a swan flower arranger. More Carnival for Tiara was made in black in the shape of a covered compote, tall tumbler, and cookie jar in a sawtooth pattern called *CAMEO*; these items were only sold through their House Party Plan.

Another boxed item: this one is Indiana's #1195 13" *EGG HORS D'OEUVRE* tray in blue. Price band B.

Indiana produced a wide range of Carnival shapes and patterns that, though no trademark is present, can usually be distinguished by the company's distinctive colors and iridescence. A *COVERED HEN* was made, as were various handled baskets and bonbon dishes (such as the *LILY PONS* and the *LOGANBERRY* aka *STRAWBERRY RELISH*, both using old Indiana moulds) plus the delightful *EGG HORS D'OEUVRE DISH* and *EGG RELISH*. A copy of Sowerby's *CHUNKY #2266* aka *ENGLISH HOB AND BUTTON* was also made by Indiana in blue and gold— they called it *WINDSOR*.

Indiana Glass Company made the *LILY PONS* bowls using old moulds—this example is in their "Iridescent Gold" Carnival. Price band A.

CARNIVAL

Whitehall Candy Box
Bonbonnière
Caja para Dulces

Indiana often individually boxed their Carnival—this is the *WHITEHALL* candy box in blue, reminiscent of Fostoria's "American" pattern. Price band A.

A Selection of Indiana's Contemporary Carnival Glass

HARVEST

Bunches of grapes and large vine leaves are the main feature of this familiar pattern. Undoubtedly a top selling line for the company in the early 1970s, Indiana's own advertising noted that this was "the line that's producing spectacular volume sales." *HARVEST* is usually found in the familiar Indiana vivid blue color with a purplish iridescence. Note that the punch set comprises a massive bowl and no base; twelve cups and a plastic ladle complete this useful set.

Shapes: punch set, water pitcher (has an ice lip), goblets, tall tumbler, sugar, creamer and tray, candy jar (cookie jar), juice glass, large open compote (also available with cover, Indiana called it the *HARVEST* Wedding Bowl/and Cover), candlestick, butter dish

Colors: blue, green, and gold (yellow-amber)

HEIRLOOM SERIES

A near-cut geometric pattern that confuses many collectors into thinking it is Classic Carnival, this was Indiana's best selling *HEIRLOOM SERIES*, sometimes called *OCTAGON VARIANT* by today's collectors. The pattern was indeed an old Indiana Glass pattern, though it was not used for Carnival production until the 1970s. Known simply as the "123 Pattern" in a range of tableware shapes made in the early 1900s (also named "Panelled Daisies and Finecut" by Pattern Glass collectors), it was re-introduced with a flourish by the company in the 1970s thus: "The exclusive new hand made Heirloom Series by Indiana makes its market debut in stunning Sunset Carnival Glass alive with an unequaled iridescent brilliance and vitality of color. The authentic near cut patterns are re-issues of the ones that are treasured heirlooms today. Each piece, carrying an Heirloom Series sticker, will be packed in a distinctive full color package for impulse sales." The color "Sunset Carnival" ranges from cherry red to amberina and is very beautiful, indeed many have believed it to be older than it really is.

Shapes: punch set, swung vase, candle holder, bowl, plate, butter dish, pitcher, goblet, handled basket, sugar, creamer, and rose bowl

Colors: red-amberina, amethyst, and black (the latter in pitcher and goblets for Tiara Party Plan—also known in the table set in black).

Indiana Glass Company's *HARVEST* pattern is quite frequently found. Two goblets flank a tall, blue tumbler. The lime green one on the left is a little harder to find than the blue ones. *Courtesy of Rita and Les Glennon.* Price band A.

The *INDEPENDENCE HALL* plate in blue Carnival by Indiana. *Courtesy of Rita and Les Glennon.* Price band AB.

A goblet in Indiana's *HEIRLOOM* series—note the paper label on the base reading *Heirloom Series. Indiana Glass - Hand Made.* The goblet is Indiana's "Iridescent Sunset"—amberina-red shading to yellow. *Courtesy of Rita and Les Glennon.* Price band A.

A Bicentennial commemorative from Indiana Glass issued in 1976, this *EAGLE* plate is in that company's easily recognizable "Iridescent Gold" Carnival. Price band AB.

219

Levay Glass Distributing Company, Edwardsville, Illinois

Gary Levi was the driving force behind Levay Glass, a mail order giftware and distributing company that was set up in June 1971. Levi's aim was to concentrate on limited editions of Carnival by using existing moulds but having the glass manufacturers produce items in short runs of specific colors. Some of these color runs were often experimental and such items are very scarce indeed. Some glass is signed and dated by Levay, and frequently a certificate of production would accompany any whimsies that were produced. Carnival was made for Levay Glass by various manufacturers, such as Westmoreland, Fenton, Imperial, Crescent Glass, and L.E. Smith. Indeed, O. J. Olson described Gary Levi as the "prime mover" who had spurred the glass companies on to produce Carnival water sets in the mid 1970s.

Fenton produced quite a lot of limited editions for Levay. In 1976, they made fourteen different shapes in vaseline Carnival for the distributor; several of them were Levay's preferred Classic Carnival patterns such as the *ORANGE TREE* (aka *FENTON'S FLOWERS*) rose bowl and the *PERSIAN MEDALLION* rose bowl. Other Fenton items for Levay include the *HOBNAIL* juice set in vaseline opal (limited to 125) and *DIAMOND OPTIC* water sets in purple (also limited to 125). O. J. Olson's advertising sheets reported in 1980 that "Fenton and Levay are now offering six pieces of aqua opal Carnival in a package deal. Specimens were displayed and advertised at the new Carnival auction and Convention at Kansas City late in April 1980." Just fifty *GRAPE AND CABLE* cuspidors were made in aqua opal by Fenton for Levay. In 1982, a range of items was made in the *CACTUS* pattern in cherry red Carnival for the company.

Westmoreland also made a lot of limited edition Carnival for Levay. Water sets in particular were produced (in fifteen or so different patterns): *GOD AND HOME* water sets were made in ice blue from Wright's moulds for Levay; the *DELLA ROBIA* water set was made in blue and turquoise; and *CHECKERBOARD* water sets were made in ice blue, dark lime green, cobalt blue, lime green, purple slag, ruby, white, blue opal, purple, and experimental black [5]. *PANELED GRAPE* was made in cobalt blue, blue opal, lime green, lilac opal, ruby, and purple slag [5]. *HIGH HOB* water sets were also produced for Levay in cobalt blue, pink, green opal, blue opal, purple, and purple slag [5]. A splendid *GOOD LUCK* chop plate was made by Westmoreland for Levay.

Five thousand purple plates in the *THREE LITTLE KITTENS* design (now owned and being made by Summit) were also produced for Levay in the 1970s. A similar number of the *HOLIDAY CHERUB* plates were also made in Carnival by Westmoreland. These are most distinctive, having a pierced, open heart edge and a lute playing cherub as the main motif. Twenty-five hundred *GEORGE WASHINGTON* plates were produced for Levay in purple—all were trademarked, dated, and numbered.

Westmoreland made various other shapes, as re-issues of their Classic Carnival patterns, in limited editions for Gary Levi's company. These include the *PEACOCK TAIL* in bowl and plate shapes (in red, black, and amethyst opal) plus the *CHERRY AND CABLE* cookie jar in cobalt, ice blue, lime green, purple slag, red, and turquoise [5]. The *STRUTTING PEACOCK* covered sugar, creamer, and rose bowl were also made for Levay in purple and red.

Imperial also produced Carnival for Levay. White and marigold *TIGER LILY* water sets and ice blue *FIELDFLOWER* water sets, plus splendid white *POPPY SHOW* vases were all made in limited editions in 1977. L.E. Smith too, produced *MOON AND STAR* water sets in white and amber/persimmon, as well as *HOB STAR VARIANT* water sets in ice blue and ice green for Gary Levi's successful distributing company.

In 1984, Gary Levi stopped having limited edition Carnival Glass under the name of Levay made for him. In correspondence with the authors about himself and his love of glass, Levi recounted that he entered the glass collectible business as a teenager interested primarily in antique glass. He further noted that he has always loved beautiful things, glass being at the top of his list. Gary's rarest and most sought after item in Classic Carnival is an old pipe humidor. He and his wife still collect Carnival and still have a deep love for the glass. Without a doubt, Levi's contribution to the growth and collecting interest in Contemporary Carnival Glass was of the utmost significance.

The *SUNFLOWER* pintray was made in 1977 by Fenton for Levay. This pretty green example is price band B.

DELLA ROBIA water sets were made by Westmoreland for Levay in cobalt blue. Price band B for a single tumbler.

Mosser Glass, Inc., Cambridge, Ohio

Mosser Glass was started by Thomas R. Mosser in the 1950s. His background was in the glass industry: as a teenager he had learned his trade working at Cambridge Glass Company where his father was plant manager. When Cambridge closed in 1954, Tom began to organize himself by buying moulds for toothpicks and salts from Cambridge with a view to beginning his own glass company. In 1959, glass production began at Mosser Glass Inc. Since then, he and his wife Georgianna have added new designs to the lines. In 1971, new premises were acquired and the business has continued to expand. Tom's children now run the family business.

Back in the 1970s, Mosser Glass became involved in what has become something of a Carnival Glass legend! In 1976, the collectors' journals *Encore* and *Carnival Glass News and Views* were full of rumors about the appearance of ice blue and amber *GRAPE AND CABLE* butter dishes and *GRAPE* nut bowls bearing what appeared to be N marks. The moulded trademark was similar overall to the original Northwood underscored N in a circle, but careful scrutiny will show that the circle isn't quite complete. Also, they were easily distinguished from the original Classic examples by the edge of the base: the original Northwood examples have a saw-tooth edge while the reproductions have a broad, scalloped edge.

The reproductions had turned up at auctions, flea markets, antique malls, and even Carnival Glass Conventions at a selling price of around $20 to $25. Finally the mystery was solved and it was discovered that the mould for the butter dish had been made by Al Motson and was owned by Mosser, who had pressed and iridized the glass. John Jennings, a wholesale dealer from eastern Tennessee, was the distributor. (Note: *GRAPE DELIGHT* nutbowls were also produced bearing the same N mark. This is of particular interest, as, during the 1970s, Dugan/Diamond—the original manufacturer of that pattern—was virtually unknown. It was only after Del Helman's "dig" at the old Dugan glass dump in 1981, plus William Heacock's research and subsequent articles, that Dugan/Diamond was fully recognized as a Carnival manufacturer. The irony is that Dugan/Diamond made the *GRAPE DELIGHT* pattern, not Northwood, thus the originals would not have borne the N mark! See entry under L.G. Wright.)

Court action was brought by the American Carnival Glass Association who, just a year or so earlier, had actually applied for and secured, the legal right for use of the original Northwood trademark. This court ruling was registered in some thirty states. The ruling was enforced by the courts with regard to the Mosser items and the "N" mark was no longer used by the company. Mosser also produced the *GRAPE AND CABLE* butter dish in cobalt blue, but this one was not trademarked in any way.

Since the 1970s, Mosser's Carnival Glass production has included an ever growing, wide range of shapes, patterns, and colors. By the end of the 1990s, they had the following iridized Carnival colors in production: purple, cobalt blue, crystal, hunter green, cranberry ice, green opal, and teal. According to Mosser, their trademark—a simple letter M or, more recently, an M within a shape formed like the state of Ohio—is now present on at least 60 percent of their merchandise (see Appendix 3). Other marks on Mosser Glass include RH within a four leaf clover on some limited edition items such as *BIMBAH* the elephant. RH represents Robert Henry, president of Mosser during the early 1980s.

Mosser's production includes a range of delightful Carnival novelties such as the *RAM'S HEAD, COLLIE, TURKEY* toothpick, and *LION*. Then there are children's miniatures such as the *GRAPE (AND*

CABLE) 3 piece table set, *CHERRY THUMBPRINT* water sets, goblets, bowls, table sets and punch sets, and the *INVERTED STRAWBERRY* mini punch set. Covered dishes, for example the *HEN ON NEST* in purple Carnival, are also popular lines. Mosser made *FLIPPER* the miniature dolphin in marigold for Pisello Art Glass of LaPorte, Indiana, dated 1983 and limited to 1000.

In 1977, an ad in Dorothy Taylor's *Encore* journal for Mosser showed several items in purple Carnival: *CHERRY AND LATTICE* table set and water set pieces plus a re-issue of the *IMPERIAL GRAPE* tumbler. Mosser also produced table sets in the *INVERTED THISTLE* pattern, but these have only been made in ice blue Carnival Glass in the butterdish shape. The *INVERTED THISTLE* water set has, however, been made by Mosser for Rosso in green opalescent Carnival (only ninety sets reported to have been made) and purple Carnival. A similar pattern called *THISTLE* was made in pink by L.G. Wright in water set and table set shapes. The *INVERTED STRAWBERRY* butterdish has also been reproduced in purple Carnival. Mosser have additionally reproduced the old Dugan/Diamond pattern *BEADED BASKET* in white Carnival.

A Selection of Mosser's Contemporary Carnival Glass

(BEADED) SHELL

An old Dugan/Diamond pattern, the *BEADED SHELL* moulds were subsequently owned by L.G. Wright for many years, but they were later sold on to Mosser for their current production. Apart from the colors in which they are made, it is not too easy to tell the modern examples from the original Classic pieces from Dugan/Diamond. An iridized base is usually present on the Mosser items (but not on the early Dugan/Diamond items) and their iridescence is usually much shinier and more even. Note that the Mosser name for this pattern is *SHELL*, while the collectors' name for the same pattern in Classic Carnival is *BEADED SHELL*.

Shapes: water set, table set (4 piece), and bowls

Colors: hunter green, emerald green, purple. Green opal, red, and black amethyst (made for Rosso in Pennsylvania).

CHERRY AND CABLE aka CHERRY (AND) THUMBPRINT

Mosser have made the large, covered cracker jar in this pattern for Rosso of Pennsylvania in sapphire blue, pink, cobalt blue, purple, white, French opalescent, green opal, and very limited examples in cranberry ice carnival (only 124 made). (The cracker jar was also previously made by Westmoreland for Levay—for details, see section on Levay Glass Distributing Company.) Other shapes have also been produced for Rosso; in fact, only the purple Carnival is in Mosser's line, all other colors have been made for Rosso. Miniatures as well as full size items are made.

Shapes: covered cracker jar, covered tobacco jar, bowl, table set, water set and goblet, miniature punch set, table set, and water set.

Colors: purple. Water set also in green opal for Rosso, for other colors in cracker jar see above.

Mosser's *BIMBAH* the elephant is shown here courtesy of Rita and Les Glennon. Price band B.

Mosser's *CHERRY AND CABLE* aka *CHERRY THUMBPRINT* pattern in a range of shapes—all these are their miniature range (approximately 2" or 3" high), but full sized versions of many shapes are also made.

CHERRY (LATTICE)

An old pattern of Northwood's, *CHERRY LATTICE* was only produced by them in crystal and not in Carnival. However, Mosser have issued the table set and water set in iridized glass. It is most attractive in Carnival—again note the iridized base.

> Shapes: water set and table set (3 piece)
> Colors: purple and black amethyst (the latter for Rosso)

DAHLIA

Originally a Dugan/Diamond pattern, today Mosser are producing very attractive water sets in this design. The pitcher is almost indistinguishable from the Classic examples, but several things help to establish the item's manufacture and age. The base of the modern examples is usually iridized (the old Classic examples of the *DAHLIA* pitcher never were). The color and iridescence of the newer items are also indicators of age: a shiny, evenly covered iridescence is more likely to be new. The Classic examples of the *DAHLIA* were only made in purple, marigold, and white (often with gilding or colors such as silver, red, or blue picking out the moulded flowers). The colors of the Mosser examples are listed below.

It is, however, easy to spot the modern *DAHLIA* tumbler. The Classic versions have four dahlia blooms around the body of the tumbler; the modern versions have three. The overall shape of the tumbler is quite different and the base of the Classic ones has a star while the modern ones are quite plain.

Mosser isn't the only manufacturer to have made the *DAHLIA* water set in more recent times: Westmoreland produced it for L.G. Wright in 1977 (purple, white, and ice blue) and Terry Crider made some examples in blue opal and green opal. See entry on L.G. Wright for more information on this pattern.

> Shapes: water set and butter dish
> Colors: hunter green, purple, French opal (crystal), green opalescent, emerald green, and white. Black amethyst (200 sets), red (172), pink opalescent (48), and sapphire blue (42) were made for Rosso.

The *DAHLIA* pattern was not made in old Carnival in this wonderful red color—this modern water pitcher and tumbler are made by Mosser. Price band D for the full water set; pitcher only, price band C.

Northwood Art Glass Company, Wheeling, Ohio

To feature Northwood in a book that covers Contemporary Carnival Glass is a treat indeed: for far too long, the name Northwood has been missing from the Carnival Glass scene. The company was one of the most successful glass manufacturing houses in the United States from the early 1880s through 1925, when the Wheeling plant was forced to close its doors. Unfortunately, the premature death of Harry Northwood's younger brother, Carl, in 1918 and Harry just a year later, left the company without the genius of talent necessary to carry on the business. Moreover, it was not only Harry's innovative glass making techniques but also his equally savvy business insight that had often kept the company at the forefront of the competitive glass tableware industry.

1998 GRAPE & CABLE SERIES

1. COBALT CARNIVAL
(EACH OF THREE SHAPES)

2. PLUM CARNIVAL
(EACH OF THREE SHAPES)

3. CRYSTAL IN GIFTWARE
(SATIN FINISH OVERALL WITHOUT IRIDIZING)

An elegant 1998 ad for the Northwood Art Glass Company that shows their superb *GRAPE AND CABLE* series vases in three colorways. Shown here by kind permission of the Northwood Art Glass Company.

Without Harry's leadership, the company survived only a few short years before it was forced into receivership. Neither Carl nor Harry had family who were prepared to manage the company. Harry's wife, Clara Elizabeth, had never been involved in the plant and did not take a role in the business after his death. Their son, H. Clarence, though very active as a territory salesman for the business, was living in Cincinnati, Ohio and had been away from the daily plant routine. Unfortunately, he too died just four years after his father. Daughter Mabel Virginia was married and her husband, Harry Robb, was employed in his own family's business. Carl's wife, Rose, returned to England shortly after his death, leaving their two daughters, Amy and Mildred in Wheeling with their respective families.

Since the works closed in 1925, the auspicious name, Northwood, had only been used in the context of old, Classic Carnival—a company without a legacy. Until 1997 that is, when a dream that had been long nurtured in the heart of Wheeling resident David McKinley began to take shape. An engineer by profession, and a passionate supporter both of family and West Virginia (Wheeling in particular), David's time and attention had mainly focused on building preservation and restoration. His progression from restoring and conserving the once glorious homes in the area naturally transferred to the contemplation of a seemingly different restoration task altogether—the renaissance of the Northwood Art Glass company! So, why would David McKinley have such a heartfelt desire to see the Northwood name on glass again? Simple—his great-grandfather was Carl Northwood, Harry's younger brother. David is "family!" Driven by one man's passion, the new Northwood Art Glass Company opened its doors in 1998, seventy-three years after the original company closed. Working closely with David McKinley is Susan Haddad, Director of the Northwood Art Glass Company. Much family support also comes from David's wife, Mary, and his younger brother, Brian, who is a Carnival Glass collector and glass historian.

Solely responsible for the new company's revival, McKinley's decision to again design glass was not surprising. An overriding principle of the new company from the very start was that the integrity and collectibility of the original Northwood Carnival Glass would not be affected. In designing the new products, David McKinley gave particular consideration to the collectors of Northwood's Classic Carnival Glass. The new glass, though reminiscent in many ways of the original Northwood product, is distinctive and marked with the new company's logo—a script signed *Northwood* moulded on the base. Old Classic Northwood was often (not always) marked with an underlined N̲ in a circle on the base.

Revered and loved, Northwood's Classic Carnival set its successors a hard legacy to follow, but coupled with the expertise and craftsmanship of the Fenton Art Glass Company, who have pressed and iridized glass for the new Northwood Company, the first offerings from Harry Northwood's descendants are of the highest quality. Using superb colors and combining different finishes is seen by the new company as absolutely essential in continuing Harry Northwood's tradition. Their contemporary products feature both color and finish in distinctive combinations and are undoubtedly of very high quality.

Fenton were chosen to produce the new Northwood glass for several reasons: not only did they have an outstanding reputation for a high quality product, but as they were also located in West Virginia, the new Northwood glass would remain "local." Further, a history had long been established with Fenton that made the whole enterprise seem absolutely fitting: in the summer of 1897, a recent high school graduate, Frank Leslie Fenton, had taken a job with the Northwood Company, which was then located at the Indiana, Pennsylvania plant. His son, Frank M. Fenton, tells the story that his father's employ almost ended several weeks after it began. "My father was late in reporting for work in the decorating department, and he was told by one of the foremen to leave the factory. On his way out, he was seen by one of the managers, perhaps Harry or Carl Northwood. The man spoke with him for a few moments and my father was sent back to work." A year later, Frank was the foreman in the decorating department! The rest is history.

1998 *GRAPE AND CABLE VASE*

Designed by David McKinley, this is the first piece that the new company has produced and is a contemporary interpretation of Northwood's famous *GRAPE AND CABLE* pattern. The design was felt to be the best way to depict a new era and honor the old at the same time. Jon Saffell made the clay and plaster mock up of the piece and from this, the mould was then produced by the Weishars of Island Mould Company in Wheeling. Finally, the vases were then pressed and iridized by the Fenton Art Glass Company. The vase stands 8" high and is a full 5" in diameter; it is produced in several color combinations and finishes. There are three different shape treatments given to the vase top: it may be cupped in, turned out, or straight up. This first release from the company honors Wheeling resident Elizabeth Northwood Robb, the granddaughter of Harry and Clara Northwood.

Shape: vase

Colors: cobalt blue, purple (plum), and crystal (pearl effect). The vase is produced in all Carnival finish (totally iridized), as well as with the grapes and leaves picked out in striking iridescence against a satin (matte, etched) background.

The splendid *1998 GRAPE AND CABLE VASE* from the new Northwood Art Glass Company. This magnificent example is in rich cobalt blue; the grapes are iridized against a matte background—a most effective treatment. Price band D.

DOLPHIN CARD RECEIVER

An old Northwood mould, this was purchased by McKinley at the closure of the L.G. Wright company (see below). In late 1999, it went into production and was pressed and iridized by the Fenton Art Glass Company for Northwood Art Glass in a rich cobalt blue Carnival. Though the mould was originally used by Harry Northwood back in the early 1900s, it was never used back then for Carnival. All Carnival examples are from the new Northwood Company and are clearly marked as such.

Shape: stemmed card receiver
Color: blue

An old mould used by the original Northwood Company (though not for Classic Carnival) has been put to use by Harry Northwood's descendants—the new Northwood Company have produced this delightful *DOLPHIN* card receiver in blue Carnival. Price band C.

Rosso Wholesale Glass Dealers Inc., Port Vue, Pennsylvania

Though not a glass manufacturer, Rosso's production is significant within the sphere of contemporary Carnival Glass. The company operates in much the same way as the L.G. Wright Glass Company used to; that is, they own many of their own moulds and commission glass to be made on their behalf. Much of their glass is made by the Mosser Glass Company, but L.E. Smith, Fenton, Terry Crider, and Summit have all made glass for them too. The difference is that Rosso's are also a mail order business, marketing their glass at both retail and wholesale levels.

The company was started in the late 1960s by Helen and Phil Rosso on a very small scale. In the late 1970s, Rosso's began to purchase glass

from the Westmoreland Glass Company. A few short years later, Westmoreland encountered hard times and when the company finally failed, Rosso purchased many of their moulds. Rosso's trademark is a letter R within a keystone (for the state of Pennsylvania). Owing to legal difficulties and marketing issues, it has not often been used. However, in 1999, following their purchase of thirteen moulds at the L.G. Wright auction, Rosso reported that they were about to bring their "R" trademark into use. Phil Rosso died in February 1999; his wife Helen had passed away almost a decade earlier. The business today is headed up by their son Philip J. Rosso and his sisters.

Covered animals and various novelties, mainly using old Westmoreland moulds and pressed by Summit Art Glass, are typical of Rosso's lines. The amusing covered *CAMEL* and the elegant *SWAN* sugar and creamer are familiar shapes, as is the *SHRINERS BARREL* toothpick, another old Westmoreland mould

---

The *SHRINER'S BARREL* toothpick in a pale lavender color is shown here courtesy of Rita and Les Glennon. Price band A.

---

that is made in purple, sometimes hand-painted. The *LUSTRE ROSE* water set, butter dish, creamer and sugar (described in Rosso's ads as an "Old Imperial mould") in black amethyst, purple, and ocean blue have all been made for Rosso by Summit. The amusing old McKee mould, the *BOTTOMS UP* whiskey glass and coasters, are also made by Summit in a range of colors including Bermuda blue and Geraldine's delight. Mosser also press Carnival for Rosso, one of their most popular lines being the *DAHLIA* water set. For details, see above under Mosser.

FILE AND FAN miniature punch set

An old Westmoreland mould owned by Rosso's is used for this delightful miniature punch set. The glass is manufactured by Mosser Glass Company, though the items can only be purchased from Rosso's. Examples of the punch set were made by Westmoreland before they closed, but the item has really had its "day in the sun" in the hands of the Rossos. A rainbow of Carnival colors has been used for this pretty little set.

Rosso's *FILE AND FAN* miniature punch set comes in a wide variety of Carnival colors (red is shown here). Price band BC.

Shape: mini punch set comprising a one piece punch bowl and stand plus six tiny cups and metal hooks

Colors: cobalt, black amethyst, purple, sky blue, Bermuda blue, pale blue opalescent, green opalescent, red, deep ruby, tangerine, chocolate, white, crystal opalescent (French opal), amber, emerald, and probably more that we have not named.

L.E. Smith, Mount Pleasant, Pennsylvania

Back in the early 1900s, Scots farmer John Duncan initiated a development plan for the area of Pennsylvania around Mount Pleasant. One of the companies that started up in response to the plan was the Anchor Glass Company. In a financial panic a few years later, Lewis E. Smith purchased the Anchor Glass Company at a bankruptcy sale and the L.E. Smith Glass Company was born. The early years saw innovations such as the original glass coffee percolator domes, juice reamers, and the vault lights seen on sidewalks. In the 1960s, they attempted iridescent ware and in 1971 they went into production with Carnival Glass. In the same year, the company was purchased by Owens-Illinois, with Smith operating as a wholly owned subsidiary. All items at Smith are still handmade—most glass is marked with their trademark letter S, though sometimes this appears with tiny letters G and C within the curves of the S.

Dorothy Taylor's *Carnival Glass Encore* reported in 1985 that Hank Opperman, president of L.E. Smith Glass (and one-time Imperial employee), stated that the company had "probably 100 to 200 moulds from Imperial." Examples include the *WINDMILL* pitcher and tumblers, the 7" *WINDMILL* bowl and the 8" oval pickle dish, the *PANSY* pickle dish, and the *OPEN ROSE* footed bowl; most of these have since been produced in red and cobalt Carnival. Interestingly, this means that Smith have produced re-issues of re-issues! (Imperial re-issued them in the 1960s and 1970s before they folded, the moulds were then subsequently bought and used by Smith). Other Carnival colors used by Smith have been amethyst, pale pink, iridized crystal, green, amber, and ice blue. Red has been a favorite Smith color, but an information note from Rossos, the wholesale glass dealers, issued to their customers in November 1998 reported that L.E. Smith Glass had been ordered by the Environmental Protection Agency to cease production of red glass until their furnaces had been renovated. The reason cited was that chemicals were being released into the air which were not permitted.

Two magnificent amethyst punch sets were manufactured by Smith in 1972: *INVERTED FEATHER AND HOBSTAR* (aka *HOBSTAR AND FEATHER)*, with eight matching cups, and the *GRAPE AND VINE* (aka *HEAVY GRAPE*) with twelve cups. *HOBSTAR* water sets in green, amber, and white Carnival as well as red *MOON AND STARS* items and several covered hen and turkey novelties are also typical Smith products. A white punch set in *HOBSTAR* was made for Levay in 1976. Commemoratives and limited editions have also been produced by Smith. In 1977, they made the HOACGA red *GOOD LUCK* hatpin holder and in 1980, five hundred *WINE AND ROSES* miniature water sets in ice blue opalescent were produced for Dorothy Taylor's *Encore*. The moulds for the miniature set (goblets and pitcher) were made in Cambridge, Ohio by Al Botson of Botson Machine Company. Smith also made Carnival Glass for Cherished Glass Wares (Mary Walrath—Walrath's Limited Editions) as "exclusives"; for example, the amberina *OHIO STAR* vase, of which only six hundred were actually released.

A Selection of Smith's Contemporary Carnival Glass

CAROL'S SURE WIN

A delightful miniature vase that stands about 5" high, the flower holder being centrally placed between the front and back of a horse! It was reported in Dorothy Taylor's *Encore* books that this whimsical item was made using an old mould. Produced in the late 1970s for Cherished Glass Wares, the vases are trademarked CGW in a heart shape on the base. The numbers were limited to 2000, though only

660 of the blue ones were actually made.

Shape: novelty vase

Colors: amber, amberina, crystal lustre, and blue

A delightful novelty vase, this is the amber version of *CAROL'S SURE WIN* by L.E. Smith (trademarked CGW, see text). Price band BC.

OHIO STAR VASE

An impressive looking, heavy item, standing 9" high and made of thick glass, the *OHIO STAR VASE* is similar to, but not the same as, its Classic Millersburg namesake: the overall pattern concept is familiar, but the individual motifs are not identical. (This isn't the only Smith pattern with a Millersburg "look" to it. Smith's *GRAPE AND VINE* punch set has a look of Millersburg's *MULTIFRUITS AND FLOWERS* pattern.) The vase was first produced by Smith in 1971-72 and then again for both Cherished Glass Wares and Levay in 1976.

Shape: vase

Colors: amethyst, green, amber, crystal lustre, amberina (limited edition for Cherished Glass Wares), and ice blue (limited edition for Levay)

The *OHIO STAR VASE* is an impressive, heavy item. Made by L.E. Smith, this one is deep purple. Price band BC.

J.F. KENNEDY PLATE

Distinguished by an open lattice edge, this commemorative plate (and it's "brother" patterns *ABRAHAM LINCOLN, JEFFERSON DAVIES, ROBERT E. LEE,* and the *MORGAN DOLLAR*) was issued in limited editions, following which the mould was broken. The first two in the series, *LINCOLN* and *KENNEDY,* were released in 1971; the other three followed a year later. Twenty-five hundred of the first two plates were produced, two thousand of *DAVIES* and *LEE,* and five thousand of the *MORGAN DOLLAR* [6]. The same open edge was used by Smith on an amethyst ICGA souvenir plate in 1973 that featured the club's motif, the town pump.

Shape: plate

Colors: amethyst and blue (100 *KENNEDY* only in 1971—individually signed and numbered by the artist)

Capturing his likeness so well, this is L.E. Smith's *J.F. KENNEDY PLATE* in purple. *Courtesy of Rita and Les Glennon.* Price band BC.

Also from L.E. Smith, a purple *ABRAHAM LINCOLN* plate. *Courtesy of Rita and Les Glennon.* Price band BC.

DANCING LADIES PLANTER

A scarce item made in Carnival in 1977, this was previously shown in L. E. Smith's "Special Listing for F.W. Woolworth & Co." back in the early 1930s in black glass. Five hundred only were produced in "Persimmon Carnival" as a special limited edition. The catalog number was #404. The planter is rectangular in shape, standing about 6" in height and almost 8" long. The moulded pattern encircles the item and features a classic portrayal of dancing females and musicians.

Shape: planter
Color: marigold

St. Clair Art Glass, Elwood, Indiana

In 1890, French immigrants John and Rosalie St. Clair settled in Elwood, Indiana. The town was thriving, based on the supply of natural gas that attracted industry—glassworks in particular. One of these glassworks, Macbeth (considered the first successful producer of optical glass in the USA), soon became the employer of John and his son (also named John). "Young" John proved to have a flair for glassmaking, spending his spare time in the Macbeth plant—inventing, creating, and improving his techniques. Soon his own young sons—John, Paul, Joseph (Joe), Edward, and Robert—became interested too, watching and learning from their father. As time went by, however, the gas supply in Elwood started to become depleted as the nearby growing cities of Chicago and Indianapolis took ever-increasing amounts. In the late 1930s, the merged Macbeth-Evans Glass plant closed its operations in Elwood. "Young" John (who by then had become known to all as "Pop") was out of a job.

Pop and his wife, Ellen, took their family away from Elwood in a search for work. Joe St. Clair, their third son, made a decision to remain behind. He and his Pop had always had a dream—their own glass plant—and Joe was determined to make it happen. In *The Story of St. Clair Glass*[7] Jane Ann Rice says "While Pop and Mom and their family were in West Virginia, Joe set the wheels in motion in Elwood. The factory that Joe built in the late '30s was a small, mod-est sheet metal structure in the backyard of the family home on North Fifth Street. There was just one small capacity furnace and the barest of glass furnishing equipment. In May 1941, the family returned and production began in earnest at the new St. Clair Glass."

Until his death in 1958, Pop supervised the glassmaking and most of the family joined in: lamps, paperweights, ashtrays, and other lines were produced. The St. Clairs never sacrificed quality for quantity and their clear, flawless crystal became known among art glass collectors and connoisseurs. In 1958, Joe St. Clair assumed full command, heralding an era of experimentation and the introduction of Carnival Glass. The 1960s saw the first St. Clair Carnival. Joe purposely aimed to use old moulds that had seen service before—but **not** in Carnival Glass. Thus, even though the shape and pattern might be old, the iridescent finish was totally new—the item was being produced in Carnival for the first time.

The scourge of the glass industry—fire—struck the St. Clair factory in 1964 and the original plant was destroyed. A larger and more modern works was built in its wake, but in early 1971 Joe St. Clair decided to retire and sold the glassworks to Robert Courtney and Richard Gregg. However, inactivity didn't sit easily on Joe—in 1974 he returned to glass making and subsequently repurchased the original plant and equipment on North Fifth Street and started again! He continued working there until his death in October 1987.

Carnival tumblers and toothpick holders were two of St. Clair's specialties. According to O. Joe Olson,[8] the St. Clair plant had three strong periods of tumbler production. In 1963-64, the *INVERTED FAN AND FEATHER* tumbler was made in marigold and white. In 1968-70, a few weeks were set aside each year for tumbler production. Four patterns were made: *INVERTED FAN AND FEATHER, HOLLY (aka PANELED HOLLY), FLEUR DE LYS,* and *CACTUS*. Blue was the main Carnival color used at that time. (See below under the pattern entry for *INVERTED FAN AND FEATHER* for more details on these other tumblers.) In 1973-74, St Clair acquired the former Breck Smith *GRAPE AND CABLE* mould (Breck Smith produced the tumbler in amethyst and white Carnival in 1965); tumblers were pressed and iridized by St. Clair in four colors—red, blue, purple, and white. Most St. Clair Carnival is trademarked with a variety of company logos: JOE ST.CLAIR or JST.C in capitals or a stylish script signature, sometimes simply ST.CLAIR (see Appendix 3).

Three St. Clair tumblers in blue. From left: *CACTUS, HOLLY* (aka *PANELLED HOLLY*), and *FAN AND FEATHER. Courtesy of Rita and Les Glennon.* Price band B for each tumbler.

When Joe finally retired, it was not the end of the St. Clair saga. For a while, youngest brother Bob and his wife Maude kept the tradition alive in Elwood by adding a small glass works to the "House of Glass" (their small antique shop), where limited quantities of Carnival and other glass items were produced. Their glass was also trademarked. Different examples of these can be seen on toothpick holders such as the *SHEAF OF WHEAT* (marked on the base ST.CLAIR and inside BOB AND MAUDE 1974) and the *BICENTENNIAL NIXON* toothpick holder (marked ORIGINAL BOB ST. CLAIR 1776—1976). These toothpicks are interesting in that they were both previously made by Joe St. Clair as well. The *BICENTENNIAL NIXON* was made in cobalt blue Carnival for Joe St. Clair in September 1974 and featured the profiles of Nixon, Washington, and a Native American Indian. Believing it would become a big seller, Joe St. Clair pressed about 20,000 of the cobalt versions; his future plan was to alter the mould and replace Nixon with Ford. However, in 1976, Bob St. Clair issued the same toothpick in red, blue, and green Carnival in much smaller numbers.

A Selection of St. Clair's Contemporary Carnival Glass

INDIAN CHIEF

St. Clair chose the *INDIAN CHIEF* toothpick holder mould for one of his first Carnival novelties. The decision was deliberate; though the mould was an old one (dating back to the 1880s), Joe felt that as it hadn't been used for the old, Classic Carnival production, its production in the late 1960s wouldn't confuse the collectors. Some of the *INDIAN CHIEF* toothpicks were made as souvenirs and bear inscriptions, indeed the one made for O. Joe Olson's Society of Carnival Glass Collectors has its club logo, Olson's initials plus the date 1964-69, and the words "Original Carnival Society." Rare examples

are signed *Antique Market, Glendale, California 1968* and also carry a dealer's name. It is thought that over 100,000 different *INDIAN CHIEF* toothpicks were made by St. Clair in various colors and finishes of glass (non-iridized custard and slag were made in addition to Carnival). However, in 1978, the moulds of the *INDIAN CHIEF* and many other pieces were sold by St. Clair to the Summit Glass Company where production continues to date.

St. Clair made a wide variety of toothpick holders using old moulds, including *ARGONAUT SHELL* (aka *NAUTILUS*), *S REPEAT*, *WREATHED CHERRY*, *CHRYSANTHEMUM SPRIG*, and *KINGFISHER*.

Shape: toothpick holder

Colors: a myriad of Carnival colors made by St. Clair, including marigold, blue, dark green, aqua opalescent, lavender, lemon, pastel green, white, ice blue, red, smoke, chartreuse, custard, and rare pink slag. Summit continue to produce the *INDIAN CHIEF* in Carnival colors including vaseline, patriot slag (red, white, and blue), Geraldine's Delight (yellow, amber to red), and more.

INVERTED FAN AND FEATHER aka FEATHER SCROLL

This is an old pattern used by Northwood and Dugan, though neither made it in Carnival Glass in the shapes that were subsequently produced by Joe St. Clair. *INVERTED FAN AND FEATHER* was made in Carnival by Dugan/Diamond as an exterior pattern only on large footed bowls in *BUTTERFLY AND TULIP* and *GRAPE ARBOR*.

In modern Carnival, however, several shapes are known—these moulds saw service with St. Clair from around 1963 but were later sold to Summit, where production still continues. Some of the St. Clair examples are trademarked, however the unmarked ones continue to fool collectors into believing they might be old. Much con-

An array of toothpicks made by the St. Clair family, plus one from Summit using an old St. Clair mould. Top row, from left: blue *WREATHED CHERRY* marked St. Clair; blue *DOG* aka *DOGHEAD* marked Joe St. Clair; green *HOLLY BAND* marked Joe St. Clair. Bottom row, from left: red *BICENTENNIAL* marked Original Bob St. Clair. 1976; *WITCH'S HEAD* aka *OLD WOMAN* not signed—this is a Summit product in blue slag; *INDIAN CHIEF* aka *INDIAN HEAD* in dark green marked Joe St. Clair in script; and *SHEAF OF WHEAT* in caramel slag marked St. Clair outside, Bob and Maude 1974, inside. Price band BC for each.

troversy surrounds the production of the marigold *INVERTED FAN AND FEATHER* tumblers that were made by St. Clair in late 1963 and early 1964, and some collectors maintain that they are old Classic Carnival. However, O. J. Olson, writing in *Carnival Glass Tumbler News*[3] in 1974 put forward plenty of evidence to show that they are indeed modern; he even stated the names of collectors who purchased them from St. Clair and named the salesmen who bought boxes of them for re-sale in 1964.

In 1967, souvenir *INVERTED FAN AND FEATHER* tumblers were made for Olson's club, the Society of Carnival Glass Collectors. Each was embossed on the base with the club's logo "Original Carnival Society, S.C.G.C. 1964-69. O.J.O." Three hundred of each of three colors (cobalt blue, ice blue, and red-amberina) were made.

St. Clair made three other tumblers that are also mistakenly thought (and sometimes bought) by some collectors as old, Classic Carnival. The first of these is *HOLLY* (aka *PANELED HOLLY*), which is characterized by its alternating plain and holly motif vertical panels and beaded borders. It was made in cobalt blue, ice blue, aqua, marigold, white, and red. Also, there's *FLEUR DE LYS*, identified by its two rows of slightly differing fleur de lys motifs. It was made in cobalt only while the *CACTUS* tumbler was made in cobalt blue, marigold, and a red/amber mix.

Shapes: toothpick, tumbler, and covered sugar

Colors: for the tumblers—marigold and white (1963-64), cobalt, ice blue, and red-amberina (1968). Marigold, ice blue, and cobalt for the covered sugar. Cobalt, ice blue, and white for the toothpick. The moulds are with Summit Art Glass at present, therefore other colors can be expected.

ROSE IN SNOW

ROSE IN SNOW was one of five old goblet designs that St. Clair chose to reproduce in Carnival between 1968 and 1970. It features a leafy rose sprig against a stippled background and was originally made in pattern glass by Bryce Brothers, Pennsylvania and the Ohio Glass Company in a wide variety of shapes during the 1880s. It was not iridized in its early use, so for that reason, St. Clair felt easy about producing it in Carnival. However, in the same way that some of his tumblers have been mistaken for old, Classic Carnival, so indeed, have these old goblets.

St. Clair's acquisition of the mould is interesting: it seems that AA Importing Company purchased this mould along with the *WILDFLOWER* and *FRUIT* moulds from a source in Ohio. They subsequently decided not to go ahead with production and St. Clair purchased the moulds from them.[8]

The other four goblets made by St. Clair around the same time were *WILDFLOWER* (made in cobalt blue only), *THISTLE* (marigold, cobalt blue, and ice blue), *HOBSTAR* (cobalt blue, ice blue, and aqua), and *FRUIT* (cobalt blue and white). The *FRUIT* goblet is the tallest of the five and features strawberries on one side, with grapes and an apple on the other. It had the shortest production period of all the goblets because the mould developed a weakness and was set aside. The *THISTLE* and *HOBSTAR* were both old Kokomo Glass Company moulds.

Shape: goblet

Color: cobalt blue

The *ROSE IN SNOW* goblet. Though the pattern dates back to the 1880s, it was only made in Carnival Glass by Joe St. Clair in the late 1960s. Price band B.

When Joe St. Clair returned to glassmaking in 1974, he marked the date with the production of this item—the *BPOE (ELKS)* Limited Edition plate in marigold, of which only 2000 were made. Price band BC.

In 1976, St. Clair produced a green *BICENTENNIAL* plate—signed JOE ST. CLAIR on the face, under the bell. Price band B.

This leaflet accompanied the *BPOE (ELKS)* plates.

Summit Art Glass, Ravenna, Ohio

Summit Art Glass, owned by Russel and JoAnn Vogelsong, was created in 1972. At the beginning, the Vogelsongs would buy moulds and have the glass made for them by other companies, such as Mosser. In 1978, Russ and JoAnn added to their growing stock of moulds by purchasing many more at the closure of the St. Clair Glass works. In Russ's own words, he bought from Joe St. Clair "all he put before me"—indeed fifty or more moulds were added to Summit's growing stock. Through the 1970s to May 1984, the Vogelsongs continued to take their moulds to various glass manu-

A few months later, in December 1984, Summit bought up a variety of moulds from the Imperial Glass Company (who were facing imminent closure). Many of the moulds had originally belonged to the Cambridge Glass Company and had been acquired by Imperial when they bought Cambridge in 1957. It was fitting for the Vogelsongs that they managed to acquire some of the original Cambridge moulds, as Russ and JoAnn were avid Cambridge Glass collectors themselves, and they experienced great pleasure at being able to acquire such historically significant moulds. Russ was allowed to roam around the dust-covered shelves in the mould rooms at Imperial, peering at items that hadn't been touched in over twenty-seven years. There he found many moulds that it was thought no longer existed; "treasures" were uncovered and brought back to Summit for production.

A selection of toothpicks from Summit Art Glass. Top row, from left: *NAUTILUS* in purple, *THREE SWANS* in Geraldine's Delight, and *S REPEAT* in green. Bottom row, from left: *COLORADO* in purple, *SIAMESE ELEPHANT* aka *DOUBLE ELEPHANT* In Geraldine's Delight, and *INDIAN CHIEF* in vaseline. Price band AB for each.

facturers to be made up, then sold the glass via a showroom attached to their house, through mail order, and by wholesale to dealers around the country. Several original moulds were also made for them by Island Mould Company, Wheeling: limited editions were then manufactured by Mosser Glass and afterwards, in Summit's own words, "the mould will be sawn into pieces and each active dealer will receive a section of the mould. Destroying the mould will insure the future value of your investment." Summit's *MAJESTIC LION*, made in 1981, was one such limited edition piece. In May 1984, however, the Vogelsongs began to make their own glass at Summit. Moulds and machinery were also purchased from the defunct Tiffin Glass Company, as well as around eighty moulds from Westmoreland.

Also in 1984, the Vogelsongs learned that the Westmoreland Glass Company was being liquidated and they worked hard to finally acquire another 109 Westmoreland moulds. Salt dips, candy containers, covered animals, candlesticks, birds, butterflies, and children's glassware were all added to Summit's inventory. A popular and familiar item is the *BULLDOG* doorstop: weighing in at over seven and a half pounds of glass, this glass eyed creature is a formidable addition to Summit's mould inventory. Indeed, over six hundred moulds are now owned by Summit Art Glass.

The Vogelsongs produce many of their items in both plain and iridized finish. Their trademark—V in a circle (for Vogelsong)—is present on some, though by no means all, of their output and indeed on some of their items, the trademark of the original owners of the moulds (for example, Westmoreland or LIG) can be found. Knowledge of the colors that Westmoreland and Imperial made their Carnival in will assist collectors in identifying certain pieces as to manufacturer. Study of the partial listings of Summit moulds below will also assist the collector in recognizing the newer Summit items and their original source.

Summit particularly like to use fascinating and unusual color mixes, sometimes in limited edition runs. Geraldine Kemple of the old Kemple Glass factory reportedly passed on many formulae for unusual glass colors to the Vogelsongs. "Geraldine used to come to our factory and would bring with her a folding lawn chair to sit on; she would spend hours here, watching and giving my husband advice on production techniques" reported JoAnn. One of the limited colors produced by Summit honors Geraldine Kemple and is appropriately called Geraldine's Delight. Difficult to produce and notoriously unpredictable, Geraldine's Delight is a red-yellow slag; no two items in the color are exactly alike. Summit produced this color in 1995-96 and stated that they would not produce it again to ensure its desirability amongst collectors. Other unusual colors made by Summit include patriot slag (a red, white, and blue mix), Princess purple (honouring Princess Diana), and emerald slag. For the new millennium, Summit has introduced Millennium Blue, a limited color made with copper to produce a rich effect that takes iridescence well.

Summit Art Glass Company's Moulds

The Vogelsongs freely gave the information regarding which moulds they owned to the *Glass Review* in the 1980s and again to the authors in 1999. We thank them for their assistance. Below we list a selection of the moulds currently with Summit. Some of these, though not necessarily all, have been, or are currently being, used for Carnival production. For example, *LUSTRE ROSE* items have been issued by Summit in both vaseline (very limited) and cobalt Carnival as well as several other Carnival colors for Rosso. It is, however, impossible to provide a definitive list of Carnival produced using the moulds listed below, as many of these are currently in production while many more are still in store and have not yet been used. Russ Vogelsongs explained that he had sometimes made items on an experimental basis and not followed through with a fuller production. A more detailed look at a few selected Carnival items produced by Summit follows the partial mould listing.

Cambridge moulds include:

BASHFUL CHARLOTTE figure (flower frog)
CAPRICE range (a small "bead" on the base distinguishes the "new Caprice" from the original)
DOLPHIN candlestick
DRAPED LADY figure (flower frog)
JENNY LIND line
LARGE BUDDHA

Imperial moulds include:

AMERICA THE BEAUTIFUL plates (#5, #7)
ATTERBURY RABBIT
BIRDCAGE covered candy
FIELD FLOWER water set (see below)
HOBNAIL water set
IMPERIAL GRAPE water set
LUSTRE ROSE water set, table set (includes the covered butter) and bowl
NU-ART HOMESTEAD and *CHRYSANTHEMUM* plates (see below)
OWL sugar, creamer, and covered jar

St. Clair moulds include:

ARGONAUT SHELL toothpick
CACTUS toothpick, salt and pepper, and tumbler
CHRYSANTHEMUM SPRIG toothpick

COVERED DOLPHIN
FLEUR DE LYS tumbler
HOLLY (BAND) toothpick and butter
INDIAN CHIEF toothpick
INVERTED FAN AND FEATHER toothpick and other items
RECLINING COLT
ROBIN ON NEST
SIAMESE ELEPHANTS toothpick
S-REPEAT toothpick
THISTLE goblet
TRIPLE SWANS toothpick
WITCH'S HEAD toothpick

Westmoreland moulds include:

BALLERINA ashtray
BULLDOG doorstop
CHECKERBOARD butter dish
COVERED CAMEL
COVERED DUCK
COVERED HEN AND CHICKS
DOGHOUSE toothpick
EASTER CHICKS plate
ELEPHANT bowl
ELKHEAD pocket watch
GARFIELD MEMORIAL plate
LAWN SWING candy
MANTLE CLOCK candy
PIANO candy
RABBIT plate
REVOLVER child's toy
SANTA ON SLEIGH and lid
SWANS tableset
THREE BEARS plate
THREE KITTENS plate
THREE OWLS plate
WASHBOARD advertising Colgate soap
WASHBOILER candy box
Plus various other small novelty candy containers, paperweights, ashtrays etc.

From an old Westmoreland mould, this blue slag *THREE BEARS* plate is an attractive novelty item made by Summit Art Glass. (This one has the old Westmoreland W over G trademark.) Price band A.

FIELDFLOWER water set

This water set is made by Summit using the original Imperial Glass Company moulds. Tumblers were reproduced by Imperial themselves in red and ice blue during the 1970s; they are trademarked IG. Summit has since produced the sets in limited numbers in various colors. It is possible to distinguish the original Classic old tumblers (early 1900s) from the new by checking the moulded scalloped line near the rim of the tumbler. On the old tumbler the top line is a double scallop that matches the double scallop below it. On the new tumblers, the top line is a single scallop that does not match the double scallop below.

Shapes: water set

Colors: cobalt blue, purple, Bermuda blue, and vaseline

HOMESTEAD and *CHRYSANTHEMUM* plates

Originally produced by Imperial back in the 1920s, these two splendid chop plates were reproduced by Imperial, Lennox, and also Arthur Lorch through the 1960s and 1970s (see section on Imperial reproduction). Still bearing the ALIG trademark on the stippled back surface, plates in both these patterns have been produced (and are still in production) in a wide range of superb colors by Summit, who now own both moulds. Some colors, such as vaseline and turquoise, were made by them in very limited quantities and are highly sought after. Geraldine's Delight (orange/yellow slag) plates were made for well-known Contemporary Carnival collector Madonna Woodward in both patterns (only 80 *HOMESTEAD* and 36 *CHRYSANTHEMUM* were produced) and each came with a letter from Summit stating that the color would never be made again.

Shape: chop plate

Colors: cobalt blue, amethyst, turquoise, vaseline, Geraldine's Delight, and Princess purple.

BUFFALO HUNT bowl

This magnificent and massive bowl is made by Summit using a Tiffin Glass Company mould that was made during the 1920s. The design was inspired by a Frederick Remington original painting that can be seen in the Smithsonian and features Native American Indians on horseback, chasing buffalo. Russ Vogelsong reports that, owing to the large quantity of glass that goes into each of these huge bowls, they are produced in only limited amounts.

Shape: master bowl

Colors: cobalt blue, Bermuda blue, chocolate, and vaseline

An impressive and heavy piece of glass, this is Summit's *BUFFALO HUNT* bowl in blue. Price band C.

Seen close up, the detail on the *BUFFALO HUNT* bowl can be fully appreciated.

An old Imperial mould, this *HOMESTEAD* plate made by Summit has the ALIG trademark (see text). The color of this plate is Summit's Geraldine's Delight. Price band C for this color, as a limited number only were produced.

SINGING BIRDS tumbler

So very similar to the Northwood original. No trademark is present on these tumblers.

Shape: tumbler and flared, ruffled, whimsy shaped tumbler

Colors: ice green, blue opalescent, vaseline

Side by side, the Northwood original *SINGING BIRDS* tumbler in green and a whimsy shape in blue opal from Summit. For the Classic Northwood tumbler in green, $80-100. For the blue opal whimsy, price band AB. *Courtesy of Rita and Les Glennon.*

Westmoreland Glass Company, Grapeville, Pennsylvania

Westmoreland Glass Company began operating in 1889 as the Westmoreland Specialty Company of Grapeville, Pennsylvania. They built quite a reputation as a manufacturer of novelties and packaging glass such as candy filled glass toys and glass containers full of mustard. These were sold via news stands and dime stores across the country. Westmoreland was one of the first manufacturers to produce Classic Carnival back in 1908. Their *Antique Iridescent Novelty Assortment* was proudly displayed in the Butler Brothers catalog at that time and they continued to produce their Carnival Glass through the late 1920s. Almost fifty years later, in 1974, Westmoreland made its first Carnival re-issues.

One of Westmoreland's specialties was covered animal containers. This purple *COVERED DUCK* is typical of their output. Price band C.

Two other companies in particular benefited from Westmoreland's Contemporary Carnival production: L.G. Wright and Levay Glass Distributing Company. A 1979 listing of Carnival tumblers made by Westmoreland was compiled by O. Joe Olson, editor of *Carnival Glass News and Views*[3]. No less than sixteen different patterns were listed, including *DAHLIA, GOD AND HOME, HEAVY IRIS, RAMBLER ROSE, STORK AND RUSHES, FLORAL AND GRAPE, GRAPEVINE LATTICE*—all made for L.G. Wright (see under L.G. Wright entry for more detail). Westmoreland also used around

fifteen of its own patterns in exclusive water or juice sets in Carnival Glass for Levay. Few were purely made for the Westmoreland Company only; the *CHECKERBOARD*, for example, was made for Westmoreland themselves and then later for Levay. Naturally, this can be confusing, as the *GOD AND HOME* water set, for example, was made for both Levay (in ice blue and scarce, as only 125 were made in 1976) and L.G. Wright (in amethyst in 1975). Red and mint green were also produced in 1979 and then cobalt blue sets were made in 1982, all for L.G. Wright.

Trademarks are not always present on Westmoreland's Carnival. The *GOD AND HOME* water sets, however, should all be trade marked with the exception of just thirty or so early amethyst sample sets. Westmoreland's trademark can be seen as the letter W over the letter G, or the full word WESTMORELAND in a semicircle above what look like three upright strokes. The *DAHLIA* water set was another matter, however. In February 1977, O. Joe Olson, writing in *Carnival Glass News and Views*[8], suggested that all readers of that journal should write to Westmoreland Glass Co., insisting that they place the L.G. Wright trademark on the *DAHLIA* moulds that Wrights were preparing to have Westmoreland manufacture. No such trademark was ever added. See section on Mosser for hints on how to identify the reproduced items in this pattern.

In the 1980s, Westmoreland fell on hard times and finally went out of business in 1984. Twelve years later, on February 28, 1996, the old factory burned down. Many Westmoreland moulds, however, had already changed hands and are now in production by other companies (see the sections on Summit Art Glass and Rosso Wholesale Glass Dealers). The Westmoreland trademarks are often still present. To determine if the item is a true Westmoreland piece, check the listing of colors that were produced by Westmoreland. The reader is recommended to the books by Lorraine Kovar on the company's recent production[5].

A Selection of Westmoreland's Contemporary Carnival Glass

DELLA ROBIA
Named after the fifteenth century sculptor, Della Robia, this is a pattern that features embossed fruit against a background of finely stippled leaves. *DELLA ROBIA* water sets in cobalt blue were made for Levay by Westmoreland in 1978, limited to 150 sets only. The water set was issued again for Levay in 1980, this time in turquoise Carnival and limited to 400 sets.
> Shape: water set
> Colors: blue and turquoise

CHECKERBOARD aka QUILT
In 1974, Westmoreland issued their Classic Carnival pattern, *CHECKERBOARD,* in the form of an amethyst water set. The demand was good and they followed up with more re-issues in ice blue and honey amber in 1975, lime green (1976), cobalt (1978), and white (1979). All were made for Levay. (Carnival juice sets in blue opal were also issued in 1976.)
> Shapes: water set and some smaller juice sizes, salt and pepper shaker, miniature punch set. (Also several shapes that are scarce: celery vase, pedestal footed bowl, square and round lidded box, cup and saucer—all these in amethyst)
> Colors: amethyst, ice blue, honey amber, lime green, cobalt blue, white, and iridized purple slag

L.G. Wright, New Martinsville, West Virginia

Lawrence Gale (Si) Wright was born in New Martinsville during the early 1900s and showed an early interest in glass, glass making, and merchandising. During the Depression years of the 1930s, Wright began buying the assets of bankrupt glass works; "paying cash for job lots and close-outs of novelty items, he travelled through the mid-West buying and selling. Wright went into partnership briefly in 1932-33 with A.A. Gralnick" (later of AA Importing Co.), and "The men bought glass and other collectibles and sold the items to dealers at wholesale."[8]

In 1937, the L.G. Wright Company was established and Si soon began to accumulate many old moulds, including some originally worked by Dugan/Diamond and Northwood. He also had many new moulds made for the company and in total, accumulated almost one thousand moulds that were used by other manufacturers on Wright's behalf, as they themselves did not make their own glass. Various companies such as Westmoreland, Summit, and Mosser made Wright's glass—final assembly only was carried out in Wright's warehouse at New Martinsville, West Virginia. A slogan was coined for the company "Cherished Today, Treasured Tomorrow."

Si Wright passed away in 1969 and his wife, Verna Mae, took the helm. Under her direction, L.G. Wright's first incursion into Carnival Glass was made in the early 1970s. It was produced for them using their moulds and specifications by manufacturers such as Westmoreland; Wright would then market the products. In fact, Westmoreland was the first to produce Carnival for Wright using mainly the old Dugan and some Northwood moulds. Purple or amethyst Carnival was the main color used, though white, ice blue, ice green, pink, and red were introduced later. Items such as the *EYEWINKER* tumblers were custom iridized by Hansen and Crider (in red, white, ice blue, mint green, and marigold) for L.G. Wright, too.

L.G. Wright's trademark is found on some, but not all items. Indeed, it has caused some difficulties in the past as they used what has been termed a "wobbly N" that can confuse new collectors into believing it is the genuine old Northwood N mark. Measell and Roetteis report[1] that Frank M. Fenton noted in the 1960s that some of the glass (not Carnival) that Fenton's were making for Wright had facsimile Northwood marks on it. Frank is reported to have said "I thought it wrong to mark the glass in this way and I told Mr. Wright that we would not continue to make these articles for his firm." Following on from this, most of the Wright moulds that had the Northwood underlined N in a circle were altered by adding a short line angled upwards from the bottom left corner of the letter N in an attempt to turn the N into a W, thus the "wobbly N." From the mid 1970s, Wright had its own trademark: an (underlined) capital W in a circle (see Appendix 3).

In 1999, the closure of the L.G. Wright business was announced and an auction of all the company's assets took place in late May of that year. The liquidation included the real estate, which comprised the house, plant site, and gift shop, as well as all the equipment, the glass inventory, and contents of the glass museum plus, of course, the many moulds. Almost one thousand moulds for glass production were auctioned, some dating from the late 1800s. The auction brochure noted that the sale included "several vintage moulds purchased in the late 1930s that have never been in production by L.G. Wright Glass Company." John Nielsen and Paul Bekemeier (of the Sunshine State Carnival Glass Association) attended the auction and reported in their club newsletter that prices ranged from $25 to $10,000 (for a group of related moulds). Moulds were bought by (amongst others) the Fenton Art Glass Company, the new Northwood Glass Company, Island Mould Company, Mosser Glass, Rosso Wholesale Glass, Aladdin Lamp Company, AA Importing Inc., and Castle Antique Reproductions.

So which company bought what moulds? Fenton is believed to have acquired around two hundred moulds including the *STORK AND RUSHES* water set. David McKinley of the new Northwood Company bought the *DOLPHIN* compote mould. Items from these two companies will be clearly trademarked. Castle Antique Reproductions (Hawley, Pennsylvania) and AA Importing Inc. (St. Louis, Missouri) also bought around one hundred and fifty. Included in the long list of moulds purchased jointly by AA Importing and Castle Reproductions were those for several well-known Carnival patterns, such as the *LATTICE AND GRAPE* and *FLORAL AND GRAPE* tumblers. Prices ranged from just a few dollars right up to $10,000 for the related set of moulds that included the L.G. Wright *PEACOCKS* bowl with the *INTAGLIO BUTTERFLY* exterior (note that this is not the Northwood *PEACOCKS* pattern, see below for more details).

Listed below are some of the old Dugan/Diamond and Northwood moulds owned in the 1970s through 1999 by L.G Wright and produced for them in Carnival Glass. Usually (but not always) these items are trademarked as detailed above. Carnival colors produced for Wright are noted, but there may have been others:

CHERRY 7" bowl (purple)
DAHLIA water pitcher (in purple, ice blue, and white—none marked—made by Westmoreland for Wright. Moulds leased to Mosser who have made it in other colors— see Mosser entry. The tumbler is a new mould).
FLORAL AND GRAPE water set (purple)
GOD AND HOME water set (see below)
GOLDEN HARVEST decanter and wine (purple—not trademarked)
GRAPE AND CABLE banana boat (10" oval in purple, ice green, and red, and 6" oval in purple and ice green)
GRAPE DELIGHT rose bowl/nut bowl (purple and ice green—also made by Mosser in amber and ice blue)
GRAPE VINE LATTICE water set
HEAVY IRIS water set (Also made by Gibson. Note that there is an inch wide band between the floral pattern and the top of the tumbler and pitcher. The purple Carnival Wright examples of this pattern have no trademark, the Gibson versions, however, have a moulded "Gibson" on the base)
MAPLE LEAF water set and table set (purple, cobalt blue, ice green, and red.
PANELLED THISTLE table set and water set (ice pink with bee trademark)
PONY bowl and plate (purple and marigold)
RAMBLER ROSE water set (purple—not trademarked)
STORK AND RUSHES water set, table set (note, no butter dish and incorrect sugar lid) and berry set (purple, marigold)
VINTAGE BANDED (aka *BANDED GRAPE*) water set

A Selection of L.G. Wright's Contemporary Carnival Glass

GOD AND HOME water set
Made using the original molds, these items were advertised thus in Wright's marketing brochure: "A Rare and Treasured Pattern in Carnival Glass, Once Again Produced From the Recently Discovered Original Old Moulds." The colors, however, are different (though note that blue has been re-issued, but should be trademarked, like most other examples with either a W in a circle or a "wobbly N"). This pattern was made for Wright by Westmoreland. Note that there is also a mini water set and table set in the *GOD AND HOME* pattern that was made for *Encore* (as souvenirs) in blue by Mosser. These are new moulds. A red mini water set was later made for Taylor by Fenton in 1981. There are also souvenir mugs made for the ACGA Conventions for E. Ward Russell that feature the *GOD AND HOME* design.

Shape: water set
Colors: ice green, cobalt blue, purple, and red

GOD AND HOME was made by Westmoreland for L.G. Wright. Here a Classic Dugan/Diamond tumbler is seen alongside the recent Wright version. Which is which? (The older Classic version is on the left—see text for ways to identify the old from the new). Classic blue tumbler, $125-200. Contemporary blue tumbler, price band B.

PEACOCKS, GRAPE AND FRUIT and others

PEACOCKS appeared in custard glass in the Wright line in 1969. The exterior pattern is called *INTAGLIO BUTTERFLIES*, which perfectly describes it. At the same time, several other interesting "new" designs also made an appearance: *GRAPE AND FRUIT* (a "look-alike" to Northwood's *FRUIT AND FLOWERS* and *THREE FRUITS* patterns, with a *GRAPE* exterior), *HOLLY* (so similar to Fenton's pattern of the same name, yet larger and with a *POINSETTIA* exterior), and *PANSY* (so very like the Imperial pattern and with an *ARCS* exterior). There is no record that we are aware of to indicate the origin of these moulds, but a likely possibility would be that they were made to resemble the patterns that they were so obviously imitating. The Wright *PEACOCK* design has only vague similarities to the Northwood pattern of the same name, though the other designs noted above are much closer to their inspirations.

We are aware of Carnival versions of the *PEACOCKS* and *GRAPE AND FRUIT* items that were made for L.G. Wright. It should also be noted that these moulds changed hands in 1999 at the L.G. Wright auction (see above for more details) and thus may well be issued in Carnival in the future. A clear difference in each case is that the new Wright moulds produced very large items—much larger than the Classic Carnival *PEACOCKS* items. The chop plate in *GRAPE AND FRUIT* is 14" in diameter and the ruffled bowl is 12"; the other three patterns are just a fraction smaller. The large size should easily serve to differentiate them from the original, Classic versions of the "look-alikes." The *PANSY* plate, however, was only 9" in diameter. The *PANSY* mould is now owned by Fenton Art Glass and has been used by them to make the 2000 HOACGA souvenir in a Millennium Blue. There was one further custard pattern in a smaller 7" plate version, also issued in 1969, that L.G. Wright called *WOVEN TWIGS*. This was virtually identical to Dugan's *VINING TWIGS* small plate.

Shapes: large bowl and chop plate (an unruffled bowl was reported in 1999)
Color: purple (blue is also reported for the *GRAPE AND FRUIT* bowl)

THISTLE

The moulds for this pattern were made by Island Mould Co., based on old Higbee moulds. A trademark bee was actually added on purpose into the new moulds to give a representational link with the old Higbee pattern. These are similar to, but not the same as, the *INVERTED THISTLE* items produced by Mosser.

Shapes: water pitcher, tumbler, creamer, sugar, spooner, and butter
Color: ice pink

[1] James Measell and W.C. "Red" Roetteis, *The L.G. Wright Glass Company* (Marietta, Ohio: Glass Press, 1997).

[2] William Heacock, *Fenton Glass, The Third Twenty-Five Years* (Marietta, Ohio: O-Val Advertising Corp., 1989), also James Measell, *Fenton Glass, The 1980s Decade* (Marietta, Ohio: Antique Publications, 1996).

[3] *Newsletter of the Collectible Carnival Glass Association*, September 1995.

[4] National Imperial Glass Collectors' Society, *Imperial Glass Encyclopedia Vol. I and II.* (Marietta, Ohio: The Glass Press, 1995 and 1997).

[5] Lorraine Kovar, *Westmoreland Glass. 1950-1984 Vols I and II* (Marietta, Ohio: Antique Publications, 1991).

[6] Rose M. Presznick, *Presznick's Encyclopedia of New Carnival and Iridescent Glass* (Lodi, Ohio: by author, 1974).

[7] Jane Ann Rice, *Story of St. Clair Glass* (Richard E. Harney, date unknown).

[8] O. Joe Olson, *Carnival Glass in the Mid-1970s* (Kansas City, Missouri: by author, 1975).

This impressive, purple *PEACOCKS* plate from L.G. Wright has superb iridescence (marked with Wright's W trademark on the base.) Price band D.

The Minor Manufacturers (and Wholesale Distributors) of Contemporary Carnival Glass

Big Pine Key Works, Key West, Florida

Lester Cunningham (former Imperial glass craftsman) established a home and small glass plant at his Florida glass works at Big Pine Key, near Key West. In 1972, he introduced a private mould plant for souvenir Carnival plates. His idea was to sell the mould and then contract to make plates to order for the owner. Initial acceptance of the idea had just come when Cunningham was killed, aged just forty-nine, in a car crash on June 8, 1973, while assisting in the pursuit of a poacher. The following 5" cobalt blue plates were issued by him:

APACHE SCOUT—design based on a famous Remington painting. Introduced in June 1972 to launch the series
STATUE OF LIBERTY—seated and surrounded by 13 stars and the date, 1776. Pressed in late 1972, signed and dated on the base by *Collector's Weekly*, Kermit, Texas
FLYING EAGLE—eagle in the sky surrounded by 13 stars. Limited edition signed on base by *Collector's Weekly*, Texas in 1973
HARRY TRUMAN—likeness of 33rd President with the dates 1884-1972. Features one of Truman's sayings "If you can't stand the heat stay out of the kitchen"
LYNDON B. JOHNSON—likeness of the 36th President with the dates 1908-1973 and the legend "Come let us reason together"—made in May 1973

Crescent Art Glass Company

This company made limited editions for Levay Glass Distributing Company in the early 1970s, including red Carnival lampshades in a *PEACOCK TAIL* pattern. In the 1980s, the *WILD ROSE* shade in both red and blue Carnival was also made by them for Levay

Degenhart Glass (Crystal Art Glass Company), Cambridge, Ohio

The history of Degenhart Glass goes back to 1845, when Charles Degenhart emigrated from Germany to the USA. Charles went straight into the glass industry and was followed by his sons Charles Junior and John. All three spent some of their time working at the Cambridge Glass Company—indeed it was where John met Elizabeth Garrett, who worked in the glass-packing department. In 1908, John and Elizabeth married; their dream was to one day have their own little glass factory and to that end they worked hard and saved even harder. In 1947, their dream was realized and the Degenhart Crystal Art Glass factory began in Cambridge, Ohio.

This blue, bicentennial bell by Degenhart is dated 1776-1976 and is marked with a D in a heart inside. Price band B.

When John died in 1964 many assumed Elizabeth would close the factory—they reckoned without her determination. She recruited Zack Boyd and later his son Bernard (see the information under "Boyd's Crystal Art Glass") to assist her—and the factory prospered. Whimsies, wine glasses, toothpick holders, owls, and other small novelties were made by Degenhart.

Most Degenhart glass was marked with the trademark D in a heart. However, Carnival Glass attributed to Degenhart was actually iridized by other manufacturers, such as Joe St. Clair, the Hansen brothers, and Terry Crider, though the actual glass was made in Degenhart moulds at Degenhart's factory. St. Clair first iridized glass for Mrs. Degenhart at his Elwood, Indiana factory in 1972. Elizabeth Degenhart finally passed away in April 1978 aged eighty-eight—Boyd's took over the factory and continued to operate in the same fine traditions of the Degenharts before them.

DEGENHART PORTRAIT PLATE

October 2, 1975 was designated "Elizabeth Degenhart, First Lady of Glass" day in the state of Ohio. This little plate, only 5" in diameter, commemorates the occasion . The Governor of Ohio signed the proclamation and the Mayor of Cambridge presented Mrs. Degenhart with the Keys to the city of Cambridge. The event was on radio and TV and was also commemorated with this plate.

Shape: plate
Color: blue

Federal Glass Company, Columbus, Ohio

Federal began its iridescent and lustre treatments during the '20s (see chapter on Late Carnival). However, limited amounts of Carnival Glass were produced by the company later on, in the Contemporary era. Federal is known for its iridized white milk glass items in the form of beer steins (for example, the *TAVERN STEIN,* which was also made in cobalt blue Carnival*),* coffee mugs, and dinner set pieces. The company trademark is an F within a shield.

In 1977, Lancaster Colony, the parent company of Indiana Glass, purchased the Federal Glass Company for $45 million (with a note of $9.8 million for six years)—at the time, Federal had reported annual sales of $50 million.

Fostoria, Moundsville, West Virginia

Though more noted for their contribution to Late Carnival, in particular their Brocaded patterns, Fostoria also produced a few Carnival items in more recent times, including the experimental *JENNY LIND* range (featuring the "Swedish Nightingale" singer), which was never generally marketed. These moulds have changed hands several times, having subsequently been purchased by Wetzel Glass and Summit Art Glass. The *AMERICAN MILESTONES* series was made by Fostoria: a set of 10" oval plates made from 1971-76 in crystal and pastel iridized. Each plate was sold in a box lined with black velvet. The moulds were retired to ensure the plates stayed collectible. Six plates were issued; their titles included "Mount Rushmore," "Francis Scott Key," and "Washington Crossing the Delaware."

Gibson Glass Company, Milton, West Virginia

Gibson Glass Company is owned by Charles and Maxine Gibson. Charlie is a master glass-maker who worked at Blenko Glass for seventeen years and then at St. Clair's. By himself, he has produced a range of interesting and unusual Carnival items. Interestingly, Gibson has also made glass for Dollywood (Dolly Parton's theme park in Tennessee), which has a "Dollywood" logo. Gibson made some Carnival souvenirs for Dorothy Taylor's *Encore* and more recently, in the 1990s, has made limited edition souvenirs for the Collectible Carnival Glass Association. The company's trademark is GIBSON.

HEAVY IRIS

Very limited in number, each set having been produced in quantities of seventy-five or less, this sought after water set is trademarked Gibson and dated. It was made using the moulds that L.G. Wright owned. The water pitcher is around 12.25 high; the tumblers are 4.25" high.

Shape: water set
Colors: made in many Carnival colors, including smoke, red, vaseline, cobalt blue, custard, Burmese, crystal lustre, burnt orange, milk glass, green, and dusty rose

Gibson's version of the *HEAVY IRIS* tumbler has superb iridescence on a smoky base glass. Trademarked Gibson 1991 on the base. Price band B.

Guernsey Glass Company, Cambridge, Ohio

Guernsey Glass was owned by Harold Bennett; the company's trademark B, or B in a triangle (for Bennett) is often confused with Boyd's B in a diamond. Guernsey made a limited amount of Carnival Glass, the most "talked-about" item being the blue *INVERTED STRAWBERRY* water set. The tumblers iridized by Bennet have a letter B on the inside of the tumbler in the middle of the base. Note that to date, only two Classic (old) Carnival *INVERTED STRAWBERRY* tumblers in **blue** are known. Most of the new ones are not signed "Crider" or "Hansen"—both of whom iridized them for Bennett. Some clear crystal tumblers were pressed by Bennet and sent to Crider for iridizing in frosty white. These are usually signed by Crider. A variety of Carnival novelties and miniatures were also made by Guernsey.

A Selection of Guernsey's Contemporary Carnival Glass

INVERTED STRAWBERRY

Tumblers and pitchers in this pattern were made in the early 1970s at Guernsey—marked B for Bennett; the pitchers had a B on the **outside** of the item. According to O. Joe Olson writing in 1975[1], there are eleven large strawberries on the old *INVERTED STRAWBERRY* water pitcher but only ten strawberries on the new ones. Don Moore, writing in *The Antique Trader Weekly* in 1983, reported that "about 30 blue pitchers were iridized in 1972 by Guernsey and an additional 100 in purple in 1977. These pitchers are smaller and shaped much differently than the old tankard which makes them easy to spot." The tumblers were iridized for Bennet by Crider and Hansen—only some of these were signed.

Shapes: water set
Colors: tumbler in sapphire blue, cobalt blue, marigold, and amethyst/purple (pitcher in amethyst and marigold)

Guernsey Glass Company made this purple *INVERTED STRAWBERRY* tumbler—their trademark (B in a triangle) is on the interior of the base. *Courtesy of Rita and Les Glennon.* Price band AB.

ROCKY

According to Dorothy Taylor, writing in "*Encore Book III,*" this novelty rocking horse was made by the Westmoreland Glass Company for Guernsey Glass and was actually a reproduction of a Cambridge Glass Company candy container from around 1915. The mould was manufactured by the Island Mould Company. *ROCKY* is easy to identify as he has his name spelled out on one of the rockers. The item is also marked with Guernsey's trademark B in a triangle as well as the date of manufacture. A smaller version of *ROCKY* (*ROCKY JUNIOR*) was also made by Bennett and is similarly trademarked and dated. A series was done in both sizes of *ROCKY*—Bennet aimed to issue a new color every six weeks or so. Fourteen colors were planned, though not all were iridized.

Shape: novelty rocking horse

Colors: for *ROCKY*—various, including white, cobalt, red, chocolate. *ROCKY JUNIOR* colors include purple, clear, pink, custard, and green.

Guernsey's *ROCKY* in caramel slag, dated 1982—note the B in a triangle trademark on the horse's flank. Price band BC.

The Guernsey Glass Company's B in a triangle trademark is on the inside of this *PONTIAC INDIAN* novelty in pink Carnival. Price band AB. Recent examples have been seen in red Carnival—it is possible that another company is now producing this item.

Mi Mi Inc., Columbus, Ohio

Back in 1973, the International Carnival Glass Association's (ICGA) newsletter, the *Pump*, reported that Mi Mi Inc., of Columbus, Ohio, were producing *FARMYARD* bowls (selling at $47.50) that looked pretty similar to the classic, old items. The glass was actually being made by the Fenton Art Glass Company for Richard "Chuck" Stone and his wife Mimi (this was the name that her grandchildren called her). The *Pump* noted that Chuck Stone had told a Fenton workman that he had purchased an old *FARMYARD* bowl for $1800 and had resold it back when it had served its purpose as a model for the new piece! The mould was made by Al Botson and bore the trademark MIMI in the center of the base. Reportedly, Fenton insisted that the mark was made more prominent and larger, to ensure that no confusion could exist.

As well as the *FARMYARD* bowls and plates in amberina (1973) and purple (1974)—limited to 1000 bowls and 1000 plates in amberina and 500 of each shape in purple—the Stones had reproduction *ELKS* paperweights made in red. The *FARMYARD* moulds were later purchased by Singleton Bailey of South Carolina, though it is reported that in the interim, the mould was used to make limited quantities of blue bowls, possibly by Mosser.

ELKS PAPERWEIGHT

Very like the original, Classic Carnival *ELKS* paperweight by Millersburg, this item from Mi Mi was not trademarked. To the casual observer, the pattern is very similar to the original, but there are in fact many differences. The easiest way to tell them apart, however, is the color: Millersburg ones were made in amethyst and green. O. J. Olson reported[1] that it was also made by Joe St. Clair and was trademarked by them.

Shape: oblong paperweight

Color: red

The splendid, red *ELKS* paperweight was produced for Mi Mi Inc. in the early 1970s. Price band BC.

Mirror Images

This company owned a number of old Westmoreland items and had them produced by Viking Glass Company in the 1980s. Various "Candlewick" items were made as well as limited numbers of the *CAMBRIDGE DRAPED LADY* flower frog in blue Carnival.

Pilgrim Glass Corporation, Ceredo, West Virginia

Pilgrim had its beginnings back in the late 1940s with a newer factory being opened in 1956 by Alfred Knobler. Pilgrim produce a fine range of glass, including impressive, multi-layered, hand-blown and hand-carved Cameo Glass. During the late 1960s and early 1970s, they also made a range of distinctive, small Carnival Glass pitchers. Their ads at the time stated that they were "mouth blown and shaped by hand" and continued "they assuredly will find a permanent place as tomorrow's antique glass."

PILGRIM PITCHER
Seventeen different shape variations were produced in this attractive, hand-blown pitcher, the average height of which is around 4" to 5". Each has a mid-blue base glass with a multi-colored iridescence; the applied handles, however, are a contrasting, strong marigold color. The surface of the glass may be either smooth or have an uneven, knobbly effect. All examples have a pontil mark on the base and were issued with paper labels that read "Hand-blown Pilgrim Glass."
Shapes: seventeen shapes of pitcher and also three shapes of bud vase (similar to the pitcher but without the applied handle)
Color: blue with marigold handle

Two blue *PILGRIM PITCHERS*. Pilgrim's paper label can be clearly seen on the pitcher on the right. Price band B.

Pisello Art Glass, La Porte, Indiana

Glass was made for Pisello by Mosser. *FLIPPER* the dolphin was made in the early 1980s in marigold and red Carnival. The item comprises a lid and base and should be dated and signed inside the lid. The mould is now owned by Summit Art Glass, who have made it in various colors including patriot slag (red, white, and blue slag) and cobalt Carnival.

Singleton Bailey, Loris, South Carolina

Singleton Bailey has glass made for him by Fenton, using his own moulds. A number of splendid limited editions were issued in the 1980s and 1990s. The *POPPY SHOW* vase is known to many collectors; the mould is the original as used and re-issued by Imperial. Fenton now make this splendid item for Singleton Bailey (trade-marked DBS and with the Fenton "F") and a wide range of colors including celeste blue, red, iridized Burmese, cobalt, and vaseline have been produced. The reader is advised to consult the HOACGA Pattern sheets on vases (third section) for details on the old and the new *POPPY SHOW* vases.

The original Imperial mould is still being used for this wonderful item—the splendid *POPPY SHOW* vase. Currently the mould is owned by Singleton Bailey and the glass is produced (and trademarked) by Fenton. Standing a full 12" high, this magnificent example is in cobalt blue. On the secondary market, price band D.

FARMYARD

Using the mould made for Mi Mi Inc., Singleton Bailey has issued a number of wonderful limited editions (made by Fenton) in this pattern. Some runs have been so small the items were numbered as low as thirty or forty pieces. Many items have individual edge finishing and all are trademarked with a small capital D and S either side of a larger capital B (as well as with the Fenton "F"). See Appendix 3.

Shapes: cuspidor, rose bowl, chop plate, bowl, and basket (basket discontinued in 1991 due to breakage problems)

Colors: a wide variety, including red, blue, green, black, iridized Burmese, sea mist green, and rose magnolia

A pale orchid pink is the color of this tightly crimped edge *FARMYARD* plate, made by Fenton for Singleton Bailey. Price band C.

main objective in starting this line of glass is to be low in volume but high in collectible value.

John Valentine reports[2] that Wetzel also made a *GRAPE AND CABLE* electric lamp for the Carnival Glass author Sherman Hand. Made in several Carnival colors including ice blue and amber, this item is very limited indeed. One of Wetzel's specialties was his glass greeting cards and business cards made in the early 1980s[2]. Examples are scarce and sought after. By 1986, however, it was re-

A Wetzel *OWL* novelty is flanked by a Wetzel *HOBNAIL* miniature water set—all items in cobalt blue. Price band B for the owl; BC for the water set.

Viking Glass Company, New Martinsville, Ohio

The Viking Glass Company was formerly the New Martinsville Glass Company, which was incorporated in 1938. In 1944, the name was changed to Viking. They pressed the *CAMBRIDGE DRAPED LADY* flower frog for Mirror Images in 1980s in blue Carnival. The company closed in 1998.

R. Wetzel Glass Company, Zanesville, Ohio

Carnival items made by Wetzel are few and far between. Writing in *Carnival Glass Encore* December 1975, Wetzel stated that he had just opened up his glass company (in 1974) and was making all his own moulds. He added:

Every piece I make is marked with my R.W. so as to one day be of a collectible value. My collectibles are at a low volume due to the newness of my small business. Since I am starting off in times of a recession, maybe my glass should be called "Recession Ware." I feel and know the mould makers skills are plainly visible in pressed glass though I feel he is the forgotten man in glass making. My

ported that Wetzel was no longer in the business and had sold his moulds to E & E Collectibles. Items produced by E & E may bear their trademark E.E. as well as the Wetzel name.

HOBNAIL

Wetzel's *HOBNAIL* is in the form of a miniature water set that was made in the early 1980s. It is an attractive little set that is increasingly hard to find. The base of the pitcher is marked in full with the moulded name WETZEL. Examples of the set can also be found with the moulded letters E.E. as well as Wetzel on the base of the pitcher and each tumbler. E & E Collectibles purchased Wetzel's moulds. Found in the USA.

Shapes: miniature pitcher and four tumblers
Colors: dark blue, amber, and light blue. Also cobalt blue marked E. E.

Wheatoncraft Glass Company, Millville, New Jersey

Wheatoncraft began to make Carnival Glass in the 1970s and they are probably most well known for their boxed series of Carnival bottles and their Colonial style *DOLLS*. The *DOLLS* were made in three Carnival colors—crystal, amber, and blue—and were styled in the fashions of the late 1700s. Dorothy Taylor reported[3] that the Wheaton *DOLLS* were probably made at the former St. Clair Glassworks for Wheaton. The three styles represented were Colonial, Southern Belle, and Victorian. Paperweights in the shape of frogs, bears, cats, and turtles are also known in crystal Carnival, as well as a splendid *SHARK* paperweight in blue Carnival. Wheatoncraft also made items for Holly City Bottle Co. including plates, decanters, and paperweights. The latter were disc shaped paperweights (including items such as the "U.S. Marine Corps or Iwo Jima" paperweight, "Paul Revere," "Spirit of '76," and "Valley Forge").

The *BOSTON TEA PARTY* paperweight made by Wheatoncraft is the same aqua blue as the *DUTCH BOY AND GIRL* bookends. A heavy piece of glass. Price band AB.

These delightful *DUTCH BOY AND GIRL* bookends were made by Wheatoncraft in the early 1970s. Price band C.

A Selection of Wheatoncraft's Contemporary Carnival Glass

DUTCH BOY AND GIRL

    These were the first bookends to be made in Carnival Glass and it is thought that they were produced in the early 1970s. Dorothy Taylor reported[3] they were illustrated in the Wheatoncraft brochure around that time. Standing 5" tall, they feature a boy and girl in traditional dress.

    Shape: novelty, figural bookends
    Color: aqua blue

PRESIDENT BOTTLES

    A range of full size bottles, almost 8" tall and featuring 15 United States Presidents, was issued in a wide variety of Carnival colors. A set of miniature *PRESIDENT BOTTLES* in three boxed sets was also made. Other bottles include those featuring the Great American series and the Astronaut Series. There is even an ICGA Commemorative showing the *TOWN PUMP*. Bottles are marked on the base with the company's name and the series to which they belong.

    Shape: bottles
    Colors: a wide range of colors, including purple, emerald green, blue, marigold, and ice blue

A 1971 ad for Wheatoncraft's *PRESIDENTIAL MINIATURES* twelve bottle set in "iridescent tones of ruby, emerald and aquamarine glass…"

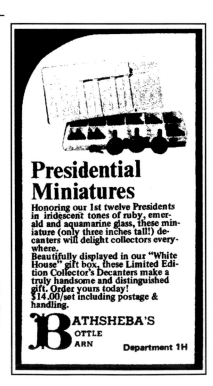

Chapter Four

Club Commemoratives and Souvenirs

The very first souvenir in Contemporary Carnival Glass was handed out at the first ACGA Convention held at Lodi, Ohio, home of the late Rose Presznick, in the late 1960s. Following a trip to the Imperial plant during the Convention, the twenty-eight members were presented with a limited edition, marigold *FASHION* compote. These were known as the "One-of-Fifty-Six" compotes; this referred to the actual number made—indeed the items were later numbered for posterity. This was to be the start of "something big," as souvenirs and club commemoratives soon became a necessary and desirable memento for all the major Carnival clubs.

Many Carnival Glass manufacturers have made souvenirs for the clubs, sometimes using existing old moulds and sometimes using new molds that have been made for this purpose. The late Dorothy Taylor commissioned a series of delightful miniatures for her *Encore* club: for example, a delightful miniature, blue water set in the *GOD AND HOME* pattern was made by Mosser as the 1979 *Encore* souvenir (only 410 sets made). Indeed, some original and outstanding items have also been produced for clubs such as HOACGA, ICGA, and ACGA. Recently, the world's first Internet based Carnival club, Woodsland World Wide (www.cga) has had souvenir

moulds made based on original designs by the co-author, artist Glen Thistlewood. One characteristic of all club commemoratives and souvenirs is that the numbers produced are limited. This fact alone makes them collectible and sought after. To cover the whole subject of Club Commemoratives and Souvenirs is impossible within this text, though the color illustrations and drawings shown here depict a number of Club souvenirs; specific information is contained within their captions. The reader is strongly advised to consult the excellent, comprehensive reference work on this subject by Diane Rosington[4].

[1] O. Joe Olson, *Carnival Glass in the Mid-1970s* (Kansas City, Missouri: by author, 1975).

[2] John Valentine's Contemporary Carnival Glass website—http://www.carnivalglass.net/

[3] Dorothy Taylor, *Encore by Dorothy. Books 1 to 3* (Kansas City, Missouri: by author, 1984-1986).

[4] Diane C. Rosington, *Carnival Glass Club Commemoratives, An Informative Guide* (Rochester, New York: by author, 2000).

Mosser made the miniature *GOD AND HOME* water set in cobalt blue for Dorothy Taylor's Encore club in 1979 (bottom right). At bottom left is the green miniature water set that was the very first Encore souvenir in 1977—the pattern is *INVERTED PEACOCK* and this set was also made for Taylor's club by Mosser. The pitcher is marked on the base Carnival Glass Encore 1977 Kansas City Missouri. DT. The mould was designed by Russ Vogelsong of Summit Art Glass—the water set has subsequently been made by Summit in other colors, for example the Geraldine's Delight (red slag) version shown at the top of the picture. Price band C for each water set.

Encore's fourth souvenir, made in 1980 for Dorothy Taylor by L.E. Smith Glass Company, was this delightful miniature water set with stemmed goblets, in ice blue. The pattern is *WINE AND ROSES*. Price band C.

Made for the 1969 International Carnival Glass Association's (ICGA) Convention in St. Louis, this commemorative souvenir Wheaton bottle features the club's motif: the Town Pump. On the reverse side, the Spirit of St. Louis plane and the St. Louis Arch are shown. *Courtesy of Rita and Les Glennon.* Price band C.

Originally an Imperial pattern, Fenton introduced their own version of *ACANTHUS* in the 1980s. This example was made for the ICGA Dallas Convention in 1995. The club's souvenir that year was an aqua blue *ACANTHUS* plate—as is usual, several whimsies were also made to raise funds for the club at the Convention. Only two black Carnival plates were made, one was plain and the other was decorated with enamelling. The decorated one is an exquisite item, hand-painted by Martha Reynolds with flowers in toning pastel shades of pink, cream, white, and blue that pick up the stretch iridescence on the plate; coralene decoration adds further delightful accents. *Courtesy of Angie Thistlewood.* Price band D (only one made).

In 1981, a new mould was made for ICGA of the Classic Carnival pattern *FROLICK-ING BEARS*—a cuspidor was the first shape produced. In 1993 and 1997, the *FROLICKING BEARS* mould was used to make (oversized) tumblers for ICGA; stippling and a band of beads was added. Shown here is the amber-marigold tumbler that was ICGA's commemorative souvenir for 1993. *Information courtesy of Dr. Jack Adams, past president of ICGA.* Price band B.

This whimsy handled mug in shell pink opal was decorated and gilded by the Fenton Art Glass Company. It was auctioned at the ICGA 1997 Convention. Price band D.

The first and second souvenirs made for the Heart of America Carnival Glass Association (HOACGA) were the red pitcher and tumbler in the *GOOD LUCK* design. The pitcher was the 1974 souvenir and was made by the Indiana Glass Company—the tumbler was the souvenir for 1975 and was also made by Indiana. It is interesting to note that the tumbler has the date 1974 on its side to match the pitcher, but inside it reads *Souvenir of 1975.* Price band D for the full water set.

In 1976 Fenton made the *GOOD LUCK* souvenir for HOACGA in the form of a splendid whiskey decanter and six shot glasses. Dorothy Taylor noted[3] that only 500 were made and the mould was destroyed afterwards to preserve the collectibility of the items. Price band D.

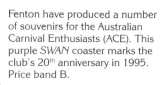

Fenton have produced a number of souvenirs for the Australian Carnival Enthusiasts (ACE). This purple *SWAN* coaster marks the club's 20th anniversary in 1995. Price band B.

In 1991, this red *EMU* coaster was made by Fenton for ACE Victoria. Price band B.

The red *GOOD LUCK* hatpin holder was HOACGA's 1977 souvenir—this time it was made by the L. E. Smith Glass Company. Price band C.

HOACGA's souvenir for 1978 was the red *GOOD LUCK* corn vase— it was made by Fenton (note the label on the base). Price band C.

"In God We Trust"—this cobalt blue miniature plate is a commemorative souvenir that was made for the American Carnival Glass Association (ACGA) by Joe St. Clair. Price band B.

This purple coaster depicting a map of Great Britain was the first souvenir made for the Carnival Glass Society (UK). Price band B.

The Woodsland World Wide Carnival Glass Association's commemoratives are made by Fenton Art Glass Company using the club's wholly owned mould and plunger. Both interior and exterior patterns are unique to the club and were designed by Glen Thistlewood. The commemoratives were issued in 1999 (Las Vegas Convention—interior pattern Thistlewood design *WOODSLAND PINE*, exterior Fenton's Imperial *OPEN ROSE* sea mist green plate) and in 2000 (Williamsburg Convention—cobalt blue rosebowl using *WOODSLAND PINE* interior and the Thistlewood *FLOWERS OF THE WORLD* exterior). Whimsies, great favorites of the collectors, were auctioned at the Conventions. The club's mould was tested in spruce green in February, 2000—only a handful of items were made in that color.

All items illustrated are 2000 issue commemoratives. Top row, from left: whimsy—unique spruce green handkerchief vase, handpainted by Fenton decorator J. K. Spindler (price band D); unique flat plate in cobalt blue (price Band D). Middle row, from left: test run spruce green rosebowl (price band D); cobalt blue rosebowl (price band B). Bottom row: tightly crimped edge, jack-in-the-pulpit shape, test run spruce green whimsy (price band D).

The *WOODSLAND PINE* design used for the Woodsland World Wide Carnival Glass Association's (www.cga) first souvenir in 1999. Based on original artwork by G. Thistlewood, it incorporates the club's motif—the pine cone—into a design that echoes the advertising patterns such as *GETTS PIANOS* made in Classic Carnival. The first souvenir (for the club's premier convention at Las Vegas) was made by Fenton Art Glass Company in sea mist green Carnival.

This is the prototype *FLOWERS OF THE WORLD* design. Discussions with Fenton identified difficulties with the intricacy and detail incorporated in the prototype. Firing and shaping would affect such a detailed design, and so a simpler, bolder concept was needed. The result is the final Thistlewood design below.

FLOWERS OF THE WORLD is the Thistlewood design that appears as the exterior pattern on *WOODSLAND PINE* souvenir items. The first souvenir bearing both patterns was issued in early 2000 in the form of an electric blue rose bowl made by the Fenton Art Glass Company. The main motif in *FLOWERS OF THE WORLD* is the sunflower, representing the state of Kansas, the home of www.cga's co-founders, Brian Pitman and Fred Stone. Test samples from a very short run in spruce green were made into a range of whimsy shapes that fetched prices from $100 to over $200 when auctioned on the club's Internet website in March 2000.

Chapter Five

Made in Taiwan and Korea

Carnival Glass from Taiwan and Korea has been on the Carnival scene for many years now. In Dorothy Taylor's *Encore* journals from 1982, a collector wrote to say she had found a blue Carnival sugar and creamer marked with a paper label saying *Made in Korea* and a purple mini punch set marked with a paper label saying *Made in Taiwan*. Similar paper stickers have been seen on black perfume or cologne bottles with ground stoppers. There is a shell like pattern on these bottles and many a collector has thought that they were old items—however, they are not.

In 1986, another issue of *Encore* featured an ad from AA Importing Company that illustrated eight separate items or groups of items. The AA Importing Company Inc. (originally AA. Sales Co.), was founded in 1934 by A. A. Gralnick in the Gas Light Square area of St. Louis, Missouri. Gralnick had actually been in partnership for a while prior to that with the late Si Wright who founded the L.G. Wright Glass Company. AA Importing became a distributor for kerosene lamp parts and accessories and, prior to and just after World War Two, it was heavily involved in the importation of fine crystal and art glass. By the mid 1970s, the company had established a name as a major player in the field of antique reproductions.

The items shown in that AA Importing ad in *Encore* were, in dark Carnival: 9" *BUTTERFLY AND BERRY* bowl on three scroll feet, 9.5" *STAG AND HOLLY* bowl on three scroll feet, 7" Squirrel candy container, 8.5" Duck candy container (covered *DUCK*), 6" *ROBIN ON NEST*, geometric patterned mini table set, and a *CHERRY BLOSSOM* water set. In white opal, two items were shown: *BUTTERFLY AND BERRY* and *STAG AND HOLLY*.

STAG AND HOLLY

These items were being imported into the USA from Korea back in the early 1980s. It was reported by Paul Miller, writing in *Carnival Glass Encore* in 1982, that they had been seen at an import show in white Carnival, marked only with a small oval gold and black sticker with the name of the importer and the words *Made in Korea*. There are, however, ways to spot the difference between these items and the Fenton originals. On some of the new items, the stags do not show their tongues, but as there seems to be more than one source of the *STAG AND HOLLY* reproduction, this detail may vary. Additionally, there are twenty-four berries on all four holly sprigs found on the large, scroll footed Classic bowls. On the fakes, however, it appears that three sprigs have twenty-four berries while one sprig has just twenty-one berries. Furthermore, there is one detail on the original Classic versions to look out for: at the bottom of the four large holly sprigs, the three lowest berries are arranged as follows: two stems have one berry at the bottom and two above it; the other two stems have two berries at the bottom and one above it. On the newer pieces, there is either one stem with no berries at the bottom, or all the stems have the two berries at the bottom with one above them.
Shapes: large, scroll footed bowls (9" to 10" diameter)
Colors: black amethyst, purple, red, white (pearlized), and possibly blue

CHERRY BLOSSOM

Reported in Dorothy Taylor's *Encore* journal in 1982 by well-known collector and writer Paul Miller, was a deep purple (almost black) Carnival imported water set from Korea, in the Depression Glass pattern *CHERRY BLOSSOM*. The pattern is lightly moulded and appears in panels around the items. On the base is a veined leaf and berry motif.
Shape: squat pitcher and pedestal footed tumbler
Color: deep (near black) purple

Fakes: one of the biggest difficulties in writing about fake Carnival Glass is the fact that, even as the reader is perusing these words, another faked item could be hitting the market. It's not possible to write a definitive listing of all the known fakes in all known variations and colors, because they will simply continue to be issued. It is also dangerous to even attempt to do so, for the reader could be lulled into a false sense of security, assuming that they are aware of all such items on the market. However, the ones that seem to be the most widespread are the trio of bowls mentioned below, *GOOD LUCK, PEACOCKS,* and, to a lesser extent, *GRAPE AND CABLE*. Who makes them? Where are they coming from? No one is quite sure.

GOOD LUCK, PEACOCKS, GRAPE AND CABLE

These are grouped together as they all come from the same (unknown) "stable" in the Far East. They are pretty good copies of the original patterns and have deceived many a new collector. They are mainly found in the UK and Australia, but have also turned up in the USA. It was reported during the 1980s that a shop in one of the London antique markets had them stacked up dozens high! Early examples (from the 1980s) were thick and heavy with a dull finish that soon oxidized, but more recent examples are lighter, thinner, and brasher looking.

The exterior pattern may be a copy of Northwood's *BASKETWEAVE* or *RIBS*. Some examples can be spotted as they have iridescence on the base, others have a solid disk of glass where the indented collar base should be. Those with the solid disk could be termed the second generation of fakes and often have an over-shiny iridescence compared to the dull, thick finish on the early examples. A third generation of fakes has also been reported. Unlike the earlier examples that were heavy, this third generation is much lighter and more like the original Northwood items in weight. On the edge, a rather poor attempt at a pie-crust finish may be evident.

So—how can you spot the fakes? For the *GRAPE AND CABLE*, it has been noted that the grapes on the reproduced items are all about the same size whereas on the original pieces the grapes appear to gradually get smaller towards the center of the bowl. Many examples bear a large looking N mark, which is cruder in appearance than the genuine Northwood N—the fake N is neither underlined nor in a circle, as it would have appeared on the old Northwood originals. The pattern seems to fill the space on the face of the bowl proportionately more than on the originals, going further out to the edge than on the original Northwood examples. The best advice to new collectors is to study examples you know to be genuine (experienced collectors are usually willing to help)—they are significantly different from the fakes. To an experienced eye, the fake is easy to spot.
Shape: bowl
Colors: marigold, blue and green

GRAPE AND CABLE hatpin holders

These were first reported back in 1987 in cobalt blue and pink and are thought to be from overseas, most likely from Korea or Taiwan. More recently they have been reported in red and other colors. The fakes are not hard to distinguish from the original Northwood versions as they have far fewer grapes and a much "thinner" looking pattern. The prongs at the top of the holder are also thin and point upward rather oddly with wide gaps between each prong. The iridescence is often poor and weak.
Shape: hatpin holder
Colors: blue, ice blue, pink, red, and more

Probably made in the Far East, this fake, green *GOOD LUCK* bowl has a poor, pinkish, oxidized iridescence— though when purchased in the late 1980s, it actually looked quite good! It has not worn well. It is typically heavy and the pattern fills the bowl closer to the edge than on the originals. More recent fakes are lighter and have a much better, often brash and shiny iridescence. Price band A.

Chapter Six

The Final Verse

"Every new beginning comes from some other beginning's end"
—Semisonic (from "Closing Time")

Almost a century has now passed since the first Classic Carnival Glass left the factories in the Ohio Valley, captivating the hearts of so many. Its beauty and commercial viability enabled it to undergo both a worldwide renaissance and a subsequent rebirth in the country where it saw its first dawn. Who knows what the future will bring?

Move out man! Life is fleeting by.
Do something worthwhile before you die.
Leave behind a work sublime
That will outlive both you and time.

—Alfred A. Montepert.

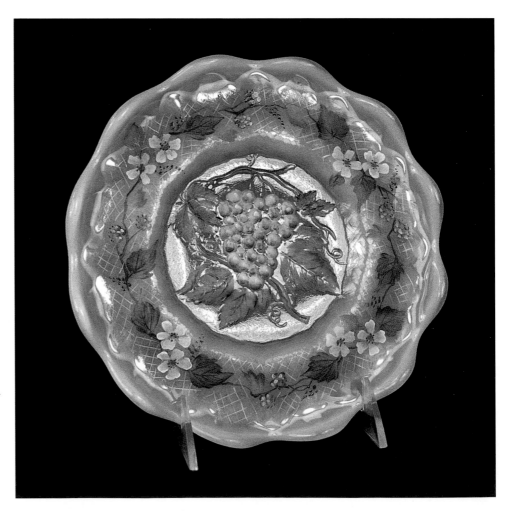

Old meets new and comes full circle. A wonderful blend of a Classic old Carnival pattern—*HEAVY GRAPE*—made from a new Fenton mould and given the modern touch by hand. This splendid piece was painted by Martha Reynolds, and was auctioned at the joint San Diego Carnival Glass Club and Southern California Carnival Glass Club's Convention in 1996. Price band D.

Bibliography

Barta, Dale and Diane and Helen M. Rose. *Czechoslovakian Glass and Collectibles*. Paducah, Kentucky: Collector Books, 1992.

Cadik, Dr. Jindrich. *Modern Glassmaking in Czechoslovakia*. Prague, 1931.

Cottle, Simon. *Sowerby Gateshead Glass*. Gateshead, England: Tyne and Wear Museums Service, 1986.

Doty, David. *A Field Guide to Carnival Glass*. Marietta, Ohio: The Glass Press Inc., 1998.

Florence, Gene. *Collectible Glassware from the 40s, 50s, 60s*. Paducah, Kentucky: Collector Books, 1994.

Foulds, Diane. *A Guide to Czech & Slovak Glass*. Prague, Czech Republic. European Community Imports. Updated, 1995.

Greguire, Helen. *Carnival in Lights*. New York: by author, 1975.

Hajdamach, Charles R. *British Glass. 1800-1914*. Suffolk, England: Antique Collectors' Club Ltd., 1993.

Hartung, Marion T. *Carnival Glass. Books 1-10*. Emporia, Kansas: by author, 1960-73.

Heacock, William, James Measell, and Berry Wiggins. *Harry Northwood. The Early Years*. Marietta, Ohio: Antique Publications, 1990.

Heacock, William, James Measell, and Berry Wiggins. *Harry Northwood. The Wheeling Years*. Marietta, Ohio: Antique Publications, 1991.

Heacock, William. *Fenton Glass, The Third Twenty-Five Years*. Marietta, Ohio: O-Val Advertising Corp., 1989.

Jargstorf, Sibylle. *Baubles, Buttons and Beads. The Heritage of Bohemia*. Atglen, Pennsylvania: Schiffer Publishing Ltd., 1993.

Karhula-Iittala Kuvasto Katalog P. 1922. Karhulan lasimuseo. Iittalan lasimuseo, Finland, 1981.

Karhula Osakeyhtio Katalog A. 1932. Kuvasto P. 1934. Nakoispainos: Finland.

Kovar, Lorraine. *Westmoreland Glass. 1950-1984 Vols I and II*. Marietta, Ohio: Antique Publications, 1991.

Lersjo, Gunner. *Glas Fran Eda*. Arvika, Sweden: by author, 1997.

Manley, Cyril C. *Decorative Victorian Glass*. England: Ward Lock, 1981.

Measell, James. *Fenton Glass, The 1980s Decade*. Marietta, Ohio: Antique Publications, 1996.

Measell, James and Berry Wiggins. *Great American Glass of the Roaring 20s and Depression Era*. Marietta, Ohio: The Glass Press, 1998.

Measell, James and W.C. "Red" Roetteis. *The L.G. Wright Glass Company*. Marietta, Ohio: Glass Press, 1997.

Mordini, Tom and Sharon. *Carnival Glass Auction Price Reports*. Freeport, Illinois: by authors, 1984-1999.

National Imperial Glass Collectors' Society. *Imperial Glass Encyclopedia. Volumes I and II*. Marietta, Ohio: The Glass Press, 1995 and 1997.

Olson, O. Joe. *Carnival Glass in the Mid-1970s*. Kansas City, Missouri: by author, 1975.

Paulsson, Ulla-Carin, Patricia Soderberg, and Gunnar Lersjo. *Eda Glasbruk*. Varmland, Sweden: ABF, 1985.

Pavitt, Wm. Thos and Kate. *The Book of Talismans*. London, England: William Rider and Son, 1922.

Presznick, Rose. *Carnival and Iridescent Glass. Books 1-4*. Lodi, Ohio: by author, 1974.

Quintin-Baxendale, Marion. *Collecting Carnival Glass*. London, England: Francis Joseph, 1998.

Revi, Albert Christian. *Nineteenth Century Glass: Its Genesis and Development*. Atglen, Pennsylvania: Schiffer Publishing Ltd., 1967.

Rice, Jane Ann. *Story of St. Clair Glass*. Richard E Harney, date unknown.

Riihimaen Lasi Oy. Kuvasto-Hinnasto P. 1939. Nakoispainos: Finland, 1993.

Rosington, Diane C. *Carnival Glass Club Commemoratives, An Informative Guide*. Rochester, New York: by author, 2000.

Taylor, Dorothy. *Encore by Dorothy. Books 1 to 3*. Kansas City, Missouri: by author, 1984-1986.

Thistlewood, Glen and Stephen. *Carnival Glass: The Magic and the Mystery*. Atglen, Pennsylvania: Schiffer Publishing Ltd., 1998.

Truitt, Robert and Deborah. *Collectible Bohemian Glass. 1880-1940*. Kensington, Maryland: B & D Glass, 1995.

Truitt, Robert and Deborah. *Collectible Bohemian Glass Volume 2. 1915-1945*. Kensington, Maryland: B & D Glass, 1998.

Weatherman, Hazel Marie. *Colored Glassware of the Depression Era 2*. Ozark, Missouri: Weatherman Glass Books, 1974.

Weatherman, Hazel Marie. *The Decorated Tumbler*. Springfield, Missouri: Glassbooks Inc., 1978.

Useful Definitions

Cameo

This is where the pattern is raised up (in relief).

Intaglio

This is where the pattern is sunk in or incised; often described as "near-cut" when the pattern is also a geometric and gives the appearance of a cut glass design.

Marie

On a bowl or plate, the center of the base within the collar.

Shear mark / Straw mark

A shear mark is a chilled rough surface caused by cutting—it has the appearance of a line across the face of the glass. Shears were used to cut off the gob of hot (elastic) glass as it was being dropped into the mould where it would be pressed. The shears slightly cooled the part of the hot glass (about 1900 degrees Fahrenheit at this point) being cut, causing it to harden a little. This formed a mark on the surface of the piece as it was being pressed. Usually, with skill on the part of the presser, this mark could be hidden by the pattern on the main face of the glass, but if there were large plain areas, the shear mark may be clearly seen.

Stuck-up and **Snapped-up**

Glass items that have a ground base (no **marie**—see above) were attached to a hot metal punty rod after being extracted from the mould. The punty had been heated so that the glass would stick fast to it. After being finished (shaped) and iridized, the piece had to be broken from the punty, and this left a rough base which had to be ground flat. The factory term for this was **stuck-up**. Often the grinding caused small chips and flakes on the **stuck-up** base. Such chips are a feature of the manufacture and are very common on ground bases.

Items which had a collar base (**marie**) could be gripped in a tool with clamp-like spring loaded jaws called a "snap" whilst being finished off. This process was termed **snapped-up**. These pieces had no need to be ground and they have smooth, as-moulded bases.

Tumble-Up

A small decanter with a matching tumbler that sits neatly upside down over the pouring neck, like a cover.

Vaseline Glass

Vaseline glass contains uranium oxide and is radioactive. The uranium is used as a colorant and makes the glass a distinct light yellow-green shade, though often the base color is masked by the iridescence on Carnival examples. When a UV (black) light is shone on vaseline, it glows a vivid translucent green—this effect is caused by the electrons being "excited" by the UV light.

The shear mark can be clearly seen on this green *TEN MUMS* bowl from Fenton.

Boyd's Carnival Colors

The information below (supplied courtesy of Boyd's Crystal Art Glass) gives a listing of all the Carnival colors that Boyd's glass has been produced in and the year in which they were produced.

COLOR	DATE USED
Mint Green	October 1983
Violet Slate	May 1984
Daffodil	February 1984
Olympic White	February to March 1984
Platinum	March 1984
Midnight	March 1984
Cobalt	September to November 1984
Bermuda	November 1984
Olde Lyme	August 1985
Misty Vale	October 1986
Fall	October 1986
Red	October 1986
Holiday	November 1986
Kumquat	November 1986
Ebony	February 1987
Vaseline	April 1988
Cobalt	January 1989
Winter	January to February 1989
Ice	March 1989
Milk White	March to April 1989
Windsor Blue	October 1989
Grape Parfait	November 1989
Mulberry	November 1989
Autumn	November 1989
Cobalt	December 1989 to January 1990
Camelot	February 1990
Sunglow	March 1990
Lime	April to May 1990
Crown Tuscan	July to September 1990
Spinnaker	November to December 1990
Cobalt	January to February 1991
Patriot White	March 1991
Vaseline	June 1991
Classic Black	September to December 1991
Cardinal Red	March to May 1992
Cobalt	May to June 1992
Columbus White	July 1992
Primrose	August 1992
Vaseline	October 1992
Ruby Red	March to April 1993
Waterloo	June 1993
Alexandrite	August to October 1993
Aqua Diamond	November to December 1993
Cobalt	January 1994
Chocolate	July to September 1994
Pale Orchid	October 1994
Banana Cream	November 1994 to January 1995
Sunkiste	January to February 1995
Milk White	March 1995
Royal Plum	April to May 1995
Vaseline	June to July 1995
Mint Julep	August to October 1995
Blue Fog	October 1995
Bernard Boyd Black	November 1995
Crystal Carnival	January to March 1996
Peach Lustre	February 1996
Milk Chocolate	March 1996
Vaseline	August 1996
Mystique	September 1996
Purple Frost	December 1996 to January 1997
Marshmallow	February 1997
Spring Surprise	May 1997
Cobalt	May to August 1997
Lemon Custard	October 1997
Alpine Blue	February 1998
Vaseline	September to December 1998
Nutmeg	January to March 1999
Rosie Pink	April to May 1999
Peacock Blue	July to August 1999
Vaseline	December 1999

Trademarks on Contemporary Carnival Glass

Below are sketches of some of the trademarks you might expect to find on modern Carnival Glass. Please note that these are hand drawings and are in "the style of" the marks on the glass. As they are drawn by hand, they will not be as exact or precise as the actual marks.

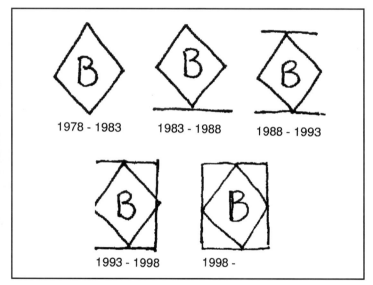

Boyd's Crystal Art Glass trademarks indicate the years when the item was made. The number and position of lines around the B in the diamond give the relevant information.

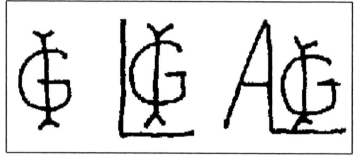

Imperial went through several trademarks along with changes of ownership. The first was the IG on the left, introduced in the 1960s. When the company was purchased by Lennox in 1972, the letter **L** was added to the trademark for Lennox Imperial Glass (see center). In 1981 the company was sold to Arthur Lorch and the letter **A** was added to the LIG—standing for Arthur Lorch Imperial Glass (see right).

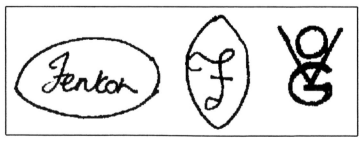

The Fenton logo on the left is easily recognized. Note that a small number under the Fenton name indicates the decade in which the item was made—this was begun in the 1980s, when an **8** was added. Items made in the 1970s have no number. The F in an oval trademark was added from around 1983 to moulds that Fenton bought from other companies. The unusual logo one on the right is Fenton too. The intertwined letters are OVG and stand for *Olde Virginia Glass* range, which Fenton made in purple Carnival in the 1970s.

Trademarks used by the St. Clair family include this trio: on the left, easily recognized, the Joe St. Clair mark. In the center, a variation in elegant script. Joe St. Clair's glass may also have the logo J ST.C or ST. CLAIR as the trademark. At right, Bob (Joe's younger brother) and Maude St. Clair also made some Carnival—this is one of the trademarks they used.

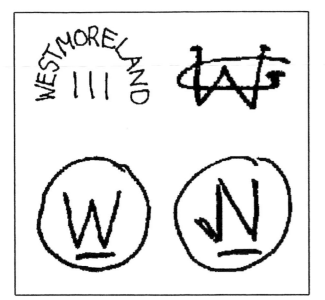

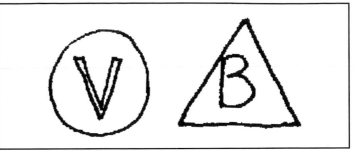

Two trademarks that are after the initial of the owner rather than the name of the factory. Left is Summit Art Glass company's V trademark, for Russ Vogelsong, the owner. The company does not use this on all their glass. Right is the B trademark for Harold Bennett of Guernsey Glass Company.

On the top are two Westmoreland trademarks—the one on the left is the latest one they used which indeed, still remains on some old Westmoreland moulds that are now being worked by other manufacturers. Bottom are two L.G. Wright trademarks. The W underlined (left) was sometimes used by them on Carnival Glass. The one on the right is the mark sometimes called the "Wonky" or "Wobbly" W.

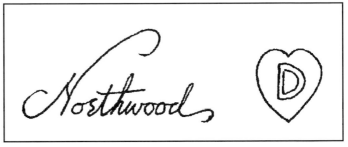

Two elegant trademarks—on the left, the script signature that is on all the glass made for the new Northwood Art Glass Company. Right, the trademark for Degenhart.

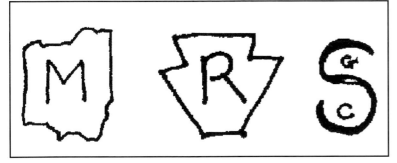

Three marks that are not seen too often. Left is the M within a shape formed like the state of Ohio, for Mosser. Center is the R in a keystone for Rosso of Pennsylvania and right is one of the marks used by the Smith Glass Company.

Three interesting logos: left DBS for Singleton Bailey. Center is OJO for O. Joe Olson of the Original Carnival Glass Society. Olson had St. Clair make glass for him and marked it thus. Right is the MiMi mark seen on some *FARMYARD* items.